Biblical Economic Ethics

Biblical Economic Ethics

Sacred Scripture's Teachings on Economic Life

Albino Barrera

LEXINGTON BOOKS
Lanham • Boulder • New York • Toronto • Plymouth, UK

Published by Lexington Books
A wholly owned subsidiary of The Rowman & Littlefield Publishing Group, Inc.
4501 Forbes Boulevard, Suite 200, Lanham, Maryland 20706
www.rowman.com

10 Thornbury Road, Plymouth PL6 7PP, United Kingdom

British Library Cataloguing in Publication Information Available

Library of Congress Cataloging-in-Publication Data

Barrera, Albino.
Biblical economic ethics : sacred scripture's teachings on economic life / Albino Barrera.
pages cm
Includes bibliographical references and index.
ISBN 978-0-7391-8229-1 (cloth : alk. paper) — ISBN (invalid) 978-0-7391-8230-7 (electronic) 1.
Economics in the Bible. I. Title.
BS670.B37 2013
261.8'5—dc23

2013016951

∞™ The paper used in this publication meets the minimum requirements of American National Standard for Information Sciences Permanence of Paper for Printed Library Materials, ANSI/NISO Z39.48-1992.

Printed in the United States of America

"Let the little children come to me . . . for it is to such as these that the kingdom of God belongs." (Mk 10:14)

For the ragpickers of Jaboneros Street,
children driven by poverty to scavenge through garbage,
even on Christmas Eve.
May you feel God's love for you despite your hard life.

Contents

List of Abbreviations

Acts	Acts
Am	Amos
Ant	Jewish Antiquities (Josephus)
Col	Colossians
Dan	Daniel
Dt	Deuteronomy
Eccl	Ecclesiastes
Eph	Ephesians
Ex	Exodus
Ez	Ezekiel
Gal	Galatians
Gen	Genesis
Hag	Haggai
Hos	Hosea
Is	Isaiah
Jas	James
Jdgs	Judges
Jb	Job
Jer	Jeremiah
Jn	John

Jos	Joshua
JW	Jewish Wars (Josephus)
Lev	Leviticus
Life	Life of Josephus
Lk	Luke
Mal	Malachi
Mk	Mark
Mt	Matthew
Mic	Micah
Neh	Nehemiah
Num	Numbers
Phil	Philippians
Phlm	Philemon
Prov	Proverbs
Ps	Psalms
Rev	Revelation
Rom	Romans
Ru	Ruth
Sir	Sirach
Tit	Titus
Tob	Tobit
Wis	Wisdom
Zech	Zechariah
Zeph	Zephaniah
1 Cor	1 Corinthians
2 Cor	2 Corinthians
1 Jn	1 John
2 Jn	2 John
3 Jn	3 John
1Kgs	1 Kings
2 Kgs	2 Kings
1 Mac	1 Maccabees

1 Sam	1 Samuel
2 Sam	2 Samuel
1 Thess	1 Thessalonians
2 Thess	2 Thessalonians
1 Tim	1 Timothy
2 Tim	2 Timothy

Preface

Whether read as Revelation or as literature, the Bible has been a perennial source of guidance and inspiration on how to flourish in life. This is even more so today in light of the new wealth created by globalization. Unfortunately, using the Bible for contemporary economic problems is not a straightforward exercise because of the vast amount of materials involved. Moreover, these teachings are of different genres—as ordinances, aphorisms, parables, paraenesis, and narratives. Furthermore, they are drawn from widely disparate books from different time periods and with their respective theologies, to boot. In addition, there seems to be contradictory teachings across different books (e.g., property ownership in the Old Testament versus the Gospels' call for radical voluntary divestment) or even within the same book (e.g., Proverbs extols wealth as a reward for virtue even as it disparages it as a danger). Besides, some norms appear to be outdated, coming as they are from a much different socioeconomic context (e.g., prohibition on charging interest on loans). Readers and scholars are left to wonder just how much of these teachings are truly applicable in a modern economy. And if they are, is there even a single coherent view of economic morality from the Old and New Testament?

The primary contribution of this book is its nascent biblical theology of economic life that synthesizes these wide-ranging teachings. In particular, it addresses three questions, namely:

- What do the individual books of the Bible say about proper economic conduct?
- How do these teachings fit within the larger theology and ethics of the books in which they are found?

- Are there recurring themes, underlying patterns, or issues running across these different sections of the Bible when read together as a single canon?

These are essential issues in any critical, intelligent appropriation of biblical economic ethics for our contemporary social challenges.

To answer these questions, we examine the sections of the Old and New Testament with substantial blocks of materials on economic morality. We let these various books and epistles state their respective concerns and speak on their own terms, instead of forcibly harmonizing them or limiting our focus to a predetermined topic, such as wealth, property, or justice. Doing so permits us to glean insights on the entirety of economic life, including its underlying nature and order. Then, we assess how these teachings flow from the larger theology and ethics of the parts of the Bible in which they are found. This book is not an exegesis of specific biblical passages but is rather a theological synthesis of the findings of exegetes and ethicists on what Sacred Scripture teaches about economic life.

The economic norms of the Old and New Testament exhibit both continuity and change. Despite their diverse social settings and theological visions, the books of the Bible nonetheless share recurring themes: care for the poor, generosity, wariness over the idolatry of wealth, the inseparability of genuine worship and upright moral conduct, and the acknowledgment of an underlying divine order in economic life. The discontinuity and change consist mainly in the Gospels' repeated call for radical voluntary divestment, which we do not find in the Old Testament.

Contrary to most people's first impression that the Bible offers merely random economic teachings without rhyme or reason, there is, in fact, a specific vision undergirding these scriptural norms. Moreover, far from being burdensome impositions of do's and don'ts, this book finds that the Bible's economic norms are, in fact, an invitation to participate in God's providence. To this end, we have been granted a threefold benefaction—the gift of divine friendship, the gift of one another, and the gift of the earth. Thus, biblical economic ethics is best characterized as a chronicle of how God provides for humanity through people's mutual solicitude and hard work. The economic ordinances, aphorisms, and admonitions of the Old and New Testament turn out to be an unmerited divine invitation to participate in God's governance of the world.

In Sacred Scripture, we find narratives of peoples and communities that are descriptive of our own lives. Their yearnings and disappointments, their sins and brokenness, their triumphs and their failures are our own struggles, hopes, and dreams. Thus, these sacred writings can lead us to a better self-understanding of who we are as individual persons and as a human community. It can imbue us with a better appreciation of our own experiences and of our possibilities going forward.

I hope this study on Sacred Scripture's teachings on economic life gives readers a glimpse into God's wisdom and unfailing love. Our economic conduct provides us with a unique opportunity to shine forth in our creation in the image and likeness of God. Often extremely demanding, hard, and even fraught with temptations and distractions, economic life nevertheless is, at its core, an occasion for humans to grow in holiness, charity, and perfection. Indeed, our economic conduct can reflect God's wisdom and love—Emmanuel!—God very much in our midst.

A word of apology. I would be the first to admit that we have just scratched the surface of an extremely rich and profound body of teachings. This book is by no means exhaustive. Many other parts of the Bible and scholarly works could and should have been included, studied, and discussed. A lot of materials had to be cut from the final version to keep this book to a reasonable length. It is the proverbial trade-off between breadth and depth of analysis, on the one hand, and manuscript size, on the other hand. Furthermore, note that this book does not go so far as to apply these biblical teachings to contemporary economic issues and policy. Neither does it include the growing literature from economists who use economic theory and analysis to examine the Bible. These require separate books of their own. Instead, my project is limited to trying to establish what Sacred Scripture teaches about economic life within the context of their respective theologies and ethics. As it is, this alone has been such a formidable, lengthy task.

A word of thanks. Colleagues and readers furnished valuable bibliography, insights, suggestions, encouragement, advice, and corrections. Over the years, various religious communities and universities extended hospitality in the use of their library and research facilities. The staff of Lexington Books was professional, extremely helpful, and a delight to work with in the final stages of this project. To all these good people, peers, and friends who have been supportive all along, I owe a deep debt of gratitude. May you share in the joy of seeing this undertaking enter a new phase. May you have a grace-filled life for your kindness, goodwill, and generosity. I pray that this work may, in a roundabout way, be a vessel of grace in making life a little easier for the poor and the marginalized.

Chapter One

Methodological Issues

Using Sacred Scripture in Economic Ethics

Exegetes, ethicists, and theologians passionately debate the proper role, use, and relevance of Sacred Scripture in contemporary ethics. On one end of the spectrum are those who believe that the words of the Bible apply to issues today in a straightforward fashion. At the other end are those who outrightly dismiss the contemporary pertinence of these ancient texts because biblical and modern cultures are worlds apart.

Most scholars take a position between these two polar opposites, although they acknowledge that the study of biblical ethics can be extremely frustrating. To begin with, there is often little consensus on the nature, content, and history of the biblical text themselves, even among exegetes. Scholarship on biblical ethics "has frequently been paralyzed by the sheer complexity of the methodological problems."[1] The literature has been likened to a conceptual cul-de-sac, with many issues left indeterminate. Others lament the often simplistic use of these sacred writings in ethics, partly due to the dearth of rigorous studies on the subject matter.[2] Moreover, exegetical studies are often incomprehensible to non-specialists. A survey of these scholarly disagreements requires an entire volume in itself. Thus, this chapter will limit itself only to interpretive issues directly related to the contemporary use of biblical teachings on economic morality.

TASKS

There are three main steps in using Sacred Scripture for present-day ethical reflection:

- Determining the role, importance, and authority of Sacred Scripture relative to other sources of moral insight (theological task);
- Ascertaining what the biblical texts say (exegetical task);
- Interpreting what the biblical texts mean for contemporary readers (hermeneutical task).

Each of these three steps has its distinct set of problems that require further methodological choices. In fact, the choices made at these conceptual "forks in the road" constitute the fourth task—the methodological task.[3] The following sections briefly summarize these tasks and their associated difficulties.

Theological Task

The first task is theological in nature as it involves selecting the proper bases for ethical reflection. This includes evaluating and taking a stand on the role and weight of these sacred writings vis-à-vis other moral authorities (e.g., law, science). Should the Bible be the exclusive arbiter in sorting through current problems in political economy? Are these ancient texts sufficient on their own in providing moral guidance on market conduct? If not, what are these other sources of moral reflection? More important, how do we rank these moral authorities relative to one another? Do biblical norms take precedence? What do we do in cases of conflicting insights from these disparate sources? What criteria do we use in adjudicating incompatible teachings and how do we justify these? Scholars differ in their responses to these questions.

There are generally three schools of thought regarding the issue of Sacred Scripture and authority.[4] First, we have those who view these sacred texts as the sole and absolute authority.[5] Second, we have those who dismiss these ancient writings as either irrelevant or of little use for modern issues and needs.[6] The cultural gap between our world and the Bible is simply unbridgeable. Between these two positions is a third approach: viewing these sacred texts merely as one of many other sources of authority. Even as Scripture is central in the life of believers, the faith community is nevertheless also formed by extra-biblical sources of ethical reflection, such as tradition, reason, experience, culture, and science.[7] Users of these sacred writings must be in dialogue with reason and be open to letting different cultures enrich our contemporary understanding and appropriation of the Bible.[8]

Most people take the third approach. Nonetheless, there is still disagreement within this middle path. Some accord a privileged position to Scripture, even as it is merely one of many other sources of moral insight. Others, however, do not reserve such a special role for the Bible. It is merely one among many voices in the secular, pluralistic, public square of ideas.

As mentioned earlier in the preface, this study is restricted only to ascertaining what the Bible teaches about proper conduct and what they might mean for contemporary economics. We will not address whether or not these sacred writings on their own are sufficient in resolving questions in economic morality.

Exegetical Task

Exegesis is concerned with investigating readers' questions regarding biblical passages and with determining what the texts say. Exegetes use a wide variety of tools, including textual criticism (establishing precisely the original Hebrew or Greek text of the passage), historical criticism (assessing the historicity of biblical events and placing the text in its historical context), source criticism (tracking down the written sources used by the biblical authors or editors[9]), form criticism (determining the life-setting and literary form[10] of biblical passages), and redaction criticism (peeling off the different editorial layers from the final text as we receive it today).

Of interest to us in this study is social-scientific criticism, that is, the study of the authors' or editors' cultural, political, and economic milieu that may have shaped the biblical text. Sociocultural criticism examines the larger social backdrop of the writers, the original text, or the redaction as a way of getting at what the authors or editors meant. For example, many believe that the prophetic denunciation against social injustice (e.g., Mic 2:1–2; Is 5:8–10) was in reaction to rampant land-grabbing in eighth- and seventh-century B.C. Israel and Judah. In the New Testament, some scholars note that the crucifixion of Jesus is best understood in light of the simmering political tension between the Roman Empire and Palestine.[11]

Biblical texts are historically and culturally conditioned. This means that to get at the meaning of the biblical texts, we have to understand their context. There is always the danger of imposing our modern categories on biblical texts instead of letting them speak on their own terms.[12] This is the danger of eisegesis in which we read our own ideas into these sacred writings. To minimize this risk, it is best to read and understand scriptural texts within their social, historical, and theological context, to the extent possible.

Unfortunately, getting at the context of these works is not a straightforward task. Take the case of the Old Testament. Given its diversity of time, place, authors, and social visions, it would be inappropriate to generalize specific biblical passages as descriptive of all Israel and across its entire history.[13] This is simply not the case. To begin with, the Bible was composed over a long period, over a millennium. Many cultures and groups were involved.[14] There is abundant evidence that Ancient Near Eastern (ANE) materials shaped biblical texts. There were numerous redactions by editors from various periods that are extremely difficult to differentiate. Thus, identifying the exact context of specific biblical passages is extremely demanding and is fraught with speculative assumptions or the use of controversial methods. Not surprisingly, there is much disagreement among scholars.

Since we are interested in economic life, social-scientific criticism in biblical studies is relevant for our study. Unfortunately, this method has its own set of problems and limitations. To begin with, many of these sociological models cannot be validated because of the dearth of hard data from ancient times. Their conclusions are often based on speculative guesswork and should therefore be interpreted merely as suggestive rather than as definitive.

Furthermore, taken to extremes, social-scientific criticism can become deterministic in forcing biblical witness to fit sociological and anthropological assumptions. Instead of serving merely as heuristic tools, these models become the lens through which Scripture is read and interpreted. Biblical text is explained solely in economic, political, and cultural terms, and religious experience is turned into nothing more than social phenomenon at its root. This is materialist, sociological reductionism[15] in which everything is interpreted solely or primarily on the basis of the material conditions or context of the era. After all, these social sciences adopt the post-Enlightenment stance that there is no room for the divine in a purely scientific, positivistic inquiry.[16] This is clearly problematic because for many readers, these ancient writings are, at their core, religious phenomena.

We can greatly enrich our understanding of biblical text by knowing as much as we can about its composition, theology, sociology, and history. However, to avoid the aforementioned problems of reductionism, social-scientific criticism is best employed merely as one of many other tools within a more robust and comprehensive exegesis.[17]

Hermeneutical Task

Hermeneutics is the science (some say art) of biblical interpretation in the contemporary use of scripture passages. It builds on the insights provided by exegesis. While exegesis ascertains what the biblical texts say, hermeneutics grapples with what they mean for the reader today. The latter is a broad task and, given our severe space constraint, I will present only its contested aspects that are directly relevant for the study of biblical economic ethics.

Issue #1: No Such Thing as Ethics in Scripture

The notion of ethics is said to be completely alien to the Bible. Thus, many argue that the use of the terms "biblical ethics," "Old Testament ethics," or "New Testament ethics" is misguided and without scriptural basis. We are imposing modern categories and language on these ancient texts. After all, the modern usage of the term "ethics" pertains to either one or all of the following: (1) descriptive ethics as an account of how people behave; (2) meta-ethics as the analytical exercise in studying both the language we use and our logical reasoning in adjudicating right from wrong; and (3) normative ethics as prescriptive of moral action. Furthermore, even as there are many rules and regulations in the Bible, critics note that these sacred writings are, nevertheless, not a handbook of do's and don'ts. They are primarily the self-revelation of a God who loves, forgives, and saves. They are an account of a God breaking into human history and inaugurating a kingdom whose building and completion define the remaining trajectory of human life.

Other scholars disagree and note that theology and ethics are inseparable in the Bible. For example, Philippians 2:2–11 and 1 Timothy 3 illustrate how profound Christological statements are often accompanied by ethical exhortations. We find a similar phenomenon in Jewish law and practice.[18] Many avoid this problem altogether by simply using the term "morality" instead of "ethics." For this study, I use "ethics" to refer to the norms, principles, rules of action, and exhortations that are normative for moral conduct.

Issue #2: Dissimilar Contexts

The historically and culturally conditioned nature of the Bible poses problems in ascertaining both what biblical texts actually meant for their time and what they mean for us today. These two tasks underscore the importance of understanding differences between the texts' original setting and our contemporary era. The circumstances in which biblical texts were written and within which we now receive them are radically different from one another.

Context is particularly important for economic ethics because economic decision-making is a practical art. Moreover, normative economics deals with questions of right or wrong; it requires much prudential judgment. In the first place, socioeconomic life is extremely complex and highly dynamic. There is no single, universal set of principles that can deal with all possible contingencies in economic life. In the vast majority of cases, we have to look at the specific circumstances before arriving at the right course of action. Second, there are many gray areas in economics. The same empirical data can often be tailored to support diametrically opposed positions. Sweeping a priori statements likely have weak foundations because adjudicating conflicting claims in economic life often requires weighing the particularities provided by context. Thus, we have to specify and then justify how we intend to bridge the contextual gap between the biblical and modern era. Two gaps are worth noting: the socioeconomic gap and the disparity in their respective eschatological horizons.

In the first place, we have a stark difference in the socioeconomic context of the Old and New Testament relative to the post-industrial age. Given this wide cultural gap, do biblical norms still apply to us today?[19] For example, many of the images, narratives, and concerns in the Bible were drawn from an agrarian setting. Furthermore, these ancient texts were written for a particular audience or in response to specific problems or needs, as in the case of the New Testament epistles. What do we do with the biblical legislation on land return, interest-free loans, and debt forgiveness vis-à-vis the modern economy which relies heavily on secure property rights and interest-bearing financial capital?

To be sure, the difference in the context does not automatically render biblical norms irrelevant. Most Christians, and even many non-Christians, accept the Ten Commandments and Jesus' two greatest commandments today. Nevertheless, most Christians would also say that the Mosaic laws' cultic and dietary restrictions are anachronistic for our time. Furthermore, people seem to be selective in the biblical laws and teachings they accept. For example, many gladly embrace passages on universal peace and turning spears and swords into ploughshares and pruning hooks (e.g., Is 2:4), even while ignoring numerous disturbing references to a warrior God leading the nation Israel in the conquest and destruction of the native inhabitants of the Promised Land (e.g., Dt 9:3).[20]

Many laws in the Old Testament are offensive to contemporary moral sensibilities. Take the case of capital punishment. Death-penalty proponents are quick to point to the scriptural warrants for the death penalty for the most heinous crimes, such as murder and kidnapping, while conveniently ignoring the many other offenses for which death was prescribed in the Old Testament, such as adultery, sorcery, homosexuality, and disrespect for parents. People take this selectivity in stride because of their commonsensical grasp of the cultural gap between biblical times and our own.[21] Values, priorities, and moral horizons are simply different. For example, purity-uncleanness and honor-shame are key Old Testament categories in evaluating moral behavior. In contrast, modern thinking revolves around individual rights and autonomy.

What controls do we use in choosing which passages to appropriate? Is it a purely subjective judgment? Is common sense the ultimate arbiter? Our moral intuitions may be sufficient for the relatively easy cases, such as the clear difference between the enduring nature of the Ten Commandments and the two greatest commandments, on the one hand, and the Mosaic cultic and dietary laws, on the other hand. Other norms are not as easy to evaluate and require reasoned argument. For example, should we apply the early Church ideal of communal property ownership to our globalized marketplace which is fraught with free-rider problems? Similarly, how practical is it to observe today the Old Testament precepts on gleaning privileges for the vulnerable? How do we determine whether a biblical teaching or law should be taken literally or metaphorically (e.g., debt remission, radical voluntary divestment)?

A second important contextual contrast is the eschatological horizon of the New Testament. Eschatology pertains to the last days, the end of the world. Paul wrote with a sense of urgency in light of what he believed was the imminent return of Jesus (the Parousia). Paul expected the second coming of Jesus Christ and the end-time to occur in his own lifetime. Consequently, he cajoled, begged, pleaded, and argued with people not to delay in embracing the Gospel. We find the same pressing urgency in the Gospel of Mark. This evangelist warned his readers that the kingdom of God was at hand, and that repentance was the only proper response, given the impending day of judgment.

It has been two millennia, and counting, since Paul's letters and the Gospel of Mark. Some are skeptical that New Testament ethics is still valid today because such ethics cannot be separated from its underlying eschatology.[22] The norms of the New Testament were given in the context of a looming end-time.

Despite this disparity in the eschatological horizon, others nonetheless argue that New Testament ethics is still relevant. Some convincingly observe that contemporary generations have, or at least ought to have, the same sense of eschatological urgency because they will not live forever. Despite the delay in the second coming of Jesus Christ, contemporary generations are nevertheless still bound by time, which means that their earthly days are numbered. It is very likely that, just like many others since the time of Paul and the early Church, they will stand before God long before the Parousia. Thus, the Pauline and Gospel appeal for a decisive conversion of hearts and their call to live as new creatures in Christ still resonate today, just as they did two thousand years ago.[23]

One could take this even further and argue that there is no substantive difference in the eschatology of the late first century vis-à-vis modernity. Pauline imminent eschatology was ultimately replaced by a Johannine nearly-realized eschatology. In the Johannine Gospel and letters, it is understood that people do not have to wait until the Parousia, nor do they have to wait until they die before they can begin to enjoy heaven. People can already have a first installment—a foretaste—of the love, peace, and joy of heaven in the here and now in the measure that they feel God's love for them and are able to love in return. In other words, they are invited to live today how they are to live in the end-time at the Messianic banquet. Thus, contemporary generations ought to find themselves on the same eschatological terrain as the first-century Christians. In light of its persecution, the early Church yearned for the immediate return of the Messiah that was taking long in coming, even as people today also endure what sometimes seems to be a prolonged vale of tears. In sum, even if we were to accept, for the sake of argument, that New Testament ethics cannot be separated from its underlying imminent eschatology, its moral teachings nevertheless still apply today because we live in the same unfolding nearly-realized eschatology of the Gospel of John.

How do we respond to these differences in the socioeconomic and eschatological contexts of the two periods? Note that the issue of how to use biblical norms properly is not a peculiarly modern problem. Recall the disagreement that pitted Paul and the Gentile Christians, on the one hand, against James and the Jewish Christians, on the other hand. The latter wanted to impose Mosaic observances on the Gentile converts (Acts 15:1–29). Their resolution of this issue is an excellent example of a discerning, prayerful appropriation of scriptural norms for our own use.

There are methods to get around disparate contexts and permit a critical and intelligent adoption of biblical teachings. Clearly, applying Sacred Scripture to economic life today requires a prior, intermediate task of selecting the criteria in determining which teachings still apply today and how urgently we are to take their demands. Moreover, there are timeless questions that transcend context, such as the perennial search to understand the purpose of life, the meaning of suffering, and the nature of interpersonal duties. Thus, many argue that differences in the underlying context should not prevent us from learning from the experiences of earlier communities of faith, including the nation Israel.[24]

Furthermore, there is a difference between being "context-dependent" and "context-specific." Context-dependence pertains to the need to take into account the larger milieu and attendant circumstances of texts. In contrast, "context-specific" refers to relevance to only one particular, specific set of circumstances. Most biblical economic insights are context-dependent and not context-specific. These texts convey a revelation that is "trans-contextual in importance and able to evaluate, effect, and transform contexts."[25] After all, these sacred writings are God's gift for all humanity.

Issue #3: Conflicting or Inconsistent Biblical Teachings

Another objection to the notion of biblical ethics is the heterogeneity in Scripture's teachings. Far from being monolithic, the Bible seems to have conflicting or inconsistent admonitions, sometimes even within the same books. For example, the prophetic literature and the Gospels view wealth with great antipathy, even hostility. There is a presumption that such riches were accumulated through sinful activity. In contrast, the Pentateuch, wisdom writings, and the historical literature depict wealth and prosperity as the fruits of a righteous life and evidence of God's favor. There are many more of these incongruities, especially on the question of property ownership.

What do we do in such cases of clashing texts? What are our criteria in accepting some of these teachings while ignoring others? How do we reconcile them? Should we even attempt to harmonize them? If not, then how do we go about justifying our selection of norms relevant for today? The deeper question associated with such heterogeneity is whether or not there is even a unified message behind biblical texts. Contemporary ethical discourse is fragmented to begin with and such biblical ambiguities only add to the confusion and discord.

We will account for some of these incongruities in the following sections and chapters. As we will see later, these seeming contradictions actually strengthen the case for using these sacred writings for contemporary ethical reflection because of what they teach us about methodology.

Issue #4: A Wide Variety of Hermeneutical Rules and Approaches

There is a daunting array of hermeneutical rules and principles in appropriating Sacred Scripture for contemporary use. While many of these are not mutually exclusive, the proliferation of methods is, nonetheless, overwhelming. Readers often give up in frustration in the face of too many choices, most of which require a separate study in themselves. Given our severe space constraint, we can only briefly describe some of these rules, especially those that have a direct bearing on our study.[26]

In the *rule of purpose*, it is the justification or the rationale behind biblical norms that is used for contemporary ethics rather than the precept itself. This addresses the problem of dissimilar contexts between biblical times and modernity. Unfortunately, the spirit behind scriptural norms is often not explicitly stated and has to be inferred.

The *rule of analogy* emphasizes the central role of analogical reasoning in applying Scripture to current issues. For example, the Old Testament mandates on gleaning privileges, interest-free loans, and slave manumission are anachronistic for the modern marketplace. Nevertheless, their underlying spirit still rings true today and is widely accepted as valid, namely, the obligation to assist those who have fallen on hard times (e.g., modern social safety net, bankruptcy relief). This rule directly addresses the problem of different socioeconomic contexts, although it requires extra work, as readers have to extrapolate similarities in the face of dissimilar circumstances.

The *rule of countercultural witness* calls for giving greater weight to scriptural passages that critique the status quo or the dominant powers and elites of their time. For example, the voices of the poor and the marginalized deserve a much greater hearing than those that promote the interests of the rich and the powerful, as in the parable of Dives and Lazarus (Lk 16:19–31), the Lukan beatitudes (Lk 6:20–26), and the strident prophetic oracles. Liberation theology and feminist hermeneutics are examples of the use of this rule.

The *rule of nonscientific scope* notes that the Bible is not meant to arbitrate empirical issues and should not, therefore, be used to resolve questions that are scientific in nature. For example, we should not look to these sacred texts to determine the economy's natural rate of unemployment.

The *rule of moral-theological adjudication* uses moral or theological norms in choosing between equally plausible but conflicting biblical interpretations. For example, do the Gospels and the Acts of the Apostles call for radical voluntary divestment, or do they sanction private property ownership? Exegetes and ethicists have relied on extra-biblical, theological, or moral arguments to justify their respective positions on this question.

Other hermeneutical rules of thumb in the literature are:

- Canon-within-a canon rule: Some parts of the Bible carry greater weight than others and serve as hermeneutical lenses with which to read it (e.g., Sinai Covenant).
- Weight-of-Scripture-as-a-whole rule: In using Scripture as a basis for making pronouncements on a particular issue (e.g., war, wealth, sex), the modern reader has to examine the consistency (or lack thereof) of biblical teachings on the subject matter, the amount of attention that the issue receives, and the degree to which the aforesaid question is central to the Bible's concerns.
- Rule of canonical interpretation: The unity of the biblical canon, including its structure, arrangement, and context, has to be considered in biblical interpretation. The meaning or contemporary application of individual biblical teachings is partly dependent on their place within the entire canon.[27]
- Rule of relevance: Contemporary relevance is a valid criterion for adjudicating competing biblical interpretations.[28]

Scholars have also differed on how Sacred Scripture speaks to us today. Some view it as the command of God; it conveys an imperative of obedience. Others accept biblical teachings as a wellspring of principles that are critical for moral action, such as love, justice, equity, and compassion. Still others take the Bible as predominantly about paradigmatic models for emulation, such as Jesus Christ. It is an essential means for character and community formation, given that Scripture reading is transformative and fruitful when read within a fellowship of faith. These sacred texts could also be viewed as a description of the symbolic world in which we live, a symbolic world from which we shape and form our own narratives. Others see the Bible as an invitation to responsive love and a call to liberation.[29]

These hermeneutical rules and strategies are not mutually exclusive. Some overlap and even reinforce one another (e.g., rules of purpose and analogy). Not surprisingly, many scholars use a variety of these approaches. Nevertheless, given the limitations of time and space, most studies make hard choices regarding which hermeneutical rules or strategies take precedence.

Issue #5: Principles-Based Hermeneutics

One of the more contested areas of hermeneutics is the issue of whether or not we can or should draw principles of moral action from Sacred Scripture as a way of applying it to contemporary ethics. This is an important question for our study because abstract principles of moral action provide the most obvious and the easiest way of bridging the disparity in the socioeconomic contexts of the ancient biblical world and the modern marketplace. In fact, it is common practice to draw universal principles from these sacred writings for use in ethical reflection.[30] Moreover, many of the aforesaid hermeneutical rules are about inferring general principles from biblical teachings, such as the rules of purpose and analogy. Furthermore, as already mentioned, economic life is complex and dynamic, and moral decision-making in this field relies heavily on prudential judgment, which often has to be guided by principles drawn from previous experience.

However, there are strong objections to the use of a principles-based hermeneutics. Moral teachings from these sacred texts come in different modes: as prescriptive rules or laws, as principles, as paradigms to be emulated, as perceptual categories through which we view and understand the world around us,[31] as "stories with ethical implications," as "narratives of approved or disapproved conduct," and as paraenesis (exhortation, advice).[32] One issue that arises is whether or not it is proper to transpose one mode of appeal into another. Hays (1990, 49) is emphatic that "texts must be granted authority (or not) in the mode in which they speak." For example, he notes that we should not turn narratives into law, as is the case when the account of common property ownership in the early Church (Acts 2:44–45) suddenly becomes a mandate for Christians to divest themselves of their property. Or we should not turn rules into principles, as is the case when the invitation to divest ourselves of possessions and give alms (Lk 12:33) is interpreted to mean detachment. Hays argues that moral imperatives should be taken on their own terms and be allowed to speak in their own mode of appeal. A principles-based approach can easily turn into a wholesale distillation of various modes of appeal (such as narratives, paradigms, rules) into general principles.[33]

Hays is against such a hermeneutical strategy because people often eventually treat the principles as far more authoritative than the biblical text itself. We can discard the text like chaff after we have gleaned the ethical principles embedded within. Or these principles might be used to override scriptural teachings themselves. Furthermore, texts are not allowed to speak on their own terms but are filtered through the lenses of these principles. In effect, principles "hijack" authority from the biblical text. This is not a far-fetched fear. Some cite the example of how the historical Jesus has trumped the biblical Jesus.[34]

The search for universal principles that encapsulate biblical teachings gives rise to other problems. First, biblical theology easily turns into philosophy, with Jesus Christ being no different from classical thinkers, such as Socrates or Buddha. Second, Christian ethics is subsumed under natural law. Human reason, rather than divine grace, becomes the guide to morality. The "moral imperatives of life" are embedded in human nature itself, and divine Revelation becomes unnecessary and redundant. There is nothing distinctive about Christian ethics, and it becomes indistinguishable from secular ethics. Thus, critics conclude that deriving and generalizing timeless principles across generations is a major pitfall in using Sacred Scripture for ethical reflection.[35]

Proponents on the other side of the debate have also much to say in defense of a principles-based hermeneutic. General principles free "the [biblical] text from its time-bound situation" and expand its reach.[36] We can further develop the biblical teaching or expand its application to other similar issues and to other time periods. For example, Psalm 144 provides rich fare when interpreted at different levels: literal reading (exodus from slavery in Egypt); allegorical sense (our redemption in Christ); moral sense (conversion from sin to a state of grace); anagogical sense (the freedom afforded by grace). Clearly, this is a reading of Psalm 144 that goes beyond the original intent of the writer and is a "re-application of basic theological principles to other peoples and situations."[37]

A principles-based approach is an "interpretative strategy" to dealing with the problem of different cultural contexts while still remaining true to the spirit behind the text.[38] Biblical texts can be applied to many cases and issues today that were not originally envisioned by their writers. Principles hold the key to this transposition. Moreover, they bridge the "cultural gap." These principles are instrumental in keeping these sacred writings alive, fresh, and relevant down through the ages by transplanting the message of the written Word from one milieu to another. After all, "Scripture has to be freed up to offer signposts in areas not on the original map."[39] Principles facilitate this.

For example, some suggest that the Church becomes an embodied metaphor to the degree that we learn from the narratives of the past and make them our own. Narratives, however, are not lived in a vacuum. Moreover, to appropriate earlier narratives as our own, we have to be able to identify with the paradigms and communities we seek to emulate. We must be able to articulate the qualities we want to imitate. Equally important, we have to justify why we choose certain qualities and not others. In other words, there is a need for metaphors that can bridge disparate narratives, different yet similar to each other. Beneath metaphors are principles at work. The use of allegory in literature is dependent on implicit principles. "Re-applications" are possible because of principles.

A second argument in defense of principles is their value in minimizing subjectivity. It is true that inferring principles from biblical text entails subjective judgment. Nevertheless, this is still much better than the alternative. Biblical hermeneutics teaches much on what the "text said," but it does not provide much guidance in moving from "that the text said to what the text says."[40] We run the danger of leaving people entirely to their own subjective judgment in making this jump. Unless we fill this vacuum with a much more objective standard, we will end up with an amorphous hermeneutics with no basis for saying why one interpretation is better than another. A principles-based approach, while admittedly subjective itself, nevertheless imposes some order, which in turn facilitates assessment and comparison between alternative interpretations. Principles are often derived from biblical text through communal prayer, reflection, discussion, and scholarship. This provides an occasion for community building. Such a communal approach has the collateral benefit of minimizing the subjective element in hermeneutics.

Third, a principles-based approach, when done properly, should not turn biblical theology into philosophy, or biblical ethics into mere natural law, because these principles are still clearly theological in their justification, use, and desired outcomes. For example, compare the principle of the preferential option for the poor with the social safety net of Western nations. Their similarities are merely material rather than formal. While secular welfare assistance is based on a social contract or even pure altruism, the biblical preferential option for the poor is founded on divine command, on the understanding that the poor are special in the eyes of God, and on the notion of humanity as a family in God. In other words, the principles derived from Sacred Scripture are ultimately theological in their foundations, even as we are able to express many of them in terms of reason. In fact, many see similarities between the Wisdom literature and natural law.

Fourth, a principles-based approach need not necessarily render biblical text dispensable. People may indeed focus on the principles, rather than on the biblical texts. Worse, they might even use these principles as a convenient and welcome shortcut in not having to grapple with the texts themselves. These are valid concerns. Nevertheless, the problem lies not with a principles-based approach per se, but with the users and their inappropriate use of these principles. Moreover, principles do not lessen the need for the scriptural writings or make them redundant because biblical texts are still treated as the foundational sources of these principles. They are essential "signposts" that guide the application of these principles. Biblical texts are the ultimate arbiters in determining the proper use of these principles.

Fifth, there will be inevitable conflicting claims among biblical texts themselves. In some cases, we cannot leave these clashing claims unresolved given their importance for social ethics, as in the case of whether or not property ownership or divestment is the proper Christian response. In such cases, how do we go about sorting through these incongruities and what criteria do we use? As we will see in part III, principles can be used to disentangle these seemingly contradictory voices.

Sixth, principles perform an integrative function for some biblical texts. Take the case of Leviticus 12:6–8; 14:21; 27:2–8 as an example. Taken as a group, these laws point to an important principle that may not be apparent when the passages are read singly by themselves: "leniencies for the poor"[41] in which the burdens of community life are spread according to people's ability to pay. Such price breaks are concrete applications of the preferential option for the poor.

Seventh, Jesus' rules on moral life are more "exemplary rather than comprehensive, and aim more at reminding the members of the community's intensive claims than at providing universal moral guidelines."[42] Since Jesus' preaching does not purport to be a complete system or even an ethical system at all, the community is left to exercise its prudential and faith-filled judgment. Thus, it is all the more important to discern the underlying spirit behind Jesus' teachings. (Recall the rule of purpose.) Such spirit would most likely be expressed in the form of general principles.

Moreover, note that the narrative of Jesus Christ is itself the "Gospel!"[43] It is from this narrative that we draw our ethics today since it continues to instruct. It is a live narrative, much as it was in the first century. After all, discipleship is about following the person of Jesus Christ. It is ever fresh in whatever circumstance the disciple may be found. Hence, we have to discern and internalize the defining formal characteristics of this narrative. This is easily or most likely expressed in terms of general principles. For example, we see Christ providing the exemplary example of love of God and love of neighbor. In addition, earlier generations pass on to subsequent generations what they have learned and appropriated from their encounter with Sacred Scripture. What is handed down will most likely include principles, even if embedded or implicit in the narratives or ethos that are passed on from one generation to the next.

Finally, we cannot deny the appeal and the utility of principles, whether for biblical morality or for ethics in general. Principles, whether explicit or implicit, are pervasive in moral reasoning. This is particularly true for social ethics because of its many gray areas that require prudential judgment. The Bible is not exempt from this phenomenon. For example, the writers of the Old Testament most likely did not intend to formulate universal principles. Nevertheless, there are, in fact, implicit or de facto principles in the Old Testament since the same moral teachings repeat themselves under different guises in the Bible.[44] There are underlying patterns throughout the Old Testament. Moreover, note the enduring power and relevance of many of these moral teachings down through the centuries (e.g., care for the poor). This continuity, potency, and unbroken relevance can be attributed to these biblical teachings' underlying implicit principles. After all, whether we reason in theological or secular terms, people most likely employ principles to distinguish proper from improper conduct.

METHODOLOGICAL CHOICES AND ASSUMPTIONS

As stated earlier in the preface, this study is limited only to the following two goals:

- Establishing what the individual sections of the Bible teach about economic life within the context of their respective social setting, theology, and ethics; and
- Discerning recurring themes on economic morality across these books and epistles when read together as a single biblical canon.[45]

Whichever methods we use will have their particular strengths and weaknesses. There is no consensus on the appropriate approach to follow and, thus, theologians and ethicists interested in using these sacred texts for ethical reflection will have to make hard methodological choices and then justify them. In this last section, I outline my choice of methodological assumptions for this study, without claiming that they are the only or even the best strategies to employ.[46]

1. Let Each Book Speak on Its Own Terms.

In the following chapters, biblical texts articulate their respective and sometimes conflicting social visions in their own voices.[47] We are not going to harmonize different books and letters of the Old and New Testament but allow them to speak on their own terms.[48] This avoids the danger of imposing a contrived unity under the guise of pulling these disparate writings into a coherent whole. This would have been unacceptable because it oversimplifies a "complex phenomenon," it dulls the "sharpness of moral dialogue" that can come about from a diversity of perspectives, and it evens out what is, in fact, a rich and varied terrain.[49]

Furthermore, the Bible is an account of a wide variety of encounters between humanity and the divine in human history and experience. In addition, social and moral life are too complex to be covered adequately by a single, much less closed, set of norms, narratives, rules, paradigms, or principles. For example, it is inappropriate to force a single view of economic life in the Bible because its books have their respective teachings. Moreover, there are contradictions or inconsistencies even within the same books or even within the same chapters (e.g., Dt 15:4; 15:11).[50]

2. Situate Each Book within the Larger Whole of the Biblical Canon.

After examining what each book has to say on economic life in its own voice and on its own terms, we appraise these teachings within the larger unity of the biblical canon in the following three sequential steps:

- First, we evaluate these economic norms within the context of the life setting (*Sitz im Leben*), theology, and ethics of the individual books in which they are found.
- Second, we assess whether or not there are recurring patterns or themes across these books and epistles.
- Third, we examine individual teachings and themes within the larger framework of the entire biblical canon.

We simply accept biblical texts as we receive them in their final form.[51] We will not differentiate the various layers of editorial work beneath these writings. This also means that we accept these biblical texts as a unified whole and not as atomistic, autonomous units.

These three steps of putting each book within the larger unity of the biblical canon are important, for a number of reasons. First, we avoid two extremes. On the one hand, letting each book speak on its own terms heads off the risk of forcing disparate biblical teachings into a false or premature unity. The wide diversity of views and the occasional contradictions are allowed to surface. On the other hand, using books singly by themselves runs the danger of presenting biblical texts as autonomous and independent of each other without any overarching framework. Consequently, the relationship of these various writings to one another is left unexplored. The unity and coherence of Sacred Scripture are, thus, ignored or given short shrift. This is an incomplete, impoverished, and deeply unsatisfactory approach to reading the Bible. More important, we run the danger of treating these writings merely as literature, rather than as the revealed Word of God.

Thus, we let each book speak in its own voice, and then we also weigh what each book says within the larger witness of the entire biblical canon.[52] The result is a unity-within-diversity or, put in another way, a nuanced unity amidst diversity.[53] We avoid the two extremes of imposing an artificial unity, on the one hand, and ignoring the biblical canon's unified message, on the other hand.

A second reason for the importance of taking the aforementioned three steps is that the Bible can be aptly described as a synergy in which the resulting whole is more than the mere sum of its individual constituent books. We will miss the insights flowing from this synergy if we limit ourselves to letting individual books speak in their own voices without examining them together as a single canon. The unified whole has a distinct message of its own that may reinforce or cast individual books' teachings in a whole new light. Note, for example, the synthesis of part III later in the book.

Third, biblical texts form a rich tapestry of God's self-revelation. In spite of the many authors and editors involved in the composition of the Bible, it is still one and the same God who takes the initiative of self-revealing divine life and love in the narratives, admonitions, ideals, and norms of these sacred writings.[54] There is one unfolding Revelation in Sacred Scripture. Despite their diversity of literary genres, social visions, and theologies, the books of the Bible describe a single phenomenon of the human encounter with the divine. There is, in fact, one narrative that emerges.

Fourth, we cannot plumb the full import of individual pericope, teachings, or books by studying them singly by themselves, in isolation of the larger biblical canon of which they are a part and to which they contribute. For example, disturbing passages that repeatedly call for the complete annihilation of all the inhabitants in the land Israel was about to conquer take on a metaphorical rather than a literal meaning when viewed within the entirety of the Old Testament, to wit: that Israel was to be decisive in shunning the idolatrous practices they were about to encounter in Canaan (e.g., Dt 7:2; 20:16–17). Moreover, note how Isaiah's description of the New Jerusalem dispels the impression one might get from the conquest narratives of YHWH as a warrior God bent on the destruction of Canaan's previous inhabitants (e.g., Is 11:7–9). And, of course, the best example of the value of reading the Bible as a whole is the Christian belief that Jesus Christ is the fulfillment of the Old Testament.

3. Sacred Scripture Continues to Speak, Even to Contemporary Generations.

Biblical texts take a life of their own by conveying new meaning beyond that which their original authors intended. Scholars have described this as the "surplus of meaning" in these sacred writings, or as the semantic autonomy of text.[55] In fact, the Bible itself demonstrates the superfluity in its meaning and the possibility of using it in ever-new ways. For example, the Exodus liberation is constantly invoked, re-interpreted, and re-appropriated by subsequent generations and writers in different contexts. We find reference to this decisive event from the celebratory hymn of Exodus 15:1–8, 20–21, to the Psalms (e.g., Ps 78, 105), to the accounts of the conquest of the land (Josh 3:14–17).[56] In addition, many motive clauses appended to the laws refer to the Exodus event as a rationale for obedience (e.g., Lev 25:38, 42, 55). Or note how Jesus uses Isaiah 61:1–2 in his inaugural lecture to characterize his own public ministry (Lk 4:16–21). We find many instances of such cross-referencing, especially in Matthew, which was written to convince its Jewish audience that Jesus brought the Old Testament to its fulfillment and completion. Christian liturgy draws heavily from Isaiah to describe Jesus as the Messiah (e.g., Advent and Lenten readings).

The semantic autonomy of text can be easily and reasonably justified. First, God is the author of Sacred Scripture and, as a result, the original intent of the texts' writers or redactors, while central and important, is neither decisive nor the last word on how the Word of God is to be used for ethical reflection. God can continue to speak to every generation through these sacred texts, long after they had been completed in the form in which we receive them today. After all, as part of Revelation, it was God who guaranteed the integrity of the oral tradition that had initially received, preserved, and transmitted divine self-revelation over many centuries. It was God who guaranteed the integrity of the oral tradition as it was finally put in writing and as the books of the canon that we now call the Bible were selected. And it is God who continues to guarantee biblical integrity as it is read, interpreted, and lived today. God can keep speaking through Sacred Scripture until the end-time. We must remember that this is a God of the living and not of the dead (Mk 12:27). In fact, the burden of proof lies with those who do not accept the semantic autonomy of text. They will have to prove why it is reasonable or likely that God's self-revelation is contained exclusively in the original meaning conveyed by the authors and editors who had composed the Bible.

Second, Sacred Scripture is God's self-disclosure that has been given as a gift, not only to the contemporaries of the original authors and editors of the Bible, but also to all humanity. This makes it even more likely that God continues to speak to men and women of every age, long after the completion of these ancient writings. Besides, there is no time in God. We cannot limit God's word to any one particular time period.

We have to consider the implications of the semantic autonomy of text for ethical reflection. First, it means that Sacred Scripture is a living document because it conveys the Word of God in ever-new ways and with ever-fresh insight and energy down through the ages, long after the biblical canon was clearly defined and closed. Biblical interpretation and appropriation provide an inexhaustible wellspring and a terrain for subsequent generations to encounter the divine.

Second, the semantic autonomy of text means that differences in context should not be an impediment for the contemporary use of biblical teachings. After all, God continues to speak to humanity today by allowing these sacred writings to take on new meaning beyond that which their original authors and editors meant for their own particular day and age.

Third, since these sacred texts take meaning beyond their original context, biblical ethics is forward-looking. It builds on lessons from the past for the sake of the present, even as it looks forward to the completion and perfection of the kingdom of God. The semantic autonomy of text explains why Sacred Scripture, far from always providing answers, often provokes probing and even unsettling questions (e.g., Job and Qoheleth).

Nevertheless, the semantic autonomy of text also poses new problems that must be addressed. For example, does it mean that Sacred Scripture is completely amorphous—putty that can be shaped into whatever form subsequent generations may desire? Is this not license to rationalize whatever it is readers may wish to draw from the Bible in order to justify their actions? Does this mean that these sacred writings depend on "private interpretation," that is, on the reader's response? What do we do with clashing private interpretations? Who adjudicates such conflicts and on what basis? Are there controls to such interpretation, or is it completely open-ended? These legitimate concerns suggest limits to the semantic autonomy of text.

Sacred Scripture is properly read and interpreted within a faith community animated by the Holy Spirit. An authentic semantic autonomy of text unfolds only within a believing community guided by the Holy Spirit. This has always been a constitutive feature of Revelation, from the Chosen People, to the early Church. Moreover, observe that the New Jerusalem envisioned in the Old Testament (Is 2:2–4) and the kingdom of God inaugurated by Christ (Acts 4:32–35) are both communal in nature. In other words, these sacred writings have been entrusted to a community of believers—a fellowship whose faith comes from and is enlivened by the Holy Spirit. It is within the safeguards provided by such a community that we find the semantic autonomy of text unfolding.

4. Inferred Principles of Action Have a Legitimate Role in Biblical Economic Ethics.

Resolving the debate on the propriety of inferring abstract principles of moral action from the Bible is beyond the scope of this book. Nevertheless, we can draw some preliminary conclusions for purposes of this study. First, recall the view that argues that sacred texts ought to be permitted to speak in their original mode of appeal.[57] I agree with this approach. However, this does not and should not preclude us from *re-presenting* moral imperatives in terms of other modes of appeal (in addition to their original mode). This claim is particularly important for principles as a mode of appeal because it is much easier to transform rules, paradigms, and even the images of a symbolic world into principles, than it is to do the reverse. In fact, this is probably the most common practice in the use of Sacred Scripture because principles are robust, flexible, and concise in the way they state the nub of the imperative or narrative.

To begin with, many biblical passages or modes of appeal readily lend themselves to re-presentation as abstract principles. In fact, such derived principles may make these moral imperatives much more accessible and comprehensible to readers. Principles can make these imperatives and narratives easier to appropriate and internalize. In fact, this is the case with many passages dealing with the proper treatment of the poor. The entire corpus of Old Testament laws on debt, slavery, land return, property, and wealth point to underlying principles of mutual assistance, preferential option for the poor, and economic security for all, even if they are not explicitly stated in such terms in the Bible. There is nothing wrong in inferring and bringing into the open the spirit implicit in many of these passages or modes of appeal. This is particularly true for those moral imperatives that recur across the canon (e.g., proper use of property).

Second, treating modes of appeal in isolation of one another may be too restrictive and may, in fact, be contrary to the nature of Sacred Scripture. For all its diversity, the Bible is nonetheless an integral whole. These modes of appeal, while distinct from each other, are in fact inseparable. They reinforce one another and often convey the same moral teachings, but from different angles and with varied perspectives. In other words, rules, principles, paradigms, and images of a symbolic world complement each other. Modes of appeal can mutually reinforce one another if used concurrently. This diversity of approaches enriches Scripture's moral teachings.

For example, in the account of the rich young man who was unable to leave all to follow Christ, the narrative's impact is reinforced by its underlying principles of detachment and finding one's anchor of security in God alone (Mk 10:17–31). Or recall the parable of the unforgiving servant that culminated with Jesus' teaching that we ought to forgive, as we ourselves have been forgiven by God (Mt 18:23–35). Or note how the parable of the Good Samaritan vividly illustrates how even an enemy is one's neighbor who deserves to be loved (Lk 10:25–37). In other words, principles work well with other modes of appeal.

Third, a synthetic task is, by its nature, reliant on drawing commonalities across different biblical texts, books, and teachings. We have to use the rules of analogy and purpose. The insights that flow from the use of these rules would in all likelihood be formulated in terms of general principles.

Fourth, principles provide an important and necessary common ground for conversation both within and beyond a faith community. An ecclesial community does not exist in a vacuum. It has to interact with the larger culture of which it is a part and to which it contributes. The faith community that is guided by Sacred Scripture is, in fact, a nested community! It is embedded within a much larger community, and one that is often pluralistic, secular, or even of another faith. An important cultural difference between the peoples of the Old and New Testament and our own era is that religion was an integral part, indeed, a central pillar of their culture. Not so in Western modernity in which religion is often viewed as a private matter, and the separation of Church and State is zealously guarded by countries such as the United States.[58]

The ecclesial community cannot hermetically seal itself off because it has to share resources with the rest of society. Absent a shared narrative of faith, the believing community and the larger culture will have to converse with one another on economic morality based on their shared citizenship or their sense of a common personhood. Principles can facilitate the use of biblical teachings in this conversation. While the two greatest commandments of love of God and love of neighbor may not be accepted in secular discourse, the principle of preferential option for the poor is one that has been part of the public's ethos. Or compare most nations' progressive taxation with the "leniencies for the poor" in the Bible. Both the ecclesial and the secular community converge in many of their social practices. Principles are an effective way of underscoring such commonalities. After all, Scripture dovetails natural law, and principles are an effective means of demonstrating this (e.g., wisdom sayings).

In sum, I concur with the position that we should preserve the original mode of appeal used by these sacred texts in their moral imperatives. However, we can go further and re-present moral imperatives, in addition to and not as a substitute for their original mode of appeal. In fact, we should supplement the original mode of appeal whenever helpful in advancing readers' grasp of Scripture's insights. In other words, for as long as we respect and present the moral imperatives' original mode of appeal, we can infer abstract principles of moral action from the Bible's rules, paradigms, narratives, and images of a symbolic world. Modes of appeal are not mutually exclusive; they can complement each other. This is especially true for principles.

5. Differences in Socioeconomic Context Do Not Preclude the Use of Biblical Insights in Other Time Periods.

The ancient agrarian economy of biblical times and our own contemporary globalized, knowledge economy are vastly different. However, this should not foreclose the use of biblical economic insights for our own day nor should such differences be exaggerated. After all, there are common features in any economy, whether agrarian, industrial, ancient, feudal, modern, or post-industrial. Humans have basic needs for food, clothing, shelter, and medical care. They are constantly confronted with opportunity costs in their choices, whether in the use of their time or material resources. Division of labor is a fact of socioeconomic life. These similar experiences across any economy form the basis for our analogical reasoning on how to use Sacred Scripture for present-day economic morality.

For example, despite the disparity between an agrarian and a knowledge economy, the Old Testament prohibition against charging interest for loans of money or grain is still relevant today. This is so because this biblical norm points to a common experience in the marketplace—there will always be people who will be vulnerable to the chance and contingencies of economic life and who will require assistance to get back on their feet. Thus, the larger and more important point of the Old Testament prohibition on charging interest is the admonition to lend a helping hand to those who have fallen on hard times and not to profit from their distress.

SUMMARY AND CONCLUSIONS

The use of Sacred Scripture in contemporary ethical reflection is not a straightforward exercise because of multiple issues, such as seeming inconsistencies in biblical teachings, wide contextual differences between ancient times and modernity, and the diversity of rules and hermeneutical approaches proposed by scholars. For this study, we let individual books speak on their own terms, but within the larger unity of the biblical canon and illumined by the faith life of a "reading" ecclesial community. Consequently, biblical texts can take meaning beyond that which was originally meant by their authors or editors.

NOTES

1. Childs (1993, 674)
2. Rodd (1993–1994, 101)
3. I take this fourfold division of tasks from Himes (1985). See Hays (1996, 212–13) for a slightly different set of tasks: descriptive (exegesis), synthetic, hermeneutic, and pragmatic (i.e., putting faith into action).
4. Davies (2006, 747–48); Wilson (1995, 60–62)
5. Wilson (1995, 60) views Kaiser (1983) and Childs (1993) as examples of this approach.
6. For example, see Knight (1939).
7. Donahue (2005, 32); Gustafson (1978, 142; 1984); Hauerwas (1984)
8. Collins and Kendall (1997, 31–36) call these the principle of philosophical assistance and the principle of inculturation.
9. For example, there is wide consensus that the Gospels of Matthew and Luke were composed using the Gospel of Mark, a yet unidentified document (Q), and sources unique to Matthew and Luke.
10. For example, we have aphorisms, miracle stories, parables, apocalyptic sayings, and prophetic oracles.
11. See, for example, Horsley (2009) and Horsley and Hanson (1985).
12. Paris (1995, 176) describes this hazard as the "heteronomy of modernity."
13. Birch (1995, 26)
14. Barton (1982, 116–17)
15. Longnecker (2009, 36)

16. DeSilva (2004, 127–28); Elliott (1993); Horrell (2009)

17. Elliot (1993, 90). For examples of such exegesis, see Perkins (1994), Verhey (2002), Cahill (1990), and Donahue (2005), who employ insights from social-scientific criticism in their work. Schmidt (1987) is skeptical of its use.

18. Longnecker (1984, 10)

19. See Birch (2001, 296–98), Davies (2006, 748–49), Marshall (1994, 131–32), Rodd (1993–1994, 101), and Wilson (1995, 56–59) for a sampling of positions on this question.

20. Rodd (1993–1994, 100–101)

21. Davies (2006, 748–49); Rodd (1993–1994)

22. For example, see Sanders (1970).

23. Hiers (1984a)

24. Birch (2001)

25. Stackhouse (1987, 390–91). See also his description of a "double hermeneutics" in using the Bible for contemporary economics.

26. Unless otherwise stated, I take the following rules from Cosgrove (2002).

27. For example, some view Qoheleth as a closing redactional commentary on the wisdom literature (Cosgrove 2002, 198). See Childs (1992) for a further exposition on the use of the canon as a reference point for hermeneutics.

28. O'Collins and Kendall (1997) propose ten principles for the contemporary theological use of the Bible. Among these are the need for a faith-filled, active, and communal reading and interpretation of Scripture; the importance of multiple attestation (biblical convergence); greater weight accorded to the consensus of centrist exegetes; attention to the metathemes that run across the entire Bible (e.g., love); openness to letting philosophy and cultures enrich our biblical interpretations; and the acknowledgment of the provisional nature of biblical interpretations because the end-time is yet to come.

29. See Hays (1996, 215–90) and Spohn (1984) for a more in-depth survey of these approaches.

30. This hermeneutical strategy started with Harnack (1901). Beed and Beed (2012) survey recent literature in the use of a principles-based hermeneutics by theologians and economists in their application of Sacred Scripture to contemporary market issues.

31. Hays (1996, 209) calls this the symbolic mode of appeal.

32. Hays (1996, 208–9); Longnecker (1984, 1–9); Marshall (1994, 132)

33. Hays (1996, 293–95)

34. Marshall (1994, 134). This is the controversy spawned by a group of biblical scholars (known as the Jesus Seminar) who proposed reconstructing the words and life of the actual Jesus who walked the earth two thousand years ago (the historical Jesus).

35. Longnecker (1984, 3–5). See also Birch (1995, 26).

36. Marshall (1994, 135–36)

37. Marshall (1994, 135)

38. Davies (2006, 749)

39. Marshall (1994, 136)

40. Marshall (1994, 136)

41. Brin (1994, 74–89)

42. Meeks (1986, 142)

43. Meeks (1986, 143)

44. Clements (1984)

45. By "canon," I am referring to the books and works constituting the Christian Bible. The Protestant and Catholic traditions differ in what comprises their respective canons. For this book, we are concerned only with those parts of the Bible with substantial blocks of materials on economic life, and all the books and epistles we examine, with the exception of Sirach, are accepted by both traditions as part of their canon.

46. See Birch (2011) for a discussion of other methodological issues and choices in the literature.

47. Most scholars acknowledge this diversity of views and the importance of not imposing a forced unity. For example, see Barton (1978), Birch (2001), E. Davies (1995), Hays (1996), Pleins (2001), and Wilson (1995, 56–59).

48. Hays (1996), Matera (1996), Pilgrim (1981), and Pleins (2001) pursue such an approach.

49. E. Davies (1995, 52); Birch (2001, 297). Birch (2001, 294, 297) cites Hempel (1964 [1938]) and Eichrodt as examples of superimposing an artificial schema on biblical texts.

50. Whybray (1989, 332)

51. I am following Childs's (1992) canonical criticism and Hays (1996) in this regard.

52. Our methodological choices #1 and 2 correspond to Hays's (1996, 212–13, 291–93) descriptive and synthetic tasks.

53. Birch (2001, 296)

54. Verhey (2011, 5, 11)

55. See, for example, how Donahue (2005, 12–13), Ogletree (1983, 2), Lee (2002), and Schneiders (1991) use Ricoeur's (1976) original insight on this point.

56. I take this example from Donahue (2005, 12).

57. Hays (1996)

58. Kloppenborg (1990, 184–85)

I

Old Testament

Chapter Two

Socioeconomic Conditions

Biblical Israel

Biblical Israel experienced numerous pivotal turning points in her socioeconomic history. The first was her gradual formation as a nation from disparate groups of marginalized people. This was followed by the emergence of the monarchy (1020 B.C.) that eventually secured the borders of a unified kingdom. The nation fractured in 922 B.C. upon the death of Solomon as the northern kingdom (Israel) split from the southern kingdom (Judah). Weakened by such internal rancor, these divided kingdoms became easy prey for the emerging empires of the era. The northern kingdom fell to the Assyrians in 721 B.C. in what has been called the Fall of Samaria. The southern kingdom collapsed in 587 B.C. when the Babylonians laid siege to Jerusalem, razed the Temple, despoiled the land, and then deported a good part of the population. In 539 B.C. the Persians defeated the Babylonians and ended Israel's exile. The surviving population returned to the Promised Land, reestablished itself as a nation, and rebuilt the Temple (Ezra 1). Israel's post-exilic subjugation under Persian rule spanned two centuries until Alexander the Great's conquests in the late fourth century. The Greeks ruled for nearly two hundred years until the Maccabean revolt. It was a short-lived independence for the nation Israel, as in-fighting led to chaos and a power vacuum that the Romans gladly filled.

These major events form the larger backdrop to much of the economic ethics of the Old Testament. For example, Israel's unavoidable exposure to the Canaanite way of life tested the nation's self-understanding and commitment to mutual assistance. This may have been the occasion for the constant biblical reminders to care for the poor. The prophets' exhortations on just conduct are often viewed as an indictment of the excessive demands of the monarchy and its elite that impoverished many. The Persian and Greek hegemony and exactions at the time of the final redaction of the Old Testament may account for its perennial call to mercy, justice, and righteousness. Indeed, to appreciate fully biblical economic ethics, we have to familiarize ourselves with its larger socioeconomic context.[1]

Unfortunately, studying the socioeconomic conditions of the times is not a straightforward exercise because of the dearth of reliable materials, especially for the post-exilic era. There at least four possible sources that can be used: biblical text, extra-biblical Ancient Near Eastern (ANE) literature and legal documents, archaeological findings, and contemporary scholarship on ancient political economies. Many biblical scholars rely on biblical text to shed light on the social conditions of these time periods. However, this must be done with great caution because many of the biblical texts often used for such an exercise were written or edited at a much later time than the period they were supposed to be describing.[2] Moreover, many of these biblical writings were not meant to be historical accounts, but were instructive, paraenetic, or theological in their aims. Furthermore, there is the danger of circularity in using biblical text to infer the socioeconomic conditions of the period, and then to turn around and use these inferred socioeconomic conditions to validate or corroborate other biblical texts. A solution to this problem is not to ignore what biblical text can tell us about the era, but to be judicious in the selection and use of the biblical texts and to know their limitations.[3]

In what follows, we examine three distinct periods: the era of the monarchs in Iron Age II (1000–586 B.C.), Persian rule (539–333 B.C.), and the Hellenistic period (332–142 B.C.). Scholars differ over their assessment of the socioeconomic conditions of Israel during the monarchical period. On the one hand, there are those who view Judah as a redistributive ancient political economy in which the ruling elite extracted peasants' surplus, thereby reducing them to the sorry plight of destitute landlessness or debt slavery. On the other hand, others point to archaeological findings suggesting a thriving peasantry able to produce and accumulate some surplus. However, scholars and archeologists agree that the plight of Judean peasants in the post-exilic period was dismal. They endured far worse conditions under the Persians compared to monarchical rule. We examine these eras and their social conditions in what follows.

PRE-MONARCHIC ISRAEL

There is no consensus in the literature on the origins of Israel.[4] Some believe that the nation began as a pastoral, semi-nomadic people who finally embraced a life of settled agriculture in the highlands.[5] Others suggest that pastoral nomads constituted only a tiny fraction of the population, no more than 10 percent. The bulk of the nation was, in fact, an ethnically and socioeconomically diverse group of people, ranging from insurgent mercenaries, tribes of organized farming communities, peasants, artisans, disaffected priests, and runaway slaves. They were bound by the common desire to live in the highlands, away from Egyptian and Caananite oppression.[6] What is clear in the literature is that the nation was predominantly peasant engaged in subsistence agriculture.

In an agrarian economy, land is the source of wealth and power. Land tenure arrangements determine the distribution of income and entitlements, and this is where we see a sharp contrast between pre-monarchic Israel, on the one hand, and the surrounding Canaanite states, on the other hand. Early Israel settled in the hill country (the highlands), while the Canaanites lived in the rich alluvial plains (the low lands).

As the nation Israel formed in the high country, they encountered a Canaanite political economy in the low lands that was a mixture of both prebendal and patrimonial land tenure arrangements. Prebendal land tenure was based on land grants awarded by the crown to royal and military officials as compensation for their loyalty and services. Patrimonial land tenure arrangements were the hereditary transfers of land from generation to generation. In the Canaanite plains, both types of land tenure arrangements were practiced since royal land grants were often also hereditary.

Recipients of these crown land grants did not do the farming themselves. Instead, they permitted peasants in search of a livelihood to work these estates. In exchange for their use of the land, peasants were obligated to pay taxes and rents which are estimated to have run up to more than half of the harvest. Clearly, the temptation for these privileged absentee landlords was to extract as much of the land's surplus for themselves and to leave the peasants with just enough to keep them alive to work the land and produce surplus. Living conditions are believed to be dire for the peasants and, not surprisingly, Canaanite states were inegalitarian societies.

The Chosen People originally grouped themselves as a tribal confederation characterized by (1) a free association among landholding families as equals enjoying full civil rights and (2) possession of land via hereditary succession. Israel was more egalitarian in the post-settlement period compared with its neighboring states. Some scholars attribute this to the people's keen awareness of their precarious state. After all, theirs was an unforgiving life fraught with much uncertainty.

Wealth was fleeting—here today and suddenly gone tomorrow through plunder or disaster. The best way to preserve it was to share it with others so that the latter, in their own turn, might share their surplus at a later time. Building neighborly good will and being able to call on others for assistance were essential in an unpredictable and hostile environment.[7] Consequently, wealth was not used to oppress others nor was it utilized to acquire even more riches, as in modern capitalism. Instead, wealth was employed to entertain, to be hospitable, to share, and to help the poor. Such altruism was, in fact, a rational strategy for mutual survival, indeed, an insurance policy on being able to call on neighbors for help later. These rational strategies for mutual survival were eventually codified in the nation's laws.[8]

No one was rich or poor because everyone was part of the clan or tribe. The village was the connection between the Ancient Near Eastern (ANE) peasant family and the larger world. The village was the lifeline of the family against the vicissitudes of life. And there were many of these uncertainties and unpleasant surprises that the family had to guard against. In the first place, there was the precarious nature of subsistence agriculture itself. They were subject to the vagaries of weather, blight, disease, floods, famine, family illness, and sheer bad luck. Second, there were pressures from the internal dynamics of the household, such as not having enough land to bequeath something to all the sons.[9] Given these pressures and demands, the family, clan, and village became important social institutions.[10]

> Pressured on all sides, peasant societies develop systems that relieve the pressure as much as possible, that spread the risk as widely as possible. So the family is never isolated. Its problems become those of every family in the village. . . . But *this reliance on village solidarity is based not on a romantic impulse or friendship but on the harshness of peasant life*. (Scott 1989, 86, emphasis added)

Peasant solidarity was a form of social insurance against the hazards of life. The ethos of mutual assistance (even if only out of expediency) worked well as a strategy for mutual survival.

The cornerstone of the pre-monarchic Israelite economy was the provision of a sufficient livelihood for all, no one excluded. It is the much-sought ideal of an equality and sufficiency for all.[11] In having a secure livelihood, these erstwhile nomads, peasants, or slaves could finally experience what it is to live free, for a change. Consequently, land was central to their identity, whether as individuals or as a nation. Land was the basis for the basic rights enjoyed by the families, from taking part in the judicial assembly at the city gate, to participating in public worship, to the right and duty of military conscription.[12] Indeed, landholding was essential for full participation in the life and governance of the community.

There is no scholarly agreement on how nascent Israel divided land. Some believe that it could have been a combination of awarding specific plots to families and of giving each family the right to be included in the periodic redistribution of communally owned land. However, one thing is certain: the right to their specific plot of land or the right to be included in the village's periodic redistribution of land was inalienable and was passed on as an inheritance to their heirs.[13]

Thus, there were two distinct approaches to land distribution and management at the time of pre-monarchic Israel. On the one hand, we have the Canaanite model that treated land as a commodity. One could accumulate as much of it as one could afford or appropriate from someone else. Canaanites were urban and mercantile in their orientation. On the other hand, pre-monarchic Israel treated land as an inheritance. It was inalienable. The nation had a rural worldview and was focused on subsistence production.

PRECARIOUS AGRICULTURE

Agriculture was the predominant economic activity of the ancient world, including Palestine. Families were engaged in subsistence farming, that is, producing primarily for their own consumption and then trading whatever surplus they may have to procure their other necessities. Cereals, oil, and wine were the principal crops, with livestock and fruit trees as supplementary sources of food and income.

Climatic and ecological conditions were of central concern. The Philistinian coastal plains and the lowlands were far more fertile compared to the Judean highlands and desert. For this reason, after the break-up of the nation, the northern kingdom (Israel) had far more resources than the southern kingdom (Judah).[14] Both the amount and the timeliness of precipitation are crucial for agriculture. In this, Judah was again at a disadvantage. It did not get as much rain as the north, and even when the rains came, they were much diminished as they moved west to east beyond the ridges of the highlands. Thus, the Judean highlands' eastern slope toward the Dead Sea is semi-arid. Furthermore, the timing of the precipitation is crucial because it has to coincide with the both the planting and growing seasons. Too early or too late outside of these two critical periods can spell disaster. It is estimated that, on the average, there were three to four bad years every ten years. Clearly, these would be catastrophic if they were bad years in a row.[15]

Farming families survived the chance and contingencies of agriculture, for at least two reasons. First was the rational decision-making of farming communities. They took to heart what earlier generations handed down in terms of what worked in that harsh environment. Best farming practices kept being refined over time as they learned new ways of coping with the vagaries of agricultural life. For example, given the rough terrain and the unpredictable rainfall of the hill country, village farming communities responded with water conservation and control, soil and fertility management, risk spreading and minimization, and labor optimization.[16]

As part of water conservation and control, they hewed terraces out of the hillside. Such terracing permitted better water retention, instead of simply letting the rainwater run off the hill. It also minimized soil erosion. The downside to this was the enormous investment of time and labor in constructing and then maintaining the terraces. As part of soil conservation and in order to maintain soil fertility, farming communities employed crop rotation and left the land fallow. As part of spreading risk and optimizing labor use, they planted different crops that were complementary in the type and degree of care needed at different times. This allowed a more even use of labor throughout the year. In addition, they also planted tree and vine crops. To be sure, these required more roundabout investments. However, they used labor during the downtime for field crops. Moreover, their output was subject to different sets of climatic conditions. It was good diversification. Most of all, farming communities raised sheep, goats, and cattle. Such herding has been described as a "disaster bank on the hoof."[17] These survival strategies, carefully learned and passed on from one generation to the next, served the subsistence farming communities well.

A second reason for their survival in the face of harsh agricultural conditions was the mutual assistance provided by families and communities to each other, even if only out of self-interest. Besides the usual crop failures and the unpredictable nature of soil and climatic conditions, there were also the seasonal fluctuations in labor requirements. They cooperated with one another on necessary large-scale projects, such as terracing, clearing forests, and hewing cisterns. Thus, the hazards of agricultural life forced communities to build interfamily and intervillage networks of cooperation. By providing help to those in need, families and clans ensured that they, too, will get help in their own moment of need. Mutual assistance was the only viable strategy for survival in such a precarious agricultural setting. An ethos of neighborly assistance was a perfect match for the requirements of agriculture, particularly in the highlands.[18] Getting ahead of ourselves, as we will see in the next chapter, these informal norms on mutual compassion were subsequently codified in the written laws (e.g., lending without interest). Equally important, by relying on communal aid as a strategy for survival, Israel reinforced even further the centrality of generosity and care for the distressed as part of her national identity.

SCHOLARSHIP ON ANCIENT POLITICAL ECONOMY

Scholars often use four models to describe the socioeconomic dynamics of ancient Israel, to wit: rent capitalism, the ancient class society, the tributary state, and the patronage system.[19] In rent capitalism, peasants work the aristocrats' land as tenants or as sharecroppers. Landowners keep most of the harvest for themselves, given the unequal bargaining power between peasant and landowner. Moreover, peasants are in constant need of loans and advances from the landowners because of the precarious nature of agriculture, such as poor weather, blight, disease, and family illness. Many peasants who till their own land eventually lose it in payment for such debts and often find themselves reduced to a life of serfdom.

The ancient class society is typical of Greece and the Roman Empire, and it is believed to have applied just as well to Israel. In this model, land is initially communally owned and periodically re-allocated among families in the community. Because of inequalities in the power structure within the community, some families reap more benefits at the expense of the weaker households. Ultimately, an aristocracy emerges and appropriates land for itself. Land becomes private and inheritable, and it is then passed on from generation to generation. In addition, liability for loans is no longer communal, but devolves to individual households. Because of this, some families lose their land due to loan default. There is conflict and tension between the aristocracy and the peasants.

In the tributary state, the primary culprit is the state itself as it seeks to siphon off peasants' surplus through taxes, forced labor, and other arbitrary exactions. This is often called the "Asiatic mode of production" or the "redistributive economy" because the state, in effect, reshuffles burdens and benefits within the nation. Peasants' output is redistributed to the favored classes, such as, the royal court, the state bureaucrats, and military officers. This model is often modified to include the elite that join the aforesaid officials in extracting peasants' output through rents, burdensome loan conditions, or outright fraud.

The patronage model is one in which peasants attach themselves to a powerful benefactor who serves as a safety net. The patron provides loans, outright grants, protection, and access to influence and to powerful people. In exchange, the client (the peasant) pledges loyalty, service, gifts, and respect.

These four models are not mutually exclusive, and it is entirely possible that ancient Israel exhibited a combination of elements from each.[20] More important, there are common features across these models:

- Peasants are at a disadvantage in the power structure of the community.
- The state and the elite live off peasants' work.
- Peasants are vulnerable and are frequently exploited.
- Peasants are compelled to give up a portion of their surplus, often a substantial part of it.
- Peasants live a precarious existence, and many end up destitute and landless.

Regardless of which model is correct, all of them point to a hard life of subsistence for peasants, if not outright impoverishment and debt slavery.

BIBLICAL TEXT

Biblical texts corroborate many, but not all, of the features predicted by the abovementioned models of ancient political economy. Consider the following plausible account of the rise of a centralized state in Israel.

Rise of the Monarchy (1020 B.C.)

Early in the Iron Age (1200–586 B.C.), the powerful Canaanite city-states in the low lands left the Israelites in the highlands relatively undisturbed. Different explanations have been offered for this. Some say that chariots were useless in the hill country and, consequently, the full weight of military power could not be brought to bear on the highlanders. Others claim that there was a general decline in the power of the Bronze Age monarchs, including the Canaanite rulers. Regardless of the reason, Israelites were able to make a living, and to do so as free men and women. Their self-sufficiency in grain allowed them to be independent of the Canaanites from the much more fertile plains, the granary of the region.

The introduction of innovations increased output in the hill country. As mentioned earlier, rock terracing permitted a more effective farming of the hills, retained more of the seasonal rains that were mostly lost to water runoff, and minimized soil erosion. Slaked lime enabled the waterproofing of cisterns. They built water reservoirs and irrigation systems. The introduction of iron—so much harder and more malleable than wood, stone, or bone—led to better farm implements. Such innovations resulted in an increase in production and surplus. Not surprisingly, when the Philistines conquered the Canaanite plains, they took an active interest in dominating and exploiting the hill country. New weaponry that allowed for more effective foot soldiers led to more military forays into the highlands. We find textual reference of this Philistine policy of subjugating Israel in 1 Samuel 13:19–22.

Saul and David led the Israelites in resisting Philistine domination. David eventually put an end to the Philistine threat and conquered the Canaanite plains, which he then absorbed into Israel. However, like any other Ancient Near Eastern king, David was now obligated to pay for the loyal services of his military officers and court officials by giving them royal land grants. He could not use land from the hill country for such purpose since these were already owned by families with secure patrimonial land tenure rights. He could, however, use land from the conquered fertile lowlands for such grants since he had the right to these by virtue of conquest. Unfortunately, this unleashed a chain of events that was to change the nation over the years. The rise of the monarchy in Israel touched off unintended consequences, many of which were inimical to the welfare of the ordinary Israelite. In particular, peasants bore the brunt of paying for the upkeep of the monarchy, there was increased competition for land, and farming families were compelled to shift from subsistence farming to raising cash crops.

Heavier Burdens

The monarchy arose as a practical necessity to have a unified defensive military leadership in the face of the external danger posed by the Philistines.[21] However, after containing the military threat to Israel, the monarchy stayed put and simply developed further to meet the administrative needs of a growing nation. It eventually became a permanent institution, serving as the core that pulled the country together. In other words, the monarchy, originally adopted only for defensive warfare, took a life of its own, evolved, and singlehandedly reshaped the nation.[22] Three critical developments deserve our attention.

First, a complex bureaucracy emerged (cf. 2 Sam 8:15–18; 20:23–26). Early Israel had been governed along the tribal divisions. This changed. The decentralized, village-based tribal confederation was ultimately replaced by administrative structures adapted from the Canaanite city-states and incorporated into David's realm, including many of these institutions' bureaucrats and religious functionaries. The nation's governance was centralized in the royal court. Moreover, Israel was divided into twelve administrative regions (1 Kgs 4:7–19). Absorbing foreign bureaucrats and religious functionaries from the conquered plains into her civil structure had enormous repercussions. In particular, the Canaanite view of land as a tradable commodity seeped into the nation's thinking, and no less than among its administrative leadership and elite.

This heralded the emergence of a new aristocracy with non-Hebrew values. Functionaries lived in the capital, even as they governed far-flung areas and districts of the country. Many of these bureaucrats were recruited from the educated upper classes of the Canaanite city-states and then integrated into Israel after David's conquest. These Canaanite recruits did not have the same upbringing in the traditional Hebrew values of fraternal solidarity and mutual assistance, of seeking an economy of equality and provisions for all, and of respect for the sanctity of land as an inalienable bequest from God. Consequently, these Canaanite functionaries had no qualms in accumulating land and building large estates. For them, there were no civic or religious restraints to self-enrichment and further land acquisition. Despite being antithetical to traditional Hebrew ethos and praxis, such attitudes were emulated by many Israelites themselves who managed to reach the pinnacles of power.[23] Indeed, the emergence of an elite civil service with non-traditional Hebrew values had a decisive, deleterious impact on the character of the nation's economy.

A second development worthy of our attention is how menacing neighboring empires added to the peasant's burdens. Israel and Judah's monarchs were compelled to divert the nation's resources for armaments. There was a new form of warfare in which citizen-farmer-warriors were replaced by a permanent, professional army of mercenaries with their own war chariots (cf. 1 Kgs 4:26; 10:26). Hence, instead of merely requiring forced labor in the form of military service, the people now needed to raise additional cash to pay for the services of an army. Moreover, this standing army had to be equipped and provisioned. A much larger army meant more horses that needed grazing land, hay, straw, and feed (1 Kgs 4:28). These military requirements directly competed with the needs of the peasants and, consequently, precipitated a rise in prices, as we would expect in the face of finite resources. Taxes had to rise accordingly. Furthermore, it also meant supporting a military elite that had to be paid.

To get an idea of the expenditures involved, consider the case of Solomon's 1400-strong chariot force (1 Kgs 10:26). It is estimated that the initial investment alone in procuring the chariots and the horses cost 1.47 million silver shekels or the equivalent of 735,000 rams.[24] And this was merely the additional tax that had to be levied on the nation just for this single military item. This does not even include the annual cost of maintaining the chariots and horses, in addition to training personnel and support staff. Thus, it has been said that the monarchs' wars against threatening foreign powers was "simultaneously and ineluctably war against the mass of Israelite peasants."[25] After all, it was the peasants who had to pay for these military actions.

The third development of interest was the crown's numerous grand construction projects. It also took responsibility for the requisite cultic sacrifices. Paying for the worship of God became the monarch's duty. Administrative expenses grew over time to match a burgeoning bureaucracy, from Saul (1 Sam 14:47–52), to David (2 Sam 8:15–18; 20:23–26), and eventually to Solomon (1 Kings 4). These additional, major expenditures had to be funded from royal coffers that were replenished by taxes. Since 70 to 90 percent of the population of Israel and Judah were peasants farming land, they constituted the economic base of the country. They became the predictable target for the crown's and the elite's revenue- or rent-raising schemes.[26] Not surprisingly, the peasantry was subjected to heavier taxes and forced labor (corvée) for both royal and military construction projects (2 Sam 12:31; 20:24; 1 Kgs 5:13–18; 9:22; 11:28; 1 Chr 20:3). The ordinary free citizen was turned into a mere subject at the beck and call of the royal court (1 Sam 8:10–18).

Besides direct levies on the citizenry, the royal coffers were also replenished by revenues from crown properties. In fact, crown lands were a principal means of defraying royal expenditures. Crown lands were augmented by conquest or by land purchases in the Canaanite areas (2 Sam 24:18–25; 1

Kgs 16:24). The chief method of expanding royal real estate was by acquiring ownerless lands that were vacated through the emigration of the owner abroad (2 Kgs 8:1–6) or through the owner's death by capital punishment (1 Kgs 21:1–19). In pre-monarchical times, families and clans took care of such ownerless properties.[27]

Given their importance as a source of income and given the need for the king to award land grants to court and military officials, there was intense pressure to acquire, develop, and expand royal lands (1 Sam 8:14; 1 Kgs 16:24; 2 Chr 26:6). Obviously, Canaanite praxis, rather than the Hebrew notion of land as an inalienable inheritance, was more suited to the requirements of Israel's monarchs. And, indeed, prebendal land tenure arrangements seemed to be a widespread practice in Israel, judging from the biblical passages that mention or critique it. For example, note 1 Samuel 22:7; 8:11–17.[28]

The peasants had to bear ever-heavier taxes from the crown. And even as they had to produce more surplus in order to pay the higher royal taxes, the peasants found themselves with even less time and less energy to work their own farms given the corvée.

Competition for Land

The royal need to expand its landholding precipitated similar behavior on the part of the aristocracy. With the emergence of the monarchy arose an elite class comprised of royal and military officials, the wealthy, and the powerful who served the crown and did its bidding. Besides receiving royal land grants, these elite enjoyed a wide variety of perks and entitlements, such as royal tax breaks, service exemptions, and tax collection privileges.[29] Unfortunately, these were not enough. The elite emulated the royal court's practice of aggressively acquiring more land. They expanded their own estates as well. The elite competed with one another in accumulating more land and the wealth and power that came with it. In the absence of war and conquest, such land acquisition was accomplished by taking advantage of those who were unable to defend themselves—the small land-owning farming families. In their desire to expand their landholding, many of the elite resorted to outright land-grabbing and exploitation. Such behavior marked a radical change in the traditional Israelite arrangements of land rights and succession.[30] It destroyed the longstanding practice of independent, small landholding families transferring land from one generation to the next as a bequest.

Ever Riskier Agricultural Practices

The peasants' goal was subsistence farming in an unpredictable environment. Their risk-reducing farming practices, carefully learned and passed on from one generation to the next, served them well. Unfortunately, these were incompatible with the aims of the royal court and the elite. The crown's goals were increased revenues through taxation and higher export revenues for the purchase of imported military equipment. The elite's goals were to extract as much surplus as possible from their lands and to raise export revenues to fund their imports. The elite and the court coincided in their goal of increasing export revenues. As a practical matter, these disparate objectives had dire consequences for crop selection. On the one hand, peasants sought to raise subsistence crops, as did their forefathers. On the other hand, the elite and the crown preferred cash crops. Not surprisingly, the peasants' agricultural best practices and survival strategies fell by the wayside, yet again another unintended consequence of the emergence of the monarchy.

From the court's point of view, the ideal agricultural produce was one that was readily taxable (i.e., easy to identify, control, and commandeer if necessary), storable, transportable, and marketable (i.e., highly desirable with a good and stable demand in the marketplace).[31] The crops that satisfied these features best were wine and oil, followed by grains (Ez 27:17; 2 Chr 11:11). Sheep and goats were the least desired. Wine and oil were excellent cash crops because of their high value relative to their unit weight or volume. Moreover, they were much sought in the international marketplace. Both the elite and the royal court replaced the peasants' subsistence crops with cash crops for export. Besides the ease of taxing or appropriating them, the royal court pushed for oil and wine because of its need for export revenues in order to procure military supplies and equipment from abroad, such as chariots and horses, not to mention mercenaries.

The elite had their own reason for extracting surplus from the peasants. They craved for luxury goods that could only be imported from abroad. Cash crops provided them with purchasing power.[32] The royal court and the elite easily compelled peasants to shift to cash crops through the crown's coercive taxation and through the land rents and interest rates charged by the elite. The consequences of such a push for cash crops were devastating for the peasants. Scholars estimate that taxes and royal impositions were no less than half of total output for the most advanced agrarian societies. In addition, taxation in kind created two vexing problems for farming communities.[33]

First, taxes in kind, for particular crops such as wine, oil, and grains, added further burdens to the peasantry. This meant that farming communities had to give up or greatly reduce their planting of subsistence crops and replace them with the cash crops demanded by the crown or by the elite as taxes or rents. As a result, households were forced to purchase some of their food from the marketplace. These farming families, who had until then produced for their own consumption, were now faced with new and unfamiliar risks: seasonal food price fluctuations and the fraudulent practices of merchants. Moreover, it also meant that besides having to raise cash crops to pay royal taxes and the elite's rents, peasants also had to raise cash crops with which to procure their food from the marketplace (most likely through barter).

Second, some of these taxes in kind had to be paid at set periods during the year. The crown divided the kingdom into twelve administrative regions. Each of these took turns in supplying the royal court's provisions (1 Kgs 4:20–28). Besides the huge quantities involved, this in-kind levy (provisions) at set periods created even more burdens for farming communities. Some crops may be out of season at the time they had to be furnished, and this entailed making additional arrangements for storage, besides having to produce extra to replace spoilage. Furthermore, there was the even-more-serious problem of natural variability in agricultural output. Farming is intrinsically fraught with uncertainty because of the vagaries of weather, soil conditions, blight, and crop disease. For example, there are accounts that the fluctuation in wheat output between a good and bad year can be as much as sevenfold.[34] Farming communities and administrative regions had to make provisions for these risks in order to meet their set quotas.

Clearly, the need to finance the monarchy led to intense pressure on the farming communities to increase their output. After all, the nation was an agrarian economy and farming constituted the bulk of its productive capacity. It was the economic sector capable of producing the surplus needed to support the lifestyle of both the royal court and the elite. In order to increase agricultural output, more land had to be brought under cultivation. That meant more hill terracing with its attendant requirements for more labor. Furthermore, less time was set aside for fallow, even as land was more intensively farmed. Moreover, grazing pastures were converted into farmland. After all, recall that sheep and goats were the least desirable agricultural output from the viewpoint of the royal court and the elite.

This push for increased output had unfavorable consequences for the peasants. They were forced to farm their subsistence crops on ever more marginal and unproductive land, if they were even able to plant these subsistence crops at all. More important, they had to give up their longstanding risk-spreading agricultural practices: fallow, crop rotation, mixed farming and diversification, and herding. Farming communities were more vulnerable than ever before to the uncertainties of agricultural life, and the result of this increased risk was immediately apparent, with even more people in debt, ironically, to the very elite that had caused the predicament to begin with.

Another consequence was the greater pecuniary risks associated with the shift to cash crops. In giving up subsistence crops, peasants had to sell or barter part of their cash crops for their other needs from the marketplace. In effect, farmers were bearing the risk of price fluctuations, something they did not have to deal with when they consumed what they produced. For example, prices were low during the harvest season and, therefore, the real cost of taxes or tributes were much higher in real terms. The farming communities were the biggest losers because they were compelled to forego their relative self-sufficiency and rely more on market exchange with its inherent price fluctuations. Of course, among the biggest winners were the merchants, because of the larger number of buyers and the increased volume of market transactions. Creditors, too, were beneficiaries because of the increased demand for cash or loans.[35]

Assyrian domination hastened the Judean economy's move to a money economy and accelerated the switch from subsistence to cash crops. The Assyrian demand for precious metals moved the economy further toward greater monetization. In addition, tributary goods were not native to Judea and, therefore, had to be bought from other nations with the use of the few exportable goods that Judea had—wine and oil.[36]

Destruction of Landholding Families and Communities

In giving up subsistence crops, the peasants were now dependent on the marketplace for their foodstuffs. As we have seen, the risks were threefold: having to barter or to raise cash to procure ever more of their needs from others, dealing with dishonest merchants, and coping with seasonal price fluctuations. These were all unfamiliar risks for them. In forgoing their risk-spreading agricultural strategies in order to increase their output of cash crops, the farming communities lost their cushion in riding out the chance and contingencies of rural life. Thus, in times of crop failures, poor harvests, foul weather, or simple bad luck, peasants no longer had the benefit of their "disaster bank on the hoof," their alternative crops, or their extra land held in fallow. These had been stripped away from them. Hill country farming was tenuous, at best, because of unreliable rainfall, pestilence, drought, and blight. With their ethos of mutual assistance, farming communities used to be able to help one another. They survived as clusters of small, independent landholding farming families. But with the advent of ever heavier royal impositions of taxes and forced labor, and with the loss of even their risk-spreading farming strategies, these communities had little surplus, if at all, to tide each other out from the vagaries of rural life.[37] They were now completely dependent on the only people who had the surplus to lend—the elite and the large landholders.

The need for hardship loans provided the occasion for the elite to dispossess independent, but weak, farming families of their land. By charging usurious interest rates and by imposing harsh loan conditions, these elite ensured that debtors could not repay their loans. Heavily indebted households eventually forfeited their ancestral land. They either became tenants (renting land from the elite) or, worse, were turned into debt slaves. Even as tenants, the peasants could not escape the demands of the elite because of the one-sided nature by which land rents were set.

Corruption of the Judicial System

In the face of these impositions, there was one recourse left for the common people to save them from landlessness—an appeal for justice and due process from the judicial system. Unfortunately, this venue was also closed to them.

During the monarchy, judges were appointed for various regions together with a supreme court in Jerusalem. It was a system analogous to the one set up by Moses (Ex 18:13–27; Num 11:16–27; Dt 1:9–18; 16:18–20; 17:8–13). In Judah, the judicial system was attributed to Jehoshapat (2 Chr 19:4–11). The justice system was subverted in two ways. First, the rich and the influential bribed judges and officials. Second, the justice system turned into a web of vested interests. Those who dispensed justice at the city gates were more interested in enriching themselves. Moreover, these elders were also likely to be the large landowners and, therefore, advanced their own claims. There were no checks and balances because it was often the same people who filled or influenced the choice of appointees to key administrative, judicial, and military posts. As a result, this small group of people became extremely powerful.[38]

In other words, the elite, who were bent on accumulating large estates by dispossessing small independent farming families of their land, were the same people or elders who carried great influence in the judicial system. Justice at the city gates was stacked against ordinary Israelites. Landholding families could not hold on to their ancestral land and their independence. Too many powerful interests were arrayed against them.

Concentration of Power

The practical consequence of unrestrained and unjust land-grabbing was the concentration of economic and political power in the hands of a few. It is estimated that large landowners and the elite, while constituting only 2 percent of the population, held over half of the land's output at this time.[39] The administration of justice that used to be dispensed at the local level by tribal elders was eventually concentrated in the royal court (2 Chr 19:8–11). The judicial system was corrupted and served as an instrument for the aristocracy's self-aggrandizement. Transit and international trade were controlled by the crown, while domestic commerce was run by the upper crust and powerful merchants.[40] Moreover, rural tenants were deep in debt to their landlords, and as a result, they were at the mercy of their urban creditors.

Given such a concentration of power, the political economy during the monarchical period became an exercise in unjustly shifting burdens and benefits across the population. This was often orchestrated by royal officials and the privileged class who enriched themselves in the process. Neo-Assyrian documents provide empirical evidence of this kind of political economy at that time, including many of the abuses harshly condemned by the prophets. It is very likely that the same conditions and abuses prevailed in Israel and Judah.[41] Biblical texts corroborate the hypothesis of contemporary scholarship and models on the redistributive nature of ancient political economies.

ARCHAEOLOGICAL EVIDENCE

The preceding account of oppressive socioeconomic conditions in Israel and Judah during the Iron Age (1200–586 B.C.) should lead us to expect widespread poverty. Peasants would have nothing left to them, and most would have been reduced to the sorry plight of landlessness and debt slavery. Moreover, the nation would have been marked by severe inequality in which pockets of great economic and political power existed amidst a vast sea of impoverishment. And, indeed, this is the position held not only by students of ancient political economy, but also by many biblical scholars.[42] The peasants were for the most part reduced to servitude during the reign of the monarchs.

Archaeological findings do not unequivocally support these conclusions. In fact, the evidence is mixed. Some findings point to a peasantry that was free, productive, and able to keep some surplus. Moreover, it seemed to be a fairly egalitarian society with thriving markets, all the way up to the destruction of the monarchy in the sixth century. In what follows, we will examine archaeological findings that both support and contradict the aforesaid claims of an increasingly destitute and enslaved peasantry during the reign of the monarchs.[43]

Corroboration of a Redistributive Israelite Political Economy

To begin with, let us examine some of the archeological findings that corroborate the account and conclusions of the preceding sections. First, archaeology confirms the emergence of centralized nation-states in Israel during the Iron Age II (1000–586 B.C.). We have evidence of population concentrations of over 20,000, such as in Benjamin, Manesseh, and Ephraim. There were urban-based settlements in the following descending order of importance: cities, towns, villages, and hamlets. There were primary seats of government, such as the Jerusalem palaces and the royal enclosure in Samaria. There were also regional centers, such as Hazor Meggido, Gerzer, and Lachish. There were frontier defenses and standing armies, as seen in the remains of stables supporting chariots. There were vestiges of a stratified society, such as the palaces at the regional centers and primary seats of government and the heterogeneity and inequality among the urban residents. Taxes, tolls, and tributes were collected, as seen in stele and the Samaria Ostraca, and there was some form of redistribution going to the elite, army, and court officials as seen in large storage facilities, silos, and granaries in regional centers. Large building projects from around 925–850 B.C. are further evidence of a centralized state. Among these were the royal Acropolis in Samaria; the rebuilding to even better standards of regional centers such as Meggido, Hazor, Gezer, and Lachish; the water systems in various regional centers and Jerusalem; and the massive temple complex in Tel Dan. These projects could only be pulled off by a centralized government with the ability and power to command the necessary resources. There were at least two and possibly three distinct periods of major building programs during the reigns of Solomon and the Omride dynasty.[44]

Second, international trade was a significant part of Ancient Israel's political economy. To begin with, the architecture and masonry of the aforesaid building projects required materials and skills that were not native to Israel. These building materials and craftsmen clearly had to be imported. Similarly, armaments and horses for the standing army and chariots had to come from neighboring lands. More important, tolls and taxes imposed on transit trade were a most likely source of funding for the monarchy. After all, south Arabian trade had to pass through Israel to gain access to the Mediterranean, Egypt, and Mesopotamia.[45] There were two major international caravan routes into and out of the western part of the Fertile Crescent, namely: (1) the Via Maris along the Mediterranean and (2) the King's Way running along the Syrian-Arabian desert. The "King's Way" ran "from Elat through Transjordan to Damascus and Tadmor to the crossings of the Euphrates." The other route extended from Elat to the west and northwest through the Negev into Israelite territory.[46] Israel controlled the via Maris from the Plain of Sharon to Damascus. She shared control of the King's Highway from Hamath in the North to the border in Edom where Judah was in control.[47]

Biblical texts corroborate the central importance of international trade for Israel. Since wealth was accumulated through imposts on these trade routes, David and Solomon established strongholds at their key points: Damascus (2 Sam 8:6) and Tadmor (2 Chr 8:4). Arabian trade routes to the countries in the Fertile Crescent passed through Transjordan, and Solomon used that to good effect by taxing Arabian sheiks reliant on the caravan trade routes (1 Kgs 10:15). In fact, the visit of the Queen of Sheba (1 Kgs 10:1–13) was more than just a social call between monarchs. It was believed to be part of a trade negotiation.[48]

Trade provided both the united and divided kingdoms access to many goods, essential raw materials, and services. Tyre was the major trading partner of Israel. In exchange for food, Tyre provided Israel timber and technical assistance (1 Kgs 5; Ezr 3:7). Ahab's military was formidable with its two-thousand strong chariot force. Note that horses were not native to Palestine and had to be bought from Cappadocia.[49]

Besides these practical necessities, international trade also provided Israel with unimaginable wealth. The biblical accounts of Solomon's vast gold holdings are impressive (e.g., 2 Chr 9:20). These could have only been acquired through trade since Egypt was the main producer of gold for western Asia. Southern and western Arabia were major sources of gold as well. Precious metals and goods came with trade with Hiram and the ships from Tarshish (1 Kgs 10:14–22). Jehu's tribute during the Omride dynasty (northern kingdom) to Shalmaneser III (841 B.C.) was said to stand out among all the other vassal nations because it consisted of gold vessels (which could have only been acquired and accumulated by Israel from trade with Egypt and Arabia). Archaeologists have discovered sizable quantities of ivory ornamental pieces in the palace in Samaria. Indeed, biblical texts corroborate the importance of international trade for Israel both during the period of the united kingdom and during the eighth century when the divided kingdoms regained some control over the caravan routes.[50]

Third, there is evidence to support the claim of a shift to agricultural specialization in cash crops. It appears that seventh-century Judah was, in fact, well integrated into the international economy of that time. Archaeological findings indicate a regional division of labor according to comparative advantage. The coastal plain of Philistia saw an increase in settlements in the seventh century. Archaeological digs point to two important cities at that time, Ashkelon and Ekron. Ashkelon was the major coastal city south of Jaffa and was believed to have had a population of as much as 12,000.[51] It was heavily engaged in trade given its port facilities. This is evident from imports in the archaeological remains. The coastal cities, including the environs of Askelon specialized in wine given its greater value relative to olive oil and grain.

The inner coastal areas, including the low lands (Shephelah), produced olive oil. Ekron, the other major city of that period, was in the Shephelah. It was the major producer of olive oil, with an estimated annual capacity of 500 tons based on archaeological findings of olive oil presses and storage. Such volume was clearly meant for use elsewhere (exports) and underscores a regional division of labor and agricultural specialization in cash crops.

Further inland, the Judean highlands and desert and the Negev planted grain. This grain was destined both for local consumption (in Judah, the low lands, and coastal cities) and for export.[52] Archaeologists have discovered Judahite wheat in Askelon, the major port south of Jaffa. This port was the gateway to international sea trade. Furthermore, Judean grain may have reached as far as Mesopotamia. A legal document from Nineveh refers to wheat being sold according to Judahite *se'ahs*, a Judean measure. Such a measure would not have been used if they had not been familiar with Judean grains.[53]

This international division of labor is further substantiated by the presence of products that are not native to Judah. For example, we have archaeological evidence of imports in Jerusalem, including different kinds of fish, shells, and wood from different countries, some of which are distant. Fish bones are said to be a significant find because they indicate the role of trade even for everyday and perishable items, such as fish. Large amounts of cedar have been found in the arid and remote regions of Beersheba and Arad (in the Negev). These cedars originated from as far north as Lebanon.[54] This indicates wealth. Moreover, the importation of such luxury items also suggests large quantities of surplus that must have been produced and then traded in order to procure expensive imports. This is evidence not only of the volume and vibrancy of trade, but also of the important role of cash crops. One needs to be able to trade something of value from Judah in order to pay for these imports. In other words, archaeology supports the claim that there was some agricultural specialization in cash crops in seventh-century Judah. This is consistent with one feature of the redistributive ancient political economy in which peasants were compelled by the rulers and the elite to give up subsistence farming in favor of cash crops.

Fourth, archaeological findings are also consistent with the claim that peasants were driven to work on ever more marginal land given the push to produce ever more cash crops even as they lost their own ancestral farms. As part of Sennacherib's 701 B.C. assault, Judah lost population and land. Its settlements in the low lands (the Shephelah) were destroyed by the Assyrians and never recovered to their eighth-century status. To make matters worse, Judah's fertile lands were taken away and given to the Philistines. Judah's king was not deposed, but the kingdom became an Assyrian vassal. Given these massive losses, many scholars view the eighth century as the zenith of the southern kingdom. It is believed that from the seventh century all the way to its ultimate destruction in the hands of the Babylonians in the early sixth century, Judah became a shadow of its former self, being severely underpopulated and on a downhill slide. Archaeological findings contradict this conclusion regarding the seventh century.

Archaeologists confirm the extensive destruction of Judah's settlements in the fertile low lands, the Shephelah. However, they have also uncovered surprising findings in what used to be the fringes of Judah. Prior to Sennacherib's 701 B.C. military campaign, the region east of Jerusalem into the desert and down to the shores of the Dead Sea, including the environs of Jericho, was hardly settled. But in the seventh century, this fringe region of Judah actually enjoyed unprecedented settlement activity instead of decline. Archaeological digs in the settlements of these areas reveal that the seventh century was, in fact, a period of growth and prosperity. This period turned out to be the peak for these erstwhile uninhabited, fringe areas. The Judean desert and the Negev were transformed to produce grain. This is a puzzling development because these are semi-arid areas. Moreover, Judah was not suffering from overpopulation given the massive loss of life it sustained from Sennacherib's predations.[55]

A plausible explanation for this counter-intuitive development is the thriving international trade described earlier in which Judah and the coastal plain were integrated into a regional division of labor producing wine, oil, and grain. Despite the shortage of manpower and the inhospitable, arid environment of the Judean desert and the Negev, these areas were settled and became the bread baskets of that time because of the increased profitability of farming and the demand for grain from overseas and the coastal areas that had specialized in wine and oil. This substantiates the earlier claim of how peasants were driven by their overlords and the elite to farm ever more marginal land.[56]

Fifth, there are archaeological sites that confirm significant income-wealth disparities and pockets of increasing affluence and opulent lifestyles during the monarchical period. The royal cities of Samaria, Hazor, and Meggido used dressed stones that were even decorated with stylized palm trees (ashlar masonry). The standard four-room houses in Hazor, Shechem, and Tirzah at this time were considerably bigger than usual.[57] This is consistent with the claims of a stratified society comprised of a wealthy propertied class with their huge estates, on the one hand, and ordinary people, many of whom had been dispossessed of their ancestral land and driven either to debt slavery or to impoverished tenancy, on the other hand. In a zero-sum, limited-goods society, this can only mean that the wealthy and the powerful enriched themselves at the expense of the poor.[58] At any rate, we can, at a minimum, claim that archaeological digs in the urban areas show a disparity in lifestyles and status among their residents.

Contradicting the Claims of a Redistributive Israelite Political Economy

There are also archaeological findings that contradict the conclusion that Israel's peasants were destitute. First, contrary to the expectations of an impoverished peasantry in a redistributive Israelite political economy, archaeologists have discovered evidence of a thriving rural population at this time. While there was indeed an emergent centralized nation-state or imperial overlords that imposed taxes and tributes, archaeological digs do not point to massive poverty in the peasant population. There are no series of huge public grain storage facilities that would have been needed for the wholesale confiscatory taxation of peasant produce.[59] There is no evidence of widespread single- or two-room hovels for impoverished peasants. On the contrary, the predominant dwelling during the Iron Age was the three- or four-room house, which measured around 110–130 square meters.[60] What is most telling about this type of dwelling is the sizable space set aside for storage, including spacious rooms and grain pits. This is clearly storage beyond mere subsistence. The architecture and layout of these dwellings show that farming households lived as extended families and were able to produce, keep, and accumulate surplus. Otherwise, there would have been no need for such storage space. The size and quality of rural dwellings and the amount of storage dispel the claims of a much-impoverished rural population. The surplus was retained locally, or at least some of it, rather than being completely siphoned off either by the landlord or by the urban elite.[61] These four-room houses were standard, were widespread, and existed all the way up to the end of the monarchical period across the various settlements in the rural areas.[62] Some villages even had boundary walls, an indication that these communities had the surplus to invest in nonessential infrastructure.[63]

Second, archaeological findings do not support the claim of severe social inequalities, as one would expect in a redistributive ancient political economy. While there is evidence of significant social stratification in the cities, archaeologists find rural villages to be cooperative and egalitarian. There are no findings of the usual evidence that point to inequality, such as, containers of luxury ointments and oils, distinctive residences, non-uniform distribution of elite goods, and preferred locations within the settlements. Furthermore, the four-room dwelling's architecture, design, and layout were egalitarian in the way people living in the house interacted. Its non-hierarchical configuration provided easy and ready access between rooms.[64] Moreover, while there were occasional instances of some households accumulating more wealth than others, the disparity in the size of the house or of the storage facilities was no more than from two- to threefold.[65] For the most part, dwellings did not differ substantially in terms of size, quality, or design. This is true not only across households in the same village, but even across different villages.[66] In addition, there is not much difference in the rural conditions between the northern and southern kingdoms.[67] These archaeological digs also suggest that these village communities were most likely governed by an elders' council rather than by a chieftain or a wealthy ruler.[68] Furthermore, there were facilities that were shared and managed cooperatively, such as grain silos, threshing floors, and oil presses. In other words, the rural areas not only showed the accumulation of some surplus, but were also egalitarian.

Third, archaeological digs support the claim that there were lands that were held privately, even as there were others that were part of large estates. The proportion between these two forms of landholding could not be ascertained at this time.[69] What is important for our study, however, is the finding that patterns of landholding were in fact mixed. Even as there were large estates, there were also many small household farms. This dispels the claim that landlessness and destitution were the inevitable or the common lot of Israel's peasants. To be sure, ordinary peasants and farming families did not live in luxury or great abundance. Nevertheless, they were able to meet their basic needs, even after having paid the various monarchical, imperial, and temple impositions. We see this in the size and quality of their four-room dwellings. Far from being reduced to debt slavery as many scholars claim, Israel and Judah's rural residents were, in fact, able to maintain their independence from predatory landlords and the urban elite all the way up to the end of the monarchical period.[70] This is contrary to what we would have expected from a redistributive scenario in which there was a massive loss of ancestral land to the elite or the royal court.

Fourth, the large building projects could have only been supported with general prosperity in the nation. The tolls and taxes from transit trade alone would not have been sufficient for the major construction initiatives of the monarchs. Much labor was also necessary, and since neither the united nor the divided kingdoms of Israel and Judah approximated the kind of imperial reach that its neighboring empires enjoyed, a large foreign slave labor force was an unlikely resource for these building projects. The monarchs would have had to depend on local labor. But even with corvée, exactions of such forced labor would have been balanced by the need to produce agricultural output that could be taxed. Hence, forced labor would have been moderated by the need for tax revenues. Monarchs could only go so far in tapping forced peasant labor because it would have been counterproductive to take so much of their time to the point of a much-diminished taxable agricultural harvest. Thus, these large construction projects would have been possible only with a growing and prosperous Israel and Judah.[71]

Biblical texts suggest that there was indeed a period of growth and prosperity for both Israel and Judah. Both Israel (northern kingdom) and Judah (southern kingdom) lost land to their more powerful neighbors and ANE empires not long after their break-up in 922 B.C. upon Solomon's death.[72] However, they had recovered much of what they had lost by the eighth century B.C. It was a propitious time for both kingdoms. Israel's rival at that time was Syria. However, Syria was conquered by Assyria in 802 B.C. In fact, Israel dominated Syria in the first half of the eighth century (cf. 2 Kgs 14:28). Furthermore, Assyria was distracted by internal problems and by its conflict with its northern neighbor Urartu. With such troubles sapping its attention and resources, Assyria could not threaten Israel. (This came to an abrupt end in 743 B.C. when Tiglath-Pileser of Assyria finally marched westward.)[73]

In this vacuum, both Israel and Judah enjoyed a period of calm and prosperity. Moreover, there was continuity given the long-lived reigns of Jeroboam II in Israel from 786–746 B.C. and Uzziah (aka Azariah) in Judah from 783–742 B.C.[74] Both kings recovered lost land, thereby nearly approximating the original landholding of the united kingdom. Jeroboam, son of Joash, extended the kingdom into Transjordan and Syria (2 Kgs 14:25, 28).

Despite Sennacherib's devastating campaign in 701 B.C., the ensuing seventh century was called the "Assyrian Century" because it ushered the *Pax Assyriaca*, a century of peace and prosperity for both production and commerce until the takeover of the empire by the Babylonians.[75] And as we have seen earlier, Judah saw an unparalleled settlement activity and growth during the century. Even as it was at the periphery of a thriving Mediterranean economy, it was nevertheless integrated into this international division of labor and shared in the benefits of peace and commerce by supplying grain both for consumption by the coastal populations and for export. The prevalence of the four-room dwellings during the monarchical period suggests that not only were peasants partly responsible for economic growth in both the eighth and the seventh centuries, but they had also shared in the fruits of the resulting prosperity.

Reconciling the Archaeological Evidence

What can we learn from these seemingly contradictory archaeological findings and inferences? First, the traditional claim is that the monarchical period was redistributive based on the Asiatic mode of production in which urban residents, the royal court, and the military elite siphoned off peasant produce through heavy impositions, rents, taxes, and interest rates. The peasants were stripped of their entire surplus and lived in debt and destitution. Despite archaeological findings that support many features of a redistributive ancient economy, we do not find support for this model's most central conclusion: the widespread impoverishment of the peasant population. On the contrary, far from showing a degradation of the ordinary peasant's life, archaeological digs show that the nation's economic production was based largely on these individual households. Moreover, these farming families were able to produce and keep their surplus, even as they had to pay taxes. For the entire monarchical period, archaeologists find that the four-room house was the predominant dwelling across rural settlements in both the united and divided kingdoms. What is decisive about this discovery is the size of these dwellings and the space set aside for storage. Such ample storage suggests a surplus that farming families were able to produce (despite the harsh agricultural conditions) and to keep (despite royal, elite, and imperial impositions).[76]

Second, these seemingly conflicting archeological findings are, in fact, not mutually exclusive. There may have, in fact, been many peasants who were reduced to penury and debt slavery, even as there were other farming households that were able to satisfy monarchical, cultic, and imperial exactions and have a modest surplus left over. Note how archeological digs pointing to social stratification are mostly in the urban rather than in the rural areas.

It should not come as a surprise to find evidence of significant social stratification in the cities. After all, urban population centers attract a more heterogeneous group of residents, from the ruling class, to the bureaucrats, to middle-class shopkeepers and skilled craftsmen, to farmers who till the land around the city, to the marginalized who eke out a living in the cities either as day laborers or through begging. Furthermore, by the nature of the anonymity of city living, urban residents were more vulnerable to the chance and contingencies of life. There was little neighborly support that the strong social ties in rural areas would have provided. Besides, there may have been a process of self-selection in that people who had fallen on hard times and could not get help elsewhere flocked to the urban areas where there were larger population concentrations. This meant a greater likelihood of either a day job or alms for these hard-pressed migrants. This is not even to mention the presence of the temple in the capitals of Israel and Judah, with their constant stream of pilgrims and their charitable giving. In addition, younger siblings may have been forced to seek employment in the cities because ancestral land was not divided but was usually inherited by the eldest son.[77] In other words, evidence of socially stratified urban centers does not necessarily mean that the rest of the country was also socially stratified. The nature of cities is such that they will generally have much more heterogeneous residents in terms of class and status.

Third, it is not necessary to claim that peasant landlessness and debt slavery were pervasive, as many scholars do, in order to make sense of Old Testament economic morality. If so, then how does one account for the well-known prophetic indictments of injustice (e.g., Amos; Is 1:21–26; Mic 2:1–5; Jer 5:20–29; 7:1–7; 22:13–19; 34:8–22; Zeph 3:1–5)? These prophets seem to be reacting to deteriorating social conditions similar to those predicted by models of redistributive ancient political economies. One explanation is that these prophets, who were largely urban-based, were referring to the socioeconomic state of the cities and their environs, specifically Samaria and Jerusalem, rather than to a generalized impoverishment of the entire nation.[78] This hypothesis is consistent with the archeological findings of significant social stratification only in the urban areas, but not in the village communities in the rest of the kingdoms.

All that is needed to make sense of the prophetic indictments is the minimal assumption that the prophets were critical of instances of injustice. There is nothing to suggest in biblical texts that these injustices had to be pandemic or utterly devastating for the prophets to indict them.[79] After all, an injustice has to be rectified, regardless of whether or not it is rampant. An injustice is abhorrent to God, regardless of whether or not it is rife (Is 1:10–17). Thus, it is entirely possible that the prophets were reacting to these urban pockets of exploitation, rather than to a national impoverishment. This would reconcile archaeological findings with the traditional reading of the prophetic literature.

PERSIAN RULE (538–333 B.C.)

There are few sources of reliable data on Judah under Persian occupation. Most are based on archaeological findings and Aramaic documents describing the life of the Jews in Elephantine in Egypt. Consequently, many commentators are compelled to rely on biblical texts, such as Ezra, Nehemiah, Haggai, Zechariah, and Isaiah 56–66.[80]

There is scholarly disagreement on what happened to Judah after the destruction of Jerusalem in 587/586 B.C. On the one hand, there are those who accept the image of an "empty land" with the wholesale deportation of the population. On the other hand, there are those who claim that only a small number was deported into exile, while the rest of the population stayed put. Still others take the middle position and acknowledge that there was massive depopulation as a result of the war, the ensuing famine and epidemics, the exile, and the flight of people to neighboring lands. Nevertheless, even as the core settlements were destroyed and depopulated, there was continuity in settlement activity in the fringes of Judah. This continuity, however, was marked by a drastic disruption in people's lives, especially compared to their pre-exilic experience at the time of the monarchs. Despite their disagreements, most scholars agree that archeological evidence reveal widespread destruction and desolation in the aftermath of the Babylonian conquest (586 B.C.). In addition, Judah endured a severe demographic decline that was to persist into the post-exilic era.[81]

The Neo-Babylonian Empire extended from 626 B.C. until its fall to the Persians in 539 B.C. Very few reliable extra-biblical sources on Judah are available for the period of the exile and the following Persian rule.[82] Little is known about the social conditions during this period. Even archeological findings are scarce. Many scholars base their conclusions on biblical text, such as Ezra and Nehemiah. Judah, also referred to as Yehud during this time and the Hellenistic era, became an insignificant province in the Persian empire. It was a small backwater, isolated area engaged in subsistence agriculture. Returnees came back to Judah gradually over many years. It is believed that the Second Temple was built around 500 B.C.

Despite the post-exilic restoration in 538 B.C., Israel did not find much of a respite. To begin with, the nation's population had been decimated and its infrastructure had been devastated. It was not only the Temple that had to be rebuilt. Both Israel's human and material capital also had to be painstakingly recreated. It is estimated that Yehud at this time numbered around thirty thousand at most, much smaller than traditionally accepted in the literature. This was a mere third of its population prior to the Babylonian exile. Jerusalem was the only urban area, and a small one at that, having around three thousand residents, about a tenth of the population. However, it is believed that the city received material support from pilgrims and from Jews who lived in the other Persian provinces and Egypt. The shift of settlements toward the coastal plain that started in the seventh century intensified even further during Persian rule.[83]

Those who returned from the exile became the minority. The consequence of this was conflict between the returnees and those who had stayed behind or those who had occupied the land from surrounding areas. Besides facing the animosity of their new neighbors, returning exiles had to fight to reclaim their ancestral land from the new owners. Some have even hypothesized that, in addition to these returnees, Persian military personnel also came and established new settlements.[84]

The Israelite peasant faced difficulties on many fronts, besides retrieving ancestral land. The geographic location of Judah was both an advantage and a disadvantage. It was an advantage in that it was isolated and was consequently spared of the constant predations of conquering armies, unlike their more exposed neighbors on the coastal plains and the lowlands in the north. The disadvantage was the difficulty of eking out a living from the land. Judah's most fertile land had already been stripped from her, the lowlands (the Shephelah). Judah did not have the kind of fertile agricultural land or the climatic conditions that the northern regions enjoyed.

Archaeological remains show that the settlements were small. Sixty-five percent of excavated sites dating from this period were just about 1.25 acres in size with less than 125 inhabitants. Besides Jerusalem, only two other sites measured more than five acres.[85] These settlements consisted of widely dispersed unwalled farmsteads or hamlets, with very few villages and towns. The material remains are poor, simple, and unadorned. There is no evidence of some of the more sophisticated goods enjoyed by the coastal settlements, suggestive either of their isolation or of their inability to produce the necessary surplus to acquire such goods via trade. The economy was primarily agrarian, subsistence agriculture, with the main crops being cereals, oil, and wine. They also raised sheep and goats. Many of these farmsteads were on land that had been previously inhabited and then abandoned at the end of the Iron Age. There were also new settlements on virgin land.[86] There is evidence of some trade with other Persian provinces and even with Greece. Communal wine- and olive-presses have been discovered around Jerusalem, as well as public grain storage facilities, indicative of imperial taxation.

Persian taxes were thorough and systematic but not much heavier than previous empires.[87] Archaeological remains show that it was a tributary economy administered from regional centers where we find most of the excavated coins and tax-related seals on pottery.[88] In addition to these imperial impositions, the population was harassed by Persian officials for bribes, gifts, and other "voluntary" contributions. It was no better under Greek rule later. The best agricultural lands became royal property ("King's Land").[89] Moreover, some believe that peasants now had to contend with two native elites—the old Judean elite and the new Samaritan elite who had made their way from the northern to the southern kingdom to take advantage of the void created by the deportations.[90] Taxes were most likely paid in kind since the widespread use of coins and a monied economy emerged only gradually and had to wait until the Hellenistic period. Surplus extracted from the peasants went to the cultural elite and the imperial coffers.[91]

The priestly class sought to fill the vacuum left by the collapse of the monarchy and emerged as significant players in the administration of Yehud, especially the high priest.[92] They, too, had their own agenda and their own impositions. They had a zeal to retrieve the religious purity of the nation from the late fifth century onward. This precipitated a push for spiritual reform that included distancing themselves from others who did not live up to the same religious purity.[93]

There is reason to believe that unlike their ancestors during the monarchical period, peasants were impoverished at this time. Yehud was much poorer and smaller in population compared to the pre-exilic period. Latifundias (large estates worked by slave labor) were not the norm for the Ancient Near East, including Judah. The bulk of labor in Yehud was not slave or indentured labor but free peasants. Nonetheless, extra-biblical texts confirm that many were falling into debt slavery. In fact, most of the Wadi Daliyeh papyri were about slave sales.[94]

The most telling evidence of poor material conditions during the Persian period is once again archaeological findings, or the lack of it. For the entirety of the Iron Age (1200–586 B.C.), the four-room house was characteristic of Israel. This type of dwelling was found in Israelite communities and not elsewhere or in any other nation in the Ancient Near East. Moreover, it was the predominant type of dwelling during the entire monarchical period. Such three- and four-room dwellings totally disappeared in the post-exilic period, and large agricultural estates emerged all the way up to Roman Palestine. The sudden and complete disappearance of these four-room dwellings after six centuries of use (as to make this architecture a part of Hebrew culture) is puzzling.[95] Many explanations have been offered, including the difficulty of finding archaeological sites for this era given the much smaller land area of Yehud and its much-reduced population base.[96] One tentative conclusion we can draw from this development is that these missing four-room dwellings would, at a minimum, suggest that there was no need to house extended families living together or to store large quantities of agricultural produce. In other words, the absence of these four-room dwellings may reflect the population's inability to produce and keep surplus.

Yehud had the telltale signs of a post-collapse society: a sudden and dramatic fall in demography, the absence of any significant architecture and construction, political and territorial fragmentation, factious governance, a much prolonged recovery time, and the dearth of archaeological artifacts.[97] The Persian period marked the low point of Judahite socioeconomic conditions compared to the nation's pre-exilic relative prosperity and compared to the recovery experienced during the Hellenistic reign. Archaeologists find a drastic decline in the number, size, density, and quality of settlements during the Persian period relative to the two other eras. There were twice as many settled sites from the Iron Age II, and many even included walled settlements.[98] In the wake of the Babylonian destruction, Judah's population dropped to as low as 10 to 15 percent of that during the Iron Age. There was some recovery, but the most that it reached during the Persian era was only a third of the population during the Iron Age and the Hellenistic period.[99]

Biblical texts corroborate this provisional conclusion on the much harder life endured by post-exilic Judah. In particular, Nehemiah 5:1–13 is a vivid account of the people's plight and desperate pleas. It presents a state of affairs not much different from that condemned by the prophets earlier when hapless landholding families and peasants found themselves heavily indebted, victimized by injustice, and constantly on the brink of destitution and debt slavery (cf. Mic 2:1–2; Is 5:8; Hos 5:10).

What little we know of the conditions in Judah during the Persian rule is significant because much of the Old Testament texts as we have received them today were written, edited, or finalized during this critical period.[100] In fact, the writing and compilation of substantial parts of what was going to be the Hebrew Scripture are said to be the key contribution of the Persian period. Two socioeconomic conditions shed light on this development. First, such writing, editing, and compilation would most likely have been influenced, indeed motivated, by the priests' religious zeal to retrieve the nation's purity and heritage during this period. This is an important consideration in understanding the theology of these texts. This felt need to retrieve their earlier religious purity stemmed in large part from the precarious existence of the nation, with Jews widely dispersed as minorities throughout the Persian Empire and with a minuscule resident population in what was already a much-reduced territory stripped of its best agricultural land. And they were materially poor compared to their neighbors and their ancestors in the monarchical period (Iron Age II). Given such a state of siege, it was necessary to make the remnant Judahite community appreciate what made them different from all the other nations in an effort to preserve their collective identity. Thus, we have the push in Ezra and Nehemiah for religious revival and recovery of the nation's purity. This ultimately led to classifying people and neighbors according to whether they were outsiders or belonged to the pure Judahite community.[101]

Second, the dire socioeconomic conditions of the Persian period shaped the milieu of the writers or editors working on Sacred Scripture at that time. This means that these dire socioeconomic conditions would most likely have been the larger social context of the substantial blocks of economic norms that we find strewn all over the Old Testament, from the law, to the prophetic literature, to the wisdom writings.

HELLENISTIC RULE (332–142 B.C.)

Alexander the Great swept through Palestine in 332 B.C., but died in 323 B.C. without an heir. The territories he had conquered were divided between Ptolemy in Egypt and Seleucus in Asia Minor. There was conflict over who was to rule Palestine and Phoenicia, and it was not until 301 B.C. that the dispute was finally settled, with Ptolemy securing Palestine and southern Phoenicia, leaving Syria and northern Phoenecia to Seleucus.

Ptolemaic Rule (320–200 B.C.)

Just like the Persians, the Ptolemies took possession of the best agricultural lands ("King's Land"). In addition, they introduced two additional exactions: tax farming and imposts on most commercial transactions. An official depot was set up in Pelusium, Egypt, for receiving goods coming from Palestine. New customs houses were established at strategic points. Goods were subject to substantial taxes ranging from 20 to as much as 50 percent.[102] These taxes were rigorously enforced. Since the goal of the Ptolemies was to maximize their tax revenues, they had officials supervising tax collection all the way down to the village level. Thus, unlike the imperial overlords of the preceding eras who governed from afar, the hand of Ptolemaic rule was ever present even to the ordinary villager. Some of these officials were their fellow Israelites, their local neighbors.[103] In fact, the high priest served as the chief administrator of the province during the Ptolemaic and Seleucid reigns.

Coastal settlements, which increased in number during the Persian period, carried on with their commercial activities and continued to flourish despite these new imposts, thanks in large part to the vibrancy of Mediterranean trade. Judah did not benefit from such trade because of her isolation and distance from the coast. This is evident in the archaeological remains of the period. Unlike excavations around the coast and its environs, which had substantial structures and assorted goods, the Judean settlements were materially poor and sparsely populated. Most of the potteries discovered were of local origin. Even Jerusalem, Judah's only city at this time, was poor and small throughout the third century.

Since there was little mercantile activity in Judea, the Ptolemies resorted to the Persian practice of a simple annual tax collected through the high priest and taxes collected in kind, such as cereals, oil, and wine. Archaeological digs have unearthed stone jars that had markings *YHD* or *YRSLM*, which scholars believe were used in the payment of such in-kind levies for the court and the temple respectively.[104] Despite the Ptolemaic impositions, Yehud was slowly recovering during this period, both materially and demographically, from the devastation wrought by the Babylonians centuries earlier. But it was an extremely slow recovery.

During the Hellenistic rule, we begin to see archaeological and literary evidence of an emerging native elite and widening inequality. For example, a mid-third-century Judean document speaks of the illicit possession of slaves. Josephus (*Ant.* 12.184) describes how Joseph, a nephew of the high priest, inadvertently became the tax collector when his uncle the high priest refused to remit Jerusalem's taxes to the Ptolemies. Joseph retained this right to collect taxes for twenty-two years and died a man of great wealth.[105]

Seleucid Rule (200–142 B.C.)

The Seleucid king Antiochus III eventually wrested control over Palestine from the Ptolemies in 200 B.C. The shift to Seleucid rule did not change the overall condition of Judah, with the exception of Jerusalem. Antiochus III was taken aback by the underdevelopment and underpopulation of Jerusalem. Accordingly, he endowed it with benefactions and tax holidays to allow the residents to improve the mean condition of their city. This seemed to have to worked in hastening the recovery of the city. Archaeological evidence reveals that Jerusalem began to enjoy greater prosperity by the early second century. Moreover, some of the city's elite were much more open to cooperating with their new overlords.[106] Based on biblical texts believed to have been written at this time, Jerusalem may have had the first significant improvement in its infrastructure through the efforts of the High Priest Simon at the end of the third century. These initiatives included repairs to the Temple, additions to the precinct walls, and the digging of a reservoir (Sir 50:1–3). The city's population seems to have also grown, judging from archaeological digs that indicate a small settlement toward the southwestern hill beyond the confines of the City of David.[107] It was not until well into the Hellenistic period before Judah finally recovered the population levels that it had enjoyed right before the Babylonian conquest.[108]

A major development at this time was the greater openness on the part of the some of the city residents and elite to adopt foreign ways. Among the artifacts of this era are large quantities of remains from foreign wine amphoras.[109] This is significant because distinctive features of Judahite lifestyle in the post-exilic period up until this time have been its simplicity, self-sufficiency, and isolation from the larger Mediterranean economy. Pottery and household items unearthed in the rest of Judah at this time were of local origin and were functional and unsophisticated. Conflict between the Hellenizers and those who wanted to keep to traditional ways eventually erupted in the open, leading to the Maccabean revolt and the rise of the Hasmoneans. We examine the socioeconomic conditions of this period in part II when we examine the New Testament.

SUMMARY AND CONCLUSIONS

Biblical Israel was not a single, homogeneous ancient economy, but "a set of economies" across a diverse geographic and fragmented landscape of intersecting markets and communities. In particular, there were two economic zones: (1) a village-centered production network of agrarian work, and (2) an urban, market-oriented center engaged, not in manufacturing or production, but in consumption. The urban center was dependent on the villages for supplies and, more important, for surplus.[110]

Rural residents produced for their own subsistence and to pay taxes to the crown and rents to their landlords. Theirs was an ancient economy based on reciprocity, kinship, and householding, rather than on market exchange.[111] The villages and peasants were risk averse; risk was minimized or spread across the entire community. They sought only self-sufficiency, rather than the accumulation of wealth and power.

Two schools of thought diverge in describing the socioeconomic conditions of the monarchical era. One school of thought follows the popular view that ancient economies, including Israel and Judah, were redistributive in nature based on the Asiatic mode of production, which involved the wholesale extraction of agricultural surplus by an urban ruling elite. The result was widespread peasant destitution, landlessness, and debt slavery. The other school of thought disputes such a dismal description of Israel's peasantry. Archaeological findings reveal that Israel and Judah were, in fact, growing and prosperous until the Assyrian predations. And even after the destruction wrought by the Assyrian army, seventh-century Judah recovered and saw a rise in settlement activity. What is most telling, however, are the archaeological findings that suggest not an impoverished peasantry, but farming families that were able to produce and accumulate surplus. The predominant dwellings of this period were the four-room dwellings that were characterized by ample space for storing produce. This indicates that Israelite peasants were able to keep at least some of their surplus. Moreover, these dwellings were not one- or two-room hovels, as the first school of thought would have predicted. Instead, the architecture, size, and quality of the remains of four-room dwellings discovered in archaeological digs show a thriving peasantry living as extended families. Archeological findings reveal a wide mix of landholding patterns, from large estates to small family farms. This points to a robust economy in which many landholding families maintained their freedom despite the heavy taxes, tithes, and impositions they had to bear.

The description of an exploited and impoverished peasantry applies more to the Persian period rather than to the monarchical era. The distinctive four-room dwellings of village communities suddenly and completely disappeared in the post-exilic period despite having been very much a part of Hebrew culture and architecture for six centuries. Scholars have yet to determine the reason for this. However, at the very least, it is clear that the absence of such dwellings suggests that farming households consisted of nuclear, rather than extended families. Moreover, they had no need for large storage spaces, an indication that they may not have had the surplus to keep. Furthermore, archaeologists conclude that excavations dating back to the Persian and Hellenistic periods reveal that the Judean highlands, including Jerusalem, were more backward and destitute compared to other settlements, particularly those on the coast. In addition, archaeological digs also suggest that Iron Age II settlements were clearly more numerous and more prosperous compared to their Persian and Hellenistic counterparts in terms of quality, size, and density.[112]

The issue of whether or not Israelite peasantry was reduced to landlessness and debt slavery in the late monarchical period is significant because many scholars believe that the eighth-century prophets were reacting to such deteriorating social conditions in their preaching and oracles. In other words, this is a case of biblical text being shaped by the socioeconomic milieu of its writers/editors. As we have seen in this chapter, archeological evidence indicates that peasants during the monarchical period were, in fact, mostly free and able to sustain a surplus.

One way of reconciling these differences is to simply expand the time frame under study. In particular, many believe that some of the biblical texts ascribed to the eighth-century prophets were in fact post-exilic, whether in their original writing or redaction. If so, then it is no longer critical to establish definitively whether or not Israelite peasants were in fact destitute during the late monarchical period. These post-exilic writers or editors would have been completing the prophetic texts at a time when they themselves were living in a much diminished and subjugated Judah under the Persians. Thus, we arrive at the same conclusion that biblical texts may have been shaped by the socioeconomic conditions prevalent at the time of their writing or final editing.

Taken together as a group, the writers, editors, and compilers of the Old Testament went through the whole gamut of life's chance and contingencies, from the harshness of nomadic life, to the uncertainties of farming that alternated between bountiful and failed harvests, to a precarious subsistence, to war and its attendant destruction, to indebtedness and landlessness, to subjugation and heavy imperial impositions, and to forced labor. The Old Testament's writers and editors had gone through both plenty and want. They knew firsthand what it was to be free and to be enslaved. Not surprisingly, this range of life experiences is reflected in the biblical texts' wide variety of economic norms and insights: from the laws' admonitions on mutual respect and assistance, to the wisdom writings' praise for hard work and virtue, to the prophetic indictment of injustice, to the entire canon's vision of God's gift of material abundance, albeit one that is contingent on the community's collective moral conduct. It is to these specific biblical teachings that we now turn our attention in the following chapters.

NOTES

1. The following account of the socioeconomic conditions leading up to the fourth century B.C. is taken from Chaney (1986; 1989), Dearman (1984), Faust (2000; 2008), Faust and Bunimovitz (2003), Faust and Weiss (2005), Grabbe (1998; 1999; 2004; 2007), Holladay (1995), Hopkins (1983; 1987; 1996), Houston (2008; 2010), King and Stager (2001), Mays (1987), Nardoni (2004, 95–98), Pleins (2001, 254–58), Premnath (1988; 2003; 2008), Schottroff (1984), Smith (2004), Stager (1998), and Wittenberg (1978).
2. For example, parts of the books attributed to eighth-century prophets are believed to have been written or redacted in the post-exilic period under Persian rule (late sixth to the fourth century B.C.).
3. See Houston (2008, 18–51) for an example of this middle-ground approach in employing both biblical text and extra-biblical sources.
4. I draw from Chaney (1986) in the following brief exposition on pre-monarchic Israel's socioeconomic conditions.
5. This was from the late Bronze Age (1550–1200 B.C.) to the early Iron Age (1200–900 B.C.). See Hopkins (1987, 189–90) and Ogletree (1983, 58–64). Coote and Whitelam (1986) believe that a decline in trade during the late Bronze-early Iron Age led nomadic people to settled agriculture in the highlands.
6. Gottwald (1976, 465)
7. Schottroff (1984, 37)
8. von Waldow (1970); Wittenberg (1978, 142–45)
9. Even more burdens were added with the emergence of the monarchy and the nation's subsequent subjugation by the neighboring empires. In addition to the burdens of farming, there were the external pressures, namely: the imperial impositions; the exactions from the cities; and the demands of absentee landlords who lived in the urban areas.
10. Scott (1989, 85–86)
11. Dearman (1984, 390); Wittenberg (1978, 142–45)
12. Schottroff (1984, 37); Wright (1990; 2004)
13. Recall the accounts of the great care with which land was apportioned within the nation after the conquest (Num 26:52–56; 33:54). Whether these accounts are historical or theological in nature, the important point is that the writers of these inspired texts saw this as the order prescribed by YHWH.
14. The upside to this is that Judah did not have to endure as many depredations as Israel did from conquering armies. Given its relative isolation and poor geography, Judah did not attract as much attention from the neighboring empires. For example, the destruction from Sennacherib's 701 B.C. campaign was said to be moderate in the Judean highlands. This allowed Judah to recover much faster and to prosper in the seventh century (Faust, 2008).
15. Grabbe (2004, 198)

16. Hopkins (1983, 179)
17. Hopkins (1983, 179, 184, 189–90, 191, fn 59)
18. von Waldow (1970). Compare von Waldow's (1970) account of the earlier circumstances for the nomadic ethos and Chaney's (1986; 1989) and Hopkins's (1983; 1987; 1996) description of the requirements of highland agriculture.
19. The following discussion comes from Houston (2008, 18–51), who provides a succinct description of these four models, evaluates them using biblical text and archaeological evidence, and then hypothesizes about the most likely socioeconomic conditions from the era of the monarchs to the post-exilic period.
20. This is the position taken by Houston (2008), who combines elements from each model in describing what he thinks was the most likely situation in Israel. Moreover, he does not believe that rent capitalism applies to Israel because there are no words in classical Hebrew corresponding to its key practices, such as "let," "lease," "tenant," "rent," or "landlord."
21. I draw from Pleins (2001, 254–58) in the following brief exposition on the burdens that followed in the wake of the monarchy.
22. Schottroff (1984, 38–39). Nardoni (2004, 95–99) claims that Israel adopted the monarchy not only or even primarily because of military necessity, as many scholars have suggested, but as a result of internal developments in the growth and evolution of the nation.
23. Dearman (1984, 389–91); Schottroff (1984, 38–39); Wittenberg (1978, 142–45)
24. Hauer (1980, 65–66) provides these estimates and their underlying calculations. He also assesses many other military expenditures at the time of Solomon.
25. Gottwald (1976, 466)
26. Chaney (1986)
27. Schottroff (1984, 38–39)
28. Ezekiel 46:16–18 refers to limits and conditions to such land grants, namely, that they should not be permanent and should not dispossess others of land in the process. Ezekiel clearly calls for reforms in the face of abuses. See Dearman (1984, 389–91).
29. Dearman (1984, 391–92)
30. Thus, Chaney (1989) notes that there were already large estates on the low lands even before the time of the classical prophets. Such land accumulation was not unique to the eighth century alone. However, it was to get more severe and more widespread in the eighth century.
31. Hopkins (1983, 196)
32. Chaney (1986)
33. Hopkins (1983, 195–97)
34. Hopkins (1983, 197)
35. Neufeld (1960); Schottroff (1984, 39). Even if the monetization of the Israelite economy did not occur until much later during the Hellenistic period, as Carter (1999) suggests, peasants were nevertheless still vulnerable because barter was still subject to price fluctuations.
36. Hopkins (1996, 138)
37. Chaney (1986)
38. Davies (1981, 83); Dearman (1984, 391–92); Pleins (2001, 258)
39. Chaney (1986)
40. Pleins (2001, 256–57)
41. Dearman (1984, 393–94). Dearman refuses to use the terms "capitalism" or "rent-capitalism" (absentee capitalism) since it would be imposing modern terms on an ancient culture. Others disagree. Lang (1985) and Wittenberg (1978) argue that absentee urban landlords simply lived off the rents that they extracted from their rural tenants.
42. See, for example, Chaney (1986, 68), Coote (1981, 32), de Vaux (1973, 169), Gossai (1993, 285), Hoppe (2004, 8–13), and Wolff (1990, 78).
43. Using archaeology and Ancient Near Eastern literature, many scholars have attempted to corroborate the Old Testament's description of the monarchical period. Grabbe (2007) notes that while the Old Testament was written as a theology rather than as history, it is possible to confirm the historicity of many of the events described during the era of the kings. Grabbe concludes that despite its theological aims, there is history in many of the accounts of the monarchy (p. 121).
44. Holladay (1995, 373–75)

45. Holladay (1995, 382)
46. Elat (1979, 531, 535)
47. Byargeon (1995, 8)
48. Elat (1979, 532)
49. Elat (1979, 541–42)
50. Elat (1979, 539–42, 546). These revenues enabled the kingdom to maintain a strong army.
51. The city was ultimately destroyed by the Babylonians in 604 B.C.
52. Cash crops could be ranked in the following descending order of value and profitability: wine, oil, and then grains. It is not surprising that in terms of land use, the coastal areas specialized in wine, the inner coastal plain in olive oil, while the hinterlands produced grain. Note, too, how the most marginal lands (beyond the highlands) were used for grazing, the least desired activity from the point of view of taxation or raising export revenues. See Faust and Weiss (2005) for an in-depth discussion of this regional division of labor based on comparative advantage.
53. Faust and Weiss (2005, 82)
54. Faust and Weiss (2005, 75)
55. Faust (2008)
56. Another explanation given by scholars is that these highlands and isolated areas were only partially damaged by the Assyrians and not occupied for any length of time. Hence, the region, including Jerusalem, recovered quickly from Sennacherib's invasion.
57. Byargeon (1995, 8); Wittenberg (1987, 62–66)
58. Blomberg (1999, 69–70)
59. Holladay (1995, 389)
60. Faust (2000, 28)
61. Holladay (1995, 392–93); Houston (2010, 102)
62. See Faust and Bunimovitz (2003) for an excellent exposition on the nature of these four-room dwellings. See also Faust (2004, 163) for further bibliography on these dwellings.
63. Houston (2008, 21)
64. Faust and Bunimovitz (2003, 30)
65. Storage for grain is an indication of the household's wealth.
66. Faust (2000, 28)
67. Faust (2004, 34, fn 13)
68. Holladay (1995, 377)
69. Faust and Weiss (2005, 78)
70. See Houston (2008, xi, 18–51) and references therein for an account of this position and the archeological evidence supporting it.
71. Holladay (1995, 374, 382)
72. The northern kingdom broke away from the nation on account of the king's abusive impositions and forced labor (1 Kgs 5:13–14; 12:4, 9–11, 14). People had had enough and they rebelled against Rehoboam, son of Solomon, who succeeded him as king.
73. Berthoud (2005, 103); Byargeon (1995, 7–8)
74. Wright et al. (1990, 1233)
75. Faust and Weiss (2005). Babylonians destroyed the Philistine cities in 604 B.C. and Judah in 597 and 587 B.C.
76. Scholars who hold that there was a thriving peasantry during the monarchy include Domeris (2007), Faust (2003; 2004), and Houston (2008; 2010).
77. Houston (2010, 106)
78. Houston (2010). Of course, one has to assume that these prophetic writings were pre-exilic.
79. Houston (2008, xi) suggests that it is entirely plausible that the prophets were preaching against injustices in the urban areas, and not necessarily about the plight of destitute peasants.
80. Grabbe (2002, 441–42). Esther, Jonah, Ruth, the Song of Songs, and the final form of Job are believed by some to have been from the Persian era. The books of Chronicles are also sometimes used, even as these came from a much later period.

81. Baron et al. (1975, 9). See Faust (2003; 2004) and Lipschits (2004) on the scholarly disagreements.
82. See Grabbe (2004, 351–60) for a concise listing of what we can know, guess, and not know about the Yehud.
83. Carter (1999, 288–94); Faust and Weiss (2005, 72). See Carter (1999, 214–48) for a more detailed accounting and for other estimates. Despite disagreements on methods, models, and point estimates, scholars arrive at the common conclusion that Yehud was a mere shadow of what Judah was in the Iron Age II in terms of demography. There was a massive drop in population.
84. Baron et al. (1975, 11); Edelman (2007, 63–64)
85. Carter (1999, 246); Mazar (2001, 72)
86. Berlin (1997, 4). As many as 75 percent of archaeological sites had Iron Age II strata (Carter, 1999, 248). Edelman (2007, 54, 63–64) notes that it did not make sense for settlers to expend the time and effort clearing virgin land, digging cisterns, and building new structures when there were many abandoned farmsteads. New settlements may have been part of the Persian settlement policy of maximizing output from the empire.
87. Grabbe (2004, 195)
88. Carter (1999, 259–70)
89. Anderson (1997, 4)
90. Gottwald (1976, 466–67)
91. Carter (1999, 281)
92. Some believe that, based partly on coins from the period, the high priest even served as the governor of Judah toward the end of the Persian empire (Grabbe, 2002, 445).
93. This is reflected in Ezra-Nehemiah.
94. Grabbe (2004, 198, 206)
95. Faust and Bunimovitz (2003, 30); Holladay (1995, 393). Similarly, the distinctive Judahite tomb also disappeared suddenly and completely at this time. Faust (2004) concludes that both puzzling disappearances point to a massive social change. The Judahite society of the Iron Age was transformed.
96. Houston (2008, 25)
97. Faust (2004, 167–69)
98. Edelman (2007, 54)
99. Faust (2007, 32, 41, 49). It took a few generations to reach the 20 percent mark, and even after 250 years, Judahite population was only up to 35 percent of what it was prior to the exile.
100. Some date the following works or groups to this period: Third Isaiah, Haggai, 1 and 2 Zechariah, Joel, Jonah, Malachi, Chronicles, the Yahwist and Deuteronomic traditions (Carter, 1999, 286).
101. Carter (1999, 315–16). Such efforts at national survival may account for some of the provisions we find in the Old Testament. For example, it has been suggested that Ezra's and Nehemiah's efforts to make the Judahite community hold on to their ancestral land was born out of a much larger concern for the preservation of what precious little land was left in Yehud.
102. For example, filtered and ordinary wine, grape syrup, and white oil were subject to a 50 percent tax. Dried figs were taxed at 33 1/3 percent, while fish (dried, salted, or pickled), honey, goat meat, and nuts carried a 25 percent charge. Pure wool was taxed at 20 percent.
103. Grabbe (2002, 447)
104. Berlin (1997, 9)
105. Biblical text corroborating this is Ecclesiates 2:4–8. In "tax farming," the elite and local officials vie with one another for the right to collect taxes on behalf of the imperial court. The highest bidder gets this concession, and while he has to make up for any shortfall from his own personal funds, he could keep anything over and above what he had promised to give to the imperial rulers as part of his winning bid. See Josephus (*Ant.* 12.169, 175).
106. Berlin (1997, 8–9, 16)
107. Berlin (1997, 16). This could have also been a splinter group living apart because of the divisions arising in the city at this time in reaction to the Hellenizers.
108. Faust (2007)

109. Berlin (1997, 17)
110. Hopkins (1996, 124)
111. Hopkins (1996, 132–33)
112. Domeris (2007, 128–50) supports this view. He notes that Judean peasants did indeed suffer from the oppressive dynamics of predatory debt that ultimately led to widespread landlessness and debt slavery, but during the post-exilic period and not in Iron Age II. He bases his conclusion on his study of the land sales, labor conditions, trade, markets, and debt from the exile onward.

Chapter Three

Covenant and Law

The Old Testament is the chronicle of God's breaking into human history to liberate an enslaved people. It is the narrative of a God who, besides providing this people relief from bondage, takes an active interest in their welfare, settles them on a land in which they could live as free men and women, and forms them into a nation. Indeed, the Old Testament is about the special relationship between God, the Lord of creation and the Lord of history, on the one hand, and a rag-tag people, on the other hand. In their Covenant, God called Israel to be the Chosen People, while Israel, in her own turn, was to have no other god but YHWH.[1]

Israel was painfully aware that it was not on account of her accomplishments that made her God's Chosen People. It was completely gratuitous that YHWH chose the most insignificant of nations to be God's own (Dt 7:7–8). Thus, despite being singled out above all the other nations, Israel knew that she was not called to an election of privilege, but to an election of responsibility.

Laws are important for the smooth functioning of any society. They encapsulate a people's self-understanding of their ideals and values and of who they are as a community. In addition, laws often rank these values in order of importance and sometimes even specify acceptable trade-offs in cases of clashing claims. In other words, laws reveal what matters most to them as individuals and as a community. Thus, the Old Testament law codes give us a glimpse of the social and moral world of the nation Israel.

For Israel, these laws were special because: (1) they came no less than from God who was forming them at that time to be nation like no other nation, (2) they articulated what God expected from Israel in her election to responsibility as the Chosen People, and (3) they were central to Israel's tradition and practices. Consequently, most scholars agree that two of the most important themes of the Old Testament are Covenant and Law.[2] The Law is central in the life of this nation. It is viewed as the codification of the revealed moral will of God.[3]

The Law is found in the first five books of the Old Testament, referred to as the Torah by Jews and as the Pentateuch by Christians. There are both narrative and legal materials in the Pentateuch. While distinct from one another, they cannot be separated. On the one hand, the narrative provides the laws' overarching context. The Law makes no sense in the absence of the larger narrative that explains the purpose of its precepts and how they came about. On the other hand, the Law is the "center of gravity" for the Hebrew scripture.[4]

Old Testament laws can make claims on the Chosen People because of the sovereignty of God, the Lord of creation, and because God had liberated them from slavery. Moreover, the Law is a divine gift that leads people to the holiness to which God invites them. It is the blueprint to blessedness—a sign of God's love, care, and concern for the people.[5]

There are four major collections of laws in the Old Testament, namely, the Decalogue (Ex 20:2–17; Dt 5:6–21), the Covenant Code (Ex 20:22–23:33), the Deuteronomic Code (Dt 12–26), and the Holiness Code (Lev 17–26). Strictly speaking, the last three are not truly "legal codes" in the full sense of the term, but collections of laws. Just like their ANE counterparts, they are neither comprehensive nor systematic.[6] Topics are arranged in a seemingly random manner.

More important, modern readers should be cautioned against reading Old Testament laws as *positive law* in the manner we understand and use the term today—as legislated norms that are used in courts of law to adjudicate disputes, assign liability, or impose penalties for injuries inflicted. These laws should be read as moral admonitions, rather than as state-mandated or court-enforced legislative prescriptions, for the following reasons.[7] First, just as with other ANE legal materials, there is no evidence that these biblical laws and codes were in fact used in legal proceedings to adjudicate actual cases. There are no legal citations or references to these laws in extant ANE legal materials. Furthermore, had these biblical laws and codes been truly positive laws, royal edicts would have used them as a basis for their pronouncements. As it is, these edicts make no mention of them and often contradict their prescriptions. Second, there were no mechanisms to enforce these laws or codes nor were there any sanctions for violations. These laws and codes were primarily self-enforced and founded on the authority and force of divine sanctions.

Third, scholars believe that these laws and codes originated from the everyday wisdom of oral tradition. These were put in writing by scribes as moral rules for a wise and flourishing life. Once committed to writing, these scribal collections took a life of their own, were widely regarded as divine in origin, and were eventually accepted by the wider population as the norm for proper moral conduct. Thus, these laws and codes have also been called "wisdom laws," indicative of their sapiential, rather than legislative, origins and function.

Fourth, some of these laws may not be law at all. For example, Deuteronomy 20:16–18 calls for the total extermination of the Canaanite residents in the conquered lands. Should this be taken as factual law? Not so. The laws on war were far more humane than this Deuteronomic pericope suggests. In fact, this passage is believed to have been written for literary purposes and propaganda five hundred years after the occupation of the land. Similarly, ANE literature has many instances of Mesopotamian propaganda disguised as law codes.[8]

It is not important for our study to assess, much less resolve, the scholarly debates on the origins, enforceability, and the legal or sapiential function of these prescriptions and prohibitions. This is beyond the goal of this project. What is critical for us is the vision of proper economic conduct that these laws and codes articulate. They express the moral will of God, non-exhaustively manifested in the written and oral collections of laws.[9] They do not describe the actual legal practice of their day.

There is a problem with dating these law codes and their respective precepts. Traditional scholarship recognizes four distinct sources in the Pentateuch.[10] These traditions overlap one another in the writing, redactions, and finalization of their respective laws.[11] Moreover, editorial changes were made over time. Given the current state of our knowledge and the evidence thus far available, it is hard to peel off and identify definitively these different redactions. In addition to these multiple editorial layers, the oral tradition incorporated in these laws compounds the difficulty of dating these legal codes. Even as they were put in writing much later, these oral traditions may be ancient and should be dated accordingly.[12]

Given these formidable hurdles, scholars agree on what we know and what we do not know. To begin with, they agree that it is extremely difficult to date many of these laws with certainty. However, we do know that these laws were not all written in the same time period. Later traditions edited or added on to earlier traditions. Within each law code, we find both early and late teachings.[13] The rough chronology from the earliest to the latest is (1) Decalogue, (2) Covenant Code, (3) Deuteronomic Code, and (4) Holiness Code. The Pentateuch was completed and took its final form in the Persian (538–333 B.C.) or Greek (332–142 B.C.) period under the priestly tradition.[14]

COVENANT CODE (EX 20:22–23:33)

The Covenant Code is the earliest of the collections of laws and may date anywhere from the thirteenth to the eighth century B.C. Many believe that it was finalized during the exile or the post-exilic period by priestly writers for remnant Israel in the Restoration. Fragments of it date from the ninth century in northern Israel.[15] In fact, it is very likely that the earliest parts of the Covenant Code are pre-monarchic and reflect a pastoral way of life. This is so because there is oddly no mention of urban life or of a king. There are numerous references to oxen, sheep, and asses—animals that are important for a semi-nomadic life. Only six of the eighty-six verses refer to agriculture in the Book of the Covenant.[16]

The laws dealing with the stranger, widow, and orphan most likely antedate the emergence of the state in Israel—to the time when the tribes, clans, and families were instrumental in shaping the life of the nation. Examples of precepts that emerged from ancient common law include not charging interest on the poor (Ex 22:25), returning a mantle (taken as a pledge) to the destitute because it may be the only covering they have (Ex 22:26–27), and the rights of the poor to harvest others' fields during the fallow year (Ex 23:11). Some themes that were most likely adapted from ANE literature are the care for the poor and securing justice for the defenseless and oppressed in court.[17]

The Covenant Code came about from the codification of the customs, oral tradition, public morality, and religious observances of Israel at a time of two major turning points in the life of the nation, namely, the shift from a nomadic life to settled agriculture in Canaan and the rise of the monarchy. There was a perceived need to codify their community practices in light of these major changes.[18]

Some scholars believe that the Covenant Code was the outcome of a struggle between tribal leaders and the royal house. For them, the Code was, in fact, a "negotiated arrangement" between village elders and the royal court given the establishment of the monarchy and the consequent disruptions that were then beginning to be felt. The Covenant Code was "a social charter" in which village elders won safeguards for their people, which were then put in writing as "laws." These became the weak's protection against a monarchy that was emerging to be disproportionately powerful.[19]

Economic Norms

The Covenant Code is divided into the following sections:

- Ex 20:22–26 (short introductory section on rules of worship and prohibition of idol worship)

- Ex 21:1–22:20 (long section of case law)
- Ex 22:21–23:19 (injunctions on caring for the poor, fulfilling cultic duties, and celebration of the festivals)
- epilogue: Ex 23:20–33 (threats, blessings, and curses regarding observance of the law, typical of ANE legal works)[20]

The Covenant Code's economic norms focus heavily on (1) the responsibilities that come with property and wealth, and (2) the duty to assist the vulnerable and the distressed. For example, male slaves are freed after six years of service (Ex 21:1–2). A daughter sold into slavery by her father and who subsequently marries the master or the master's son must be treated properly, even if the marriage fails (Ex 21:7–11).[21]

Strangers are not to be harassed or exploited (Ex 22:21). Not only are the Chosen People to lend to one another without charging interest, but they are also not to act like an extortioner (a usurer) in harshly treating or looking down on those who are driven to borrow from others.[22] Collateral may be secured only under strict conditions that protect the well-being of the debtor (Ex 22:26–27). Anything the land produces during the sabbatical fallow is reserved for the poor (Ex 23:10–11). The Sabbath rest is to be enjoyed by all, including servants, slaves, aliens, and farm animals (Ex 23:12).

Similar to contemporary torts, people are held responsible for the damages they cause through their negligence or recklessness (Ex 21:18–19, 22–36; 22:4–7, 13–16). Restitution and retribution are required for theft of farm animals (Ex 22:1–4, 9–12). Dishonest appropriation must be corrected with proper amends (Ex 22:9).

The Covenant Code calls for truthfulness in providing testimony and impartiality in judging (Ex 23:1–3, 6–7). Moreover, there is a clear admonition against accepting bribes (Ex 23:8). There is a duty to help an enemy's farm animals in distress or at risk. This is a pointed reminder of the deeper underlying obligation to prevent harm (Ex 23:4–5).

While not explicitly about money or property, some obligations to God also have an economic dimension. For example, the stipulation not to put God on a par with other gods implies not letting wealth or property compete with God for the nation's attention and affection. Nothing and no one ought to be valued more than God (Ex 20:23). In addition, the Covenant Code calls for promptness in offering the requisite cultic sacrifices (Ex 22:29–30; 23:15–17, 19). Finally, fidelity to God's Law leads to prosperity, health, and victory over their adversaries (Ex 23:20–33).

Theology and Ethics

Like other ANE legal literature (e.g., Code of Hammurabi), the Covenant Code was not meant to be comprehensive.[23] It merely provided a glimpse into God's will for the Chosen People. Thus, it becomes even more important to discern the spirit of these laws and their underlying cosmic divine order.

Among the distinctive features of the Covenant Code are the care and extensive protections for the alien, widow, and orphan. Justice toward the poor is the core message of this law code.[24] This concern for the poor was not merely imitated from ANE literature, but was a well-considered choice, as seen in the structure of the Covenant Code itself. For example, the God who legislates the Covenant Code is the God of the Exodus liberation. The language employed in telling the reader not to oppress the stranger is similar to the language used in describing the oppression in Egypt (Ex 3:9; Dt 26:7). Moreover, the laws were embedded in history itself by giving them binding power based on what God had done for Israel in her moment of need and who, now in her own turn, had to take care of the poor in her midst.[25]

Consider, for example, the treatment of slaves. It is the first concern expressed in Exodus 21:1–11, unlike ANE literature in which discussion on the treatment of slaves is usually relegated toward the end. This priority given to the humane treatment of slaves may reflect Israel's appreciation for her own liberation from slavery (Ex 20:2).[26] Similarly, notice the admonition not to wrong or oppress the stranger (Ex 22:21). Israel is pointedly reminded that she, too, had been a stranger in Egypt and, by inference, should therefore empathize with the alien. It is a theology of obligation or reciprocity. In the same way that God heard Israel's pleas during her bondage in Egypt, God also hears the cries of the alien, widow, poor, and orphan.[27] In other words, these laws and the strength of their claims flow from Israel's own experience of the favors God had lavished on her. This is true as well during the final editing of these laws in the post-exilic period. Israel's experience of bitter exile was still fresh. Note how narrative and law cannot be separated from one another. Israel's liberation is the basis for the claims of these laws.

Thus, Exodus is said to be a theology of creation and redemption. The theology of creation affirms the goodness of creation and the divine order put in place by God. Even more important for our study is the theology of redemption, because it is God who holds chaos and evil at bay and then restores the good that had been lost. God confronts and rectifies the tyrannical oppression of Pharaonic Egypt. The People of God were liberated and then rejuvenated and established in the Promised Land.

Consequently, the Law has to be viewed as a divine gift for Israel's own good, so that she might be the nation God created her to be—a nation held up for emulation by other nations. This is Israel's vocation in the priesthood—mediating between other nations and God, even while serving as a model. This is the larger context within which the Law was given.[28] This accounts for why the Law insists on solicitude for the poor and concern for one another's well-being.

DEUTERONOMIC CODE (DT 12–26)

The Deuteronomic Code was part of the reform of laws during the time of Josiah and the decline and downfall of the Assyrians (late seventh century B.C.). There had been repeated attempts to revise Israel's laws and to reappropriate the old customs. Deuteronomy was the outcome of such an attempt at reform. It builds on the Covenant Code, overlaps it, and revises existing laws, but it also adds new precepts. It rearranges the Covenant Code and structures itself around the Ten Commandments.[29]

The Deuteronomic Code affirms the continuing importance of care for the poor in Israel and actualizes such concern through law and practice. It includes traditions from the seventh century B.C. and probably from Josiah's reforms. The Code was incorporated into the larger Deuteronomic history after the exile.[30]

If the Covenant Code was indeed a negotiated settlement between village elders and the royal house, then the Deuteronomic Code can be viewed as a continued effort at balancing the needs and demands of the royal court and the villages in the face of changing socioeconomic times. In addition, the Deuteronomic Code was a response to the shift from rural concerns (e.g., Covenant Code) to new urban issues.[31] The Deuteronomist has been described as essentially about giving "a theological accounting of the Law and its place in Israel."[32] It was about keeping the laws relevant and responsive to the fresh challenges and needs of the time.

Economic Norms

A major theme of the Deuteronomist is solicitude for the well-being of the vulnerable and the distressed. The Deuteronomic Code calls for debt forgiveness at the end of seven years for loans made to fellow Israelites (Dt 15:1–2). It requires the Chosen People to lend generously, freely, and without ill will to fellow Israelites in economic distress, even with the approach of the seventh-year remission (Dt 15:7–11). No interest is to be charged on loans of food, money, or anything else for which interest is usually paid (Dt 23:19).[33] Moreover, lenders may not to go into borrowers' homes to choose a pledge. They have to wait respectfully outside the house and let debtors choose and bring out whatever collateral they select (Dt 24:10–11). Furthermore, they are not to take millstones or the upper stone as surety because these implements are essential for the borrower's livelihood (Dt 24:6). Similarly, lenders are not to take the cloak of the poor or the widow as collateral (Dt 24:12, 17).

Slaves are to be set free after six years of service, and they are to be provisioned by their masters in proportion to the blessings they themselves had received from God (Dt 15:12–14).

Sanctuary and hospitality are to be extended to runaway slaves. They are not to be oppressed, exploited, or returned to their masters, but allowed to live in their midst (Dt 23:15–16). An enslaved female prisoner of war who is subsequently taken by an Israelite as a wife may not be resold as a slave should the marriage fail. She is to be given her freedom (Dt 21:10–14).

Tithes every third year are to be set aside for the Levite, strangers, widows, and orphans (Dt 14:28–29; 26:12). Cultic sacrifices and offerings are to be shared with slaves and the Levites (Dt 12:17–19), including those from the Feast of Weeks (Dt 16:9–12) and the seven-day Feast of Booths or Tabernacles (Dt 16:13–15). Landowners are to let aliens, widows, and orphans glean through their fields, fruit trees, and vineyards (Dt 24:19–22). Passers-by may "scrump" through these fields and vineyards, but not use a sickle or a basket (Dt 23:24–25).

Another theme of the Deuteronomist is the importance of truthful, just, and respectful conduct. Judges and officials are to dispense justice impartially and be immune to bribes (Dt 16:18–20). People are not to remove landmarks (Dt 19:14). Merchants are to use honest weights and measures (Dt 25:15–16). Hired laborers have to be paid at the end of the day because they depend on such wages for their daily sustenance. They are not to be defrauded or exploited just because they are needy, poor, and defenseless (Dt 24:14–15). Fathers have to be unprejudiced and show no favoritism in dividing their estate and leaving a bequest to their children (Dt 21:15–17). Defaming a bride (and her family) on her virginity requires compensatory and retributive justice in the form of a heavy fine (Dt 22:13–19).

Such respect carries over even to animals and plants. An ox treading grain ought not to be muzzled (Dt 25:4). The enemies' fruit trees are to be preserved and not destroyed during sieges or war (Dt 20:19).[34] People are to exercise paternal care and prevent harm or loss for their kinsfolk's properties that may be at risk or for their farm animals lost or in distress (Dt 22:1–4).

Gratitude for life's blessings is another concern of the Deuteronomist, and such thankfulness has an economic dimension to it. In particular, the Chosen People are to tithe in thanksgiving for God's gift of abundance and in order to support the Levites for their priestly ministry (Dt 14:22–27; cf Num 18). The people are to bring the first fruits of their fields, vineyards, orchards, and olive trees before the Lord as a thanksgiving offering (Dt 12:5–7, 10–12, 17–19). These offerings to God are to be in proportion to the blessings they have received from the Lord, and they are to be presented before God during the Feast of Weeks (Dt 16:9–12), the seven-day Feast of Booths (Dt 16:13–15), and the Feast of Unleavened Bread (Dt 16:16–17). The firstlings of their farm animals are to be consecrated and offered to God (Dt 15:19–20). But no animals that are defective or blemished may be used in such offerings (Dt 17:1). These sacrifices are then to be eaten before the Lord in a shared feasting, with everyone partaking, including the Levites, the servants, and the aliens (Dt 26:1–11). In light of their service before the Lord on behalf of the people, the priests-Levites are to receive a portion of the cultic sacrifices and first fruits of the land, flocks, and wine press (Dt 18:1–4, 8).

The Deuteronomist envisions a land flowing with milk and honey in which no one is in want. There is the promise and optimistic expectation of material abundance so much so that there will be no poor in Israel (Dt 15:4). However, this is a conditional promise that is premised on upright conduct on the part of the nation. And herein lies another clearly discernible theme running through the book of Deuteronomy that scholars refer to as the Deuteronomic doctrine of divine retribution or just deserts.

Material prosperity, harmony, and success come about only through fidelity to the law. The book of Deuteronomy makes a bold promise that there will be no poor in Israel, but only if the nation follows the will of God. With such docility and fidelity, the Chosen People will never ever have to borrow from neighboring empires, and none will rule over them (Dt 15:5–6). In fact, God will raise them above all the other nations in praise, renown, and glory if they are faithful to the law (Dt 26:16–19).

The link between material prosperity and upright moral conduct is repeatedly employed by the Deuteronomist to motivate the Chosen People to care for one another. Thus, those who lend generously and freely without ill will to their fellow Israelites who have fallen on hard times will themselves be blessed abundantly by God (Dt 15:7–11). God will reward masters who set their slaves free after six years of service (Dt 15:18). Care in dispensing justice will lead to life and abundance in the land (Dt 16:18–20). Those who lend to their fellow Israelites without any interest will be blessed by God in all their undertakings (Dt 23:19–20). Similarly, landowners who leave something on the threshing floor, the vineyards, and the olive trees for the aliens, widows, and orphans to glean will flourish in life (Dt 24:19). Indeed, the people are clearly admonished that it will go well for them and their children if they follow the statutes and ordinances of the Lord and do that which is good and right in the eyes of God (Dt 12:28).

Note that this connection between material prosperity and success, on the one hand, and obedience to the will of God, on the other hand, extends beyond the Deuteronomic Code (Dt 12–26). For example, Deuteronomy 28–30 is a lengthy admonition on the blessings (including material prosperity) that come with obedience and the punishment attendant to disobedience.

Theology of the Deuteronomic Code

Sabbath release is believed by some to be the underlying theology of the Book of Deuteronomy.[35] To begin with, the Sabbath points to an earlier gift—the gift of God's creation that had been the object of divine activity and from which God rests. That earlier gift of creation and existence is, in itself, reason to be thankful. The Sabbath is a second, additional gift to humans—the gift of rest.

The Sabbath is about surcease from toil and daily concerns. It is about relief so that people might have the time and space to open themselves to God. It is a rest dedicated to and spent on God. Moreover, the Sabbath is a gift for all, even for the beasts of burden, slaves, and the aliens, that is, for all who would otherwise not have had the occasion to stop work and to rest.

But these themes apply not only to the Sabbath day but also to the sabbatical year and the Jubilee year. Observe that in all three cases, we have the same theme of release—from work, from debt, from bondage, and from landlessness. These releases are not merely about rest, but about new beginnings, especially for the sabbatical and the Jubilee year. They are about being refreshed and renewed, but always in reference to God.

If Sabbath release is indeed the underlying theology of Deuteronomy, then the Deuteronomic Code fits right in with the rest of the book. After all, note that the Deuteronomic Code is about protecting the person and easing the harshness and the chance and contingencies of life for those who are distressed. The Code is about providing new beginnings. And it is not the king or the state or the Temple that provides such new dawns. Rather, it is the people themselves who will furnish one another with a fresh start as needed. They are God's instruments in providing such releases and new chances to each other. And in living up to these releases, they actualize the *Shema* in their own lives: to love God with all their heart, soul, and strength (Dt 6:4–5).

Ethics of the Deuteronomic Code

There are at least three distinctive features in the ethics of the Deuteronomic Code. First, the Deuteronomic Code is a deliberate effort in the seventh century B.C. to bring Israelite life in conformity with God's mandates. Thus, the Code restates the key provisions that it believes preserve Israel's divine election to responsibility. Recall that Israel's existence itself was at risk at that time because of her wanton infidelities. The object of Deuteronomic reformers was to codify (via the written law) and to conform to the moral will of God. Thus, the Deuteronomic Code has been described as a "parenetic restatement of the law."[36]

Second, the Deuteronomic Code humanizes the laws of the land. This is apparent from a comparison of the provisions of the Covenant and Deuteronomic Codes. Note the statutes that are found in the latter but not in the former, such as: the care with which one avoids injury or danger to life, as in the construction of roof battlements (Dt 22:8); the need to take down the body of an executed, hanged person before nightfall (Dt 21:22–23); the proscription against excessive and dehumanizing punishment (Dt 25:1–3); humane treatment of women war prisoners (Dt 20:11, 14; 21:10–14) and runaway slaves (Dt 23:15–16); proper treatment of the poor (Dt 15:1–11); non-discrimination of a hated wife and her son (Dt 21:15–17); respect for others' property (Dt 23:24–25); no cruelty to animals (Dt 22:6–7; 25:4); restrictions on taking a millstone as collateral for debt (Dt 24:6); the use of honest weights and measures (Dt 25:13–16); tithing in support of the Levites (Dt 26:12–15); proper care and respect for fruit-bearing trees in the enemies' city even in time of war (Dt 20:19–20); payment of the day wages of a worker (Dt 24:14–15).[37]

In addition, Deuteronomy closes loopholes or improves the provisions of the Covenant Code. Unlike Exodus 21:2–4, Deuteronomy requires the release not only of male servants but also of maid servants after six years of service. In addition, masters are required to provision freed slaves with goods and necessities to ease their way to a fresh start (Dt 15:12–18). Unlike Exodus 23:4 that merely calls for the return of stray animals, Deuteronomy 22:1–3 requires that they be cared for until their restoration to their owners. Deuteronomy 24:10–13 goes beyond Exodus 22:25–27 in explicitly stating that no pledge may be taken from the poor.

Unlike Exodus 22:26–27, Deuteronomy 24:6, 10–13 imposes further restrictions on debt pledges. In addition to the earlier ban on taking a cloak as a pledge, it prohibits getting hold of millstones as collateral since these are needed by people for their livelihood. Moreover, Deuteronomy instructs that no surety should be taken from the poor and that, out of respect for the debtor, creditors should not enter a borrower's house but wait outside for the pledge to be brought out by the debtor. Deuteronomy is far more detailed in specifying the proper manner by which debt collateral is to be handled.

In Exodus, there is ambiguity as to which types of loans are not subject to interest rates (e.g., consumption or commercial loans). Deuteronomy 23:19 dispels this uncertainty with its blanket prohibition that covers all items for which interest is usually charged. Deuteronomy 23:19–20 likewise clears earlier questions about Exodus 22:25 by noting that the ban on charging interest applies regardless of whether or not the borrower is poor. Deuteronomy not only regularizes debt forgiveness (Dt 15:1–3), but also closes an earlier loophole by explicitly stating that it is a moral obligation to lend to the distressed, even with the approach of the seventh-year debt-release (Dt 15:7–11). In other words, Deuteronomy adopts the Decalogue and the Covenant Code and then adapts these for its own times and concerns.[38]

In addition to the preceding contrasts, consider, too, the great importance accorded by the Deuteronomic Code to the human person. Unlike the Covenant Code, there is little on property protection in Deuteronomy, except for the admonitions against moving a landmark (Dt 19:14) and using false weights and measures (Dt 25:13–16). Most of Deuteronomic legislation is about the protection of the human person. Moreover, even in terms of cultic observances, the concern is not with the rituals themselves. Deuteronomy is interested more in ensuring that these festivals included everyone (Dt 14:22–29; 16:1–17). Note the motive clause in Deuteronomy 16:12. Moreover, observe how the interest in these sacrifices stems partly out of a desire to see that those without access to land and the destitute are fed.[39]

A third feature of Deuteronomic ethics is its daring vision of eliminating destitution in the land: there will be no poor in Israel. The Deuteronomic Code is said to be far bolder than either the Covenant or the Holiness Code in this regard.[40] In fact, the Holiness Code tones down the Deuteronomist's goal, perhaps thinking of the Deuteronomic Code as being utopian.

Prior to Deuteronomy, authors or editors were not careful in the choice of words to describe the poor. In contrast, the Deuteronomist took great care to distinguish two groups as the object of laws. The first group is comprised of slaves, Levites, strangers, widows, and orphans, that is, people who do not have access to land. The second group consists of those who are adversely affected by the chance and contingencies of life.

Numerous economic provisions of the Deuteronomic Code are intended to ensure that those who are landless do not end up being poor and destitute. Thus, recall the Deuteronomic mandates on participation for slaves and Levites in the festivals and freewill offerings, the tri-annual tithes for the poor, Sabbath rest even for the strangers and slaves, and gleaning privileges for the landless. Note the primary beneficiaries of these statutes. Even as slaves, Levites, strangers, widows, and orphans do not own land, they will not be left in want because the community ensures that they have access to the fruits of the earth. This goes a long way toward fulfilling the Deuteronomic vision of not having any poor in Israel. Despite having no land of their own, these people are nonetheless still able to participate in the feasts and in the life of the community.

There are also provisions for the second group: those who have fallen on hard times and are impoverished. Recall how Deuteronomy stipulates lending without interest, debt remission, slave release, restrictions on debt pledges, and the daily payment of wages.[41] These ordinances facilitate much-needed assistance to small farmers who are in distress so that they are not made permanently poor. These provisions give them a realistic chance of rising above their economic setbacks. These laws are about relief, recovery, and restoration.

For both groups of people (those who are landless and those who have fallen on hard times), the Deuteronomic Code provides a safety net to ensure that they do not become permanently destitute. This is how Deuteronomy 15:4 is to be fulfilled in having no poor in Israel (cf. Dt 15:11).[42]

In sum, God's in-breaking in human history by liberating Israel revealed the end (*telos*) to which people ought to direct their economic activities.

> In this command [observance of the Sabbath] Israel broke decisively from the Pharaonic system of production and consumption. Israel asserts that "rest" for self, for neighbour, and even for God is the goal and quintessence of life . . . which precludes hostility, competition, avarice, and insecurity. . . . [It] anticipates a community of peace, well-being and joy. There could hardly be a bolder refutation of Pharaoh's brick quotas than in this sabbath principle. (Brueggemann, 1994, 16)

And, indeed, the Chosen People were to build an economy that was a complete antithesis of their experience in Egypt: every Israelite family with an inheritance of land for its own use and a livelihood, in contrast to the Pharaonic monopoly in land ownership; freedom in the Promised Land, in contrast to Egyptian slavery; rests, feasts, and festivals in Israel, in contrast to unceasing hard toil under the Egyptian yoke; respect for the dignity for every person as an end, in contrast to the use of people as expendable slaves and chattel; a decentralized, sharing, and caring Israelite community of tribes, in contrast to the concentration of power in Pharaoh; Israelite egalitarianism, in contrast to great inequality in Egypt; and justice and love in the Promised Land, in contrast to chronic injustice in Egypt.[43] There was a rich economic content and context to God's breaking into human history on behalf of Israel. As mentioned earlier, Sabbath release is said to be the theology of the Deuteronomic Code. Thus, the ethics of this law code may be said to be about actualizing "a Sabbath economy."

HOLINESS CODE (LEV 17–26)

Many scholars date the Holiness Code as post-exilic and attribute it to the priestly class.[44] The Holiness Code has wide-ranging materials and detailed prescriptions, from ritual observances to the manner by which the exchange value of ancestral land is determined. What ties such diverse materials together is their common underlying foundation—the invitation to be holy as God is holy (Lev 19:2; 20:7–8).

Economic Norms

The Holiness Code calls for solicitude for the poor. The Chosen People are to welcome into their households those who have fallen on hard times. They are to extend to these distressed fellow Israelites the same privileges and care as they would to tenants or aliens who live in their midst (Lev 25:35). In fact, those who have to sell themselves are to be treated with respect and be welcomed as tenants or as hired hands, and not purchased as slaves (Lev 25:39–43). The impoverished should not be exploited by lending them money or food at interest, or by selling them food at a profit (Lev 25:36–37). The produce of the land during the Sabbath fallow are for the servants, slaves, and hired hands (Lev 25:1–7). Landowners should let the poor and the aliens glean through their fields and vineyards (Lev 19:9–10; 23:22).

Strangers living in Israel are not to be abused (Lev 19:33–34), and the protection of the law applies equally to both aliens and native Israelites (Lev 24:22).[45] The deaf and the blind are not to be cursed or mistreated (Lev 19:14).[46] Sabbath rest is to be observed after six days of work (Lev 23:3) and during the Day of Atonement (Lev 23:31–32) and the Feast of Booths (Lev 23:33–38). Land is to be left fallow every seventh year (Lev 25:1–7).

Ancestral land is returned to their original holders on the Jubilee year (Lev 25:8–16).[47] Sellers or their kinsfolk have the right to redeem ancestral land previously sold. After all, land cannot be sold in perpetuity because land belongs to God (Lev 25:23–28). Similarly, Israelites sold into slavery maintain the right to redeem themselves or to be redeemed by their kin (Lev 25:47–55).

People are not to defraud their neighbors or to withhold pay from workers (Lev 19:13). They are not to steal (Lev 19:11). They are to use honest weights and measures (Lev 19:35–37). Justice at the city gates must be impartial and honest (Lev 19:15). Those who injure others are subject to retributive justice (Lev 24:17–21).

Gratitude calls for acknowledging God's blessings. The first fruits of a newly planted tree are offered to God (Lev 19:23–24). Similarly, the first fruits of the fields are reserved for God (Lev 23:9–14). No deformed or defective animals may be offered to God in cultic sacrifice (Lev 22:20–25).

Just as in Deuteronomy, we find a link between moral conduct and material prosperity. The nation's fidelity to the law, including resident aliens, is a necessary condition for continued tenure on the Promised Land (Lev 18:26; 20:22–26; 25:18–22). God will provide sufficient harvest for those who observe the Sabbath fallow. Their harvest on the sixth year will be enough to supply their needs for the seventh and eighth year, until the ninth year's harvest (Lev 25:20–22). Offering first fruits in gratitude to God is a necessary condition for continued abundance (Lev 19:23–25). In other words, Israel's material prosperity and success are dependent on her fidelity to God (Lev 26).

Theology and Ethics of the Holiness Code

Holiness is the goal of human activity.[48] And as we will see repeatedly for the rest of the Old Testament, such holiness requires both legal-cultic purity and moral rectitude. First, the Holiness Code is said to be "an exegetical harmonization of the Priestly Code, the Decalogue, the Covenant Code, and Deuteronomy." After all, it was the priestly class that finalized the Pentateuch as we receive it today. The Holiness Code seeks to codify the norms of justice, just like the other two law codes.[49] In terms of structure, Leviticus 19 and 25 are described as the Code's two pillars. On the one hand, Leviticus 19 is an ethics for the individual centered on the love of neighbor including one's enemy (Lev 19:17–18). On the other hand, Leviticus 25 is a social ethics that underscores community and social solidarity.[50]

Second, the ethics of the Holiness Code must be viewed within the context of the larger priestly agenda of filling the vacuum after the monarchical debacle and collapse that lost Israel everything she had received as God's Chosen People (post-exilic era). The priestly program was then one of national renewal and restoration, even as it had a political dimension as well, namely, bolstering the power base and position of the priestly class.

This priestly agenda was well served both in the Code's prescriptions on rituals and in its admonitions regarding the poor. The early chapters of Leviticus (1–15) are about purity and ritual. They describe Israel's sacrifice system and detail pure and impure practices. Their underlying premise is that God is holy and, as a result, people will also have to be pure in order for them to have a relationship with God (Lev 11:44–45; 15:31). And, of course, since the priests are mediators between the divine and the earthly (by the nature of the priestly office), this plethora of rituals and purity regulations enhance priestly power and influence because priests become indispensable. The more people have to deal with rituals and questions about or remedies for impurity, the more invaluable is the service provided by the priestly class.[51]

The overriding focus of priestly writing is said to be the self-serving political agenda of the priestly class, and not the interests of the poor. Nevertheless, as argued later, the Holiness Code is bold in its vision for the poor. However, cynics hold that even this pro-poor posture was a calculated move. These priestly writings were intended to show concern for the destitute because such solicitude ultimately strengthened the priestly class itself.[52] After all, recall that care for the poor dated all the way back to the earliest days of the nation. It gave the priests credibility as the guardians of the nation's traditions.

Third, scholars disagree over the audacity of the social vision of the Holiness Code relative to the other two law codes or even the prophets. Some claim that the Holiness Code has an impressive social program on behalf of the poor.[53] Despite its self-serving political agenda of maintaining its own power, the priestly class did articulate an impressive call for relief and restoration for those who had fallen on hard times. In fact, in some cases, Leviticus has provisions that are even more radical than either the Covenant or Deuteronomic Code.

Consider, for example, the priestly (*P*) version of the Decalogue (Lev 19:1–18). It can be aptly described as an activist social agenda that is inclusive. After all, it has far more on social justice than *D*'s (Dt 5:6–21) or *E*'s (Ex 20:1–17) versions and explicitly includes theft, fraud, wages, and the physically disabled. Furthermore, it requires extra attention and assistance for the poor and the stranger (Lev 19:9–10). To its credit, the priestly agenda includes holiness for all, even for the least. Thus, *P*'s version of the Decalogue is said to be the most far-reaching of the various formulations.

Beyond the Decalogue, we see a similar boldness in *P*'s concern for the poor in the other provisions of the law. It goes beyond the practice of debt slavery to question the very institution of slavery itself. Leviticus 25:39–43 stipulates that the distressed should not be purchased as a slave, but should instead be welcomed into the household either as a tenant or as a hired hand. Its Jubilee Law is much more radical than the sabbatical year, the seventh-year slave manumission, or debt forgiveness, because it even calls for the return of ancestral land to their original owners.

In light of these differences, we can dispel two observations that are often made about the Holiness Code. To begin with, many characterize the priestly writings as interested more in purity and rituals and not with social issues. In addition, many mistakenly relegate the Priestly (*P*) tradition to the background when it comes to matters of social justice. It is often overshadowed by the Elohist (*E*), the Deuteronomic (*D*), or the prophetic traditions, which many deem to be the prime proponents of social justice in the Old Testament.

P is also an important social-justice exponent. The priestly social vision can stand toe-to-toe with the Covenant Code, the Deuteronomic Code, or even the prophets in terms of its inclusiveness and daring. Its scope is more extensive because it covers the shrine, community, families, and the marginalized. Its social program is even more demanding in its requirements (e.g., Jubilee Law).[54]

To be sure, the priestly class was assiduous and bold in its advocacy for the poor for larger ends. They believed that it was a necessary condition for the successful re-establishment of Israel in the post-exilic period. The priests took to heart the prophetic claim that ritual purity cannot be separated from moral integrity. Genuine worship entails social-justice work.[55]

Other scholars disagree with these claims. In contrast to the Deuteronomist, the Holiness Code resigns itself to always having the poor in Israel. The priestly class was not even aiming for the elimination of destitution in its social agenda. For example, as mentioned earlier, the Deuteronomic Code provides a social safety net for the landless. Even if slaves, strangers, widows, the poor, and orphans do not own land, the laws made sure that they were not destitute and were still able to access the fruits of the earth.[56] We do not find comparable provisions to these in the Holiness Code.

Sabbatical releases in Deuteronomy occur every seven years. Leviticus 25 takes place every fifty years. This is beyond the life expectancy of people during this era.[57] Thus, many will not get to recover either their freedom or their ancestral land in their own lifetime. The seven-year period is much more realistic and effective in making sure that there were no poor in Israel.

Consider, too, the gleaning law (Lev 19:10; 23:22; cf. Dt 24:19–22). Unlike Deuteronomy, Leviticus uses the word "poor" for the beneficiaries of this law. This presupposes that there will be poor in Israel.[58] On the celebration of the feasts of Pentecost and Tabernacles, Deuteronomy 16:14 calls on all, including the stranger, to partake as equals with the rest of the community. In contrast, Leviticus 23:42 mentions only citizens, but not aliens. Deuteronomy is much more inclusive.[59]

In sum, there are strong arguments that can be presented for both sides of the debate regarding the Holiness Code's advocacy for the marginalized. Regardless of which tradition has the bolder social program, what is important for our study is that the three law codes of the Old Testament present a wide array of social legislation on behalf of the poor.

SUMMARY AND CONCLUSIONS

Despite differences in their theology, ethics, and social context, the three Old Testament law codes converge in the themes underlying their economic norms, to wit:

- There is a constitutive economic dimension to God's order of creation.
- Care for the poor, the distressed, and the vulnerable is a defining formal characteristic of what it is to be the Chosen People of God.
- Laws provide a concrete venue for imitating God by showing the path to holiness and righteousness through proper conduct in economic life.[60]

We will discuss these in greater depth in part III when we examine recurring themes in both the Old and New Testament.

The norms underlying these themes are not mere abstract generalizations. They are concrete and specific in what they require. In contemporary language, these laws are formulated as both positive and negative duties, as do's and don'ts. The biggest blocks of materials are those on how the Chosen People were to use their wealth and possessions and on how they were to treat the poor, the vulnerable, and the distressed in their midst with compassion, justice, and love.

Furthermore, in responding to the particular problems of their day, the Covenant, Deuteronomic, and Holiness Code illustrate how to use Sacred Scripture for ethical reflection under different socioeconomic contexts. Note that the writers and editors of the Old Testament adopted many ANE legal provisions that were then adapted for the special Covenant relationship between Israel and YHWH.

NOTES

1. There is an unresolved scholarly debate on whether the Covenant was a historical reality early in the formation of the nation Israel, or whether it was in fact a much later theological concept that emerged from the eighth-century prophets who emphasized that what was distinctive about the nation Israel was its election to responsibility, that is, living righteously according to God's will. This is a debate that we need not resolve for our project. See Nicholson (1986) for an in-depth survey and evaluation of this issue. It is sufficient for our study to note that: (1) the Covenant reflects a unique relationship between YHWH and the nation Israel, and that (2) this special relationship required a particular moral conduct that is consistent with divine will. This includes the many economic norms that we study as part of this covenantal relationship.

2. The other important theme of the Old Testament is land. In fact, some would go so far as to argue that land may be a far more important theme than Covenant (von Waldow, 1974, 493). See also Wright (1990; 2004).

3. Kaiser (1983); Ogletree (1983); McKenzie (1990, 1299); Otto (1995, 162)

4. Pleins (2001, 42, fn 2)

5. Ogletree (1983, 51–52)

6. Wenham (2006, 352)

7. For an in-depth exposition on this issue, see Fitzpatrick-Mckinley (1999), Jackson (1989; 2006), and LeFebvre (2006).

8. See Lohfink (1982, 243).

9. Historical criticism concludes that these laws did not all come from the time of Moses because substantial parts of these codes were written centuries later. However, the goal of these codes is to be unambiguous about the authority and the source of these laws—God's will as mediated through or as communicated to Moses.

10. For the narratives on the origins of the nation, we have the Yahwist or *J* source (ninth century B.C.) and the Elohist or *E* source (eighth century B.C.). For the legal traditions, we have the Deuteronomist or *D* source (seventh century B.C.) and the Priestly or *P* source (post-exilic) (Murphy, 1990a, 4). This is Wellhausen's "documentary hypothesis." Ceresko (1992, 68–74) provides a concise description of these four sources.

11. Pleins (2001, 74–75) refers to this as the process of "traditioning."

12. Some claim that the Covenant Code may have even been redacted by a Deuteronomic hand according to the Deuteronomic Code, although other scholars dispute this claim (Lohfink, 1991, 38–39).

13. Thus, von Waldow (1970, 182) notes that an ordinance within a particular law code does not necessarily indicate its age because of the mix of early and late materials in all three law codes.

14. Barton (1982, 118) adopts the view that the Pentateuch took its final form during the exilic or post-exilic eras. Donahue (2005, 19) puts the completion after the exile.

15. Donahue (2005, 19); McKenzie (1990, 1299); Nardoni (2004, 69)

16. Stein (1953, 164)

17. Lohfink (1991, 39–40); von Waldow (1970, 184–85). However, Lohfink (1991, 40) surmises that the laws on the proper treatment of strangers (e.g., Ex 22:21; 23:9) were not drawn from the outside but came from within Israel itself.

18. Mendenhall (1954, 37)

19. Pleins (2001, 53, 80–81). Von Waldo (1970) also argues that these laws were a priestly counter-reaction to the social crisis unfolding in Israel because of its worsening conditions.

20. Wenham (2006, 354)

21. However, for all its compassion, the Covenant Code also has provisions that treat slaves as property (e.g., Ex 21:3–4, 7–11, 20–21, 32).

22. Goldingay (2002, 199) notes that the Covenant Code does not merely ask that no interest be charged. It goes further and calls for a change in attitudes. After all, even if lenders do not charge interest, they may nonetheless be cruel or disrespectful in demanding a collateral or repayment.

23. Clifford (1990, 53)

24. Pleins (2001, 51, 54)
25. Lohfink (1991, 40–42)
26. Wenham (2006, 354–55)
27. Pleins (2001, 52)
28. Fretheim (1991)
29. Mendenhall (1954, 44); Pleins (2001, 54–61)
30. Donahue (2005, 19–20)
31. Pleins (2001, 59, 60, 80–81)
32. Toombs (1965, 399)
33. Debt remission is only for fellow Israelites and not for foreigners (Dt 15:3). The latter may also be charged interest (Dt 23:20).
34. However, non-fruit-bearing trees may be cut down and used for the siege works.
35. The following points on the Sabbath theology of Deuteronomy are drawn from Miller (1985).
36. McKenzie (1990, 1299)
37. See Weinfeld (1961, 241) and Pleins (2001, 55–58).
38. Pleins (2001, 54–56)
39. Weinfeld (1961, 243–44)
40. Although Pilgrim (1981, 151) suggests that the goal of the sabbatical year legislation that we find as early as the Covenant Code is to have no poor among the people.
41. Lohfink (1991, 45, table 3)
42. Lohfink (1991, 43–47)
43. Brueggemann (1994)
44. For example, see Donahue (2005, 19). In contrast, McKenzie (1990, 1299) views it as earlier than the exile.
45. There are exceptions. For example, Leviticus 25:44–46 permits foreign slaves to be owned as chattel and to be treated differently compared with Israelite slaves.
46. We do not find such special consideration for the disabled when it comes to rituals. For example, Leviticus 21:16–23 limits the extent to which the lame, the blind, and the deformed are able to participate in cultic offerings. They are barred from priestly offices and functions.
47. Houses have to be returned as well during the Jubilee, but not for those in walled cities. These can be redeemed within one year of sale and then become a permanent sale (Lev 25:29–31). Levites are exempt from this rule and will always have the right of redemption. Moreover, the pasture and land belonging to Levite cities cannot be sold (Lev 25:32–34). The releases called for in the Jubilee Law are said to have been practiced as early as two thousand years prior to the writing of Israel's laws. For examples of such releases in ANE, see Hudson (1999, 29–31). For Israel, we have the release proclaimed by King Zedekiah (596–587 B.C.), which he promptly rescinded after the war emergency was over. He was duly punished for it (Jer 34:8–11; cf. Neh 5). Other than these two passages, there is no other mention of actual Jubilee releases in Sacred Scripture.
48. Faley (1990, 72)
49. Pleins (2001, 65)
50. Otto (1995, 164)
51. Pleins (2001, 61–64)
52. Pleins (2001, 65)
53. See Pleins (2001, 50ff) for a further exposition of the following thesis.
54. Pleins (2001, 50, 61)
55. Pleins (2001, 70)
56. See Lohfink (1991, 43, table 2) for a listing of these fourteen laws.
57. The average life expectancy for that period is believed to be forty years for males and thirty years for females (Lowery, 2000, 8).
58. Moreover, it also denotes the widow and orphan as among the "poor" compared with the careful wording in Deuteronomy as we have seen in the preceding section.
59. Nardoni (2004, 79–90) suggests another difference. Deuteronomy is particularistic and ties in with ancient traditions. In contrast, the priestly writings are more universalistic in their thinking.

60. See Baker (2009) and Hiers (2002) for alternative syntheses of Old Testament economic norms.

Chapter Four

Prophets

Prophets served biblical Israel through most of its history, namely: the preclassical prophets, the classical prophets, and the apocalyptic prophets. We find the preclassical prophets in the books of Joshua, Judges, Samuel, and Kings. The classical prophets constitute the biggest and the most well-known group that comprises Isaiah, Jeremiah, Ezekiel, and the twelve minor prophets, such as Hosea, Amos, and Micah. Daniel is an example of an apocalyptic prophet.[1]

Of immediate interest for our study are the classical prophets, covering the second half of the eighth to the fifth century B.C. The strictly classical prophets are Amos and Hosea in the northern kingdom (Israel) and Isaiah and Micah in the southern kingdom (Judah) during the Neo-Assyrian Empire (934–609 B.C.). A distinctive feature of the classical prophets was their call. They were individually commissioned by God, operated on their own, and were not part of a band of wandering prophets. The classical prophets did not come from a single cultic, tribal, or occupational class. Jeremiah and Ezekiel were from priestly families. Isaiah was a wisdom teacher from Jerusalem. Micah and Amos were free peasants.

Prophets were commissioned by God for very specialized tasks. Note, for example, Amos 7:14ff, Isaiah 6, Jeremiah 1, and Ezekiel 1–3. In addition, the classical prophets did not seek such charge from God. In fact, some even tried to avoid God's call (e.g., Jer 1:6). These prophets suffered greatly on account of the message God gave them to preach.

The prophetic books have been traditionally used as the principal source of our knowledge of the historical prophets to whom these works are attributed. However, ascertaining the actual historical setting of each prophetic book is extremely difficult. Scholars acknowledge that it is a highly speculative exercise. These books were most likely written by later authors and not by the historical prophets themselves. Moreover, these books underwent a long period of redaction of two or three centuries, with the final editing occurring during the Persian period. Differentiating the various editorial changes entails much guesswork. Nevertheless, most scholars agree that each prophetic book has a core set of teachings that date back to the historical prophet itself.[2] To get around these difficulties, we simply take these texts as integral wholes, in their own right, without having to delve into the scholarly disagreements on the details of specific passages, such as their authorship or dating.

Central to our study of biblical economic ethics are the classical, eighth-century prophets because of the socioeconomic ills they addressed. The classic expression of justice commonly associated with the prophetic tradition is attributed to this period. In fact, these pre-exilic prophets are often called the social prophets. They were the conscience of the nation at a time of grave sin and danger.[3] Of all the prophetic books, Amos stands out because of the prominence of justice as an issue.[4] This has led many to conclude that Amos was clearly reacting to the deteriorating socioeconomic conditions of his time. Thus, we will devote more attention to Amos and less so to the other prophets or to the other time periods.

AMOS

The book of Amos is the earliest example of classical Hebrew biblical prophecy. By his own account, he functioned as a prophet during the reigns of Azariah (aka Uzziah) of Judah (787–736 B.C.) and Jeroboam II of Israel (787–747 B.C.). Amos was a prophet in the northern kingdom, Israel. He preached in Samaria, its capital (Am 3:9; 4:1; 6:1; 8:14), in the sanctuary in Bethel (Am 3:14; 4:4; 5:5–6; 7:10, 13), and possibly in the sanctuary of Gilgal (Am 4:4; 5:5). Amaziah, the priest at the royal sanctuary, expelled him from Bethel (Am 7:10–17). Judean by birth in Tekoa in the Judean highlands, Amos was a herdsman prior to his call from God (Am 1:1; 7:14–15). In addition, he gathered leaves and fruits from sycamore trees as feed for his livestock. We cannot assume that he was from a poor social background because of his ability to express himself and his working knowledge of Hebrew educational traditions.[5] By his own account, he was neither a professional prophet, a cultic prophet, nor a prophet's disciple (Am 7:14). His ministry was a direct commission from YHWH (Am 7:15), and he ended up preaching in the northern kingdom.

Condemnations

The external events at this time were propitious for both Judah and Israel. There were rivalries among the Aramean states and given her weakened and distracted condition, Assyria was unable to pursue her imperial ambitions and impose her authority on the surrounding states. This allowed Israel and Judah to recover some of the territory they had lost. (Amos 6:13 speaks of two victories.) However, Israel's problems were really internal rather than external.[6]

Given this period of peace and prosperity, the people were complacent in thinking that their relationship with God was coming along smoothly. After all, by the doctrine of divine retribution (just deserts), prosperity was a reward from God for righteousness. Israel and Judah would not otherwise have been doing so well if God was not pleased with them.

Amos was pessimistic despite the successes of Kings Joash and Jeroboam II in regaining land, in establishing a period of peace, and in enjoying some economic prosperity. After all, the primary, if not the sole, beneficiaries of these were the upper classes. What was even worse, such prosperity came at the expense of ordinary people. Thus, Amos shocked the people by warning them that the destruction of Israel was imminent on account of her transgression of God's will. King Jeroboam II's reign marked the end of their period of prosperity. Israel had brought down evil upon herself (Am 5:18–20). She could not be spared either by her cultic observances (Am 5:21–27; 5:4–6) or by her boasting of God's election of Israel (Am 3:1–2; 9:7–8).[7]

Amos was critical of the elite at the time of King Jeroboam II because of their self-indulgent consumption and the manner by which they acquired their wealth.[8] It is believed that these were the urban-based aristocrats in Samaria, including the royal officials, tax collectors, and merchants.[9] Amos indicted the ruling elite for exploiting and oppressing the weak and the poor. The rich and the powerful impoverished the rest of the nation so that they could enjoy their lifestyles and their luxuries.

Archeological evidence supports the claim of new wealth and opulence during this period. This is evident in home-construction activity. In the city of Tirzah near Sechem, a former capital of the northern kingdom (1 Kgs 14:17), archaeologists confirm wide wealth disparities. The houses of the poor were small, shabbily built, and crammed in the city. In contrast, the houses of the rich were large, clearly expensive, solidly constructed, and set apart from the city in a separate section surrounded by walls.[10]

This is consistent with the scathing indictments we find in Amos. The rich were not satisfied with merely having shelter. They wanted separate lodgings for the winter and summer (Am 3:15a; cf Jer 36:22). Moreover, these homes were built of expensive materials, such as hewn stones (Am 5:11a), and were lavishly furnished with ivory (Am 3:15b; cf 1 Kgs 22:39). They had plush furniture and couches for extravagant banquets (Am 3:12; 6:4–6; cf Is 28:1–4).

The elite indulged in a life of inordinate feasting, carousing, and drinking (Am 4:1; cf. 2:8; 5:11; 6:4–7). These feasts were filled with music and song

(Am 6:5–6; also 6:7; 8:3a). As further evidence of opulence, meat was a standard fare at these banquets even as it was rarely eaten by the masses at that time because of the expense. And they were meats of the best kind, such as calves fed in the fields and fattened in the stalls (Am 6:4b). Banqueters were massaged by servants using the best olive oil (Am 6:6a).

Amos harshly condemned such self-indulgent consumption in the face of great poverty.[11] But even more reprehensible than this lifestyle was how the rich and the powerful paid for them. They could afford such disordered pleasures because they robbed the defenseless and the poor whom they drove ever deeper into debt slavery.

Debt slavery was permitted in Israel (Ex 21:2–6; Lev 25:39–43; Dt 15:12–15), and the upper classes used this practice for their own further enrichment. The poor and even ordinary people incurred debt because of the unforeseen contingencies in life, and the elite took advantage of such unexpected needs by imposing harsh loan conditions. To be sure, there were laws governing debt collateral (Ex 22:25–26; Dt 24:12–13, 17; Jb 22:6). But these precepts were routinely ignored, and pledges were not returned. Creditors took garments as collateral despite proscriptions against such practice (Am 2:8a). After all, recall the earlier point that these laws were not positive laws that we have today but were mere moral exhortations without legal enforcement mechanisms or sanctions. They were self-enforced, from the heart.

Unconscionable creditors extracted as much grain as possible from debtors in arrears (Am 5:11). Moreover, both people and their possessions were subject to sale (Am 8:5). Creditors confiscated debtors' vintage (Am 2:8b). Furthermore, an insolvent debtor could be sold into slavery (Am 2:6) or bought as a slave (Am 8:6) even for a trifling debt (e.g., price of a pair of sandals). People were treated as objects (Am 2:7b).[12] Amos 2:8 suggests that even the temple was complicit in exploitative lending practices.[13] Thus, for most people, debts turned into an unrecoverable slide into slavery. Amos and the other prophets condemned such conduct as morally unacceptable.[14] They preached that Israel will be punished for driving many people into slavery and destitution. And as we will see later in her history, Israel was indeed enslaved and impoverished.

Unscrupulous merchants violated the Sabbath, used false measures and weights (cf. Lev 19:36), foisted off inferior merchandise (Am 8:6), and exploited the poor (Am 8:5–6; cf. Mic 6:10–11). In effect, the well-to-do enriched themselves even further from the little that the poor had to begin with.

The powerful prevented the prophets from speaking out (Am 2:12). Moreover, they perverted the judicial system and manipulated the administration of the law for the rich's advantage (Am 5:7, 12, 15; 6:12; cf. 1 Kgs 21; Is 1:21–23; 5:20; 10:1–2; Mic 3:1–3, 9–11). Justice was supposed to be dispensed at the city gates. The law called for due process (Dt 10:17–18) and warned against accepting bribes (Ex 23:8). Legitimate fines imposed by the law were not to be used as occasions for extortion (e.g., Ex 21:22), which is no different from outright robbery. In practice, judges were venal and easily bribed (Am 5:12). Thus, the poor's claims were not heard, and justice at the city gate was denied (Am 2:7; 5:10–12).

Amos also corroborates the practice of land-grabbing at that time and the formation of big estates. These drove many families off the land, turning them overnight into landless poor peasants. The destitute were treated as merchandise (Am 2:6–7; 4:1; 5:11–12; 8:4, 6). And they bore heavy impositions from the royal court and landowners who exacted exorbitant rents and unfair grain taxes (Am 5:11).[15] The poor and the defenseless were victimized at every turn by the wealthy, the powerful, the merchants, and the officials. The elite's wives, too, were condemned for their indifference and complicity (Am 4:1). Indeed, the poor found no relief from anywhere or from anyone, but God. After all, God rejects the mighty and the strong (Am 2:9a), while staying by the side of the weak and providing them with the necessities of life.

These offenses were even more reprehensible in light of Israel's long-standing tradition of mercy and compassion, and in view of her Covenant relationship with YHWH. Israel should have been marked by genuine solidarity in line with her history and in view of the favors shown her by God. Instead, the nation was marked by violence, repression, intimidation, and oppression (Am 2:7a; 8:4).

Amos underscores the irony in the jarring disparity between the cultic observances of the leadership and the elite, on the one hand, and their exploitation of the poor and the weak, on the other hand (Am 3:1–2, 9–10; 4:4–5; 8:5). Israel's worship was, consequently, empty and meaningless (Am 5:21–22, 24).[16]

There is also a paradox in the eight oracles against the nations (Am 1:3–2:16). Israel was held up as a model of justice and equity for all the nations (Am 3:1–2), only to be exposed as one of its most egregious violators (Am 2:6–7). For such injustice, Israel was headed toward complete destruction (Am 5:18–20; 6:11; 9:1).[17] She was to be punished for having driven her own people, God's Chosen People, to utter destitution.[18] This doom and God's judgment were a certainty (Am 8:2; 4:1–2). The Law and Israel's Covenant obligations to God demanded nothing less (Am 2:4, 9–10). Israel was to be judged, just like the Amorites (Am 2:10–16).

Theology and Ethics

Central to the theology and ethics of the book of Amos is the call for Israel to live up to its Covenant obligations. Amos was not a social subversive, but a theological revolutionary who was bent on bringing Israel's social practices in line with the Covenant. He was not interested in changing Israel's governance or social structures.[19] To this end, note how his criticisms were based on the Covenant relationship between YHWH and Israel.[20] Moreover, his addressees were not the poor or the oppressed. In fact, Amos did not promise a bright future for the poor or a vindication for their sufferings. Unlike the other prophets, Amos was concerned more with addressing the oppressors rather than the oppressed.[21] We can summarize the key elements of his preaching as follows.

First, as mentioned earlier, Amos stunned Israel when he announced the imminent end of their period of peace and prosperity. After all, the people had been expecting the coming Day of YHWH, marked by light and brightness, and heralding God's blessings and salvation for the people, as God crushes Israel's enemies (Am 5:18–20). Was her prosperity, after all, not a sure sign that God was pleased with Israel? Was this not a reward from God according to the widespread belief in the doctrine of divine retribution (just deserts)? Thus, the people were outraged at the effrontery of Amos in going against the public's belief and expectation. His woe-oracles were, in fact, shockingly about a looming day of judgment rather than a day of salvation.[22]

This was the immediate context of Amos's criticism of Israel's empty cultic practices (Am 3:14; 4:4–5; 5:4–7, 21–24; 8:10; 9:1). What was more important was what was in their hearts, rather than the externals of their ritual observances. All that was required was that they seek YHWH (Am 5:4-5) and live in justice (*mišpāt*) and righteousness (*tzĕdāqâ*).

Second, the juxtaposition of justice (*mišpāt*) and righteousness (*tzĕdāqâ*) as a combination is said to be one of Amos's major contributions to prophetic ethics.[23] We find this in his famous line from Amos 5:24: "let justice roll down like waters, and righteousness like an ever-flowing stream."[24] When combined together, *mišpāt* and *tzĕdāqâ* refer to the divine order's characteristic features of mutual compassion, mercy, and faithful goodness.[25]

Third, Amos preached care for and just treatment of the poor. This was a bedrock requirement not only for Amos, but for the other prophets as well. After all, God is not the god of a political or social system. Rather, Amos's God is "the God of the lowly, the victims who were crushed without pity in the economic machinery of Israel of that age."[26] Thus, instead of their hedonism and their pre-occupation with lavish feasts, the rich and the powerful should have been solicitous of the innocent (victimized people) [*tzaddîq*], the needy (those in absolute need, that is, the destitute) [*'ebyônîm*], the poor (those in relative need, that is, the have-nots) [*dallîm*], and the afflicted (suffering people) [*'ănāwîm*].[27] Not surprisingly, the nation's cultic observances were not merely hollow but were, in fact, abominable before the Lord.

Fourth, despite his message of Israel's certain doom, Amos preached repentance and hope. There is disagreement among scholars on this particular feature of Amos's theology and ethics. On the one hand, some scholars claim that unlike other prophets like Isaiah, Amos was singularly focused on the forthcoming destruction of Israel. He was emphatic that the looming punishment will give no concessions at all. On the other hand, there are exegetes who claim that Amos did offer an alternative for the people if they would only repent (cf. Jer 18:5–10). Amos was not merely about condemnation.[28] In fact, Amos held out hope for a remnant and the future restoration of the nation under a Davidic king (Am 9:9, 11–15).[29] To this end, he repeatedly called for repentance and a return to the Lord. But such conversion necessarily entailed embracing *mišpāt* (justice) and *tzĕdāqâ* (righteousness), and all the other Covenant requirements that the Chosen People had failed to practice thus far (Am 5:4–7; 14–15; especially 5:24).[30]

Implications for Economic Ethics

How do the economic norms of Amos fit within the book's theology and ethics? Besides pointing out what was patently wrong in Israel's moral conduct, Amos had no specific economic norms. As already mentioned, his central point was that Israel live up to the Covenant requirements of *mišpāt* (justice) and *tzĕdāqâ* (righteousness).

In terms of his economic ethics, Micah 4:4 is said to be a good summary of what Amos sought as a paradigm in his social ethics, that is, of every Israelite living in freedom with a house on the ancestral land bequeathed by YHWH. This was a return to the traditional communitarian, pre-monarchial tribal constitution. Note how this is comparable to and converges with Proverbs 30:7–9 in which wisdom asks for neither wealth nor poverty, but only for sufficiency. Values that were clearly important for Amos were the good (Am 5: 14–15; cf. Mic 6:8), the right (Am 3:10), protecting the needy as the righteous person (*tzaddîq*) (Am 2:6b), and, of course, the tandem of justice (*mišpāt*) and righteousness (*tzĕdāqâ*) (Am 5:24; cf. Is 1:16–17, 27).[31]

In sum, Amos did not break new ground in advancing a novel set of ideals for the people to pursue. All he did was to point out how far Israel had strayed from the well-known ideals and requirements of her election as God's Chosen People. It was simply a matter of living up to what they already knew and understood.

ISAIAH

There are at least three distinct blocks of materials in the book of the prophet Isaiah, namely: First Isaiah in the eighth century B.C. (Is 1–39), Second (Deutero-) Isaiah during the exilic period (Is 40–55), and Third (Trito-) Isaiah in the post-exilic period (Is 56–66). The bulk of materials related to economic life are found in First Isaiah, and because of our space constraint, we will devote most of our attention to this first part.

First Isaiah

The prophet of First Isaiah preached in Jerusalem between 742–700 B.C., with social justice as a major concern, just like the other eighth-century prophets.[32] Of interest for our study are the failure of Israel's leaders and God's promise of a future vindication.[33]

The Lord God looked for justice and righteousness in Israel and Judah, but found only bloodshed and cries of distress instead. Consequently, a day of reckoning was forthcoming (Is 5:1–7). Their sacrifices and prayers were abominable and worthless before the Lord because of their evil deeds (Is 1:11–17). Families were dispossessed of their land (Is 3:14; 5:8–10; cf. Mic 2:1–2).[34] The wealthy enriched themselves by exploiting the poor (Is 5:18–23). The orphan, widow, and defenseless were ignored or maltreated (Is 1:21–23; 5:7, 22).

Justice at the city gates had been corrupted, bribery was rampant, and the innocent were condemned. The rich and the powerful used the laws for their own gain and advantage at the expense of the poor. Laws that should have protected the distressed and the orphans were co-opted instead by the wealthy to scheme against the poor (Is 1:21–23; 10:1–2; cf. Am 5:12). Israel's legal institutions had become instruments of injustice that inflicted suffering on the very people they were meant to serve (Is 5:23; 32:7). The elite and the elders of the people were indicted, for it was they who exhausted the produce of the poor (Is 3:13–15). They misled the people and brought them down the wrong path (Is 3:12). Women lived in frivolity and had been lulled by their comfortable and seemingly secure lives into complacency (Is 3:16; 32:9).

But a day of judgment was at hand. The leaders and the elders of the people will be stripped of their power (Is 3:1–5). Their sins had brought about the imminent collapse of their nation (Is 3:8–9). Jerusalem will be besieged by her enemies (Is 29:2–3). They will lose their crops, their land, their fortress, and even the city itself (Is 32:9–10, 14). And the leaders and elders will be judged for what they had done to their own people, especially the poor (Is 3:14–15). Their ill-gotten wealth will be plunder for their conquerors and new masters (Is 3:25–26).

Despite the ills Israel had brought down upon herself, there will nonetheless be a day of vindication, for the Lord is a merciful God (Is 24–27). The ruler of Israel will be toppled (Is 28:1–6). A new ruler will come who will be completely different from those whom they had known and who had brought them so much harm (Is 11:1–5). The poor will find relief with this new king (Is 9:6–7). Even those who suffer from other lands will find comfort and refuge in Zion under this new reign (Is 14:30–32). It is the poor and oppressed who will walk through the city (Is 26:6). The poor will exult in YHWH (Is 29:19). It will be the end of Israel's and Judah's foreign alliances that have allowed alien gods, kings, and values to lord it over God's Chosen People (Is 26:13–14). Injustice will cease (Is 29:20–21). God's saving action and justice will prevail and cover the nation (Is 32:1–20).

Just like the northern kingdom, Judah was beset by the same problem of the elite indulging themselves in lavish feasts, opulent lifestyles and homes, and conspicuous consumption (Is 5:22; 28:1–4, 7–13; Mic 2:11; cf. Am 6:4–6). Their drunken celebrations in Jerusalem began early in the day (Is 5:11–12). Jerusalem's women preened themselves with cosmetics, expensive clothing, and other adornments (Is 3:16–24; cf. Am 6:6a).[35] In general, Judah suffered from the same malaise found in the northern kingdom during the second half of eighth century. This elicited similar condemnations from the other prophets (Is 10:1–2; cf 5:8, 20; Mic 2:1–2; Jer 5:26–28; 22:13–17; Ez 34:2–6). Consequently, punishment was forthcoming for both Judah and Jerusalem (Is 3:1–18; 5:25–30). And it was going to be a painful chastisement from the Lord in order to purify and to bring the Chosen People back to faithful righteousness (Is 1:25–27).

Theology and Ethics of First Isaiah

Consider three observations on First Isaiah's theology and ethics. First, the expectations are high. Moral obligations flow directly from the nature of who God is. The book of the prophet Isaiah calls God the "holy one of Israel" and acknowledges the transcendent and awesome sovereignty of God over all creation. But God's holiness brings forth moral obligations that includes social justice (Is 6:3–13). It is a point similar to Amos 5:21–24, Hosea 6:6, and the wisdom literature (Prov 14:31; 15:8; 21:3, 27). Consequently, Isaiah is critical of worship in the face of gross injustice (Is 1:10–15).[36] Isaiah 1:16–17 explicitly states what Judah has do: to be just, to do right, and to defend the marginalized.

Second, just like Amos, the prophet Isaiah was emphatic that God's judgment was certain. Judah was headed for a severe chastening for all that she had done. Third, we also have the certainty of God's saving grace. Despite the imminent punishment, a day of vindication was also forthcoming. There is reason for hope. Isaiah is distinctive among the prophetic books because of its strong message of hope. The certainty of God's saving action stems from the intrinsic qualities of God and is rooted in the promises made to David (Is 2:2–4; 9:6–7; 11:1–10). God will not renege on these promises. Moreover, God will be directly involved in saving Israel. A future king will emerge who will live up to everything called for in the Covenant, such as defending the poor and oppressed and bringing peace and order in the land (Is 9:7; 11:4–5; cf. Ps 72:4). There is a pronounced Isaianic hope that Israel will yet be saved (Is 7:14; 8:9–10; cf. Ps 46:5–8, 11). Those longing for justice can be reassured that God will redress evil and bring forth peace and harmony (Is 1:26).[37]

In sum, First Isaiah (Is 1–39) could be aptly described as a work about desolation and hope. There is a noticeable shift and development within First Isaiah which moves from dire pessimism on Judah's then current state of affairs, to steadfast hope in God's future saving action.[38]

Deutero-Isaiah (Is 40–55)

Running through the oracle of Israel's salvation is the theme of God's saving justice (Is 51:1–8). Those who seek justice are addressed (Is 51:1); their hopes for justice will be satisfied (Is 51:3). It is God's justice that will liberate the people and the nation, return the land to them, and rebuild Jerusalem. And the promise made to David will be an assurance given to every Israelite (Is 55:3). Thus, Isaiah 51–52 describes God's justice as one of liberation and restoration. And it will be enduring and not merely transitory (Is 51:6, 8).[39]

Trito-Isaiah (Is 56–66)

Trito-Isaiah addresses the people in the post-exilic period who are experiencing the same evils as in the monarchic era. In response to this resurgent problem of injustice, Trito-Isaiah preaches the need for justice and equity (Is 56:1) and criticizes the lack of concern for the value of life as seen in the murder of innocent people (Is 57:1). God always champions and helps the poor (Is 66:2b). Justice is a necessary condition for the fulfillment of the promise made to the people regarding their restoration (Is 58:10–14). Material abundance will come in the wake of fidelity to God (Is 58).

In addition, Third Isaiah (Is 58:3–14) articulates the famous critique of hollow cultic practices in the face of injustice. God will chastise selectively, that is, only those who persist in their injustice (Is 65:11–16). And, of course, there will be a great reversal (Is 65:13; 61:1–3a). In sum, God is making a new creation that will endure, be centered in Jerusalem, and benefit the remnant people (Is 65:13–25; 60:1–22).[40]

Ethics of Deutero- and Trito-Isaiah

There is continuity in the critique of social injustice in moving from First Isaiah to Second and Third Isaiah. In particular, there is still:

- a critique of the powerful steeped in violence and bloodshed (Is 59:1–4, 6–8).
- a critique of the venal motives of the leaders ("shepherds") of the land (Is 56:10–11).

- a critique of the thinking that ritual observances substitute for social justice. This is empty worship because the Lord asks for justice, not empty cultic practices (Is 58:3b, 6–7).
- the famous promise of a "new jubilee" in Isaiah 61:1–4 that is eventually used in Luke 4:16–31.
- the promise of an end to oppression. People will be able to keep and enjoy the fruits of their own labor (Is 65:22a).

MICAH

Micah worked in the southern kingdom (Judah), was a contemporary of First Isaiah, and was a generation after Amos. Some believe that Micah concentrated on the rural areas, while First Isaiah was more urban in focus.[41] Micah was most likely an elder of the small town of Moresheth who defended the interests of the rural peasants against the encroachment of the urban elite and the royal court.

It is extremely difficult to dissect, much less date, the book of the prophet Micah because of its numerous overlapping redactions. It consists of both pre-and post-exilic passages. Many of the key texts are related to the exile and restoration, rather than to the eighth-century abuses (e.g., Mic 4:8, 9–13; 5:1–5; 7:8–20).

Economic Life

The book of the prophet Micah seems to have been a reaction to land-grabbing, land consolidation, injustice, and greed. This is succinctly summarized in Micah 2:1–2, 9 (cf. Is 5:8).[42] The elite and the powerful enriched themselves by taking advantage of the weak. They stole homes from women, most likely defenseless widows (Mic 2:9). They corrupted the judicial assembly at the city gate (Mic 3:9–10; 7:2–3). Their exploitation of the poor was so abhorrent as to be likened to cannibalism (Mic 3:2–3). The elders and leaders of the people (i.e., royal officials, false prophets, and priests) were responsible for this sad state of affairs and were condemned for their wrongdoing (Mic 3).

Micah 6:1–8 summarizes God's case against Israel and Judah (cf. Hos 4:1–3; Is 3:13–15). Their worship was hollow because of their evildoing (cf. Am 5:21–24; Hos 6:6; Is 1:12–17). God called the people to steadfast love and justice (cf. Am 5:24; Hos 2:19; 12:6; Is 5:7).[43] The leaders and the elders were warned of an imminent great reversal in which the wealthy and the powerful will end up with nothing (Mic 2:4–5), while the poor and oppressed will dwell in peace and abundance on their own land and will no longer have to live in fear, subjugation, and want (Mic 4:4).

Theology and Ethics

We find both a theology of judgment and a theology of renewal in Micah.[44] Just like the other eighth-century prophets, Micah believed that Jerusalem will be destroyed (Mic 3:12). Nevertheless, Micah assured the people that it was not to be their terminal condition because there will be a day of restoration (Mic 4:6–7). The book situates itself between the time of God's judgment and the forthcoming salvation (Mic 7:18–20).

This judgment-renewal theme is rooted in the call for economic justice and proper economic conduct (e.g., Mic 4:1–5). Moreover, it is steeped in the language of covenant and history. Micah 6:1–12 is an excellent example of these two features. Micah 6:1–5 is a brief reprise of what YHWH had done for Israel and for which Israel was now bound by covenantal obligations. These duties are concretely specified in Micah 6:6–12 regarding the use of honest weights and scales, that is, proper economic conduct (cf. Dt 25:13–15; Lev 19:35–36). Of course, the hope is that "a recovery of the exodus tradition would induce a social embodiment of God's exodus intentions."[45]

HOSEA

Hosea preached in the northern kingdom. The book uses the imagery of God bringing a lawsuit against Israel for her violations of the Covenant (Hos 4:1–3). In particular, Israel had lost steadfast love, loving kindness for one another, and an appreciation and respect for God's sovereignty. With the loss of these three important qualities, Israel was well on her way to self-destruction. Consequently, all creation, including the land, languished (Hos 4:3). The blessings of the Covenant had ceased so that the nation might realize how she had mistreated God and who God really is—the source of life (Hos 2:9–13). The book of Hosea is critical of the people's useless cultic observances because not only were they unjust in their treatment of one another, but they also lacked two vital inner dispositions for genuine worship: steadfast love and an acknowledgment of God's sovereignty. Just like Jeremiah 9:23–24, Hosea 2:14–16, 19–20 sees knowledge of God as a condition for righteousness.

Nevertheless, unlike unredacted Amos, Hosea also has a message of hope and salvation. God so loves Israel as a parent (Hos 11:1–9), and therefore calls for conversion and confidence in the loving mercy of God (Hos 6:1–2). This necessarily includes righteousness (*tzĕdāqâ*) and steadfast love (*hesed*) in people's mutual relations (Hos 10:12; 12:6). Note that there is a universality in its message. Hosea 14:9 explicitly instructs and invites subsequent generations to heed the teachings put forth in these writings.[46]

JEREMIAH

Jeremiah is set in the southern kingdom. The book has a core set of materials that most likely came from the original Isaiah. However, materials were subsequently redacted by Deuteronomistic editors. The larger context of the work was the Babylonian siege, conquest, and exile. It is a narrative description of the end of Jerusalem and Judah (Jer 37–45, 52) and addresses the exiles.[47]

Jeremiah was unusual among the prophets because he openly and vehemently censured the king (Jer 21:11–23:8).[48] King Jehoiakim was criticized for his injustice and infidelity, unlike his father, King Josiah (640–609 B.C.), who initiated reforms and was considered a good king (Jer 22:15–17). King Jehoiakim enriched himself and lived opulently, but at the expense of the poor. Violence was a means to economic gain (Jer 22:17), and workers toiling on royal construction projects were not paid their wages (Jer 22:13–14). This was contrary to the responsibilities of Judah's kings who were supposed to dispense and maintain justice (Jer 21:12–14; 22:1–5, 13–19; 23:5–6). In fact, the administration of justice was constitutive of the monarch's obligations and functions as God's agent (cf. Ps 72). And the substance of this justice was the protection of the weak and the marginalized.[49] Failure to live up to this duty put the monarchy itself and Judah at risk. In fact, an exploitative king did not deserve to be called king at all, and King Jehoiakim was warned that unless he reformed, he will be buried just like a donkey (Jer 22:19). Thus, the prophet repeatedly called on the king to practice justice (*mišpāt*) and righteousness (*tzĕdāqâ*) (Jer 22:3, 16–17). There will be a sure day of judgment for the king on account of his abuses (Jer 22:19, 22).

Jeremiah goes further to note that dispensing justice was an obligation of the whole nation and not only of the king (Jer 7). Judah's very survival depended on it. Just conduct is a necessary condition of worship. People should not be lulled into a false sense of security on account of their cultic observances, because worship is rendered hollow and empty by evildoing. Moreover, the people did not have a genuine disposition for the Law in their hearts (Jer 7:1–15; 21–23).[50] The rich grew wealthy and powerful through deceit and oppression, and they corrupted justice by withholding it from the weak and the poor at the city gate (Jer 5:26–29; 9:1–8). Theft, murder, perjury, and adultery were rampant (Jer 7:5–11). Moreover, Jerusalem had walked away from YHWH to follow other gods. She had abandoned the Law of God that had provided order until then. Instead the nation preferred the chaos of evil and the murder of the innocent poor (Jer 2:34). They had such disrespect for humans as to enslave them (Jer 5:26). Judah had sought all sorts of alliances with neighboring powers, rather than devote her time and attention to taking care of the poor in her midst (Jer 2:34–37). Though not destitute himself, Jeremiah nonetheless identified himself with the poor because he himself was a victim of injustice by the elite.[51]

Infidelity was widespread. Jeremiah (5:1–9) lamented that not a single just person could be found in Jerusalem. Thus, he addressed an oracle to the whole people and indicted them for their failure to take up the cause of the vulnerable and to give justice to the weak and the poor. They were also taken to task for exploiting the weak (Jer 5:20–31). Their reprehensible conduct reflected a broken relationship with God whose judgment will be sure and swift (Jer 5:29). Wealth unjustly acquired will soon be lost (Jer 17:11). The city can be saved from its looming destruction, but only if people practiced justice and ceased their violent conduct and oppression of the aliens, orphans, and widows (Jer 7:5–6).[52]

Theology and Ethics of Jeremiah

Jeremiah belonged to the Deuteronomic school of thought which held that tenure on the Promised Land was dependent on the people's fidelity to the Sinaitic (Mosaic) Covenant. In other words, their blessings were merely temporary and conditional. They were contingent on the people living up to their Covenant election of responsibility. Unfortunately, their apostasy and idolatry had broken the Covenant (e.g., Jer 3:1; 31:32).

Another theological-ethical insight from the book of Jeremiah is the link between idolatry and injustice.[53] As we have seen from the preceding list of Jeremiah's indictments, his social critique is similar to that of the eighth-century prophets. However, the book of Jeremiah differs from Micah and First Isaiah in that it links the exploitation of the poor to idol worship.[54] Injustice and idolatry go hand in hand (Jer 1:15–19; 2:5–8, 20–28; 4:1–9; 5:26–31; 8:8–12). Not a single just person could be found in the city streets because people were ignorant of what they owed YHWH (Jer 5:1, 4). Jeremiah 7:8–9 suggests that the Decalogue shows a similar link between maltreating neighbors and idolatry.

Idol worship and injustice were related because unlike other gods, YHWH is deeply concerned with justice (Jer 7:5–7). YHWH and Baal have different priorities in their understanding of justice and righteousness. For Baal, in the event of conflict, survival takes precedence, even over the claims of orphans, widows, and the weak. In contrast, for YHWH, the preferential option for the poor is constitutive of justice and righteousness.[55] Thus, in Jeremiah 2:32–37, idolatry leads to injustice. Israel sought Baal and therefore, not surprisingly, she had innocent blood on her hands (cf. Jer 22:17).

Nevertheless, it is not only idol worship that spawns injustice. In fact, any cult could do so or be misused for wrongdoing. As Amos 2:8 vividly illustrates, even Israel's worship of YHWH was co-opted and became an occasion for the exploitation of the poor. Similarly, Hosea 8:11 and Jeremiah 7:8–11 decry the corruption of cultic worship for iniquity.[56]

Finally, another theological insight we can draw from Jeremiah is how knowledge of God is a sure foundation for growth in righteousness and moral conduct.[57] Righteousness is rooted in the knowledge of God. The key to understanding the nature and the source of justice is Jeremiah 9:24: "let those who boast boast in this, that they understand and know me, that I am the Lord; I act with steadfast love, justice, and righteousness in the earth."[58]

Righteousness is an innate quality of God; it is a constitutive feature of God. It is in the very nature of God to act with steadfast love, justice, and righteousness. This being the case, to know and to understand God is to emulate God and to strive for steadfast love, justice, and righteousness in one's own life. This is *not merely theoretical knowledge but a lived knowledge* of God.[59] *Imitatio Dei*! In contrast, most people put their trust in wisdom, might, or wealth (Jer 9:23). These are false ends because they do not lead one to God, but only to death, after a deceiving period of seeming prosperity and complacency. In underscoring the importance of knowing God, Jeremiah 9:23–24, in effect, also highlights the centrality of justice in moral life.

EZEKIEL

Ezekiel is a careful balancing between the prophetic social critique and the priestly temple authority involved in the nation's post-exilic reconstruction. It is a priestly prophetic piece of work. The prophet enumerated the sins of the people and their leaders and warned them of God's sure and severe punishment. He exposed the sins of the people by contrasting the deeds of the righteous, whom God will allow to live, from the unrighteous person, whose life God will not spare. The righteous does not worship idols, is chaste, does not oppress others, returns pledges for a loan, does not rob others, feeds the hungry, clothes the naked, does not lend to the poor at interest or profit from them, is fair and impartial in rendering judgment, and faithfully observes the laws of God (Ez 18:5–9; 15–17). In contrast, the unrighteous is violent, sheds blood, worships idols, oppresses the needy and the poor, robs his neighbors, is an adulterer, charges interest for loans, and does not return pledges for loans (Ez 18:10–13).

Ezekiel went beyond the aforesaid comparison of the righteous and unrighteous person and explicitly identified the sins of Jerusalem, namely: idol worship; bloodshed and violence; oppression of aliens, widows, and orphans; desecration of the Sabbath; slander; impurity and sins of the flesh; bribery; murder; robbery; usury; profiting from the poor; extortion; unjust gains from neighbors; and the corruption and denial of justice (Ez 22:6–12, 29). The people refused to follow God's laws but conformed instead to the standards of the nations around them (Ez 11:12). They listened to the words of the Lord and spoke of love, but their hearts were avaricious and were set on unjust gains. They fell short of putting God's word into practice (Ez 33:31–32). They were no different from Sodom, guilty and punished for hoarding wealth and for self-indulgent consumption (Ez 16:49). The rich and the powerful were not satisfied with what they already had, but robbed others of their inheritance (Ez 46:16–18).

God will judge those who perpetrate such evils. And the punishment will be thorough and fearsome (Ez 18; 22). Merchants were doomed; the loss of their wealth was imminent. Their riches had led them to sin, and their wealth could not save them on the day of reckoning (Ez 7:10–13, 19). Severe punishment awaited those who had inflicted much suffering on others and had caused much evil (Ez 7:25–27; 11:5–12; 22:15).[60]

Theology and Ethics of Ezekiel

Unlike other prophets who focused on the emptiness of Israel's cultic practices given her injustice (Am 5:21–25; Hos 6:6; Jer 7:21–23; Is 58:1–12), Ezekiel stressed the link between worship life and social justice. The latter flows from the former. In this he followed the Holiness Code that sees an intrinsic connection between worship and social ethics (Lev 19:2–18; Lev 17–26). Thus, the book of the prophet Ezekiel sees cultic and ethical demands as mutually reinforcing and inseparable (Ez 18:5–9, 14–17; 22:1–12). Idolatry, disrespect for the sacred, and violation of the Sabbath inevitably and unsurprisingly lead to disrespect for one's parents, unjust treatment of the weak and the vulnerable, sexual excesses, murder, and a whole variety of other sins (Ez 22:6–7, 9, 12). Worship and moral integrity go hand in hand.[61] By stressing this link, the book of Ezekiel stays within the prophetic pattern of criticizing social injustice, even while affirming the centrality of cultic observances. The preferential option for the poor and the protection of the oppressed are still critical concerns, even in the midst of the post-exilic, priestly era of reconstructing the nation.

SUMMARY AND CONCLUSIONS

The prophetic literature provides a glimpse into the nature and dynamics of economic wrongdoing. In the process, they reveal the ideal conduct and duties expected in an upright economic life. Prophetic economic ethics is not abstract in its teachings. It has practical content to it—of do's and don'ts.

Prophetic teachings do not constitute a homogeneous body of literature. They exhibit a wide diversity of concerns, goals, and socioeconomic contexts. Nevertheless, we can discern distinct patterns running through the prophetic books. Various scholars have suggested different lists of common elements in these writings.[62] Three are particularly relevant for our study of prophetic economic ethics, namely: the reprehensible nature of injustice, the link between apostasy-idolatry and injustice, and the certainty of judgment for wrongdoing.

First, justice is a central concern in the prophetic literature. The prophets were critical of rampant land-grabbing, the oppression of the weak, the corruption of the administrative and judicial system, and the venality of the leadership. In condemning the abuses and exploitation of their era, the prophets were, in effect, also (1) identifying the requirements of moral economic conduct and (2) affirming the importance of economic life in God's order of creation. We should not dismiss economics as mundane or unworthy of the holy. The prophets show us that there is a constitutive economic dimension to God's governance of the world. Economic life is neither peripheral nor unimportant. It is part of God's creation.

Second, the prophets indicted Israel's and Judah's unjust conduct and apostasy-idolatry. These two failures were, in fact, mirror images. On the one hand, the Chosen People's cultic observances were hollow because they maltreated one another, especially the vulnerable. On the other hand, they were unjust and unrighteous in their treatment of their neighbors because they did not truly know God, whom they had abandoned in their pursuit and worship of idols. As Jeremiah 9:23–24 notes, to know and to understand God is to imitate God in steadfast love, justice, and righteousness. Injustice is the predictable fruit of apostasy and idolatry. Indeed, *imitatio Dei* is the theological foundation of economic morality, and of justice for that matter.

Finally, the prophetic literature underscores a distinctive feature of the divine order of creation: There are consequences to our wrongdoing. Humans bring down judgment upon themselves in maltreating one another, contrary to God's order of creation.

NOTES

1. Wolff (1978)
2. Blomberg (1999, 69, fn17)
3. Mays (1987, 145); Vawter (1990, 196)
4. Schottroff (1984, 33–40)
5. Schottroff (1984, 28–29)
6. Schottroff (1984, 33–40)
7. Schottroff (1984, 39–40)
8. The following summary of indictments from Amos are taken from Dearman (1984, 386), Finley (1985, 416), Pleins (2001, 369–77), Schottroff (1984, 35, 36), and Wittenberg (1978, 146).
9. Houston (2008, 64–65)
10. Schottroff (1984, 34)
11. Schottroff (1984, 34–35)

12. Amos 2:7b condemns the father and son for having sexual relations with the same girl. A common reaction is to view this sin as the violation of the laws of consanguinity (i.e., having sex with the same woman). However, Dearman (1984, 386) notes that this, in fact, is a crime against property. In Exodus 21:7–11, a daughter who is sold into slavery has the right to be the wife of either the master or the son, but not both. Thus, in Amos 2:7b, the slave girl is not the wife of either, but is used as a sexual object.

13. Temples often served as banking or lending institutions (Neufeld 1955). Neo-Assyrian temple practices were likely adopted in pre-exilic Israel and Judah. Money and property could be deposited with the temple under the name of the deity and depositor. These funds could then be lent out at interest, although the interest did not go to the depositor but to the creditor (the temple). Thus, it was a mutually advantageous proposition for all parties in that depositors had a safe place to keep their capital, the temple had a source of revenue, and debtors had access to loans. The garment and wine in Amos 2:8, once brought to the temple, were technically no longer the property of the debtor. Dearman (1984, 387) suggests that this was what Amos was criticizing. Furthermore, he notes that Amos was critical of "worship centers" on many other occasions (Am 2:8; 3:14; 4:4–5; 5:4–5, 21–24; 7:17) because of their complicity and role in these social sins. This also explains the animus Amaziah held against Amos. Recall that it was Amaziah who drove Amos out of Bethel (Am 7:12–13).

14. Pleins (2001, 369–77) notes that Amos was not condemning the institution of debt slavery itself, but its corruption and abuse as a means of exploiting the poor.

15. In fact, the law prohibiting charging a poor person interest (Ex 22:25) may be extended to cover the case of heavy rents and unfair grain taxes (Finley, 1985, 416, fn 17).

16. Nardoni (2004, 95–121). Pleins (2001, 369–77) suggests that by juxtaposing the violation of the law on pledges within the context of cultic use in the temple, Amos 2:8a is an implicit indictment of the hypocrisy and emptiness of their cultic and religious observances. It is devoid of justice.

17. Nardoni (2004, 103)

18. Pleins (2001, 266)

19. Byargeon (1995, 9)

20. Finley (1985, 417)

21. Schottroff (1984, 40)

22. Byargeon (1995, 8–9); Wittenberg (1987, 60–61)

23. Schottroff (1984, 40). See Nardoni (2004, 101, fn 21–23) for a further discussion and examples of the parallel, conjoined, and analogous use of justice (*mišpāt*) and righteousness (*tzĕdāqâ*) in Amos and the other prophets. Williamson (2012) is an excellent brief study of this word pair across the Old Testament and ANE.

24. Bible quotes are taken from the New Revised Standard Version. www.biblegateway.com/passage (last accessed March 1, 2013).

25. Nardoni (2004, 102). Such a combination is called a hendiadys, a figure of speech in which a word pair is used to express a complex idea.

26. Schottroff (1984, 40)

27. Finley (1985, 413–15); Guyette (2008, 17)

28. Byargeon (1995, 10)

29. Finley (1985, 412)

30. Finley (1985, 412–13); Nardoni (2004, 103)

31. Schottroff (1984, 40)

32. Nardoni (2004, 106)

33. The following description is drawn from Nardoni (2004) and Pleins (2001).

34. Dearman (1984, 388) says that Isaiah 10:1–2 is possibly also about land accumulation.

35. Schottroff (1984, 34–35)

36. Nardoni (2004, 106–7)

37. Nardoni (2004, 106–7); Pleins (2001, 213–57)

38. Pleins (2001, 217)

39. Nardoni (2004, 113–14)

40. Nardoni (2004, 114–15)

41. Dearman (1984, 389); Nardoni (2004, 110–11); Wittenberg (1978, 147)

42. Micah 2:1's reference to how the evildoers plot at night and execute their plans in the daytime because of their power to do so most likely refers to the corruption of justice at the city gates. It is at the judicial assembly at the city gates that they strip the poor and the weak of their land and what little they have. See Nardoni (2004, 79) and Pleins (2001, 381–90).
43. Nardoni (2004, 110–11)
44. These insights are drawn from Nardoni (2004, 110–11) and Pleins (2001, 381–90).
45. Pleins (2001, 385)
46. Nardoni (2004, 104–5)
47. Nardoni (2004, 112–13); Pleins (2001, 276–318)
48. Bracke (2002, 389); Pleins (2001, 284–88); Nardoni (2004, 112–13). For an exegesis of Jeremiah 22:13–17, see Wessels (1994).
49. Bracke (2002, 388)
50. Bracke (2002, 391)
51. Pleins (2001, 290, 298–301). Jeremiah was not a poor man because he had the means to purchase land (Jer 32:6–14).
52. Bracke (2002, 388–90); Nardoni (2004, 112–13); Pleins (2001, 283–91, 298–301)
53. The following points are drawn from Bracke (2002) and Pleins (2001, 283–91).
54. The connection between idol worship and injustice in Jeremiah is similar to Amos 8:4–8, which also linked idol worship and economic injustice, but this time in the northern kingdom.
55. Bracke (2002, 392, fn 6)
56. See Houston (2008, 81–82) for a critique of the claim of Pleins (2001, 283–91) that Jeremiah shows an explicit connection between idolatry and injustice.
57. Obviously, this, too, is an additional reason for why there is a link between idolatry and injustice. Idolatry prevents one from getting to know and then emulate God.
58. Bracke (2002, 393–94) also notes the importance of this passage.
59. Wessels (1994, 106)
60. Pleins (2001, 321, 336–37)
61. Nardoni (2004, 112–13)
62. For example, Wolff (1978, 23–25) suggests two perennial features of the classical prophets' teachings: a critique of the abuses of their day and the judgment that is sure to come. Mays (1987) summarizes the major teachings of the prophets as care for the poor, justice in land tenure arrangements, and integrity in dispensing justice. Blomberg (1999, 71–81) notes that prophetic teachings on possessions can be organized under two main headings: (1) what Israel has done wrong (worshiping idols, empty worship, exploitative land accumulation, idolatrous materialism and overindulgence, and corrupt leadership) and (2) what the nation is supposed to be doing (justice for the marginalized, generosity in sharing possessions, repentance, and faith in the promise of restoration).

Chapter Five

Wisdom Literature

The wisdom literature is essential for the study of biblical economic ethics, for a number of reasons. To begin with, it has an enormous amount of materials on the subject matter. Take the case of the book of Proverbs. Close to a third of this work is related to economic life. Of its 513 verses in the short-sentence segments (Prov 10:1–22:16; 25–29), there are 120 direct references to wealth or its cognates and 70 verses on poverty or low status. Taking into account the overlaps, 158 out of 513 verses deal with wealth or poverty.[1] Second, some believe that the wisdom literature, especially Proverbs, greatly influenced the New Testament's wariness over wealth, its dangers, and its lesser worth relative to other values in life.[2]

Third, wisdom writings are not as vulnerable to objections that they are context-specific since they are gleaned from knowledge learned from daily life. This is an ethic that has universal appeal since it is rooted in the experience of life, rather than on some historical event, such as the Exodus. Wealth and poverty are treated as topics in their own right because wisdom literature is widely believed to be based on popular morality. Unlike the economic norms of the rest of Sacred Scripture, these teachings are less likely to have been shaped by cultic, legal, prophetic, or reform theology or ethics.[3] Fourth, sapiential literature is a "living exchange with the corresponding institutions and traditions of the neighboring peoples."[4] They provide insights that are appealing even to people do not believe in God. Given these reasons, we will examine key sections of the wisdom writings with substantial blocks of materials on economic life.

PROVERBS

Setting in Life

Dating

There is no consensus on the precise dating of the book of Proverbs. Many believe that it may have been written anywhere from the eighth century B.C. to its finalization either in the Persian (Achaemenid) or Greek (Hellenistic) era.[5] Some ascribe an eighth-century provenance because the nation would have had a scribal caste by then to begin the composition of this book.[6] Furthermore, some of the passages speak of the royal court as a present reality. Moreover, some texts exhibit similarities with the known literature from this period (e.g., Prov 25:1; 21:1). Compare, for example, Proverbs 21:3 with Amos 4:4–5, Isaiah 1:10–20, and 1 Samuel 15:22.

Scholars are divided over whether the book of Proverbs was finalized during the Persian (539–333 B.C.) or Greek (332–142 B.C.) reign. Some consider the Persian period as the terminal date based on the language, structure, and themes of Proverbs.[7] Materials that had developed in previous centuries were put together and finalized during the Achaemenid rule when the sages were among the lay leaders of the Restoration community. Moreover, the economic activities described in Proverbs are believed to be consistent with the economic conditions prevalent in the Persian period. The writers or editors were most likely reacting to the socioeconomic problems of their day.[8]

Others see a much earlier beginning and a much later date of completion. Some date wisdom literature from Israel's pre-monarchic tribal beginnings, to as late as the Hellenistic period.[9] At any rate, Proverbs could not have been written any later than the second century B.C. because Sirach (180 B.C.) was clearly using it as a source. Moreover, the book has concerns over wealth and other economic issues very similar to those of Sirach and Qumram.[10]

The oldest texts are Proverbs 10:1–22:16 and 25–29. The last parts to have been written are Proverbs 1–9 and 31:10–31. Proverbs 1–9 is believed by most to have been the last part written since it is a description of how the rest of the book ought to be read and used. Many view it as the introduction to the work.[11] Moreover, its lengthy instructions and didactic poems (most of which are found in Proverbs 1–9) require greater theological sophistication, in contrast to the pithy sayings that are considered to be of earlier origins, from folk-village life. It is composed of collections of materials from the early post-exilic or Persian period.[12]

Audience

For whom were the sages writing? What was the need for documenting oral tradition? It was probably for the benefit of the literate, the ease of transmission to later generations, or as part of an educational process, or all the above. Proverbs was the output of the learned strata of Israelite society, for the immediate benefit and use of their educated peers.[13] If so, it would have reflected the views, mindset, and practices of the aristocracy of its time.

There are good reasons to believe that the target audience of Proverbs was primarily the socio-political-economic elite. That the oral tradition had to be put in writing and become tradition as text meant that it had to be collected, edited, and written by an educated scribal-class elite, for an educated elite. After all, the use of text, instead of oral transmission, is already indicative of the uncommon class status of both those writing it and those who will read it.[14] Thus, the wisdom sayings were clearly for the benefit of those with the leisure and the education to be literate in order to access the work.

Furthermore, Proverbs 3:9–10 describes the rewards God gives to the faithful: full vats and full barns. This pertains to propertied people. Proverbs 22:12–24:22 speaks of the proper attitude to have toward the poor, most likely addressed to the well-off. In addition, Proverbs 3:9–20 is a summary of the paradigm of success, which requires instruction in acquiring wisdom. All these suggest that the book of Proverbs was not meant for the masses, but for a select group who had the time and the opportunity to pursue such disciplined training in acquiring wisdom—scribes, court officials, landowners, and upper classes. There is a certain exclusivity to the work, or at least parts of it, such as the prologue (Prov 1–9).[15]

Economic Norms

Proverbs has been widely viewed as equivocal in its views on wealth and poverty. A comparison of the views on wealth between Proverbs 1–9 and Proverbs 10–31 immediately reveals seeming inconsistencies. Not only is the work marked by much ambiguity, but it even has many passages that contradict one another. On the one hand, the book is clearly marked by a cause-and-effect dynamic, also known as the virtue-wealth nexus, wisdom-prosperity link, or act-consequence connection. From this perspective, prosperity and wealth are the reward of virtue, hard work, and righteousness. Poverty is the lot of the indolent, the foolish, and the wicked. People receive their just deserts. (Recall the Deuteronomic promise of material abundance as a result of fidelity to the Covenant.)

On the other hand, the book is also critical of wealth, which it views as impermanent and distracting in the pursuit of the better goods in life. Moreover, it acknowledges that poverty can also arise because of the injustice and oppression of others or because it may be the will of God (Prov 22:2; 29:13). Furthermore, the poor are deemed to be special in the eyes of God and worthy of assistance. However, the unjust often seem to get away with their evildoing as they prosper while the righteous wallow in poverty, want, and suffering. Not surprisingly, many scholars find Proverbs to be incoherent in its teachings on wealth and poverty.[16]

Numerous theories have been offered to account for these apparent contradictions in Proverbs. Some say that these inconsistencies should not come as a surprise. The writings clearly came from different sources. The influence of ANE literature is evident. Proverbs' sentence-exhortations resemble Egyptian and Mesopotamian literature and draw from a diversity of sources, in terms of both geographic and social setting. Proverbs 22:17–24:22 is widely acknowledged to have been shaped by the Egyptian *Instruction of Amenomope*, which advocates for the poor.[17] Proverbs 30:1–14 (from Agur) is from Aramaic wisdom, as is Proverbs 31:1–9 (from the mother of King Lemuel).[18] Unfortunately, this explanation is inadequate because it does not address contradictory teachings in sections that came from the same origin (e.g., Prov 10:1–22:16; 25–29).

One must also remember that Proverbs was compiled over a long period of time, stretching from the Davidic or Solomonic monarchical period, all the way to the Persian or even the Greek era (second century). The book has multiple layers of editorial redactions. As we have seen earlier, Proverbs 1–9 is a much later addition from a different century. Different periods have their respective needs and concerns. For example, some believe that the early writings came from the upper-class elite who were self-serving in rationalizing their privilege and wealth.[19] Later scribes then changed or softened these in light of human experience and the realization that the retributive doctrine was not entirely consistent with empirical reality. Others suggest that the harsh and demanding sayings (e.g., poverty as the lot of the indolent) emerged out of a rural, folk, non-stratified setting in which hard work was necessary, given the small farmer's precarious world.[20] (Note that there are not many seeming inconsistencies in the short-sentence segments of Proverbs.) These harsh sayings, however, were then later toned down by sages who added the distinctively Hebrew ethos of solicitude for the poor. Thus, we should expect heterogeneity in the book's teachings given the long period of time that it took to complete it and given its many authors and editors, not to mention its manifold ANE antecedents.

Another explanation is that writers may have been using a wide variety of literary techniques, such as exaggeration or irony. Moreover, some of the passages are merely descriptive of what is, while others may be normative on what ought to be. Still, another position is that the writers may have been simply inconsistent or illogical in their views. They may have held either conflicting or sophisticated, complex views that allowed for both sets of teachings to hold true. For example, they may have subscribed to a virtue-wealth dynamic, even as they acknowledged that this did not always hold in life.[21] We have to accept the possibility that Proverbs was written by scribes who held clashing views on wealth and poverty or who later changed their thinking. Furthermore, there is nothing that requires Proverbs to be governed by "absolute logic and consistency."[22] Scribes that put together Proverbs may have simply preserved sayings that were emerging out of different social contexts.

Making Sense of Contradictions: A Shift in Focus

One approach to making sense of these seeming contradictions in Proverbs is to shift our focus. Instead of looking for consistency and universal applicability, readers would probably be better off taking the wisdom literature as a straightforward description of the world and how it works.[23] Wealth is a gift from God (Jb 1:10). Too much of it or too little of it can be trouble, and the ideal is just to have a sufficient amount (Prov 30:8–9). Wealth is not limited only to hardworking or virtuous people because even the wicked prosper (Prov 11:16; 17:8; cf Jer 12:1ff). However, wealth gained through wickedness will not truly benefit the person (Prov 10:2; 11:4; 13:22; 22:16). For example, wealth can distract the person from righteousness (Prov 11:24–26; 22:16, 22–23).

Wealth is not the goal of life (Prov 8:10–11; 23:4), but it brings many advantages and makes life so much easier. The life of the poor is difficult, vulnerable, and fraught with uncertainty (Prov 10:15; 13:8, 11; 14:20; 18:11; 19:4, 7; 22:7; Sir 40:28–30). Indolence (Prov 6:9–11; 10:4–5; 12:11; 24:30–34) and self-indulgence (Prov 21:17; 23:20–21) are causes of poverty. Wealth is to be used for meeting basic needs, whether for oneself or for others, especially the poor (Prov 14:21, 31; 11:24–25; 17:5; 19:17).

In other words, the various parts of Proverbs speak to different groups of people. Israel was going through a stage when it was increasingly polarized into different classes. The hard-work paradigm applied to the more traditional, free landholding peasantry. In contrast, the social-order paradigm (i.e., the call to be generous and to remember old tribal practices) addressed the new rich. The sayings on the link between wisdom and wealth (Prologue) may be meant for the emerging court class.[24]

These sayings are generally descriptive of human experience, *ceteris paribus*. They are to be understood within a particular setting in life or a set of parameters that are considered commonplace, and such set of conditions normally encountered in daily life will necessarily differ across time and across groups. Thus, it is wrong to read Proverbs as dogmatic because "Proverbs are inherently *partial utterances*."[25] Far from weakening the work, the seeming incongruities in Proverbs actually strengthen the credibility of the book's economic insights. They describe life both as it should be and as it is.[26]

Another View: A Harmonious, Consistent Whole

A more complex account of Proverbs' cohesiveness is Timothy Sandoval's *The Discourse of Wealth and Poverty in the Book of Proverbs*. Sandoval claims that Proverbs is, in fact, a coherent whole with the goal of lauding "wisdom's virtuous way."[27] Even if the materials were drawn from numerous ANE literature and folk sayings from oral tradition, they all ultimately had to be compiled and put in writing by an educated elite. These scribes and redactors sorted through the various proverbs and decided what were chosen, what were dropped, what were modified, and how they were presented. The input of the scribe in Proverbs is not only critical but also inevitable.[28] It would have been unlikely for the final editors to have left contradictions as is and not to have added their own materials or redacted the folk proverbs in line with their own worldviews.

For Sandoval, Proverbs has an editorial unity and is coherent in its outlook. The seeming contradictions in the work are, in fact, due to the failure of readers to distinguish texts that are (1) figurative and metaphorical in nature, (2) historical and descriptive of the world around them, and (3) didactic in their aims. Not everything in Proverbs should be read literally.

Sandoval proposes the following two theses:

- That Proverbs is about changing the values of most people who would equate material prosperity with success or the good life. Wealth is a much lesser good compared to the real and greater value of virtue.
- That the writers of Proverbs used material prosperity as a metaphorical, rhetorical, and literary device in showing the great worth of wisdom. In effect, the sages employed the imagery of the lesser good of wealth in teaching people about the true and far more enduring value of wisdom.[29]

Wealth as a Metaphor

Proverbs uses discourse on wealth and poverty in two ways: (1) as a figurative, motivational device, or (2) as a direct, literal instruction on proper economic conduct.[30] It is the latter that directly pertains to economic ethics. Readers have to switch between these two uses as needed. Through the use of metaphors, Proverbs constructs a symbolic moral world.

Wealth is used by Proverbs as a metaphorical symbol of that which is desirable. It associates wealth with wisdom. Wealth imagery is "the text's most important rhetorical motivation."[31] After all, most people desire riches, are unlikely to be jaded by them, and will want to keep acquiring even more. Similarly, there is no end to which we should be pursuing wisdom. There are no limits to wisdom. Both wealth and wisdom are desirable, and they have a certain unattainable quality to them. Besides wealth, other powerful motivational symbols are honor, social status, and sexual fulfillment. We find all three in the book of Proverbs.[32]

Examples of teachings on wealth that are directly about economic conduct are the call to honor God with our wealth and produce (Prov 3:9–10), the admonition on timely sharing and giving as characteristic of generosity (Prov 3:27–28), and the warning on the folly of risky behavior (Prov 6:1–5).

Whether as a motivational symbol or as a literal teaching on proper economic behavior, the two uses of wealth in Proverbs point to the same moral vision—the attainment of a good, flourishing life that entails virtuous living, including social justice. Wealth as a motivational symbol is used for the much larger didactic end of promoting virtue and righteousness instead of folly and wickedness. Not all sayings in Proverbs on wealth or poverty should be taken literally.

Finally, the fundamental moral vision of the work is summarized in Proverbs 30:7–9 (neither poverty nor riches but just enough). This moral vision is characterized by balance. While it appreciates the practical utility of wealth in life, it nevertheless does not idolize or exaggerate the value of wealth. Material prosperity is viewed merely as a means to grow in wisdom's virtuous ways without undue economic difficulty. The goal is not to accumulate wealth for its own sake, but to have enough of it so that one might have the time and the means to pursue wisdom without undue care. The book is not about teaching the path to success (e.g., prosperity), but about moral instruction (virtue and character). The sages were not interested in describing the world and conveying its values. Wealth and poverty are central to Proverbs because of their use both as the images and as the motivation for promoting "wisdom's virtuous way."[33]

Despite its seemingly contradictory aphorisms, the book of Proverbs does not differ on substantive points, such as, on how socioeconomic life unfolds, and more important, on how virtue and wisdom, rather than material wealth, are what truly matter in the end. This convergence should not come as a surprise because these sayings were drawn from longstanding lessons learned from daily life that had been transmitted by oral tradition from generation to generation. Moreover, putting such oral tradition in writing was clearly meant to be instructive—on the incomparable value of striving for virtue and wisdom in life.

NON-TRADITIONAL WISDOM LITERATURE

The tensions that we find incipient in Proverbs finally come out in the open in Job and Qoheleth. Proverbs is classified as traditional wisdom, while Job and Qoheleth are called non-traditional, critical wisdom. Note their key differences. First, in terms of literary format and rhetoric, Proverbs is didactic, educational, and sentential. In contrast, Job is in a dialogue format and argumentative. There are two sets of dialogues in Job: with other people and with God. A peculiar feature of Job is that it is a combination of the dialogue and the complaint genre. Qoheleth takes the form of philosophical musings.

Second, in terms of social vision, Proverbs focuses on virtue and wisdom rather than social change. In contrast, Job is oriented more toward the prophetic social vision and is described by some as a direct assault on the fundamental beliefs of traditional wisdom. Job is part of the dispute tradition that examines particular aspects of the wisdom literature. Qoheleth, too, is part of the dispute tradition and questions the utility or even the value of wisdom in the face of a transient world marked by uncertainty, death, and seeming futility.[34]

Job

Sociologists conceptualize society in terms of either a paradigm of order or a paradigm of conflict, or both. The book of Proverbs espouses a paradigm of order. In contrast, Job employs a paradigm of conflict.[35] In this paradigm of conflict, there is an ongoing battle between divine order and chaos in the cosmos. Order is not intrinsic to the cosmos. Hence, the structures and order of life are constantly under threat, requiring vigilance and unceasing effort. Such chaos emerges from human flaws, sinfulness, and failures. The role of Wisdom is to curb this destructive tendency, thereby making Wisdom central to the establishment and maintenance of the social order.[36]

There is also a difference with respect to ethics. Job goes against traditional wisdom's ethics of results. The cosmology behind an ethics of results is that God has embedded an order in the cosmos in which the virtuous are rewarded with a good life while the wicked are punished. It is a latent beneficent order that is actualized by the righteous and the virtuous in their moral lives. Hence, traditional wisdom is an active ethic, that is, an active ordering of the world around it.

In contrast, Job goes against this traditional thinking. There is no beneficent order implanted in the creation of the cosmos. The cosmic order is not based on a mechanical cause-and-effect dynamic. Instead, as per the paradigm of conflict, there is an ongoing struggle between divine order and chaos. Suffering and death are an inevitable part of life and not necessarily the result of wickedness or folly. Justice and ethics for Job, therefore, are about the constant struggle against chaos to sustain order in life. In the face of inevitable suffering and death, human righteousness comes with participating in God's creative act of confronting chaos. Out of this participation comes true life, borne out of a struggle to secure order.[37] Note the dependence on God rather than on human power to defeat Leviathan (Jb 40–41). Job trusts that it is God who will set things right.

Nevertheless, this is a mysterious God. Job is a disputation on the justice of God. The book has been described as a clash between two freedoms: between "human responsibility and divine inactivity."[38] The world of humans is ruled "despotically by an omnipotent deity, a deity whose actions disclose neither justice nor love in its dealings with mankind."[39] It is a fragile, futile life marked by suffering and pain. God seems to be indifferent to humanity's fate and suffering.[40]

Traditional and critical wisdom differ in their views on wealth and poverty. In contrast to Proverbs that views sloth and frivolity as causes of poverty, Job sees the exploitation of the poor as the cause (Jb 22:5–9; 20:15, 18–23). In contrast to Proverbs that sees the accumulation of wealth as the result of industry and virtue, Job ascribes such riches to God choosing not to punish wickedness (Jb 21:7–13; 24:1–4). Regarding the question of what to do about the problem of evil, Job calls for solidarity with the poor who suffer in the face of God's silence. He calls for empathy in sharing their grief and pain, just as Job did. Furthermore, Job differs from traditional wisdom in using strong language to describe God as the active defender of the poor (Jb 5:15 cf Prov 22:22–23). In fact, Job is closer to the prophetic literature than to traditional wisdom in its attitude toward the poor. Proverbs never goes beyond charity in dealing with the problem of poverty. It is just a fact of life that God permits. In contrast, Job clearly recognizes poverty as a consequence of injustice (Jb 24:4, 9, 14; 29:12; 30:25; 31:16–21; 34:28; 36:6, 15).[41] Nevertheless, there is a major difference between the prophets and Job. Most of the prophets are confident and certain in the judgment of God. In contrast, Job is not as optimistic about God's intervention based on his experience that evil and injustice persist in the world without any relief. This is a cause for Job's resentment directed against God. Hence, an important part of Job's social vision is his language of lament, protest, and resignation.[42]

Implications for Economic Ethics

Key to the economic ethics of Job, are the YHWH speeches in which humanity and its institutions are shown to be peripheral, if not irrelevant, in the unceasing struggle against disorder. Job 40–41 describes the battle of God with Leviathan and God's victory. Justice and order are clearly dependent on the sovereign power of God. Thus, justice in the human sphere is about participating in God's fight against chaos in order to establish order in the cosmos and in human affairs.[43]

This is exactly the same phenomenon and dynamic in economic ethics. It is God who desires and restores order in the economic realm despite its unremitting tendency toward chaos because of avarice and human sinfulness.

Humans cannot be Pelagian in thinking that they can restore order in economic life on their own. It is part of a much larger battle against evil that only God can win. Thus, an important part of economic ethics is the acknowledgment of the leading, central role of God.

Qoheleth

Despite their shared skepticism of traditional wisdom, Job and Qoheleth differ substantially in their cosmology, ethics, and implications for normative economics. Job is concerned with the problem of moral evil. A possible response is to repent and reaffirm belief in God's justice despite the inexplicable nature of suffering. In contrast, Qoheleth is concerned with natural evil and with death. A possible response is to despair, to deny meaning in life, or to doubt God's justice and care for humans.[44] In both Job and Qoheleth, we see a convergence in their humble acknowledgment that we cannot fathom everything in the mind of God.

As mentioned earlier, sociology uses two lenses with which to conceptualize society, namely, order and conflict. In contrast to Job's use of the paradigm of conflict in describing society, Qoheleth is similar to traditional wisdom in using a paradigm of order.[45] Nevertheless, Qoheleth's cosmology is different.

Unlike traditional wisdom in which order is beneficent, Qoheleth sees the order of the cosmos as tyrannical and rigid. Instead of the trust in divine beneficence in traditional wisdom, Qoheleth sees an aloof, absent, uncaring God. It is a God to be feared, rather than a God in whom one can place trust and hope. Humans cannot comprehend the order of the cosmos nor can humans influence this cosmos or how it operates. Thus, the best response is passive joy and to take each day as it comes and to enjoy it. God alone determines what is to happen. Moral conduct makes no difference.[46]

Just like traditional wisdom, Qoheleth is founded on a theology of creation. The work makes no reference to the historical encounter between God and Israel. Instead, it has clear, strong statements on the beauty and majesty of God's creation (Eccl 3:11; cf Gn 1). Moreover, humans are not privy to the timing of events, including their own death. Only God knows this. There is a mystery to God's plans that people cannot fully discern. In this regard, Qoheleth serves an important function in the wisdom literature. It exposes the limits of wisdom literature in its inability to provide humans with a complete roadmap to living life, since there is a mystery to God's plans that they cannot hope to unravel. Wisdom, in fact, comes from accepting such constraint and, then, making the most of whatever God reveals or gives to humans in daily life.[47] Such an attitude not only acknowledges the limitations of wisdom, but also discloses its down-to-earth realism.

Implications for Economic Ethics

In Qoheleth's cosmology, humans are created "upright" but they have tendencies toward evil, and often give in. It is rare to find a righteous person (Eccl 7:25–29). They are utterly dependent on God and helpless in the face of the inevitability of death. Just like Job, Qoheleth (Eccl 8:14; 9:2–3), too, rejects the traditional theory of virtue-rewards nexus. Moral character does not count. All depends on the whims of God. In fact, God's will and governance of the world is mysterious and unfathomable. But God is distant and inaccessible, indeed, absent and indifferent to human suffering. Ultimately, the only "good" for humans is the joy that they can get from this life from festive celebrations, family relationships and friends, and human labor. It is to enjoy whatever is possible to human nature and whatever else God permits. This has been called an ethics of well-being.[48] The person should simply accept and seize every moment of joy as it is encountered.

There is no protest or prophetic critique of the abuse of power in Qoheleth, only helpless resignation. Neither does Qoheleth put its hope in the establishment of an apocalyptic community to make sense of life. Rather, it is all about submission to God, to foreign rulers, and to wherever one may be led. In effect, Qoheleth calls for meek acquiescence to the political status quo. The key is to simply enjoy whatever life brings.[49]

SIRACH

Sirach was written sometime in the second century B.C.[50] The complete text as we received it is the Greek translation, although fragments of the Hebrew text have been discovered in the last century. The book draws heavily from Proverbs and is accepted by the Catholic tradition to be part of its canon. In contrast, neither the Jewish faith nor the Reformation traditions consider it to be part of their canon. The latter views it as apocrypha. In the wisdom literature, Sirach has the second most number of passages (after Proverbs) on economic life, primarily about wealth and poverty.

Sirach was clearly reacting to the "crisis of Hellenism" in Judaism at a time when Greek practices and customs were being imposed or pushed on the nation Israel.[51] Sirach was conservative in its response by holding fast to the unchanged and unchanging truths of the past in dealing with current problems (e.g., Sir 2:12; 41:8; 33:2–3; 1:26–27). The writer urged the people to be faithful to their laws and traditions, reminding them of the glories and heroes from Israel's past (e.g., Sir 2:10; 24:8, 23; 44:1–50:21).

Sirach exemplifies the post-exilic sage, one who was from the Temple, rather than the royal bureaucracy and who, consequently, forged a close alliance between the wisdom and the priestly tradition. Thus, there is a clear convergence of the Torah, wisdom, and Temple in Sirach. While Ben Sira drew from popular Greek philosophy and combined it with Hebrew wisdom, he was nonetheless emphatic in his position that wisdom can be found in the Torah.[52] Both the Torah and creation are sources of wisdom (Sir 39:1–35).[53]

Insights on Economic Life

Righteous Wealth

It is much better to be wealthy than to be poor because riches make for a much easier life. Moreover, the rich enjoy a privileged social standing and command better deference and respect from everybody else in the community. People are more likely to excuse or overlook their mistakes (Sir 10:30–31; 13:3, 21–23). In contrast, the poor face ceaseless toil, and for all their efforts, they receive meager earnings. They cannot stop working, lest they sink into even more abject destitution. In fact, so abhorrent it is to be a beggar, that it is better to die than to have to beg for a living (Sir 31:4; 40:28–30). Food, clothing, and shelter are the basic necessities of life (Sir 29:21).

Nevertheless, there are intrinsic dangers to wealth. It is not evil in itself, but wealth can cause manifold problems. Wealth can lead to presumption in which the rich anchor their sense of security in their possessions and think that they are invincible and can do whatever they please. This is folly because God punishes such arrogance (Sir 5:1–3). Moreover, wealth is deceitful because it does not provide genuine assistance on the day of calamity when help is needed the most (Sir 5:8). Wealth is evanescent and can disappear overnight without warning (Sir 18:25–26). The inordinate desire for riches can be all-consuming as to leave one bereft of life. It can be a stumbling block as it causes anxiety and robs one of sleep and peace of mind (Sir 6:1–4; 31:1–2, 5–7; cf. Ps 52:7). Wealth can ruin people's virtue and character. Business has intrinsic dangers because it presents numerous occasions for dishonesty, sin, and division (Sir 8:2b; 26:29–27:2). Trade and commerce are closely associated with sin. Many enrich themselves at the expense of the defenseless. Such wealth will surely be lost, with the evildoers punished (Sir 13:4–7; 21:8). Moreover, injustice ruins social harmony, and no one can live in peace (Sir 13:18–19).

Riches are good and laudable, if they are free from sin (Sir 13:24). Righteous wealthy persons are even more laudable because they act justly and do not succumb to the great power and the numerous occasions of sin that riches bring in their wake (Sir 31:8–11).

Proper Use of Wealth

Righteous wealth must not merely be acquired in a just manner; they must also be used properly. Wealth is not an end in itself to be accumulated, but to be used and shared with generosity with friends and the distressed. Unlike stinginess, generosity is a virtue that deserves high praise (Sir 14:3–11, 13; 31:23–24). Equally important, one is to be generous in tithing and in offering the fruits of one's labor to God. One is not to think of this as bribing God or putting God in one's debt on account of such offerings. After all, riches and the fruits of the land and of one's toil come from God to begin with (Sir 35:10–15).

Almsgiving is particularly pleasing before the Lord: "One's almsgiving is like a signet ring with the Lord, and he will keep a person's kindness like the apple of his eye. Afterward he will rise up and repay them, and he will bring their recompense on their heads" (Sir 17:22–23). It atones for sins (Sir 3:30). Despite the grief and the risks that come with loaning to others, one must nevertheless lend to the needy, be a surety for them, and not let them leave empty-handed. To give alms is to obey the commandments and to store heavenly treasure (Sir 29:8–14).

One must readily assist the poor and not avoid them. One should never reject the pleas of the poor nor oppress them. They are to be treated with respect. The vulnerable and the oppressed are to be defended. One ought to exercise paternal care for the fatherless, assisting their mother as a husband would (Sir 4:1–10; 7:32). Great will be the reward of those who take care of the poor, for God hears their cry and will surely answer their prayers. To take care of the poor is to be like the son of the Most High and to be loved by God (Sir 4:6, 10; 35:16–26).[54]

On Proper Conduct

Treat friends, faithful servants, slaves, and hired hands with fairness, respect, and charity. Give them their due, including freedom for the deserving slave held in bondage. One is to treat farm animals with care (Sir 7:18–22; 33:30–33). Give graciously to all the living, to those who mourn or are sick, and even to those who are dead (Sir 7:33–35).

One is to live a virtuous life. Wealth comes from temperance, hard work, modesty, and prudence, which is why the indolent will never be rich and are doomed to indigence (Sir 10:27; 18:30–19:1; 20:28). No one respects a lazy person (Sir 22:1–2). Do not be a fair-weather friend, but stick with your friend in poverty and in adversity (Sir 22:23). Be honest and prompt in paying debts, even if there is the opportunity to defraud the lender. Always be truthful with scales and measures and in one's dealing with others (Sir 42:1–5). Be appreciative of the risks guarantors have undertaken on our behalf in extending us assistance in our moment of need (Sir 29:1–3, 15). Be moderate in everything, including food (Sir 31:19–20, 22; 37:29–31).

And strive to live an upright life that will not bring us disgrace; sinful living is a cause of shame and regret (Sir 41:17–22). The joyful have better health and a longer life expectancy, while the angry, the distressed, and the envious ruin their health and their life (Sir 30:21–24).

Hard-Nosed Realism

The realism in Sirach is clearly evident in its down-to-earth advice. Giving assistance today makes it easier to ask for help someday (Sir 3:30). Borrowers are deferential and obsequious when they are asking for a loan, but they turn arrogant, belligerent, and even dishonest at the time of payment. Lenders should be prepared to incur much grief in lending. Not surprisingly, many hesitate to lend, not out of meanness, but because of fear of being defrauded (Sir 29:4–7). One might as well write off as a loss whatever one lends or pledges as surety (Sir 8:12b–13).

Be wary because things are not always what they seem to be. Adversity may bring success, while a windfall may end up in a loss (Sir 20:9). Some gifts return nothing, while others may have to be repaid twofold (Sir 20:10). One may buy for little, but pay for it seven times over, being "pennywise, pound foolish" in our modern language (Sir 20:12).

Be cautious in what we do. Building our house from borrowed money is like gathering stones for our burial mound (Sir 21:8). Market exchange or transactions must always be recorded in writing (Sir 42:7). We should not give away property until near death, lest we put ourselves at the mercy and generosity of our own children and kin after handing over their inheritance too early (Sir 33:20–24). Never contend with the rich and the powerful (Sir 8:1–3). Do not judge before we investigate, do not answer before listening, and do not be associated with a wrongdoer (Sir 11:7–9). Keep those under our charge busy with work, because idle hands cause trouble (Sir 33:25–30).

Balance

Because of its unflinching realism, Sirach is balanced in its advice. For example, it admonishes its readers always to assist as best they can, but not to the point of harming themselves. They ought to exercise prudence in acting as a guarantor and should not be a surety beyond their means. Almsgiving and helping the poor are important values, but one should not impoverish oneself in helping others (Sir 8:12–13; 29:16–20). This refreshing balance is also seen in its acknowledgment of the value of trade as an occupation. There is no shame in earning a profit with merchants (Sir 42:5).

We also see this balance in Sirach's appreciation of enjoying the present moment. Life is fragile, unpredictable, and even ironic. One works hard and saves all his life, only to die as soon as he decides to take it easy and enjoy his wealth (Sir 11:18–19). Just like Qoheleth, Sirach admonishes people on the folly of hoarding wealth as a miser. Riches are to be used and enjoyed in the present because misers will see the fruits of their labors dissipated by those who did not toil for them (Sir 14:3–6). These are blessings from God meant to be enjoyed in the here and now (Sir 14:12–19).

On the Order of God's Creation

There is an order to God's creation (Sir 42:15–43:33). God always set things right and restores the order that chaos and evil mar. Thus, there is reason for the poor and the righteous to hope. In the first place, there are great reversals in life. The mighty and exalted fall while the oppressed ascend the throne. Thus, one should never judge people by their appearance (Sir 11:1–6). God can turn the poor rich in the blink of an eye (Sir 11:21–22). Hence, it is folly to build one's confidence on wealth, because God can easily reverse everything (Sir 11:23–26).

Second, Sirach subscribes to a cause-and-effect dynamic.[55] There are consequences to our moral choices. Evildoing comes back sevenfold (Sir 7:1–3). God rewards people according to their conduct on the day of death (Sir 7:36; 11:26). The good that we do to the devout will be duly repaid by God, while those who persist in evil will come to a bad end (Sir 12:2–3). Almsgiving is particularly pleasing before the Lord and will bring many signal divine blessings in its wake (Sir 17:22–23). There is a sure day of judgment when God hears the cry of the poor and rectifies the wrong against them (Sir 9:12; 14:12; 35:16–26). To be sure, there will be suffering and great distress in the here and now, but only as a test (Sir 2:1–5). God always makes things right and restores order. This doctrine of just deserts is perhaps best summarized by the ending verse: "Do your work in good time, and in his own time God will give you your reward" (Sir 51:30).

In sum, there is a hierarchy of values in God's order of creation as it pertains to economic life. All things—good or bad, poverty or wealth—come from God. It is better to be rich than to be poor, because God did not intend humans to be destitute. Nevertheless, it is better to be healthy and joyful than to be rich (Sir 30:14–16). Best of all, however, is to fear the Lord and be a wise person (Sir 40:25–27). With fear of the Lord, the person is in good hands and will want for nothing (Sir 1:16–19; 2:7–18; 51:28). After all, the deeds of the righteous are pleasing sacrifice to the Lord. Obeying the commandments is a sweet offering to the Lord (Sir 35:1–9). The fear of the Lord is wisdom and such wisdom includes living up to the law (Sir 1:1–20; 19:20; 21:11). The core of Sirach's message is fear of the Lord.

THEOLOGY OF WISDOM LITERATURE

Theology of Creation

The theology of the wisdom literature is rooted in a theology of creation. God is not called the God of Israel or Abraham by the sages. Instead, they refer to God on many occasions as the Creator and Maker of all. Wisdom did not emerge from a historical encounter between God and humanity. It is not based on a theology of covenant election or exodus liberation. Instead, wisdom literature conveys an appreciation for creation as a special gift of God to humanity. That the human person is even allowed to give names to creatures (a privilege reserved to the king) is reflective of God's gift.[56]

Not surprisingly, the theology of Proverbs and the wisdom literature is a theology of creation.[57] Proverbs 8:22–31 is a description of God creating the universe through wisdom. Proverbs 3:19–20 refers to God's creative act. God's word keeps chaos at bay (Prov 8:29). God is the divine architect creating beautiful structures (Prov 3:19–20; 8:26–29). In Proverbs 1 and 8, the world is a city that Lady Wisdom visits. Proverbs 9:1–6 describes the seven-pillared house of Lady Wisdom to which all are invited to learn and to share in her offerings. Proverbs 8:22–31 is about Lady Wisdom being fathered by God, the first child of creation. The sages used the metaphors of word, artistry, fertility, and battle to describe God's creation and maintenance of the world.[58]

Sociological Roots of a Theology of Order

Living in harmony with the cosmic order is the underlying theme of the wisdom writings. The sociological background of the sages may account for this.[59] Wisdom literature was finalized at a time when Israel's world was upended both in the exile and in the foreign domination and subservience of the post-exilic era. Prior to 1000 B.C., the family was the anchor of stability and a source of self-identity for the Israelites. This was replaced by the monarchy that became a focal point of their nationhood. This order that held together their individual and common life was shattered with the fall of Jerusalem (587 B.C.) and the subsequent exile. There was chaos and a loss of identity with the destruction of the monarchy. Moreover, Israel had to endure the impositions and exploitative practices of the occupying imperial powers even after the return from exile and restoration.

The immediate post-exilic task was the recovery of their self-identity. They had to appropriate for themselves a worldview that provided hope and made sense of what they were experiencing. Thus, we find their belief in a cosmic order anchored no less in the creative act of God. This gave rise to their theology of creation that provided an unchanging reference point of stability, regardless of what their uncertain times brought. Moreover, no imperial power can match the sovereignty of the Almighty Creator. It was a vision of a cosmic order that the Israelites knew was beyond the reach of their foreign masters. God, the Creator, is in charge and would make all things right. God, the Creator, keeps chaos at bay. Order always triumphs in the end.

As part of this order, the sages wanted to bring back the family as a focal point for the nation, just as it had been before the era of the kings. This accounts for the passages in which family and relationships are emphasized (e.g., Prov 19:26). It also explains why Lady Wisdom figures so prominently in Proverbs 1–9, the last part of Proverbs to have been written around the early post-exilic period.[60] Note that it is also the period for the composition of parts of the Pentateuch, including Genesis, by the priestly tradition—a time when they needed to have a semblance of order and stability. The order of creation restored the Israelites' identity, hope, and direction.

SUMMARY AND CONCLUSIONS

There is nothing new under the sun that people have not already seen (Eccl 1:9–10). There is much about economics in the wisdom literature because wisdom is partly about achieving success, and economic life is a constitutive part of human nature.[61] Despite their wide diversity, the books comprising the wisdom literature converge on the following common points:

- There is an underlying divine and natural order in life that permits us to discern regular patterns in the events of life. Regularity and predictability in human affairs stem from this underlying order.
- Socioeconomic life is multifaceted and covers a wide range of life experiences, from the harsh realities of destitution and injustice, to the blessings of prosperity, to the profound meaning and sense of accomplishment in life that come from virtue and hard work.
- Despite the good things and the easy life that flow from riches, the crown of human experience is clearly the attainment of wisdom through virtuous and honest living. This is the treasure par excellence, and not material wealth.
- Wisdom literature is descriptive of the various stages and facets of life. Their contradictions should not come as a surprise because they match the richness and complexity of economic life, one that is fraught with chance and contingencies. One should, therefore, expect diverse perspectives.

Nevertheless, wisdom literature is undergirded by a theology of creation and an ethics of order. Its sayings should not always be taken literally, that is, as promising material benefit. More important, they point readers to a cause-and-effect (act-consequence) dynamic underlying creation in which virtue holds the greatest value and brings its own set of rewards. The cosmic order is designed to support a virtuous life. The sages tout the great, indeed incomparable, value of wisdom and virtue. Wisdom is about recognizing and discovering the patterns of life and then living life accordingly and in harmony with this given order.[62] Economic life is a constitutive part of this order, and Sacred Scripture has much to contribute in imbuing economic ethics with wisdom.

NOTES

1. Whybray (1990, 11–15, 60). This is not even counting indirect references, that is, terms that are usually associated with or imply the wealthy, such as "proud" (Prov 15:25), "ill-gotten gains" (Prov 15:27; 28:16), and "wicked."
2. Schmidt (1987)
3. Whybray (1989, 333)
4. Lohfink (1982, 242)
5. Fox (2000, 6)
6. Sandoval (2006, 41, fn 35)
7. Fox (2000); Washington (1994, 111–33, 203); Yoder (2001)
8. Seouw (1997, 21–36); Yoder (2001, 39–72)
9. Crenshaw (1989, 32); Perdue (1990a, 457)
10. Sandoval (2006, 41–43, 211–14)
11. Fox (2000, 6, 48–49)
12. Perdue (1997, 79). Perdue (1997, 80) cites many other reasons for why Proverbs 1–9 is widely held by scholars to be the last part of the work to have been completed (late sixth and fifth century B.C.).
13. Pleins (2000, 453–55)
14. Pleins (1987)
15. Habel (1988, 28–31, 32–34, 42–43)
16. Sandoval (2006, 31, fn 11). Pleins (2000, 465–74) concludes that Proverbs is ambivalent in its attitudes toward poverty.
17. Habel (1988, 42–43); Pleins (2000, 452); Washington (1994, 185ff, 203)
18. Crenshaw (1989, 32). See Fox (2000, 17–27) for a brief exposition on the wisdom literature that preceded Proverbs and that followed the wisdom writings of the Old Testament. See Pleins (1987, 69–76) for further evidence of ANE influence on Proverbs.
19. Crenshaw (1989); Pleins (1987)
20. Washington (1994, 183–85)
21. Sandoval (2006, 62); Van Leeuwen (1992)
22. Whybray (1990, 11–74, 62–63)
23. Hembrom (1996)
24. Habel (1988, 48–49)
25. van Leeuwen (1992, 29, emphasis in original)
26. Gladson (1978) argues that these jarring incongruities were the precursor of the "dissent" or "pluralism" that eventually breaks out into the open in Job and Qoholeth.
27. Sandoval (2006, 209)
28. Fox (2000, 6–11)
29. Sandoval (2006, 45–49)
30. Sandoval (2006, 63–66)
31. Sandoval (2006, 58)
32. Sandoval (2006, 6, 57)

33. Sandoval (2006, 66, 209)
34. Pleins (2000, 452, 485–86)
35. The social location of Job may partly account for the use of a paradigm of conflict. It is believed that Job was most likely composed during the Babylonian exile or the early post-exilic period. The paradigm of conflict reflects the suffering of the people.
36. Perdue (1990a, 459–60)
37. Perdue (1990a, 470–71)
38. Pleins (2000, 452, 485–86), citing Gutierrez (1987, 67)
39. Gutierrez (1987, 98)
40. Pfeiffer (1976, 98)
41. For this reason, Pleins (1987, 70–72) disagrees with Malchow (1982), who classifies Proverbs' concern for the poor as social justice. For Pleins (1987, 71), social justice entails addressing the institutional source of poverty. In his view, Job can be classified as social justice, but not Proverbs.
42. Pleins (2000, 500–508)
43. Perdue (1990a, 475)
44. Crenshaw (19780, 299) claims that these are among the most popular responses to dealing with the problem of theodicy, that is, the question of why God permits evil in the world.
45. Perdue (1990a, 457)
46. Perdue (1990a, 468–69)
47. Zimmerli (1964, 155–58)
48. Perdue (1990a, 471–72)
49. Perdue (1990a, 477–78)
50. Fox (2000, 6); Sandoval (2006, 41–43)
51. See di Lella (1966, 140–41) and 2 Maccabees 4 for an account of this conflict.
52. Sirach was not the first to associate wisdom with the Torah. Psalms 19 and 119 talk of the Torah as the source of wisdom (Perdue 1990a, 461–62).
53. Perdue (1990a, 461–62, 476–78)
54. See Gregory (2010), Morla Asensio (1998), Wright (1998), and Wright and Claudia (2001) for an extended discussion of wealth, generosity, and almsgiving in Sirach.
55. di Lella (1966, 144–45)
56. Zimmerli (1964, 148, 151)
57. Ceresko (1995); Habel (1988, 31–32); Murphy (1990b); Perdue (1990a); Yee (1992)
58. Habel (1988, 31); Perdue (1994, 79–80)
59. The following sociological explanation is drawn from Ceresko (1995, 226–32).
60. Ceresko (1995, 221–22)
61. Hembrom (1996, 232)
62. Perdue (1990a, 470–71)

II

New Testament

Chapter Six

Socioeconomic Conditions

First-Century Palestine

Understanding the socioeconomic conditions and mindset of the Mediterranean world in the first century is essential because the New Testament, or any other written or oral tradition for that matter, did not arise in a vacuum. It was a product of its time. Jesus, the evangelists, and the early Church had to teach and speak in terms and images that were accessible to their target audiences. For example, given the agrarian nature of that era, it should not come as a surprise that the New Testament employs the images of the good shepherd watching out for wolves (Mt 7:15), separating sheep from goats (Mt 25:31–33), lost sheep (Lk 15:1–7), vine and branches in need of pruning for further growth (Jn 15:1–8), and seeds and weeds (Mt 13:24–30). We can enrich our understanding and appreciation for New Testament teachings on economic life by examining their socioeconomic context. This includes studying the history, social practices, and mores of first-century Palestine.[1]

HISTORY

First-century Palestine was an agrarian society with 70 percent of the land used for agriculture and 90 percent of the population engaged in farming. The peasantry was comprised of small landowners and the landless, who had to work either as tenants or as day laborers. In addition, there were those who resorted to banditry or who were reduced to beggary. Landholding peasants farmed anywhere from one to fifteen acres, with the average at around four to nine acres. Most families engaged in subsistence agriculture, producing primarily for their own consumption rather than for exchange or cash. The region enjoyed agricultural self-sufficiency with grains, wine, and oil as the most important crops.

Jerusalem was the center of the Jewish economy because of the wide variety of services and goods needed for the cultic observances in the Temple. Over seven thousand priests and Levites had to be supported. Pilgrims required provisions and housing. Animals for sacrifice had to be brought in from the surrounding regions. All this spawned ancillary employment, such as metal workers, incense makers, bakers for shewbread, and moneychangers. This does not even include the ten thousand workers involved in the rebuilding of the Temple. These, too, had to be housed and provisioned. Besides the tithes collected from across the nation, the Temple was also an important magnet for drawing funds from overseas. Jerusalem benefitted from the regular contributions sent in by the Diaspora Jews. Every male Jew, thirteen years old and up, was supposed to pay an annual half-shekel due. Based on the 48 A.D. Roman census of Jews in the empire, there were around 8 million Jews including those not subject to Rome—in Mesopotamia, Iran, and southern Arabia. Even if the actual figure was only a quarter of this, with half a million in Palestine and the rest in the Diaspora, and even if only one-third of those in the Diaspora paid, it is estimated that the half-shekel dues alone would have amounted to a million denarii annually. This represented around 10 to 15 percent of Herod's income.[2] These remittances were critical for the nation's finances. This is not even to include the special gifts, requisite offerings, and extra donations made to the Temple and the priests. Indeed, Jerusalem was the linchpin of the Jewish economy.

International commerce, while significant, was not a major economic activity. Chief exports were dates, opobalsam, and wheat. Some oil, wine, and native spices were also sold overseas. These exports were mostly grown on imperial land or were in-kind payments for taxes. Consequently, the ordinary peasant was neither dependent on nor enriched by trade with the neighboring states or cities. The nation was agriculturally self-sufficient, able to provide for its own citizens.

Power Structure

Life in first-century Palestine was shaped by the power structure and dynamics of an imperial culture. The first-century Mediterranean world is best described as an advanced agrarian empire.[3] The structure was pyramidal with the emperor, Caesar, at the apex. Next were the ruling classes, the elite, and the native aristocracies who advised and served the emperor and who governed on his behalf. These court officials and military officers were generously rewarded with land grants and privileges. Beneath them were the retainer classes, that is, the bureaucrats who served the ruling elite. Next in line were the landholding peasants whose subsistence livelihoods were greatly at risk. These small landowners were constantly on the verge of being impoverished and losing their land due to heavy impositions from imperial taxation. Finally, at the bottom were the landless peasants who either never had an inheritance or had lost their farms and were now reduced to tenancy, begging, banditry, or selling their services as day laborers. Power, privilege, wealth, and prestige emanated from the top down. Overlaying these class divisions were further categories that determined status: urban versus rural, free versus slave.

Galilean and Judean Political History

The Persians ruled Judah from the 539 B.C. until the arrival of Alexander the Great around 330 B.C. After the death of Alexander the Great, his empire was divided between Ptolemy in Egypt and Seleucus in Asia Minor. Judah was ruled first by the Ptolemies (320–200 B.C.) and then by the Seleucids (200–142 B.C.). Seleucid control over Judah disintegrated, hastened by the Maccabean revolt in reaction to attempts at Hellenizing Jewish life. Much of what is known about this period is drawn from biblical text, 1 and 2 Maccabees in particular. Even Josephus relies on these texts. The Maccabeans, often also called the Hasmoneans, eventually succeeded in winning political control of Judah. There were at least two significant developments that are relevant for our study of New Testament economic ethics.

First, archeological evidence confirm the Hasmonean program of "Judaization." Hasmonean rulers expanded the territory of Judah, established new Jewish settlements, and harassed and drove away Gentile residents of settlements in Idumea and Samaria, replacing them with Jewish settlers. They embraced the post-exilic quest of retrieving the purity and identity of the nation. We find evidence of this in the archaeological remains of the period.[4] Unlike settlements on the coast, the Transjordan, the Negev, Idumea, and the north, Jewish communities seem to have deliberately segregated themselves from international trade and from non-Jewish communities. Material remains from Jewish communities show that wares and household goods were remarkable in their uniformity—all locally manufactured, despite the vibrant international trade of the period and the region. Archaeologists do not find in these Jewish settlements pottery, wares, wine amphoras, or other goods from Phoenicia, Alexandria, Greece, or southern Italy that are commonly found in the remains of other settlements in the region for this particular period. This has been interpreted as evidence of a Hasmonean a policy of economic independence.[5] More important, such findings are consistent with a nation trying to retrieve its religious purity. These archaeological findings reveal Jewish simplicity, as they forego the sophistication of the many fine imported goods enjoyed by their neighbors.

Such isolation from international trade also confirms the Jewish self-understanding of being a people distinct from Gentiles and all the surrounding settlements. From the depths to which they had sunk in the Neo-Babylonian and Persian periods, the Jewish nation now emerged as a self-confident people asserting their distinctive claims as God's own people. Not surprisingly, a century later, we find in New Testament texts many accounts in which concerns over purity, shame, honor, and belonging shaped their conduct toward one another and strangers (e.g., Mt 9:11).

A second development relevant for our study is the emergence of native conspicuous consumption at this time. This is unusual because up until the early second century, archaeologists have found Jewish settlements to be simple and egalitarian. Not anymore. Archaeological remains show that the Hasmonean rulers had a taste for elaborate and expensive architecture. Archaeologists find evidence of this in the tombs and private residences that the Hasmoneans built for themselves. The Hasmonean rulers were keeping up with the rest of the Hellenistic world in which public displays of wealth and power were the norm. Clearly, the Hasmonean rulers failed to practice what they preached as part of their program of "Judaization," the retrieval of national purity and the assertion of their Jewish identity. Besides adopting Hellenistic attitudes regarding conspicuous consumption and palatial construction, the Hasmoneans also followed the Persian and Hellenistic practice of appropriating the very best lands for their own use and benefit—"King's Land."[6] Note that Herod would later follow the same practice.

At about this time, a group of Jews left Jerusalem and settled in isolation on the northern edge of the Dead Sea. This eventually became known as the Qumran community. Archaeological remains show a stark simplicity of life, as evident in their architecture and the absence of imported or luxury goods. This was clearly a protest and a desire to get away from the affluent lifestyles of their Judean rulers and the Hellenized ways of the elite of Jerusalem.[7]

The Hasmonean adoption of Hellenistic attitudes on the accumulation and public display of individual wealth and power and the emergence of a Qumran community of stark simplicity are relevant for our study of New Testament economic ethics. These events provide the larger socioeconomic backdrop for the "hostility toward wealth" that many scholars find strewn throughout the Gospels. The New Testament texts disparaging wealth and the rich may reflect the continuing tension between adopting scandalous foreign (Greco-Roman) ways, on the one hand, and remaining pure and true to the Jewish simplicity of life and religious fervor, on the other hand.

The period of independence after the Maccabean revolt and the ensuing Hasmonean rule proved to be short-lived. The nation was soon wracked by bitter internal rivalries for power. In the resulting chaos, Pompey besieged and ultimately conquered Jerusalem in the summer of 63 B.C. Rome filled the void by appointing the Herodians, an Idumean dynasty, as client kings to administer the Jewish territories.

Herod the Great was the first in line and reigned from 40 to 4 B.C. He is notable for his benefactions and grand construction projects, many of which were record setting for the era. The Temple Mount was built on an expansive artificial esplanade, said to be the largest in antiquity. The Royal Portico of the Temple was the longest building at that time. His palace—the Herodium—was the largest in the world, until Nero built his in Rome. Caesarea was said to be most technologically advanced harbor in antiquity.[8]

Herod rebuilt and expanded the Temple in Jerusalem. He added a theater, an amphitheater, and a fortified royal palace in Jerusalem—Hellenistic touches that displeased the faithful Jewry. He built new cities (Caesarea Maritima and Sebaste) and temples to honor his Roman patrons. Enamored of Hellenistic culture, Herod the Great extended his largesse and major construction projects beyond Palestine: the isles of Chios, Cos, Rhodes, and the cities of Laodicea, Tripolis, Byblos, Berytos, Sidon, Tyre, Ptolemais, Ascalon, Nicopolis, Olympia, Sparta, Athens, Pergamum, Antioch, and Damascus. Herod's Jewish subjects derived little to no benefit from these overseas benefactions despite having paid for them. In fact, Josephus writes of Herod, "He had not ceased to adorn neighbouring cities that were inhabited by foreigners although this led to the ruin and disappearance of cities located in his own kingdom" (*Ant* 17.306–307).[9] In addition to their showcase projects honoring their Roman overlords, Herodian client kings curried Roman favor through their tributes, gifts, and bequests. For example, Herod the Great left bequests for Augustus and his wife totaling 1,500 talents or 9 million denarii (a denarius is a day's wage).[10]

Upon the death of Herod the Great, Caesar Augustus divided the region among Herod's sons. Herod Archelaus governed Judea, Samaria, Idumea, Jerusalem, Sebaste, and Joppa from which he drew an annual income of 600 talents until he was deposed and exiled in 6 A.D. by Augustus, and his properties confiscated on account of his cruelty (*Ant* 17.319, 342; *JW* 2.111).[11] He was replaced by a Roman procurator who lived in Caesarea Maritima, while Jerusalem was controlled by the priestly aristocracy.[12]

Herod Philip reigned in Batanaea, Trachonitis, and Auranitis in northern Transjordan and drew an annual income of 100 talents. Herod Antipas was given Galilee and Peraea from which he drew an annual income of 200 talents (1.2 million denarii), in addition to special levies for his building projects (*Ant* 17.318). Antipas is of immediate interest to New Testament readers because it was he who governed Galilee at the time of Jesus. Herod Antipas continued his father's practice of honoring Roman emperors through massive building projects in Galilee, such as the rebuilding of Sepphoris (the administrative center of Galilee that has been described as "the ornament of

Galilee") and Tiberias, a new city built on the lakefront honoring Tiberius, who succeeded Augustus.[13]

Imperial Impact

While most scholars agree on the redistributive nature of imperial economics, they differ on its consequences for Palestine and the degree to which the social conditions of the Greco-Roman world shaped New Testament text. In particular, some claim that the economic norms of Jesus, the evangelists, and the early Church were a direct reaction to the brazen injustice of the ruling elite and the resulting impoverishment of the population. New Testament teachings and views on economic life merely reflected the dire socioeconomic conditions of their time. Jesus was preaching against rampant economic iniquity, the prophet Amos of his time. Other scholars disagree with this grim assessment and note that despite the abuses of the Romans and their Herodian collaborators, there were, in fact, vibrant markets, with the peasantry enjoying some measure of sufficiency. Both schools of thought present strong literary, historical, and archeological evidence to support their respective views.

Impoverished Palestine

Given the mode of production in the Roman world, many conclude that first-century Palestine must have been a highly unequal society in which an elite few, centered on imperial Rome and its client rulers, impoverished the vast majority of the population. There are numerous literary and historical accounts of Herodian excesses and increasing inequality.

Josephus describes Herod the Great as a cruel tyrant who lusted for honors, power, and wealth (*Ant* 16.151–157). Herod had only modest resources at his accession. In fact, he was compelled to melt his ornaments and valuables to mint ready money (*JW* 1.358; cf *Ant* 15.306). Not long thereafter, however, he filled his coffers through the police state that he had created with the use of foreign mercenaries, informants, and fortresses across the country. His subjects had no choice but to underwrite his ambition and vast expenses because of his brutality (*Ant* 16.154). Herod the Great received anywhere from a quarter to a third of Palestinian grain and as much as half of the produce of fruit trees. This was similar to the Syrian rates of taxation in second century B.C. (cf 1 Mac 10:30).[14] Moreover, Herod confiscated or plundered his subjects' properties (*Ant* 15.5). And then, there were the frequent arbitrary, special taxes. This is not even to mention the tribute sent to Rome and the Temple tithes.

In addition to these impositions, ordinary people were harassed by Herod's underlings for their own share of bribes and gifts. The ruling elite were comprised of members of the royal court, aristocrats, high military officers, and religious leaders. Even the priestly class was corrupt, became political, and sought the same aristocratic lifestyle. Just like their Greco-Roman counterparts, the elite disdained manual labor and were supported by the productive work of the rest of the population. For ordinary peasants, land was their only source of livelihood; for the elite, land was the source of wealth and power. For peasants, land was acquired through inheritance; for the elite, land was acquired through conquest, expropriation for unpaid debts, or royal grant as a reward for loyalty and service. The goal of the ruling class was to accumulate as much land as possible, with peasants furnishing the labor, mostly under great compulsion through a combination of slavery, corvée, or obligations to a patron. Living in the cities, these absentee landlords extracted produce from the countryside through heavy taxation, burdensome rents, usurious interest, or outright exploitation and theft. Their aim was to draw as much surplus as possible from the peasants, leaving just enough to keep them alive to work the land. The elite even resorted to violence to extract dues from the people (*Ant* 20.180–81, 206–7).[15]

As a consequence, literary and archeological evidence point to a concentration of land ownership. The crown and the ruling elite owned ever-larger land estates spread all over the nation. Much of this growth in the size of estates was due to peasant forfeitures from indebtedness. The peasantry was increasingly left landless, with most ending up as tenants, day laborers, or beggars. Some resorted to banditry. This state of affairs in Palestine was consistent with the land concentration observed in other parts of the Roman Empire.[16] It is reminiscent of Nehemiah 5:1–12 and its description of ever deepening indebtedness for peasants and the eventual loss of their land.[17]

Taxes and religious impositions alone absorbed 28 to 40 percent of the peasants' produce. After setting aside seed for the next planting season and covering farming expenses, peasants had about 8 to 20 percent of their harvest left for their subsistence.[18] Clearly, peasants bore the brunt of financing the Herodian dynasty's lifestyle and foreign benefactions. After all, an agrarian society is heavily dependent on the productive labor of its peasantry.[19] Consequently, they also became a tempting source for easy revenues.

Fishing was a vital industry for Galilee, and many depended on it for their livelihood. Even this, however, was tightly controlled by Imperial Rome and the ruling elite. They were able to extract the produce of this industry as well.[20]

Even the nobility were not spared. Many were murdered and their properties confiscated by Herod. Bitterness against Herod's abuses was widespread. In fact, people complained that Herod inflicted calamities on the nation that were even worse than all the misfortunes and forced deportations endured by their ancestors. At his death, the nation was impoverished (*Ant* 17.304–10; *JW* 2.84ff, 1.524). As much as 80 percent of the population was estimated to be at subsistence level, defined as the struggle to meet daily needs for survival.[21]

Increased disaffection in the population was evident in the rise in banditry and prophetic protest movements.[22] Peasants refused to pay tribute and burned debt records (*JW* 2.403–4, 427).[23] During the first Jewish revolt, the people attacked Sepphoris and Tiberias due to their resentment for these cities' residents (*Life* 66–68).[24] It was also probably due to Antipas's burdensome levies that went toward refurbishing and maintaining these cities.

Some suggest that the withdrawal of the Essenes from the rest of society and the Pharisees' espousal of a simple lifestyle (*Ant* 18.12, 18) were, in fact, about making a statement that being poor was nothing to be ashamed of, as Greco-Roman society thought. In particular, the Essenes wanted to be a counter-cultural witness and indictment of the grasping conduct of the elite.[25]

Most of the aforesaid conclusions are heavily based on the accounts of Flavius Josephus. In dealing with ancient literature, readers have to be cautious, lest they take "rhetorically fraught depictions . . . as though they were factually accurate."[26] It is not always clear whether these ancient writings are descriptive of reality or mere rhetoric in espousing the ideal. Ancient authors may not have been writing for data keeping or history, but may have been promoting a particular worldview or advancing a personal agenda.[27] In the case of Josephus, his objectivity has been questioned because of his role in some of the events that he was describing, and he may have been self-serving in some of his accounts. Moreover, his writings are said to have a pro-Roman bias because he wanted to ingratiate himself with his Roman patrons.

We can correct for this problem by looking for corroboration from other Ancient Near Eastern materials. For example, take the case of the Romans in Egypt. Ancient court documents and tax receipts recorded on papyri and ostraca in Egypt reveal Roman tax practices around the first century.[28] Unlike the Greeks who put the burden of the costs of government on the wealthy, the Romans shifted the tax burden to their subjects. Those who worked the land bore the bulk of these impositions. There were over a hundred different types of taxes, from the head tax, to taxes on artisans and land, to imposts at harbors and tolls, to levies on some contracts and market transactions. In addition, there were ad hoc levies and requisitions of goods to pay for special administrative or military needs. And then, there were the "liturgies," that is, requisite unpaid work done on behalf of the community (e.g., clerks, transporters, inspectors, councilmen, magistrates).

Romans were efficient and well organized in collecting taxes. Tax collection was contracted out to the urban elite who served as tax brokers or as tax and toll collectors. Rome was thorough, methodical, brutal, and unrelenting in tax collection. Soldiers were used as enforcers to coerce the population. In the process, the burdens of taxation became heavier for the ordinary peasant because the soldiers were abusive and demanded bribes for themselves.

Those unable to pay their taxes became fugitives. So burdensome were these impositions and so poor was the countryside that those who were in arrears for a year or two in the payment of taxes were as numerous as those able to pay on time. Ancient records show a large number of fugitives. However, Imperial Rome made sure that it did not lose tax revenues by compelling the rest of the community to make up for the shortfall caused by these fugitives. Furthermore, since idle land did not produce any revenues for the Romans, the local community was forced to work unused or abandoned land.

These tax practices in first-century Egypt were replicated across the Roman Empire, including next-door Palestine, where the Romans were just as brutal and demanding in the collection of taxes. Note the disparaging descriptions of Roman predation in literature of the era (e.g., Revelation 17 and 18; Sibylline Oracles).[29] The *Jewish War* (1.220–22) recounts the enslavement of the residents of four cities just because they were tardy in meeting a special levy.[30] Tacitus notes that in 17 A.D., Syria and Judea appealed for a reduction in taxes. So onerous were the impositions that respectable teachers and citizens like Hillel were driven to join in widespread tax evasion. It has even been claimed that the siege of Jerusalem in 70 A.D. was over the nonpayment of taxes and tribute (*JW* 5.405–6).[31] Roman taxes were oppressive and harshly administered. Herod the Great and his sons were merely following the example of their Roman overlords in maltreating their subjects.

While archaeologists find that Galilee had a mixed land ownership of large estates and family-run subsistence farms, the trend was, nevertheless, toward ever-larger estates. Peasants were experiencing the widespread loss of land at the time of Jesus. In addition, archeological sites provide evidence of luxury among the aristocracy.[32]

The Jewish revolts of 66–70 A.D. and 132–135 A.D. suggest that first-century Palestinian socioeconomic conditions were unbearable. Roman retribution was swift and cruel. The first Jewish revolt (66–70 A.D.) had devastating consequences for first-century Palestinian socioeconomic life. Even if Jewish peasantry had not been destitute prior to 70 A.D., they were now. To begin with, there was a massive loss of life. Josephus estimates over a million casualties in Judea, though this is widely viewed to be an exaggeration. Tacitus puts the besieged population in Jerusalem at 600,000. Of these, as many as half a million may have died, with the rest taken as prisoners.

The destruction of the Temple was catastrophic for the nation's economy, given the market activity generated by the pilgrimages and their associated ancillary services. In addition, it also meant an end to the inflow of overseas funds from the regular contributions from Diaspora Jewry. What remained of the nation's economic infrastructure beyond Jerusalem was either ravaged or expropriated. The population was compelled to support and furnish provisions for the occupying troops. Moreover, the Romans confiscated the land of those who were involved in or who supported the rebellion, both living and deceased. Jewish peasants found themselves suddenly forced off their land or turned tenants on their own lands. A new class of landlords emerged: Roman consuls, senators, military officers, and aristocratic women. A few of these were Jews who received land as a reward for their loyalty or services during the rebellion. This massive loss of life and property, the pillaging of villages and towns, and continued Roman exactions pushed the population into deeper poverty. Not surprisingly, there was a second revolt in 132–135 A.D.[33]

In sum, the Palestinian economy in the first century was extractive, redistributive, and tributary. This was typical of the lands subjected by Imperial Rome at that time.[34] In such a political economy, a central institution siphoned off resources from the countryside to the city. This was accomplished through taxes, tithes, interest on debts, and rents. Consequently, many scholars believe that first-century Palestine endured much hardship. What little surplus the peasants reaped from farming, if there was even any at all, was appropriated by Rome and its Herodian client kings for unproductive purposes. As a consequence, there was an increase in social banditry, especially between 40 and 66 A.D., and a rise in peasant landlessness, with ever more people driven to seek work either as tenants or as day laborers. Thus, many believe that the Jesus movement was comprised primarily of the poor and the disenfranchised.[35]

Robust Palestinian Economy

Other scholars dispute such a dismal view of a highly unequal and impoverished Palestinian society in which a small elite exercised great economic and political power amidst a vast sea of peasant destitution.[36] There are also strong literary, archeological, and historical evidence suggesting a robust first-century Mediterranean economy with a resilient peasantry that was neither indigent nor enslaved. While not living in carefree abundance, most peasants were able to satisfy their basic needs. Despite the redistributive and extractive nature of Roman political economy, there were also thriving markets. In fact, many supported themselves and their families as free householders working off the land.[37] Later rabbinic sources show that peasants had a vibrant economic life, as seen in these works' discussion of markets, village trades, and laws governing trading.[38] There are also archeological findings showing small family-run farms. First-century Jewish peasants in Galilee continued to own modest plots of land, lived according to the nation's Covenant tradition, and enjoyed some measure of sufficiency.[39] While there was indeed social banditry, this was not the dominant experience of the nation.[40]

The Jewish revolts are not unmistakable evidence of an impoverished population. The poor are not the only ones who have the motivation and the means to stage collective action. Those who enjoy stable sufficiency (the middle section of the population) are just as prone to protest if they see the possibility of improving their position or if there is a deterioration in their condition.[41] Thus, we should not be quick to conclude that the Jewish uprisings were precipitated by widespread poverty.

Galilean studies reveal some surprising insights on this issue. Herod Antipas is usually portrayed as the immediate context for Jesus and his preaching. The common belief is that the grand construction projects of Antipas impoverished many people who were driven to debt and then to poverty. Jesus was reacting to Herod Antipas and his ruling elite's economic injustice. This is a traditional assessment. However, recent studies suggest that Herod Antipas was, in fact, a minor player, and ironically, one who served a stabilizing role. His main contribution was acting as a buffer that cushioned Galilee from what could have been an even harsher Roman rule. By keeping Rome happy and at bay, Antipas bought time and peace for the region, thereby ushering in a period of growth and prosperity for Galilee, and not only for the urban centers, but also for the rural areas. Population expanded, agriculture thrived, and public buildings rose.

The rebuilding of Sepphoris (after the disturbances on the death of Herod the Great in 4 B.C.) and the building of Tiberias point to the increasing marketization of Galilee. These two cities were the administrative centers of an emerging vibrant market economy. Archeological findings show the proliferation of olive presses, frescoes in private dwellings, and specialty production, such as ceramics. The remains of wine and oil presses and storage silos suggest intensive cultivation and a flourishing domestic market that served not only local needs but also other regional and even far-flung centers of trade.

There was specialized manufacturing: an indigenous pottery industry at Kefar Hanania (between upper and lower Galilee) and a stone-jar industry in Shihin in lower Galilee. The pottery industry was believed to have supplied common kitchen wares not only for Galileans, but also for export trade to the Golan, the Decapolis, and Phoenician cities. The existence of these specialized industries, their use of indigenous raw materials, and their sale to far-flung areas beyond local needs dispel the view that first-century Palestinian peasantry wallowed in destitution and landlessness.[42] Selected villages seemed to thrive, all the way up to the Jewish revolt of 66–70 A.D. There was small-scale industrial activity.

Furthermore, the social-scientific theory of oppression predicts greater urbanization because urban centers are parasitic on rural produce. It also calls for greater monetization because peasants have to join the money economy. They need cash in order to purchase their food and other necessities from the marketplace, since they have been compelled to give up subsistence farming and shift to export crops. Moreover, they need to raise cash in order to pay their taxes. In the case of Galilee, it was not as urbanized or as monetized as one would expect from such a theory of oppression, despite its growing market economy.

Herod Antipas's two signature cities Sepphoris and Tiberias were modest. There is no evidence of grand or expensive public buildings, great wealth, or imported building materials. Based on literary and archeological evidence, Herod Antipas was a "minor ruler with a moderate impact."[43] He could not have caused dire and widespread poverty in the population. Far from it, he brought some stability and peace that allowed the Galilean economy to grow.

The debate among scholars on whether or not first-century Palestine was destitute or thriving also plays out in the field of Pauline studies. Most scholars conclude that the Pauline communities were urban Christians. Some claim that the early Church was predominantly a community of the disenfranchised and the poor. Others disagree and see a much more diverse faith community, and one that was largely supported by its more affluent members.[44] Biblical texts themselves suggest an economy with some surplus. The letter of James and the Pastoral Epistles show that the urban Christian churches had wealthy benefactors who were part of the elite. In fact, they may have even dominated these church communities.[45] If Roman Corinth was typical, then there is reason to believe that there was a lot more disposable income at that time, as seen in the city's spending on religious temples, games, and temporary lodgings for guests. Archeological evidence points to some economic prosperity and growth during this period.[46]

In contrast to the view that the first-century Mediterranean world was comprised only of either the very rich or the destitute, studies suggest that there was, in fact, a sizable middle section of anywhere from 29 to as much as 42 percent of the population. These were the merchants, traders, freed persons, artisans, military veterans, regular wage earners, large shop owners, and some farm families who either produced a moderate surplus or were just slightly above subsistence level.[47] In other words, there was a wide range of economic conditions for the vast majority of the population: from large estates, to family-owned farms, to landless peasants dependent on day labor or tenancy, to the destitute reduced to beggary, to those in debt slavery. According to this view, one cannot assume a completely or uniformly impoverished population for that period.

Assessment

Was the first-century Mediterranean world, including Palestine, destitute or was it a robust peasant economy? Did Jesus and his contemporaries live in precarious subsistence or did they enjoy some measure of self-sufficiency?

There is no conclusive evidence on which view is correct. Ancient historical, archaeological, and literary sources are fragmentary and do not provide definitive answers. They support conflicting views. The danger is to arrive at conclusions based more on interpretative assumptions than on hard data. However, this lacuna should not stymie us in our study of New Testament economic ethics, for at least two reasons.

First, the seemingly contradictory archeological evidence and literary accounts may not, in fact, be mutually exclusive. They may be describing different sectors or groups within the economy. For example, in an economic history of this period, we find an account of both a thriving economy and poverty existing side by side.[48] Agriculture and a modest industry were said to be flourishing during this period. Agriculture kept up with population growth. Dates, grapes, olives, and figs continued to be the main produce of the nation. These were not merely consumed domestically, but were also exported. They were of such quality as to compete even with the very best of Italy, Spain, and Greece, making it even to the imperial tables in Rome. While pursued on a very small scale, some specialized crafts were well established, such as textiles, linen in particular. During the First Jewish Revolt, certain quarters of Jerusalem were described in terms of the predominant markets or products therein—metals, wool, and clothes.

However, despite these thriving sectors, there were also many small farmers who could not keep their land because of the heavy fiscal impositions. In fact, Rome had to reduce the state's share of the land's produce from a third to a quarter. Landless peasants in search of work flooded the urban areas. For this reason, it is believed that slave-holding did not make economic sense because one could hire day laborers at a much cheaper cost. This economic history of the later Second Temple Period only goes to show that there are accounts of both a thriving economy and destitute peasants. The archeological findings and the literary works may be descriptive of different segments or geographical areas of the economy. It may have been a robust economy of small farms and large estates, interspersed with pockets of destitute peasants.

Second, it is not essential to establish conclusively whether or not there was widespread landlessness and poverty in first-century Palestine in order to make sense of New Testament economic norms. These teachings may have also been in response to the prevailing public ethos of the period (e.g., greed, materialism), whether espoused by the populace or by the ruling elite. In other words, these biblical economic passages may not necessarily have been in reaction to the dire socioeconomic conditions of their day. They may, in fact, have been addressing the misplaced values of the people of their time. A wrong or an injustice has to be addressed, even if it is not rampant. After all, Sacred Scripture aims to instruct and form hearts and minds. Hence, even if scholars are unable at this time to establish definitively the actual economic state of the first-century Mediterranean world, we can nevertheless still appropriate biblical economic ethics for contemporary use. It is sufficient that we have an appreciation for the most likely socioeconomic conditions of the time for what they may reveal regarding the public morality of the period.

SUMMARY AND CONCLUSIONS

There is a multiplicity of factors that comprise a person's social standing in the ancient world, namely, "ethnic origins, *ordo*, citizenship, personal liberty, wealth, occupation, age, sex, public offices or honors, and family heritage."[49] Nevertheless, access to resources (economic power) was a major determinant of a person's social standing. Moreover, there was a self-reinforcing dynamic to this in that even as economic power enhanced social status, such social status in its own turn opened the door to even more or new sources of wealth and power. Consequently, those who have more to begin with, will have even more at the end of the day.[50] In other words, economics matters enormously in understanding the dynamics of any society, including the Ancient Near East.

NOTES

1. The following brief account draws from Applebaum (1976), Freyne (2004), Harland (2002, 514–22), Kyrtatas (2002), Hanson (1997), Hanson and Oakman (1998, 107), Horsley and Hanson (1985, 32–33), Jeremias (1969, 124–26), May (2010), Perkins (1984, 183–85), Theissen (1978, 33–46), and Verhey (2002, 253–62).
2. Broshi (1987)
3. The following is a description of Lenski's (1966) model, which most scholars use to describe ancient empires.
4. Berlin (1997, 22–43)
5. Berlin (1997, 29–30)
6. Berlin (1997, 32–34)
7. Berlin (1997, 34–36)
8. Broshi (1987, 31)
9. Josephus (1980, v. 8, 513)
10. Hanson (1997, 102). In the last twenty years of his reign, Augustus is said to have received bequests from client kings totaling 350 million denarii.
11. Ant = Josephus, *Jewish Antiquities*; JW = Josephus, *Jewish War*.
12. Freyne (2004, 23)
13. Freyne (2004, 32)
14. Hanson and Oakman (1998, 114). This is also consistent with the findings of Lenski (1966) on ancient agrarian economies. He concludes that the ruling elite in ancient agrarian economies received anywhere from at least a quarter of the land's income (most likely half), to as much as two-thirds (Hanson and Oakman, 1998, 99–129). See Broshi (1987) for a description of the revenue sources for the Herodian economy.
15. Freyne (2004, 34); Hanson and Oakman (1998, 99–129)
16. Freyne (2004)
17. Freyne (2004, 30)
18. Harland (2002, 514–22)
19. In 39 A.D. during the reign of Gauis Caligula, peasants refused to work their land to protest the building of the emperor's statue in the Temple. Rome and the ruling elite backed

off, which only goes to underscore the importance of peasant labor in producing extractable surplus (*Ant* 18.271–89; Freyne, 2004, 3).

20. See Hanson (1997) and Hanson and Oakman (1998, 107).
21. Oakman (1986, 37–91); Perkins (1994, 46)
22. Horsley and Hanson (1985)
23. Freyne (2004, 34)
24. Life = *The Life of Josephus*.
25. Freyne (2004, 34)
26. Johnson (2008)
27. For example, the prologue of the Code of Hammurabi makes expansive claims about the king as champion and protector of the poor. Yet there is not a single piece of legislation for the poor in the entire Code. See Lohfink (1991). It turns out that many Ancient Near Eastern prologues and epilogues were self-serving royal propaganda.
28. The following account is based on Lewis (1983, 156–84) and Perkins (1986, 183–85).
29. See Perkins (1994, 53).
30. Horsley and Hanson (1985, 31)
31. Jeremias (1969, 124–26)
32. Frenye (2004, 34)
33. Applebaum (1976, 692–99)
34. Hanson and Oakman (1998, 113) contrast three alternative methods of distribution. (1) In general reciprocity, people get what they need and contribute what they can. Exchanges are viewed more as gifts with no need to be reciprocated immediately. (2) Balanced reciprocity entails an exchange of goods or services of comparable value. It is a quid pro quo, descriptive of modern markets in which people get what they pay for. (3) In redistribution, a central authority appropriates goods or services and dispenses these to its favored supporters and according to its political ends. See also Polanyi (1968).
35. See Schmidt (1987, 19, fn 3 and 4) for scholars who view New Testament economic teachings as a reaction to the impoverishment of first-century Palestine.
36. For example, see Freyne (1988; 1994; 2004) and Schmidt (1987).
37. See, for example, Scheidel (2006) and Rathbone (2006).
38. Safrai (1994, 224–72). See also Noell (2007).
39. May (2010, 491)
40. Freyne (1988, 155–67; 1994)
41. Theissen (1978, 39)
42. Freyne (1994). See Jensen (2006) for the preceding points regarding the minor but useful role of Herod Antipas.
43. Jensen (2006, 252, 254, 256)
44. For example, see Meggitt (1998) for the former view and Meeks (1993) and Theissen (1982) for the latter position. See also Longnecker (2009).
45. Kidd (1990, 61–95)
46. Engels (1990, 121–30); Greene (1986)
47. Longnecker (2009, 44); Friessen (2004)
48. Baron et al. (1975, 16–18)
49. Longnecker (2009, 37, emphasis original); Meeks (1983, 54–55)
50. Longnecker (2009, 42–43); Veyne (1990, 44)

Chapter Seven

Mark

The traditional view is that the Gospel of Mark's audience was the Gentile Christian community in Rome about the time of Nero's persecution. In their suffering and helplessness, Mark re-presents Jesus Christ as one who had also suffered and had been persecuted. Jesus Christ is re-presented as one with whom they could identify as they struggled to make sense of their own travails.[1]

THEOLOGY OF MARK

The distinctive features of Mark's theology are his eschatology and the identity of Jesus Christ. Mark 1:14–15 is programmatic for the Gospel.[2] Note the three elements of this pericope: (1) It proclaims God's reign in the here and now. (2) It is Jesus who brings this kingdom to fruition. (3) It requires a response of faith and conversion from all to whom the Gospel is preached.

Eschatological Fulfillment

The Gospel of Mark has an imminent eschatology in which the nearness of the kingdom is a constant refrain. Mark's audience was an "eschatological community" because of their conviction that they were living in the last days, characterized by the in-breaking of the reign of God.[3] The fullest manifestation of the kingdom of God was yet to come, at the end-time. However, they held that it was already mysteriously present in the person and ministry of Jesus Christ. It was already present to those who believed in his Gospel.[4]

Mark attributes his programmatic pericope to Isaiah, but it is in fact a combination of Exodus 23:20, Malachi 3:1, and Isaiah 40:3. These are all about the promised restoration of Israel by God.[5] They flow from the Old

Testament view of God as king who wields absolute sovereignty over creation and over human history.

The kingdom of God is a "metaphor for God's rule over creation and history."[6] This kingdom is yet to be fully revealed. Nonetheless, it is already present. It is faith that enables people to see the reality and the presence of such kingdom unfolding in the here and now. Hence, note the importance of believing as part of Mark's programmatic pericope so that people might recognize and participate in the in-breaking of this kingdom. Only in discipleship can one grasp the mystery of the kingdom of God.[7]

Who is Jesus?

Jesus brings the Old Testament understanding of kingship to completion. The good news is that God is finally fulfilling the promise made to Israel in the person of Jesus Christ. His miracles are the manifestation of God's reign and goodness in the here and now.[8] Thus, the ill are healed, the dead rise, and evil is banished. In fact, everything that Jesus does in his public ministry of preaching, teaching, and healing is about effecting the kingdom, the in-breaking of God's rule.[9] Jesus' ministry can be described as sacramental because it effects what it signifies. He does not merely proclaim the coming of the kingdom; he actually brings it about. The kingdom and its fulfillment are inextricably linked with Jesus (Mk 4:11; 8:31, 38; 9:1; 11:9–10).[10] But there is an added twist to Jesus as the eschatological fulfillment of God's Old Testament promise. It is no ordinary eschatological fulfillment of God's promise. It is, in fact, a prophetic eschatological fulfillment. Jesus also turns out to be the Isaianic Suffering Servant. Just like the Suffering Servant in Isaiah who bore the sins of many, Jesus also suffers for the sins of others.[11]

Jesus' messiahship is different from and is, in fact, superior to the Old Testament Davidic kingship because Jesus is a suffering messiah who will rise from the dead and return at the end of the ages. Moreover, it is a messiahship of humble service. Nevertheless, it is a kingship of sovereignty and power because it is Jesus who will judge everyone in the end.[12]

The identity of Jesus is kept a mystery all along in the Gospel of Mark until the very end. The climax of Mark's narrative is the discovery of who Jesus truly is: the son of God (Mk 15:39). Note a twofold paradox. In the first place, Jesus is recognized, not in his eloquent preaching or in the stunning wonders of his miracles. Instead, Jesus is revealed as the son of God in his helpless, brutalized condition as he is nailed to the cross. Indeed, genuine "power is not self-attesting."[13] The second irony is that it is an outsider, a Gentile (and a Roman soldier at that) who recognizes and acknowledges Jesus for who he truly is.

For Mark, Jesus and the kingdom of God are correlates. The Gospel is about the messenger (Jesus) rather than the message itself. Mark has turned eschatology into Christology. His main theological themes become clear only as the narrative unfolds: (1) Jesus is the Messiah, and (2) the Messiah is to suffer and die and then rise from the dead.[14]

In sum, the proclamation of the in-breaking of the reign of God is not meant to be a threat, but good news. But what is "good" about the Gospel when it is all about suffering in what it offers?[15] The good news is that the kingdom of God, inaugurated by a suffering Messiah, opens breathtaking possibilities for humans. It is to this that we now turn our attention in the ethics of the Gospel of Mark.

ETHICS OF MARK

It is said that there is little ethical material in Mark.[16] The narrative nature of the Gospel and its imminent eschatology may account for this perception of a dearth of ethical teachings in Mark. After all, Mark is a straightforward account of the life of Jesus. In contrast, Matthew and Luke appropriate materials from Q that has a wealth of paraenetic, short sayings believed to have originated from the historical Jesus himself. Furthermore, Mark's imminent eschatology may account for why there is no need for a comprehensive exposition on the moral life.[17] What is the point of an extended treatise on morality since the end-time is expected at any moment? Moreover, some would even go so far as to claim that whatever little ethical materials may be in Mark are not applicable for any other time period. After all, because of the imminence of the Parousia (Jesus' second coming), Mark's ethic is, at best, merely an "interim ethic." Thus, not even his call to love, or any other admonition for that matter, can be applied in its original meaning and context because it was clearly intended for a short duration, what with a looming end of the world in sight.[18] Other scholars disagree and find much ethical materials in Mark.[19]

Narrative Genre

Unlike Paul who uses paraenetic letters to directly provide instruction, the evangelists employ the narrative genre in which moral teachings are drawn from the stories and biographies of people. "Didactic biographies" were common in the ancient world (e.g., Plutarch's "Lives"). Furthermore, note that the biography itself is the "gospel," the good news.[20]

Such narrative genre is particularly true for Mark because, unlike Matthew or Luke, it has no materials similar to Q's, that is, sayings that provide direct, explicit teachings on the moral life. Hence, readers have to look at the entirety of the narrative and distill the Gospel's ethical teachings.[21]

Mark's ethics is rooted in the story of Jesus. It is a "kerygmatic narrative" because the Gospel is preached in the narrative itself. "To proclaim the gospel is to tell the story of Jesus."[22] "To know the story is to be shaped by a new ethical vision whose horizon is none other than the in-breaking Kingdom of God."[23] The evangelist's narrative of Jesus' life has, in fact, an abundance of ethical materials: service to others, patient suffering, table-fellowship with the outcasts, help to the needy, confrontation with injustice and self-righteous behavior, and observance of the true spirit of the law. Thus, the Gospel of Mark can be described as a "narrative form of moral exhortation."[24] The narrative genre necessarily points to a response of action. The story becomes the reader's own narrative.

Because of the imminent second coming of Jesus, Mark is eschatological both in its theology and in its ethics. As already mentioned, since Christ is expected soon at any time, moral life in Mark is merely an interim ethic, and a very short transitory period at that. This interim ethic is characterized by (1) immediate, necessary changes in the status quo and (2) an elicited response of discipleship.

Change in the Status Quo

The requisite immediate change in the status quo involves a confrontation with evil, a reversal of outcomes and values, and the proper interpretation and observance of the law. God's in-breaking in human history heralds divine sovereignty, an end to the status quo, and a consequent pro-active fight against the evils that weigh people down.[25] Not surprisingly, it is a divine initiative that will be received with mixed reaction by people with different interests and concerns. Since they are the primary beneficiaries, the poor will welcome God's in-breaking, while the rich and the powerful will feel threatened because their privileged position is put in jeopardy. They are the ones with the most to lose.

Reversal of Outcomes and Values

In the first place, there will be a reversal of outcomes. The outcasts, the outsiders, and those whom society had excluded suddenly take center stage and receive the honored places in the kingdom of God: the ill and the blind (Mk 5:25–34; 10:46–52), the Gentiles (Mk 7:24–30; 15:39), and the little children (Mk 10:13–16).[26] Prostitutes, sinners, and tax collectors will enter the kingdom of God first before the ritually clean, law-abiding Pharisees who, in their self-righteousness, have no room for God's forgiveness and grace.

There will also be a reversal of values, especially with respect to power and suffering. These take new meaning, contrary to the public's usual understanding. True power is not in oppressing or dominating others. Rather, true power is in serving and even suffering (with Jesus) for others.[27] This reversal of values also flows from following the example of Jesus and from the

kingdom of God already present, even if only for those who have faith. Thus, disciples are imbued with a new way of thinking. They surrender their lives, rather than pamper themselves (Mk 8:35); they serve, rather than demand to be served (Mk 10:43–44); and they seek to be the last, rather than to be the first (Mk 9:35). This new way of thinking is emphasized on those three occasions when Jesus predicts his own suffering and death.[28] In contrast to the ethos of domination and oppression characteristic of the civil and religious leadership of that time, Jesus' disciples embrace an ethic of service.

These reversals of outcomes and values stem from God's absolute sovereignty. God's claims trump all else, even those of family ties. The kingdom of God takes precedence over all other interests or concerns. Thus, Jesus' kin are those who do the will of God (Mk 3:31–35). The apostles are rewarded a hundredfold for leaving all, including their families, in order to follow Christ (Mk 10:28–31). Those who deprive and divest themselves of everything for the sake of Christ, end up gaining everything, including perfection (Mk 10:17–22). And those in the eschaton neither marry nor are given to marriage (Mk 12:18–27). In other words, the kingdom of God "relativizes" the value of everything.[29] Corresponding changes are, therefore, also required in the way people live so that they might reflect this new scale of values even in the here and now. The kingdom of God has upended disciples' way of thinking.

Confrontation with Evil

Besides the reversal of values and outcomes as part of the change in the status quo, we also have the confrontation with evil. Controversy stories form about a fifth of Mark.[30] In fact, some observe that "Jesus' miracles possess an ethical dimension since they are powerful protests against the suffering caused by hunger, sickness, chaos, and Satan."[31]

Key elements of justice in the Gospel of Mark include freedom from the oppressive use of power and authority; liberation from the restrictions imposed by legal purity; the restoration of dignity to the marginalized, the outcasts, the lowly, the defenseless, and women; and the creation of a new family—the community of faith—in accord with God's will.[32]

If people are to appropriate the story of Jesus as their own, if the narrative of Jesus' public ministry is to be the blueprint of their moral lives, then his numerous confrontations to right wrongs and redress evil must surely have implications for how they ought to live. Surprisingly, scripture scholars and ethicists have not picked up on the ethical implications or significance of the controversy stories. These stories, I propose, point to an ethic of courageous, pro-active confrontation with evil. As we will see in a later section on discipleship, the virtue of fortitude is constitutive of discipleship. But the daring required of discipleship is not merely about patiently bearing oppression and persecution. It is also about facing off and rectifying evil. This is not an ethic of passive acquiescence. While it calls for patience, it is nevertheless vigorously engaged in rectifying iniquities. All this is about imitating Jesus as part of discipleship.

Observance of the Law

The proper interpretation and observance of the law is another area in which the kingdom of God changes the status quo. As we have seen earlier, Mark's imminent eschatology "dramatically relativizes the norms of the old order" (including the Torah).[33] Jesus does not abrogate the law. Rather, he transcends the Pharisees' legalistic and mediocre interpretation of the law and gives it new life. And Jesus radicalizes and even goes beyond the demands of the law in what he expects of his disciples. We see this in the case of divorce, which was permitted under Moses, but not under God's divine plan (Mk 10:2–9). We also find this in the invitation extended to the law-abiding rich man in search of eternal life to go further and sell all he has for the benefit of the poor, and then to follow Jesus (Mk 10:17–22).[34]

Jesus is free to interpret the law and to act accordingly. He is not bound by the law as interpreted by the religious leadership. But such freedom of Jesus "neither stems from nor flowers in license."[35] Rather, it leads to much tougher standards when it comes to guarding the human heart (Mk 7:1–23). Jesus is concerned with the interior disposition itself and not with superficial, outward observances. His freedom to interpret the law and to bring it to a new and higher degree of obedience comes from his power as the Son of God. It is an authority that flows from the absolute sovereignty of God heralded by the in-breaking of the kingdom.

No doubt, the observance of the law from the heart and the mind is a far more demanding ethic than one that is judged in terms of external appearances. Jesus takes it to a whole new level, not for the sake of God, but for the disciples' own well-being. He inaugurates a new terrain where disciples can be true to who they are and were created to be. For in embracing morality from their hearts and minds, they become the freest of men and women. Thus, one can say that Jesus' re-interpretation of the law inaugurates an ethic of freedom.

Discipleship

The change in the status quo requires a corresponding transformation and response from all, but especially from people who have been privileged to receive the gift of faith and who thereby see and recognize the in-breaking of God's reign in their midst. The response elicited is nothing less than discipleship. The predominant thinking among scholars is that Mark's ethic is an "ethic of discipleship."[36] His programmatic pericope (Mk 1:14–15) is followed immediately by the call of the apostles, who respond decisively to the invitation of Jesus (Mk 1:16–20). Discipleship is initiated by Jesus, as in his invitation to the apostles and the rich man in search of eternal life. More than the other Synoptic Gospels, Mark openly writes about the failings of the apostles. Nevertheless, these apostles struggle valiantly to follow Jesus despite their flaws and lack of understanding. This call to discipleship is not only central to Mark's theology and ethics, but also a constant theme running through the entire Gospel (Mk 1:16–20; 2:14; 3:13; 8:34; 10:52).[37] In what follows, we examine some of the key characteristics of such discipleship.

First, such discipleship requires a definitive response. The imminent Parousia has "compressed time."[38] There is great urgency with little time to waste. Immediate action is called for. Thus, the programmatic proclamation of the kingdom in Mark 1:14–15 includes an urgent call, indeed, a plea for repentance and belief.[39] The imminent end-time accounts for such haste. However, such decisiveness goes further than mere immediate response. Such commitment must also be evident in the willingness to embrace an uncompromising ethic.[40] Thus, Mark's ethics is extremely demanding in what it expects. We have already seen this in the invitation to the rich man to sell everything, to give to the poor, and to follow Jesus. We see this in the invitation extended to all to take up their cross and to follow Christ (Mk 8:34). In fact, the apostles provide examples of what it is to be decisive in one's discipleship. They immediately respond to follow Jesus, leaving all behind even before being promised or assured of any recompense in exchange (Mk 1:16–20).

A second key quality of discipleship is repentance. We find this in the programmatic proclamation (Mk 1:14–15) that summarizes the Gospel: (1) the reign of God is at hand, and (2) it requires both repentance and belief in the Gospel.[41] This pericope is a straightforward imperative that illustrates the impact of theology on ethics. It also provides a succinct answer to the question of why one ought to be moral.

Repentance consists of the following. It entails a readiness or even actual abandonment of everything to follow Jesus, as in the case of the apostles (Mk 10:28). It also requires a new way of thinking, one that is conformed to the reversal of values inaugurated by the in-breaking reign of God in which service takes precedence over being served, being last is better than being first, and losing one's life becomes key to saving it (Mk 8:35; 9:35; 10:43–44).[42]

Repentance must find expression in a new way of life. A new way of thinking must find fruition in a new way of living. Belief implies action.[43] An excellent example of such contrite response is the apostles' perseverance. Despite not always understanding what Jesus teaches and despite their shortcomings, they nonetheless persist in living their new life as his followers. The call to repentance and belief underscores the much larger point that faith requires action and is not merely about words or good intentions.

Third, discipleship is communal in nature. Discipleship blossoms to its fullness within a community of believers. Mark's ethics is, in fact, an ethics of discipleship within community.[44] This is significant because it highlights the social dimension of God's gifts. Faith, repentance, the call to discipleship, the response to such an invitation, and then the ability to persevere in such a response—all these are gifts from God. But they are gifts given not only for the benefit of the recipient but for others as well, including nonbelievers. On the one hand, the individual finds support from the rest of the community and is uplifted by the faith of fellow believers. On the other hand, the individual contributes to the vibrancy of witness within the community and supports others in their own appropriation and practice of the faith. Thus, believers mutually support and reinforce one another in their communion of faith. This social dimension to discipleship is best appreciated by juxtaposing the beginning and the end of the Gospel of Mark. It begins with the bold proclamation of the Gospel's programmatic synthesis (Mk 1:14–15), and it ends with an equally bold proclamation in commissioning the apostles to go forth and preach the Gospel to all creation (Mk 16:15). Disciples are vessels of grace for others in God's in-breaking reign. And even this seeming imposition of a duty turns out, in fact, to be yet another gift—the gift of participating in the work of God.

The communal nature of discipleship has another ethical implication to it. Disciples do not get to pick whom they serve or with whom they associate. It is God who makes these choices. Thus, the community of believers may be an odd mix of people. They may find themselves sharing the same faith, breaking bread, working side by side, or even living with fellow believers whom they would have never chosen on their own. Note, for example, how Jesus invites a rag-tag mix of apostles, including a tax collector (Mk 2:14; 3:14–19). Again, this is consistent with how the in-breaking of God's reign relativizes everything and upends long-held, unquestioned values and prejudices. Thus, it has been said that for Mark, "following Jesus inevitably entails imitating his deeds and words, seeking to obey his ethical teachings while emulating his life of self-sacrifice *in a loving acceptance of others, whoever they may be*."[45] Disciples are to be a paradigm themselves of what it is to be an inclusive community.

Jesus is critical of the manner by which the laws of purity had been misused to denigrate and exclude people. He welcomes into his community of faith those considered unclean. Thus, Jesus expels the demon from the daughter of the Syrophonecian woman with great faith (Mk 7:24–30). His second miracle of multiplying loaves of bread and fish to feed the multitudes is in pagan territory (Mk 8:1–9; 7:31). He commissions the apostles to preach to the ends of the earth (Mk 13:10). Indeed, Jesus challenges the conventional practice of purity laws in his time and is emphatic that what is important is what is in the heart, and not in the hypocritical, empty observance of rituals (Mk 7:1–23).[46] And, of course, there is the tax collector in Jesus' inner circle.

A fourth characteristic of discipleship is the imitation of Jesus. Markan ethics, just like the other Gospels, is not merely deontological. To be sure, obedience to God's will is central to the life and example of Christ and the message he preaches. Nevertheless, moral life is also teleological, in showing disciples the kind of person God created and calls them to be. In the Incarnation, Jesus provides a vivid, living example of what it is to be truly and fully human. He shows people who they truly are and the possibilities open to them. Consequently, at the heart of Mark's ethics, and the other Gospels for that matter, is the imitation of Jesus. "Discipleship and conformity to Jesus' way are the central features of Markan ethics."[47] Such an ethics of emulation is consistent with the narrative genre of the Gospel in which the ethics is drawn from the entirety of the story itself and in which the narrative of Jesus becomes the disciple's own. Jesus is the "model of moral behavior," obedient to the will of God, compassionate and faithful.[48] The Gospel invitation entails more than just following Christ. It involves imitating Jesus in "word and deed, life and death." Thus, disciples have to deny themselves and carry their cross (Mk 8:34), serve others (Mk 10:42–44), and preach the Gospel (Mk 16:15).[49]

In recognizing who Jesus truly is, people discover their own self-identity—as followers called to re-present Christ. "When we embrace Mark's answer to the question, 'Who do you say that I am?' we are not just making a theological affirmation about Jesus' identity; we are choosing our own identity as well."[50] To know Jesus is to follow him. Moreover, in being Christ-like in their moral choices, disciples shine forth in the divine image and likeness in which they were created.

A fifth feature of discipleship is its sacramental nature. In imitating Jesus, disciples in effect re-present Emmanuel, God with us.[51] This entails preaching the Gospel to the ends of the earth by continuing the work of Jesus in revealing God's reign in the here and now.[52] And just as Jesus makes the kingdom of God tangibly present through his miracles, deeds, and preaching, so too the disciples in the way they live and love together as a community of believers. Hence, theirs is an instrumental, sacramental discipleship, whether as individuals or as a group. In such self-identification with Jesus and in re-presenting Jesus through their discipleship, they become prophetic and proleptic. They are prophetic to the degree they live lives of witness and holiness. They are proleptic to the degree they already live in the eternal freedom won for them by Christ.

Such re-presentation is instructive because it reminds the followers of Jesus that discipleship is about making vivid and tangible once again that initial Jesus-event, but this time in their own lives (to the extent humanly possible). Disciples are not merely agents of Jesus (as in representing him), but they are real instruments in making Jesus truly present in the here and now, in the manner they live and love. Disciples are prophetic in such re-presentation, in the same way that the Old Testament prophets re-presented in their own lives what it was that YHWH expected of the nation Israel. It is an unmerited privilege to be chosen and empowered to do so.

Jesus is sacramental in effecting the in-breaking of God's reign in human history. He is the personification, the sacrament, and the foundation of the kingdom of God. As disciples continue his work of preaching, teaching, healing, suffering, and even dying for the sake of the Gospel, they too become sacramental in the continued unfolding of the kingdom of God. They are participants in Jesus revealing such kingdom down through history via the Holy Spirit.

A sixth element of discipleship is service. This is made clear in Mark 10:35–41 when James and John and the other apostles compete for status, honor, and power. It is a teaching moment, another illustration of the reversal of values that the reign of God inaugurates. Jesus notes that far from seeking self-aggrandizement and authority, true discipleship is about an ethics of service.[53] The kingdom of God is not merely one of many kingly reigns nor is it meant to complement Roman rule or Pharisaical-priestly religious leadership. Rather, the kingdom represents a whole new ethos, a new way of thinking and acting in which service, rather than power or dominance, is sought (Mk 10:42–45). In fact, Christ's messianic justice is characterized by service, especially to the needy and the marginalized. His is a servant authority in which power is used for the benefit of those unable to fend for themselves. Not surprisingly, we find the fullness of this servant authority, this messianic justice, in Jesus helplessly crucified for the sins of others and dying so that others might live.[54]

A seventh quality is the suffering that characterizes Mark's discipleship. Mark's ethics entails more than just ordinary service. It is, in fact, an ethics of "suffering servanthood."[55] Mark's imminent eschatology shapes his resulting "interim ethics" by requiring both a readiness in waiting for the Lord (Mk 13:33–37) and docility during this temporary period. Moreover, the imminence of Jesus' second coming gives strength to disciples for such patient endurance. They will have relief soon. Part of this perseverance is also animated by the promise of entering the kingdom as a reward for those who have been faithful. Thus, Mark's ethic has also been called an "interim ethic of suffering."[56]

To believe in the Gospel is to follow Jesus, and to follow Jesus is to suffer with him. Jesus himself explicitly links discipleship with suffering (Mk 8:34–35).[57] In fact, suffering is central to the Gospel. Recall the climatic resolution of what had slowly built up throughout the narrative on the mystery of Jesus' identity. Jesus is fully and profoundly revealed for who he truly is in the crucifixion: the Son of God, the Messiah. Disciples are invited to join Christ crucified, abandoned, forsaken, and mocked.[58] Thus, the ethics of Mark flows from his Christology.[59] This stress on suffering is consistent with the most likely life setting of the Gospel of Mark: that it was addressed to a persecuted Gentile Christian community in Rome at around the time of Nero. It was meant to encourage them to persevere in the face of their great distress.

An eighth feature of discipleship is the central role of faith. Much faith is needed. In the first place, Mark's ethics is eschatological because it entails watching and waiting. It is aptly called an "eschatological ethic of watchful discipleship."[60] Openness and docility are required because the precise dynamics and outcomes of God's ways and of the kingdom are hidden.[61] The identity of Jesus in Mark's narrative is a mystery and takes many twists and turns before being revealed in a surprise, indeed shocking, ending. This warns disciples against self-righteousness, dogmatism, and complacency in thinking that they know exactly the will of God. They cannot claim to know the fullness of God's will. All they can know with certainty is that such divine plans continue to unfold from a loving God.

Thus, discipleship requires humility and sincere prayers in constantly discerning the will of God. It also calls for a spirit of openness in whatever it is God may ask of the disciple, no matter how difficult, counterintuitive, or countercultural. God, the Lord of history, has a track record of surprising people with impossible or unusual tasks (e.g., Abraham, Moses, John the Baptist). In fact, Mark's intended readers (the persecuted Christians of Rome) have firsthand experience of such unusual and surprising demands from God. Discipleship has brought them nothing but grief, pain, and suffering. These exacting encounters with God merely underscore the importance of not shrinking from the difficult or even impossible things that God may ask of the disciple. Not surprisingly, Mark's ethics has been called a heroic morality.[62]

God has plans even if they are obscure to the disciple at the moment. The narrative of Jesus' life, death, passion, and resurrection is a case in point. Equally important, the disciple has to have a lively sense of mystery and never underestimate whatever surprising outcomes God may have in mind for the disciple. Creation-Salvation history itself has been fraught with such unexpected twists and turns, such as the creation of humanity, God's inbreaking in history, God's pursuit of human friendship, the Covenant relationship, the Incarnation, Calvary, and the special divine favors bestowed on the poor.

Openness and docility are essential, lest disciples impose their own views of how God's plan ought to unfold and, as a consequence, miss altogether God's graces right before their eyes. The prime examples of this were the Pharisees and the religious leadership of that first century who, despite their religiosity and their desire for a vibrant relationship with God, failed to recognize and accept Jesus for who he truly is, the Son of God. And this failure was due to their preconceived idea of how God was going to answer their prayers. Such requisite openness and docility are dependent on the depth of the disciples' faith. Profound faith enables disciples to accept and persevere in the surprising impossible or difficult tasks God often asks of them.

Great faith is also required because suffering and pain are integral to discipleship. Unlike Matthew or John, Mark does not provide his intended audience with the consolation of Christ's presence to assuage the afflictions they bear on account of Jesus in this interim period. They bravely soldier on, with the promise of a coming Parousia to sustain them. Thus, discipleship is made that much more demanding and difficult in not feeling the company of Jesus in their midst.[63] Suffering is borne without even a clear idea of the end for which they suffer, except for some vague promise of the reign of God taking hold. It is not at all clear how God's promised help in their torments will come about, as in the case of the spirit helping them in Mark 13:9–11. It is not at all clear how the promised hundredfold return for all that they had abandoned for the sake of Jesus will come about (Mk 10:30; 4:8, 20). Such knowledge would have eased the burden of the cross a bit and would have made the suffering more tolerable. Unfortunately, such concrete information is part of the hidden and mysterious ways by which God's reign and God's plans unfold.[64]

Furthermore, enormous faith is required because the motive for such heroic discipleship is not love. Unlike the other Gospels, Mark does not present love as the motive for discipleship, or even of Jesus dying on the cross for love. Instead, the motive is pure and simple obedience to the will of God.[65] Discipleship is not pursued in expectation of a reward (cf. James and John jockeying for position in Mk 10:35–45). Unwavering trust is called for.

Indeed, the demands of discipleship are enormous, and perhaps even unreasonable, from a human point of view. It requires a resolute and decisive response. It calls for sustained action. It entails bearing heavy burdens and crosses. And all these are to be done in the dark, that is, without any knowledge of how God's plans are to unfold precisely, except for the assurance that God always fulfills divine promises. Many of these unknowns and difficulties compound each other to form a synergy of uncertainties that make discipleship that much more exacting. These uncertainties are dispelled on the weight of God's word alone. The disciples are to take God's promise and invitation in Mark 1:14–15 at face value, on the basis of faith alone.

In sum, Mark's community of faith believes that since his resurrection, Jesus is now enthroned in the kingdom of God. The disciples realize that they are living in the period between the inauguration of the kingdom and its consummation. Their lives in this intermediate period have to be imbued with values that are consistent with and in anticipation of the Parousia. Moreover, it is important to live fruitful lives during this period of waiting (Mk 11:20; cf. Is 5:1–7).[66]

Why be Moral?

What is the basis for moral conduct in Mark? Why be moral? As mentioned earlier, Christology is the starting point of the Synoptic Gospels' ethics. The freedom of Jesus in correcting the misinterpretation and observance of the Mosaic moral precepts by the religious leadership of his time underscores the source and basis of morality: "Moral obligation is no longer determined by external observance of the prescriptions and prohibitions of the law; moral obligation is determined instead by the nature and activity of God and his Christ."[67] It is a theonomous ethic. It is God who wills such conduct, the God who exercises absolute sovereignty over creation and history.

Despite the claim that the interim nature of Mark's ethic renders it inapplicable for other generations, the discipleship elicited by the Gospel is, in fact, not limited merely to the contemporaries of Jesus, or the Gentile audience of Mark, but is meant for other time periods as well. After all, Jesus and the proclamation of the in-breaking of God's rule are intertwined, so much so that to do things for the sake of Christ is to do them for the sake of the Gospel and vice versa. Since the yet unfolding kingdom transcends the historical Jesus, discipleship continues down through the ages.[68]

Moreover, observe that there is no closure to Mark's narrative. It is simply an account of the disciples continuing the work of Christ. Readers are invited to supply the ending in the narratives of their own lives (hopefully in taking up the cross and in discipleship). In fact, the Gospel of Mark is best read and understood "rightly only through following Jesus in self-involving, self-sacrificial service."[69] Only in immersing oneself in the narrative that one reads does the Gospel come to life and bear fruit.

Finally, even the imminent eschatology of Mark is still relevant for current generations. His belief in a looming Parousia imbues his ethics with pressing urgency. An immediate and decisive response of discipleship is thus called for. Today, with the benefit of hindsight, people are aware of the delay in the second coming of Christ. No one knows when the end-time is to take place. Nevertheless, the same decisive response of belief, repentance, and conversion apply just as well to people of this age because of the shortness of temporal life during which they are able to requite God's initiatives. Moreover, in addition to such brevity, people do not know when their earthly journey is to come to an end or how it is to end. Consequently, Mark's ethics of watchful waiting is applicable today, even if under very different circumstances and expectations.

MARKAN PERICOPAE ON ECONOMIC MORALITY

The impact of Mark's theology and ethics on his teachings on economic morality is immediately apparent. To begin with, scholars' observation that there is little ethical material in Mark is borne out by the paucity of explicit moral norms on economic life relative to Matthew and Luke. In what follows, we distinguish passages that are clearly intended to be about economic life from those teachings on economic morality that are drawn by inference.

Explicitly Economic Pericopae

There are at least five pericopae that are directly and explicitly about economic morality, to wit:[70]

- Worldly concerns and the deceit of riches prevent the word of God from taking hold of people's lives and producing abundant harvest (Mk 4:18–19). [Immediate context: the parable of the sower and the seeds (Mk 4:3–8, 13–20).]
- Theft, covetousness, and deceit defile the person (Mk 7:22). [Immediate context: Jesus instructs the Pharisees and the scribes that what is even more important than external observances is what is in the human heart (Mk 7:1–23).]
- It does not profit people to gain the whole world but forfeit their souls in the process (Mk 8:36). [Immediate context: Jesus lays out the conditions of discipleship as self-denial, taking up the cross, and following him (Mk 8:34–9:1).]
- The rich are warned that it is only with great difficulty that they will be able to enter the kingdom of God. In contrast, those who have abandoned all for the sake of the Gospel will receive a hundredfold reward in this and the next life (Mk 10:17–31). [Immediate context: the rich man in search of eternal life.]
- Widow's mites (Mk 12:41–44): This is either a call to heroic generosity (to give from one's substance and not merely from one's surplus) or an indictment of the religious leadership's exploitative greed.[71]

In sum, these five explicitly economic pericopae warn about the dangers of wealth (Mk 4:18–19; 8:36; 10:17–31); condemn sinful economic conduct (Mk 7:22); laud complete trust in God alone (Mk 12:41–44); and promise manifold rewards for all that the disciple gives up for Christ (Mk 10:17–31).

Insights on Economic Morality by Inference

Besides the preceding passages, Mark's narrative has much more to offer on the ethical foundations of economic life. Since Mark is predominantly narrative (rather than paraenetic), the lives of Jesus, the apostles, and many others in the Gospel are potential sources for economic teachings. It is by inference or by imitation that we arrive at these economic norms. The most obvious ones are those from the lifestyle of Jesus: simplicity of life; charity and graciousness in humbly accepting gifts and support from others; and holy indifference with respect to possessions. Jesus rejoices, is thankful, and puts material gifts to good use when he has them (e.g., dining with others in table-fellowship), but he is just as content when he has little or nothing. Material goods are merely means for the larger end of promoting the kingdom of God.

In addition to these examples from the life of Jesus, note the following insights from many other passages. Radical dispossession and utter trust in God alone are praiseworthy, as seen in the examples of John the Baptist[72] and the disciples (Mk 1:6, 16–20; 2:13–17; 6:8–11). People reap what they sow; what they give will be measured back to them (Mk 4:24–25). There is value in itinerant mendicancy for the Gospel, as seen in Jesus sending the apostles to preach with no bread, bag, or money (Mk 6:8–11). Divine solicitude for people's material well-being is evident in Jesus being moved with compassion and feeding the multitudes (Mk 6:32–44; 8:1–9). Status or power should not be sought, for the greatest is the last and the servant of all (Mk 9:33–35; 10:35–45). Be cautious of venality and corrupting that which is holy, as seen in Jesus' cleansing of the temple turned into a "den of robbers"[73] (Mk 11:15–17; 12:38–40) and in Judas' betrayal of Jesus for money (Mk 14:10–11). Love ought to be the motive of economic agency, or moral agency for that matter, as seen in the two greatest commandments (Mk 12:28–34). People should hold nothing back from God, not especially their best, as seen in the anointing of Jesus with expensive perfume in Bethany (Mk 14:3–9). In sum, we can infer norms of economic morality from the various narratives and the little paraenesis that we find in Mark.[74]

SUMMARY AND CONCLUSIONS

How do these direct and indirect teachings on economic morality fit within the theology and ethics of Mark? To begin with, it is important to note that economic morality is not the principal motif of the Gospel. Mark is about the eschatological fulfillment of the Old Testament promises in the person of Jesus Christ and about the imminence of the end-time. Consequently, it would be wrong to use the Gospel of Mark as a handbook for upright economic conduct because that is not the intention of the work.

Nevertheless, both the explicitly economic pericopae and the inferences we can draw from the rest of the Gospel are consistent with and support Mark's theology and ethics. Clearly, these insights on economic morality fit within the imperative of change in the status quo and the call to discipleship. Radical dispossession, sole reliance on divine providence, spurning self-aggrandizement in power and status, and expending oneself in service for others—all these upend worldly values. Equally important, they are vital conditions of true discipleship.

Furthermore, some of these insights fit within an interim ethic in which the end-time is imminent. For example, the direct teachings clearly stress the danger of wealth in impeding people from pursuing and embracing wholeheartedly the kingdom already made present through faith (Mk 10:17–31; 4:13–20). Or wealth can prevent people from fully living their discipleship and discharging their duties (Mk 10:28–31; 6:8–11). Some would even say that the widow who gives her two small coins is an example of authentic liberation from slavery to wealth (Mk 12:41–44).[75] By any measure, wealth pales in comparison with the magnitude and enduring value of the kingdom. It is folly, indeed laughable, to even compare material possessions with living in God's reign.

Besides Markan theology and ethics, we can also use insights from social-scientific criticism to sharpen our understanding of some of these passages. Take the case of Mark 10:28–31. Peter reminds Jesus that he, along with others, had left everything to follow him.

The apostles left not merely their livelihoods or their properties; they had also left their families. The "kinship-economics" of that period accentuates the enormity of what Peter and the other apostles had given up. To give up not only livelihood or property, but even kin is to give up everything—economic survival, physical safety, community life, and social status. Worse, it is to endanger one's own kin because the family will be short-handed in farm work and may itself be put at risk in being unable to produce enough for its subsistence. This may even be the immediate cause of the persecution mentioned in verse 30. Their kin and the rest of society may persecute or hold in contempt those who had left their families in such a lurch.[76] It is unheard of in a kinship-economics to simply leave the family. (Mark 1:19–20 describes James and John leaving immediately their father and the hired hands in order to follow Jesus.) Families depended on one another for mutual sustenance and survival. This is particularly important in an ancient culture in which honor-shame and social status are central to one's self-identity and the extended family. To follow Christ is a profound sacrifice beyond mere economic deprivation. It is literally giving up everything.

Moreover, Mark 10:28–31 also speaks of divesting property. Viewed within the politics-shaped economics of that period, this was sheer folly. Such property presumably includes not only leaving behind a fishing boat, but walking away from land as well. This was significant because land was an inheritance. Ancestral land was treasured and was core to every Hebrew's security and identity. Not only was it essential for ensuring the family's livelihood and survival, but it was also the family's bequest from God, their tangible sign that they were part of the Chosen People.

Furthermore, such conduct was counter-cultural, particularly in an agrarian setting. The competition for arable land was intense, and estate accumulation was assiduously pursued because land was the source of wealth and power. This was especially so in a limited-goods society in which land was scarce. One could have more of it, but only at the expense of everybody else. Thus, giving up property, land, and kin could be viewed as a prophetic action—a prophetic critique of the social arrangement at that time in which power was used to amass even more land, thereby driving others to landlessness and destitution in the process.[77]

Viewed within the kinship-economics and the politics of that period, the call of Jesus to the apostles and to the rich man in search of perfection in Mark 10:17–22 was not merely radical. It was downright foolish! It was, in effect, stripping away the essential anchors of one's life that provided security and stability—property and social relationships. However, for the followers of Christ, such divestment was not folly but was about trusting in God alone. Kinship-economics and politics-economics underscore what to many will appear to be the unreasonable, if not ludicrous, price of discipleship. It was not a surprise that the wealthy man in search of eternal life walked away sad.

Social-scientific insights give us a better appreciation for how Jesus calls for a completely different set of values in these economic admonitions. His call and example of simplicity of life sharply contrasts with the royal and aristocratic lifestyles. His invitation to voluntary poverty is the antithesis of the elite's preoccupation with acquisition and accumulation. His selflessness is a counterpoint to their grasping ways. Instead of power and privilege, it is much better to be last and to serve others. Given the chance and contingencies of agricultural life, Jesus calls for generosity and assistance to the poor. Indeed, given these sharp contrasts, it is not surprising to see Jesus and the religious leadership of his time clash repeatedly.[78]

In sum, while these direct and indirect insights on economic morality are not principal themes in the Gospel of Mark, they are nevertheless important because they reveal how Markan theology and ethics can be put into practice in economic life. Moreover, viewed within their socioeconomic context, these teachings provide alternative core values to that of the ruling elite of that era.

NOTES

1. Verhey (1984, 75)
2. Matera (1996, 15–20)
3. Matera (2007, 22)
4. Duling (1992, 56–57)
5. Thielman (2005, 64–65)
6. Matera (2007, 12)
7. Marshall (2004, 81); Matera (1996, 20; 2007, 23)
8. Matera (1996, 24)
9. Matera (2007, 12, 15)
10. Schrage (1988, 138–39)
11. See Thielman (2005, 68–74) for a further exposition on the parallelism with the Old Testament.
12. Davies (1995, 329); Matera (2007, 18)
13. Hays (1996, 76)
14. Marshall (2004, 79, 93–94)
15. Hays (1996, 79); Marshall (2004, 60)
16. For example, see Houlden (1973, 41–42) and McDonald (1998, 108).
17. Burridge (2007, 168)
18. Sanders (1975, 31–33)
19. For example, see Burridge (2007, 159), Matera (1996), Verhey (1984, 78), and Via (1985).
20. Meeks (1986, 138; 1993, 189–92)
21. Burridge (2007, 156); Hays (1996, 73–75); Matera (1996, 13)
22. Matera (2007, 5, 9)
23. Matera (1996, 35)
24. Verhey (1984, 78)
25. Hays (1996, 88–91)
26. Hays (1996, 90)
27. Hays (1996, 88–91)
28. Matera (1996, 22)
29. Burridge (2007, 172–77)
30. For specific examples, especially the conflicts with the authorities, see Burridge (2007, 172–77) and Verhey (1984, 77, 79).
31. Matera (1996, 24). See also Marshall (1989, 63–64).
32. Nardoni (2004, 201)
33. Hays (1996, 87–88)
34. Burridge (2007, 172)
35. Verhey (1984, 79)
36. Burridge (2007, 179, fn 92)
37. Verhey (1984, 75)
38. Hays (1996, 89)
39. Mark uses "immediately" eleven times just in the first chapter alone (Hays, 1996, 89). See also Marshall (2004, 60).
40. Hays (1996, 87–88)
41. Burridge (2007, 179); Matera (1996, 15)
42. Matera (1996, 20–23)
43. Matera (1996, 21–22)
44. Burridge (2007, 182–83)
45. Burridge (2007, 185, emphasis added)
46. Nardoni (2004, 211–13). Note that this inclusiveness is also seen in the proper treatment and respect accorded to women. See Nardoni (2004, 213–14).
47. Schrage (1988, 139)
48. Matera (1996, 31–34)
49. Burridge (2007, 183–84)

50. Hays (1996, 79)
51. Verhey (1984, 74–82)
52. Matera (2007, 11–18); Verhey (1984, 74–75)
53. Burridge (2007, 177); Hays (1996, 81–82); Verhey (1984, 76–78); Via (1985)
54. Houston (2010, 101–3)
55. Hays (1996, 81–82)
56. Burridge (2007, 168, 172); Matera (1996, 30–31)
57. Verhey (1984, 75)
58. Hays (1996, 73–92)
59. Burridge (2007, 166); Hays (1996, 75–85)
60. Verhey (1984, 75–76)
61. Hays (1996, 88–91)
62. Verhey (1984, 74–82)
63. Hays (1996, 87–88)
64. Hays (1996, 83)
65. Hays (1996, 84)
66. Nardoni (2004, 205)
67. Verhey (1984, 80)
68. Matera (2007, 10)
69. Hays (1996, 91)
70. Clearly, there is a subjective element behind deciding which biblical passages are directly or indirectly about economic life. For example, Schmidt (1987) lists only two explicitly economic pericopae: Mark 10:17–31 and Mark 12:41–44. Of "secondary interest" to him are Mark 1:6; 1:16–20; 2:14; 4:19; 6:8–9; 8:34–37; and 14:3–9.
71. Myer (2008, 318–23) and Resner (2010) interpret this passage not as praise for the widow for her generosity, but as a prophetic indictment of the Temple's greed. Instead of receiving assistance from the Temple, the widow was, in fact, shaming the Temple by giving everything she had to live on—as if to underscore the exploitation of the Temple. (She should have been the one receiving assistance from the Temple to begin with.) Thus, note the following passages in which Jesus predicts the doom of the temple with not a stone standing on another (Mk 13:2b). See also May (2010, 492–93). An even stronger case can be made by looking at the preceding passages. From Mark 11:15 onward, we see the clash and testy exchanges between Jesus and the religious leaders. Immediately preceding the pericope on the widow's mites is Jesus' condemnation of the hypocrisy of the scribes, including an explicit reference to how they "devour widows' houses" (Mk 12:38–40).
72. Freyne (2004, 23) suggests that John the Baptist may have been persecuted by Herod Antipas, not for the reasons stated in Mark 6:14–29 but because of Antipas's concern that John the Baptist's popularity combined with his championing justice for the poor may provoke an uprising, which would cast him (Antipas) in an unfavorable light before his Roman patrons. This was the reason proposed by Flavius Josephus (*Ant.* 18.116–19).
73. The reference to the "den of robbers" is from Jeremiah 7:11. This is significant for our purposes because its immediate context in Jeremiah 7:5–11 is about the condemnation of economic injustice in Jerusalem. See Nardoni (2004, 205).
74. Mark 11:13–14, 20–24 is clearly an economic metaphor for a much larger point being made, such as the importance of bearing fruit for the gifts given to us. See Hanson and Oakman (1998, 105–6) for their exposition on how this episode on the fig tree refers to the nation Israel, its welfare, and its failure to live up to her calling.
75. Nardoni (2004, 210)
76. May (2010, 489–90)
77. May (2010, 490–95)
78. See Myers (2008) for an example of a political-liberationist reading of the Gospel of Mark that relies principally on social-scientific models.

Chapter Eight

Matthew

Matthew is believed to have been written in Greek for a Greek-speaking Jewish audience, most likely in Antioch (Syria). Most scholars date it in the last quarter of the first century, after the destruction of the Temple in Jerusalem (70 A.D.) and after Christian Jews had finally been expelled from the synagogue. The Gospel was clearly shaped by this internal clash among the Jews, as evident from the numerous conflict stories and the contrast between the church community and rabbinic Judaism. Moreover, note the scathing denunciations of the scribes and Pharisees. Far from being conciliatory in reaching out to win over its Jewish opponents, the Gospel asserts that the Christian community is, in fact, the Church that fulfills and lives up to the Covenant relationship of the Old Testament. Matthew is keen to make the case that far from abrogating the law, Jesus brings it to a genuine observance that is both internalized and more radical. The rift between the Jewish religious leadership and the Jewish Christians seemed to be deep and irreconcilable at the time of Matthew's writing. Nevertheless, despite their expulsion from the synagogue, Jewish Christians were still concerned (1) about the role of the law and commandments in their new life in Christ, and (2) about the sources and modes of authority, that is, whether they ought to follow the legalistic path of the priests or the more charismatic approach of the prophets.[1]

MATTHEW'S THEOLOGY

The Gospel of Matthew is drawn from at least three sources: Mark, Q, and an unnamed and unknown collection (many call it "M") that provides materials not found in the other Synoptic Gospels. Matthew reproduces 80 percent of Mark.[2]

Just like Mark, Matthew is a biographical narrative in which both its theology and ethics flow from the entire narrative itself and not from a piecemeal extraction of teachings. And just like Mark, Matthew's main interest is not in the message but in the messenger himself. Christ is the eschatological fulfillment of the law and the prophets. He is the Isaianic Suffering Servant who dies to atone for the sins of many.[3]

Matthew is also eschatological in its outlook. Jesus will come a second time, and this will mark the apocalyptic end of temporal life. However, Matthew's eschatology is different from Mark or even Paul in that the Parousia is not as imminent. There is an implicit acknowledgment of a delay in Christ's second coming, and as a result, Matthew does not have the same urgency that we find in Mark or in the Pauline letters. Moreover, in contrast to Mark, Matthew's delayed Parousia is mitigated by the consolation that Christ is already present in their midst within the Church. In addition, Matthew stresses the forthcoming judgment in the eschaton and is distinctive for its good news on the kingdom that Jesus had inaugurated.[4]

Matthew goes to great lengths to show the link and continuity of his Gospel with the Old Testament. For example, note how it traces the genealogy of Jesus all the way to Abraham through David (Mt 1:1–17). Note the dreams, the astrological signs, and the conflict with oppressors (Mt 2). Observe the parallelisms in the life of Jesus and Moses. We have the slaughter of the innocents (Ex 1:15–20; Mt 2:16–18), the flight from danger (Ex 2:15–22; Mt 2:13–14), and the return to their birthplace (Ex 4:20; Mt 2:19–21). Moreover, just as Moses gave the law, Jesus in his Sermon on the Mount is the new teacher. And like Ben Sira, Jesus is also a teacher of wisdom. And just as Moses presented Israel with the Pentateuch, Jesus in Matthew presents five sermons. Each of these sermons ends with "When Jesus had finished these sayings (parables)" (Mt 7:28; 11:1; 13:53; 19:1; 26:1), reminiscent of a Moses typology (Dt 32:45).[5]

MATTHEW'S ETHICS

Matthew includes nearly all of Mark's materials and then strategically inserts large blocks of didactic materials, such as the Sermon on the Mount [from Q], the parable of the ten virgins [from M] (Mt 25:1–13), and the parable of the last judgment [from M] (Mt 25:31–46).[6] We examine some the distinctive features of Matthew's ethics in the following sections.

Jesus Christ

Just as in Mark, the starting point of Matthew's ethics is his Christology.[7] After all, as noted earlier, the evangelist is interested more in the messenger than in the message. Matthew's "principal ethics" consists of the claims that

God has come to be with humanity through Jesus, that Jesus fulfills the law and the prophets, and that Jesus builds a new community of faith.[8]

Jesus is presented as a teacher and as a new and greater Moses.[9] He is the embodiment of Wisdom, and it is in Jesus that we see the revelation of the will of God. For this reason, Jesus can interpret the law. This new interpretation is conveyed through his instructions (as the new and greater Moses) and through the example of his life. Not only does he teach his disciples to be merciful (Mt 5:7), but he himself also shows what it is to be merciful (Mt 9:27–31; 15:22–31; 20:30–34). He himself demonstrates how to accept persecution for the sake of righteousness (cf. Mt 5:10 and 27:17–26), how to turn the other cheek (Mt 5:39; cf 26:52–53), and how to carry one's cross (Mt 16:24; 26:47–27:50).[10] The law is sometimes viewed in Jewish circles as the embodiment of Wisdom. In the new dispensation, Jesus is the embodiment of such Wisdom.[11] Matthew is an ethics of "proper righteousness in the kingdom of heaven" as revealed in the life and the preaching of Jesus.[12]

Some describe Matthew's ethics as sectarian because it offers a specific vision of the good that must be embraced and followed, namely: that which is revealed by the Gospel and by the life of Jesus Christ. It is sectarian in that the authority of Jesus is foundational.[13]

Kingdom of God

The kingdom of heaven (God) is at the heart of Matthean theology and ethics. For example, while Mark refers to the kingdom only fourteen times, Matthew has fifty references to it, of which thirty-two are unique to him. (Nine of the fifty come from Q). Many of these are found in the parables. Matthew has the same understanding of the kingdom as Mark, namely, as God's reign already present in the here and now and in the future. Matthew 13 constitutes the centerpiece of his teaching on the kingdom of heaven.[14]

Matthew prefers to use "kingdom of heaven" as a circumlocution to avoid using the divine name of God. It is equivalent to the "kingdom of God." Besides, the kingdom of heaven may be the more appropriate and accurate term to use because heaven is the realm where God's reign is already fully and firmly acknowledged. Thus, it is more explicit and highlights the Gospel's ethical dimension and its call for greater righteousness.[15]

This kingdom refers to God's sovereignty, reign, or rule. It pertains to God's governance of the world. God is sovereign even of history (Ex 15; Is 30:7; 41:9; Ps 87:4; 89:11; 136). In the Old Testament, the use of "kingdom" is heavily apocalyptic, and the reference to God as king implies the triumph of God's reign over earthly kingdoms and the eventual relief of those persecuted and oppressed.[16]

The kingdom of heaven is already present "spatially and temporally" because of Emmanuel ("God with us"; Mt 1:23). Not surprisingly, the kingdom of heaven has ethical implications. To begin with, it calls not only for great joy but also for bold and decisive risk-taking, as in the cases of the man who sells everything in order to buy the field with the treasure or of the merchant who sells everything he has in order to buy the one fine pearl of great value (Mt 13:44–46). Admission to the kingdom requires repentance. Moreover, it demands "fruits" from people's lives (Mt 7:16, 20; 21:28–32; 21:43; 25:40). Such "fruits" must be in the form of greater righteousness (Mt 5:17–20).[17]

There is a certain mystery associated with the kingdom. Chapter 13 of the Gospel is descriptive of the kingdom: Matthew 13:1–9, 18–23 (seeds and sower); 13:24–30, 36–43 (weeds); 13:31–32 (mustard seed); 13:33 (leaven); 13:44–46 (hidden treasure and pearl); 13:47–50 (net); 13:51–52 (householder). Common to these is the hidden nature of the kingdom's growth and development. It blooms ever so slowly without people noticing or understanding it. It is assailed by wickedness (Mt 2:16; 4:3–11; 6:13; 12:25–37; 13:19). Nevertheless, it prevails over evil and flourishes.[18]

In sum, the kingdom of heaven is the ethical horizon for Matthew. The Sermon on the Mount, deemed by many as a summary of Matthew's moral teachings, is an ethics for the kingdom. Jesus himself exemplifies the Sermon on the Mount. Moreover, the law is interpreted in light of the kingdom. In other words, the kingdom is the reference point for Matthean theology and ethics.[19]

Righteousness

Matthew builds on Mark's point on the importance of doing the will of God and puts it within the Jewish understanding of "doing righteousness."[20] Righteousness (*dikaiosynē*)[21] is the central concern of Matthew's ethics (Mt 3:15; 5:6, 10, 20; 6:1, 33; 21:32). The key passage is Matthew 5:20 on the importance of surpassing the righteousness of the Pharisees and scribes. Such greater righteousness is reflected in the disciple's moral life and choices (Mt 6:19–7:27).[22]

Faith and action are essential and inseparable in Matthew. Behavior is just as important as belief. In fact, the proof and test of people's deeply held convictions are their moral conduct. In other words, belief and action work in tandem with one another.[23] Thus, note the importance accorded to hearing the word of God and then acting accordingly (Mt 7:15–23, 24; 23:1–12; 23:23; cf Hos 2:19). Recall the parable of the sheep and the goats (Mt 25:31–46). The final judgment is about right action.[24] Or consider Jesus' constant admonition to produce fruit and not to follow the example of the Pharisees.[25] It brings to mind the warning of Jeremiah 7:4. Not everyone who cries out, "Lord! Lord!" will escape the judgment, but only those whose faith finds expression and fruition in their lives. The kingdom requires a new way of life for the disciples, new wine in new wineskins. Bearing fruit is essential in Matthew's moral world. Thus, note how the Gospel's parables (Mt 24–25), interspersed with the need to be watchful, are about yielding harvest while there is still time.[26]

Matthew's call for greater righteousness can also be described as an ethics of character formation. For example, in the six antitheses in Matthew 5:21–48, Jesus stresses the importance of virtue and the person's interior disposition, rather than the external observance of the law.[27]

The emerging majority opinion of scholars is that righteousness in Matthew pertains to "the performance of righteous deeds in obedience to God." It is about doing the will of God. This has been called "ethical righteousness."[28]

Matthew's call for a fruitful righteousness does not give rise to the problem of "works-righteousness"[29] for at least two reasons. First, the fruit expected of disciples is that of a self-forgetful response to the invitation extended by Jesus. For example, in the parable of the sheep and goats (Mt 25:31–46), we find that those who were about to be rewarded were not even aware of why they were being singled out for such distinction. Their past actions were not a calculated response to get them in God's good graces. Rather, their actions of feeding the hungry, clothing the naked, and visiting the sick and imprisoned were spontaneous acts—from the heart. Matthew ethics is not about a contrived, rewards-seeking works-righteousness, but a virtuous, self-forgetful righteousness.[30]

Second, Matthew's ethics is not works-righteousness because it is ultimately founded on grace. We see this in the centrality of the saving effect of Jesus' death—the soteriological significance of the Christ event (Mt 1:21; 20:28; 26:28). Grace is clearly manifest in discipleship because it is Jesus who initiates and sustains that discipleship, and not the disciples themselves. Thus, it is Jesus who invites the early followers, culminating with Jesus promising to send the Holy Spirit to strengthen and enlighten them (Mt 10:20). Furthermore, Jesus reveals to the apostles what was not given to others (Mt 11:25–27). In addition, we also have Christ's healing ministry and his presence in the Church (Mt 1:23; 28:20). The parables on the kingdom speak of grace as God's gift, as in the parable of the vineyard owner (Mt 20:1–16) and the wedding banquet (Mt 22:1–14). Matthew's righteousness is steeped in God's grace at every step of the way.[31] The entire Gospel is founded on the gratuitous gift that is the kingdom of God. Ethical righteousness is merely a response to this earlier divine gift.

Righteousness (*dikaiosynē*) is central to both Matthean and Pauline thought. However, they differ from each other in their emphases. Matthew's righteousness underscores right conduct in following the will of God in the observance of the law. In contrast, Paul's righteousness refers to three things: as a quality in God, as God's eschatological gift, and as descriptive of how a person stands before God. For Paul, righteousness is a gift stemming from the death and resurrection of Jesus. For Matthew, righteousness means right conduct. Just like James, Matthew believes that authentic faith necessarily manifests itself in action.[32]

Another way of explaining the difference is to pose this issue in terms of the indicative and the imperative. The "salvific indicative" is inseparable from the "ethical imperative."[33] For Paul, the indicative makes the imperative possible. Hence, it is a gift. In contrast, in Matthew, the "full and final expression of the indicative" is seen in living up to the imperative.[34] By putting the Sermon on the Mount soon after the initial proclamation of the kingdom (Mt 4:17), Matthew is accentuating the link between the salvific indicative (kingdom of heaven) and the moral imperative (Sermon on the Mount).[35] Only by wholeheartedly embracing their duties do people see and appreciate the fullness of who they are as new creatures (the indicative). In other words, "ethical conduct does not accomplish salvation, but without it the personal appropriation of salvation is impossible."[36]

Even as Matthew and Paul differ in their emphases, they nonetheless share the same understanding of righteousness as being comprised of two constitutive components. First, we have the gift of God's action in liberating people from their distress. Second, we have the requisite ethical conduct that follows in the wake of such salvation. Thus, righteousness has two sides to it, to wit: the primary gift and empowerment (the indicative) and the demand for a corresponding response that flows from such grace (the imperative). Paul emphasizes the gift, while Matthew highlights the attendant ethical responsibilities. The two go together, even in the case of Paul. With salvation comes a corresponding demand for action.[37]

Perfectionist Ethic

Besides upright living, Matthew's call for greater righteousness presents a second, related requirement. Many interpret the six antitheses in Matthew 5:21–48 as the internalization and radicalization of the law. Some disagree with such a reading. For them, it is much more accurate to say that Matthew's morality is a perfectionist ethic.[38] Clearly, these antitheses invite a much deeper and more profound observance than the Pharisees' lackluster or, worse, self-righteous observance of the law. What is most telling, however, is how Matthew ends these antitheses. The climax is in the invitation extended to the disciple to be perfect as the heavenly father is perfect (Mt 5:48; cf Lev 19:2).

This call to greater righteousness and to be perfect as the Father is perfect is not a mere abstract call to holiness or an empty invitation that is short on specific content. As we have seen earlier, Matthew's ethics is ultimately based on a bedrock foundation: the will of God. This, too, is not a mere hazy, abstract will of God. In the first place, it is a divine will that is concretely revealed in the life and preaching of Jesus Christ. Jesus is the model of what it is to obey the divine will and to imitate God. Indeed, Jesus Christ is the paradigm of what it is to be truly and fully human.

Second, besides the aforesaid six antitheses, the teachings of Jesus Christ present specific ways by which one grows in perfection in the ordinary course of the day (e.g., giving to all who beg or borrow, loving one's enemies, turning the other cheek). These teachings are not exhaustive, but they highlight the general direction and spirit of the will of God concerning human conduct.[39] Actual deeds, and not bold but empty words, lead to greater righteousness and the imitation of God's perfection (cf. Pharisees).

Reward and Punishment

Matthew stresses accountability and judgment, reward and punishment more than any of the other evangelists. There is a clear link between the Parousia and judgment. Note the numerous references to Gehenna (Mt 5:21–30; 10:28; 18:9; 23:33), judgment (Mt 16:27; 5:21–22; 7:1–2; 10:15; 11:22, 24; 12:36, 41–42; 13:24–30, 49–50), reward (Mt 5:12; 6:1–18; 10:41–42; 25:34), punishment, and unimaginable weeping and gnashing of teeth in the afterlife (Mt 7:23; 8:12; 13:42, 50; 22:13; 24:51; 25:30, 41).[40] Eschatology is a critical reference point in Matthean ethics. Ethical behavior is appraised relative to its consequences and divine judgment. The litmus test is whether or not an act is in accord with God's will. God's will is the standard for what is good or evil.

Clearly, accountability is a major theme in Matthew. Implicit in such accountability is an acknowledgment of the following set of premises: (1) There is a divine order and, therefore, there are objective expectations. (2) There are consequences to moral choices. (3) Evil will come to an end, and good will be revealed and rewarded. (4) There is hope for those who persevere in doing good. (5) Only goodness has enduring value.

In addition, such divine judgment implies a human duty of stewardship. After all, people can be held to account only for something entrusted to their care. This is important for economic ethics, or for moral life for that matter, because it is a warning against adopting a proprietary attitude in which people have an exaggerated notion of autonomy in doing whatever they please with whatever they own, including their freedom.

Community Ethics

For Matthew, discipleship takes place within the setting and support of a community of believers, in particular, the *ekklēsia* (church) (e.g., Mt 18:15–20). Just as the Chosen People were supposed to be a nation different from all the other nations in the way they cared for one another, the community of disciples is also called to be a "contrast society." Thus, note the beatitudes in the Sermon on the Mount. Or consider the radicalized and internalized observance of the law following the example of Jesus. Thus, we have a communal ethics of perfection, that is, a community of character and virtue in which doing good becomes second nature to people.[41]

Just as we have seen in Mark, there is a social dimension to discipleship. The discipleship elicited takes place in community and is never a purely individual or private endeavor. Furthermore, discipleship entails being a community and working with whomever Christ may have invited. Thus, note the "unclean" people (e.g., tax collectors) in the table-fellowship of Christ. Moreover, there will be the hungry, the naked, and the needy, whom disciples should receive gladly and serve (Mt 25:31–46). Such inclusiveness and unconditional welcome for those whom they would have otherwise avoided is an occasion for personal growth and community formation.[42] It is also an important stepping-stone to learning what true love of God and neighbor is.

On Law

Jesus is neither antinomian nor legalistic like the Pharisees and scribes. He firmly affirms his continuity with and reverence for the law (Mt 5:17–20).[43] The life of Jesus is, in fact, the fulfillment of the law. He is the eschatological completion of the Old Testament prophecies and narratives.

Matthew underscores the role of Jesus, not as a new lawgiver but as the "true interpreter of the law."[44] There is really nothing new in Matthean ethics, only a re-appropriation of what has been there all along. Jesus strongly affirms the law (Mt 5:17–20; 23:23), even oral tradition (Mt 23:2).[45]

What is distinctive in Jesus' approach to the law is the manner by which he internalizes and radicalizes the observance of the law, taking it to a much higher set of standards. In particular, the law is to be lived in love and mercy, along the lines of the prophetic tradition. Thus, the law and the prophets depend on the two great commandments (Mt 22:40). *This is the hermeneutical key to interpreting the Gospel of Matthew: Jesus as the true interpreter of the law who lived and fulfilled it in love.* Thus, to imitate Jesus is to fulfill and to live the law in love and mercy. Righteousness is merely about living up to Christ's interpretation of the law.[46]

Jesus is going to take the law to a higher level of observance, that is, to "a more radical righteousness of the heart, intensifying the demand of God far beyond the letter of the law."[47] In Matthew 5:21–48, we see the juxtaposition of six antitheses to emphasize this new, higher standard of observance from the heart. The law is not merely about murder, but about anger or calling someone a fool; not merely about adultery, but about lustful thoughts; not merely about divorce in certain cases, but about a universal prohibition. The law is about moving from oath-taking to plain honesty, from retaliation to total nonviolence, and from the love of one's friends to the love of one's enemies.[48]

The Sermon on the Mount presents a new and surpassing righteousness compared with how the law had been lived until then. Christ looks beyond the minimum requirements of the law to examine what lurks in the human heart (Mt 5:22, 28; 6:21; 12:34; 13:15; 15:8, 18; 19:8). The beatitudes present the qualities disciples ought to have. Jesus interiorizes the observance of the law.[49]

Mercy and Compassion

Mercy and compassion are hallmarks of Matthew's ethics. Consider, for example, the numerous people healed by Jesus. Or recall how Jesus takes on the burdens of others' sins (Mt 8:17; cf., Is 53:4). Such compassion is not in competition with the law. Thus, Jesus instructs the cured leper to present himself to the priest and to follow the prescriptions of the Mosaic laws for those who are healed (Mt 8:4).[50] Note how Matthew 22:40 is appended to Mark. Love and mercy are foundational, not only for observing the law, but also for the entire moral life itself. Consider, too, Matthew 20:1–16 on the vineyard owner and Matthew 25:31–46 on the sheep and the goats. In both of these parables unique to Matthew, love and compassion are the central points. In this regard, Matthew's ethics is very much along prophetic lines. Compare, for example, Matthew 22:40 with Hosea 6:6. This is consistent with Jesus presented as a lawgiver (Sermon on the Mount), as another Moses. This is yet another point of intersection and continuity with the Old Testament.[51]

The importance of mercy and love as key hermeneutical lenses is illustrated by how Matthew resolves the tension inherent in his Gospel. On the one hand, it calls for greater righteousness in the observance of the law. But, on the other hand, there is also need for compassion and love. Matthew resolves these competing claims by stressing the central role of forgiveness.[52] At the end of the day, mercy trumps the rigorous demands of justice and greater righteousness.

Eschatology

Matthew's eschatology affects his ethics in manifold ways. First, because of the delay in the second coming of Jesus, we find more explicitly ethical materials in Matthew than in Mark. Ethics takes on even greater importance in the face of a much longer temporal existence.

Second, Matthew stresses consequences, judgment, and punishment for people's actions as part of the end-time.[53] The eschaton is an important reference point for ethical life. Thus, note the five sets of additional materials in Matthew 24:36–25:46 that are not in Mark on the implications of the eschaton for accountability: the suddenness of the end (Mt 24:37–46), the faithful and wise servant (Mt 24:45–51), the parable of the wise and foolish maidens (Mt 25:1–13), the parable of the talents (Mt 25:14–30), and the final judgment (Mt 25:31–46).

Third, the presence of Jesus in the here and now is important for ethics because it is an empowerment and encouragement that disciples need not shrink before that which is difficult or impossible. It is also a reason for why disciples need not be anxious (about what they are to eat or drink) and why they ought to keep their gaze fixed intently on the kingdom of God. After all, "the world according to Matthew is *a world stabilized and given meaning by the authoritative presence of Jesus Christ*."[54]

Fourth, even as the eschaton is the reference point, the present is, nonetheless, as important, as seen in the mandate to preach the Gospel to the ends of the earth, to be a city set on a hill, and to be watchful in waiting. (Thus, recall the aforesaid additional block of materials in Mt 24:36–25:46.) This period of waiting is important; it has high expectations regarding moral conduct.[55]

Confrontation with Evil

There is a tension in Matthew between the call for greater righteousness and the call for mercy and compassion, between the indictment of the scribes and the Pharisees and the call to love.[56] The call for mercy, forgiveness, and love of one's enemies trumps all else and has the final say, if only because of the example of Jesus forgiving and never giving up on the Pharisees. Hence, Matthew does reconcile these competing tensions. Nevertheless, one teaching we can infer from the Gospel narrative of Jesus' life and public ministry is the duty to confront and redress evil. Acquiescence to evil is neither humility nor meekness. Nor is it what forgiveness and mercy are about. There is an obligation to meet evil head-on and to rectify it (e.g., Mt 18:15–20), although at the end of the day, there has to be always a readiness to forgive and to love despite the harm inflicted by evil. Forgiveness and mercy, on the one hand, and confronting and rectifying evil, on the other hand, are not mutually exclusive.

Moreover, such tension can also be resolved within the "need to shepherd vulnerable sheep."[57] This is an obligation not to give up on those who have strayed and to treat one another with great compassion and forgiveness (Mt 18:12–35).

MATTHEW'S MORAL NORMS ON ECONOMIC LIFE

Matthew incorporates all of the pericopae we examined in Mark that directly or indirectly teach about economic morality.[58] The only exception is Mark's account of the widow's mites (Mk 12:41–44) which we do not find in Matthew. In what follows, we again distinguish insights that are explicitly stated in the Gospel from those that are merely inferred. In addition, we will also differentiate passages that are unique to Matthew and those that come from Q. We will not repeat the pericopae that we had already examined in Mark.

Explicitly Economic Pericopae from Q

On hope for the poor: The kingdom of heaven belongs to the poor in spirit (Mt 5:3). *On property and possessions*: Disciples are to be unmeasured in their self-donation, giving to everyone who begs from them and refusing no one who borrows from them (Mt 5:42). Store heavenly treasures that are enduring, that neither moth nor rust can destroy, and that thieves cannot steal (Mt 6:19–21). People can only serve one master, and they have to choose between letting their lives center on God or on mammon (Mt 6:24).

On confidence in God's providential care: God knows people's needs and will provide for them bounteously, even before they ask. They should be uninhibited in asking God for their daily provisions (Mt 6:7–15).[59] Moreover, they should not worry about what they are to eat or drink and how they are to be provisioned for tomorrow, for God cares for them profoundly. Rather, they should set their hearts on the kingdom of God (Mt 6:25–34). People should never hesitate to ask, to seek, and to knock, for they are God's children (Mt 7:7–11).

In sum, Matthew's explicitly economic pericopae drawn from Q include a warning on the dangers of wealth and the folly of people setting their hearts on it (Mt 6:19–21, 24), a call for unconditional generosity (Mt 5:42), an invitation to trust in the providential care and love of God (Mt 6:7–15, 25–34; 7:7–11), and a message of hope to the distressed in assuring them of their ultimate vindication (Mt 5:3).

Explicitly Economic Pericopae Unique to Matthew

Good deeds such as almsgiving should not be done with the goal of drawing others' praise or esteem. Rather, they are carried out for the sake of God alone, who in turn will reward such meritorious works in good time (Mt 6:1–4). To feed the hungry, clothe the naked, welcome the stranger, and visit the sick or those imprisoned is to do so to Christ Himself. This is the parable of the final judgment in which people will get their just deserts (Mt 25:31–46).

In both of these passages unique to Matthew, note the importance of both self-forgetfulness and solicitude for others' well-being. Both pericopae call for disinterested self-giving. As mentioned earlier, those who were being commended were completely spontaneous and devoid of self-consciousness or expediency in responding to the plight of those who were in need. They were not even expecting a reward for their acts of kindness.

Inferred Teachings on Economic Morality from Q

On discipleship's exacting demands: Jesus has not even a place to lay his head (Mt 8:19–20). There is need to follow Jesus without delay, with not even time to bury one's own father (Mt 8:21–22).[60] *On material support for the preaching of the Gospel*: In sending the apostles to itinerant mendicancy, Jesus reassures the apostles that the laborer deserves his food (Mt 10:9–10). *On the providential care of God*: Jesus encourages the apostles not to be afraid of persecution because they are worth more than the sparrows under God's care. Nothing will ever happen to them without God's will (Mt 10:28–33).

On the fatal danger of materialism and the folly of self-indulgence: Jesus tells the tempter that people do not live by bread alone but by the word of God (Mt 4:1–11). Jesus contrasts John the Baptist's simplicity of life with the frivolity and luxury of Herod's court (Mt 11:8–9). There is need to be ready for the end-time, unlike the people of Noah's time who were too preoccupied with eating and drinking and, consequently, were oblivious to the evils they had wrought upon themselves (Mt 24:37–41). *On stewardship and accountability*: The returning master puts his faithful steward in charge of his possessions (Mt 24:45–51). In the parable of the talents, the faithful servants exercised initiative and care for the properties entrusted to them by their master (Mt 25:14–30).

On how faith must be reflected in our economic conduct: John the Baptist calls for changed lives that befit repentance (Mt 3:7–10). *On amity and the value of prudential peacemaking*: It is better to settle with one's opponents before reaching the courts (Mt 5:21–26). *On an optimistic engagement with the world and on the goodness of material goods*: Unlike John the Baptist, Jesus eats, drinks, and enjoys the hospitality of his hosts (Mt 11:18–19). *On the importance of justice and mercy*: The Pharisees take great pride in their observance of the law to its minute details, but fail in its larger and more consequential demand for just and merciful conduct (Mt 23:25).

Inferred Teachings on Economic Morality Unique to Matthew

On unconditional generosity as part of stewardship and gratitude for what have been received: The apostles received the Gospel without pay; they are to give to others without pay (Mt 10:8). The unmerciful indebted servant is unable to extend to others the same generosity that he himself had received in being forgiven of his even larger debt (Mt 18:23–35). The vineyard owner kept bringing in the unemployed until the last hour of the day, but nevertheless still pays them a full day's wage (Mt 20:1–16).

On the just use of properties: The vineyard owner uses his property to provide employment and dignity for those who could not find work (Mt 20:1–16). *On the inevitable forthcoming reversal*: The meek shall inherit the earth (Mt 5:5). *On the forthcoming accountability and judgment*: The weeds will be separated from the wheat at harvest time (Mt 13:24–30). The good fish will be kept and the bad ones discarded when the net is sorted at the end of the day (Mt 13:47–50). *On recognizing the authentic value of faith and giving up all for it*: The man sells all he has in order to buy the field with the hidden treasure (Mt 13:44). The merchant sells all he has in order to buy that one pearl of great value (Mt 13:45–46). *On venality and corruption*: Judas betrays Jesus for thirty silver pieces (Mt 27:3–10).[61]

Comparison with Mark

In contrast to Mark, Q adds "a strong ethical tone to [the] portrayal of Jesus."[62] This is apparent in the many direct, explicit teachings on economic life we find in Q. This disparity may also be partly explained by Mark's dependence on narrative, from which we draw his ethics and theology. In contrast, Q is paraenetic (exhortations and direct sayings).[63] Thus, note how Mark has only a handful of explicit teachings on economic morality, with the rest being inferred from his narratives.

The materials drawn from Q clearly reflect the same concerns over possessions and wealth that we find in Mark. Q also warns of the danger of riches in impeding discipleship and fidelity to the will of God. It also affirms the exacting demands of following Jesus: radical dispossession and decisive, total response. However, Q pushes into new terrain by highlighting the futility, indeed the folly, of pursuing earthly riches in lieu of heavenly and enduring treasure. Moreover, it not only reiterates the need for unconditional generosity but also explicitly states reasons for doing so—because people themselves have received much from God.

Unlike Mark, Q dissuades disciples from anxiety for their daily provisions by repeatedly presenting them with various images: of how God has even numbered the hairs on their head and of how they are more valuable than the lilies and grass of the fields and the sparrows in the sky for which God provides. God's providential care is real, constant, and effective. Q also provides hope to the poor and the distressed by assuring them of their certain relief and vindication from all that afflict them.

The materials that are unique to Matthew repeatedly stress (1) the importance of good works, (2) the need for an active concern for the well-being of others, especially the distressed, and (3) a forthcoming day of judgment, punishment, and rewards. Faith must find expression in good works. Stewardship for the many tangible blessings people receive requires not merely gratitude. They also have to use these gifts for others' welfare. In moving from Mark to Matthew, we find a much more vivid imagery of what God expects (e.g., parable of the sheep and goats at the final judgment) and many more teachings that are relevant for economic morality (e.g., parable of the vineyard owner). And, of course, Q introduces paraenetic passages.

MATTHEAN ECONOMIC ETHICS IN THE CONTEXT OF ITS THEOLOGY AND ETHICS

Matthew's economic ethics readily flows from and is shaped by the Gospel's theology and ethics. To begin with, recall that for Matthew, discipleship occurs within community, that is, the Church (*ekklēsia*).[64] Economic issues will inevitably have to be addressed whenever people live in community. After all, there will be need to allocate, to collaborate, and to share. Given the finitude of the earth's resources and people's material needs as embodied beings, there will be competition for the gifts of the earth. People's economic conduct will either build up or tear down communities. Not surprisingly, Matthew's economic ethics explicitly emphasizes people's moral obligations for one another's well-being.

Second, accountability is a major feature of Matthew's economic ethics. Recall the parable of the sheep and the goats and the positive obligations for sharing and solicitude for others' welfare (Mt 25:31–46). Or note the parable of the wise and foolish virgins and the need for prudential planning and foresight (Mt 25:1–13). These are in addition to the parables drawn from Mark on the talents and the importance of stewardship and a work ethic (Mt 25:14–30) and on the wicked tenants who kill the vineyard owner's son (Mt 21:33–41). Common to these parables is the day of reckoning when people will be asked to render an account of what had been entrusted to them. *There is an eschatological dimension to Matthew's economic ethics. Alternatively, one could say that there is a constitutive economic dimension to his apocalyptic-eschatological ethics.*[65]

Third, Matthew's economic ethics provides a message of hope for the marginalized and the defenseless. Note Jesus' ministry to the tax collectors and sinners (Mt 9:10–13; cf Hos 6:6 on the primacy of mercy over sacrifice); the integration of outcasts in the eschatological community (Mt 8:11–12); the people with whom Jesus identifies in the parable of the sheep and the goats (Mt 25:31–46); and the little ones who are welcomed by Jesus (Mt 18:1–6).[66]

Furthermore, the notion of the kingdom of God, which is central to Matthew's ethics, is best appreciated in its larger socioeconomic context. In the Ancient Near East, the king is the protector of the weak and the one who restores justice and equilibrium in the order. Thus, to say that the kingship of God is at hand is to provide hope for the poor, because it is God who will take up their cause and provide them protection and look after their needs. It is in this context that one ought to read Isaiah 61:1.[67] In other words, reference to the kingdom of God has immediate economic ramifications because it has a direct link to those who are oppressed or distressed. We cannot just spiritualize the kingdom. It has a this-worldly consequence. It champions the poor and the powerless.

Fourth, Matthew's economic ethics is about character formation and internalizing the law. The law is radicalized and brought to a much higher level of observance by Jesus in Matthew. This naturally includes its economic ordinances and statutes. Such interiorization is part of Matthew's call for greater righteousness. It can also be described as an ethics of character formation. For example, in the six antitheses in Matthew 5, Jesus stresses the importance of virtue and the person's interior disposition, rather than the external observance of the law.[68] Of course, an excellent example of such surpassing righteousness in economic life is the parable of the sheep and the goats (Mt 25:31–46). The duty of mutual assistance, dating all the way back to the Old Testament statutes, is not enforced by the royal court or the Temple, but by people's conscience and good will. It is enforced in the human heart, for which people will ultimately be held to account on the day of judgment. Besides, belief is manifested in action; belief and action are mutually reinforcing.

Fifth, insights from social scientific criticism can sharpen our understanding of these passages relevant for economic life. These teachings advance a set of values that are the exact opposite of the elite's conduct at that time—inordinate wealth acquisition, unrestrained land accumulation, exploitation of the weak, enrichment at the expense of the poor, and conspicuous consumption. Just as in the Gospel of Mark, Jesus presents an alternative way of life, one that is characterized by simplicity, generosity, mutual care and assistance especially for the poor and marginalized, trust in the providence of God, and service. In understanding the socioeconomic conditions of that era, we get to appreciate how Greco-Roman attitudes and practices are incompatible with discipleship in Christ.

SUMMARY AND CONCLUSIONS

Matthew calls for a greater righteousness. The Gospel affirms Jesus as the new interpreter who radicalizes and internalizes the law. Matthew and the other synoptic teachings on economic life are non-legislative, but are instead aimed at voluntary compliance from the heart. They are enforced in the internal forum—a matter between the person and God. Examined in terms of continuity with the Old Testament, Matthew does not cite or cross-reference Mosaic statutes or ordinances on economic morality. However, in terms of the spirit of the law, Matthew is very much in line with the longstanding Jewish ethos and praxis of care for the poor and helpless, as seen in the parable on sheep and goats. This is true for all four Gospels.

NOTES

1. Burridge (2007, 194, 199); Hays (1996, 109); Matera (1996, 37); Meeks (1986, 137); Verhey (1984, 82)
2. Luke reproduces only 65 percent of Mark (Brown, 1997, 263, 265).
3. Burridge (2007, 188); Thielman (2005, 88)
4. Hays (1996, 104–7); Matera (2007, 29)
5. Burridge (2007, 190); Hays (1996, 95); Meeks (1986, 141)
6. Hays (1996, 95); Matera (1996, 36)
7. Burridge (2007, 189) goes so far as to conclude that "Matthean Christology has a conspicuous ethical dimension."
8. Burridge (2007, 199)
9. Hays (1996, 93ff); Thielman (2005, 91–93)
10. Thielman (2005, 90)
11. Thielman (2005, 89–91)
12. Burridge (2007, 203)
13. Meeks (1986, 136–43)
14. Burridge (2007, 203); Matera (1996, 37; 2007, 27, 29)
15. Duling (1992, 50); Matera (2007, 27–28)
16. Duling (1992, 50–52)
17. Duling (1992, 57–58)
18. Burridge (2007, 204)
19. Matera (1996, 43, 49, 53)
20. Matera (1996, 49)
21. This is the Greek translation of the Hebrew *tzĕdāqâ*.
22. Verhey (1984, 86–87)
23. Meeks (1986, 136–37)
24. Donahue (2005, 26)
25. Thielman (2005, 105–10)
26. Marshall (2004, 125); Matera (2007, 35–36, 49); Theilman (2005, 105–9)
27. Verhey (1984, 87)
28. Hagner (1992, 101, 118)
29. "Works-righteousness" means that we can earn our own salvation or justify ourselves before God through our works alone.
30. Verhey (1984, 90–92)
31. Matera (1996, 59–62)
32. Matera (1996, 44, 59, 61; 2007, 31)
33. The "indicative" describes who we are, while the "imperative" mandates our duties. The salvific indicative describes how we are now new creatures in Christ. This is followed by the ethical imperative, which is a statement of our obligations that come with being new creatures in Christ.
34. Matera (1996, 61)
35. Matera (2007, 30)

36. Matera (1996, 62)
37. Nardoni (2004, 234); Furnish (1968)
38. Meeks (1986, 136–43)
39. Meeks (1986, 136–43)
40. Burridge (2007, 202); Hays (1996, 106–7); Matera (1996, 56). See also Matera (2007, 47–50) for a detailed account of the forthcoming judgment as part of the Parousia.
41. Hays (1996, 96–99). Hence, as I will argue later, Matthew's ethic is more teleological than deontological.
42. Burridge (2007, 220–21); Hays (1996, 93ff)
43. Hays (1996, 95–96); Verhey (1984, 82)
44. Burridge (2007, 211–12)
45. Burridge (2007, 207); Keck (1984, 51); Verhey (1984, 83)
46. Burridge (2007, 207, 211–12); Marshall (2004, 118–20); Thielman (2005, 88–89)
47. Hays (1996, 95)
48. Hays (1996, 95–96); Matera (1996, 46; 2007, 33); Thielman (2005, 88–89)
49. Thielman (2005, 89); Verhey (1984, 86). This is very much along the lines of virtue ethics and character formation.
50. Matera (1996, 52–53)
51. Hays (1996, 101, 107); Matera (1996, 35, 52–53)
52. Hays (1996, 101–4)
53. Hays (1996, 106–7)
54. Hays (1996, 109, emphasis in original)
55. Hays (1996, 109)
56. Hays (1996, 101–4, 109)
57. Thielman (2005, 107–9)
58. The following pericopae are identified as pertinent to economic morality by Donahue (1989), Esler (1987, 165–69, 196), Gillman (1991), Johnson (1981, 12–13), Karris (1978, 117), Oakman (1986, 8–9), Pilgrim (1981, 184), Schmidt (1987), Squires (2006, 179), and Zimmerman (2003).
59. Cf. manna in the desert (Ex 16:4) (Nardoni, 2004, 229).
60. Discipleship demands a decisive and total response that entails leaving everything behind. This requirement of a definitive break with the past is underscored by the intentionally exaggerated admonition to turn one's back on the sacred filial duty of burying one's father. The hyperbole is used for its shock value as in the case of the seeds producing thirty-, sixty-, or a hundred-fold (Mt 13:8).
61. Other passages that scholars have cited as related to economic life include: Mt 22:1–14 (parable of the great feast), Mt 17:24–27 (temple tax), Mt 21:28–32 (parable of two sons, one obedient and the other disobedient), and Mt 13:51–53 (parable of the householder).
62. Brown (1997, 265)
63. Burridge (2007)
64. Hays (1996, 97) notes that only in Matthew (16:18; 18:17) do we find explicit reference to *ekklēsia*.
65. Hays (1996, 106–7)
66. Nardoni (2004, 233) likens Christ's acceptance of these people to the Suffering Servant in Isaiah, who takes on himself others' infirmities.
67. Dupont (1977, 38–41)
68. Verhey (1984, 87)

Chapter Nine

Luke-Acts

Economics-related passages from the Gospel of Luke and the Acts of the Apostles[1] are as extensive as they are impressive. These two works taken together form the longest part of the New Testament. Any serious study of biblical economic ethics requires a careful consideration of Luke-Acts because of the amount of attention they devote to economic morality.

SETTING IN LIFE

Setting

The majority opinion is that the author of Luke-Acts was a Gentile Christian because these works were written in impeccable and stylish Greek. Some suggest that the author must have been a Jew since Luke-Acts clearly demonstrate extensive knowledge of the Old Testament. However, this view has been rejected because of the error in Luke 2:22 concerning the purification of the parents of Jesus at the temple. Any Jew would have known that only the mother, not both parents, is subject to this purification rite. Consequently, most scholars believe that the author was most likely a proselyte or a Gentile "God-fearer," that is, a non-Jew who had adhered to the Jewish faith and attended synagogue prior to subsequent conversion to the Gospel of Jesus Christ.[2]

Both Luke and Acts name their intended recipient: Theophilus, a Latinized Greek name (Lk 1:3; Acts 1:1). While some say that Theophilus is symbolic of all "lovers of God" as the intended recipient, others are quick to note that Theophilus is addressed as "most excellent," indicative either of the author's patron or of someone with high rank in society. Moreover, such respectful salutation was standard, indeed expected, in Hellenistic circles.

Furthermore, it is evident from Luke 1:4 that Theophilus had already been taught the faith and that Luke-Acts were meant to build further on such initial instructions. Many scholars believe that the Gospel and Acts were written for a Greek audience.[3] Thus, unlike Matthew, Luke's genealogy of Jesus goes all the way back to Adam and Eve and not merely to Abraham (Lk 3:23–38). Jesus belongs to all of humanity and not merely to the nation Israel.[4]

This Hellenistic audience may also partially explain why Luke-Acts, in contrast to Matthew, have many more explicit admonitions on economic life. Matthew addressed a Jewish audience and, consequently, we can presume that they were familiar with the numerous Old Testament ordinances governing economic morality and with the Jewish ethos of concern and care for the poor. Luke, on the other hand, was writing for a Gentile audience. They were unlikely to be conversant with Hebrew economic norms or with Jewish practices regarding assistance to the poor. Moreover, many of them were from the wealthy classes steeped in the Greco-Roman mindset of looking down on the poor, associating only with people of their own class, and building patron-client relationships. Thus, Luke faced the double task not merely of educating readers on caring for the marginalized, but also of changing ingrained cultural practices among his intended audience.

Luke-Acts were not meant to be a response to critics, cynics, or adversaries of the faith. These works were "internal" documents in that they were intended to reassure Gentile converts about the certainties and the firm foundations of their faith, in light of the fierce opposition and socio-political persecution they endured. Moreover, they were written to give these Gentile Christians a deeper understanding of the larger theological-ethical context of their beliefs. Luke's audience consisted of suffering Christians in a Greco-Roman society who wanted practical advice on how to live the Gospel, who needed to be reassured that their sacrifices were for a purpose much larger than themselves, and who were keen to know where they fit within God's salvation history and plans.[5]

Since Mark is widely accepted to be a source of Luke, the latter could not have been written earlier than the 80s. Most authors date it anywhere from the late 70s to the mid-90s, at the latest.[6] Together, Luke and Acts constitute about a quarter of the New Testament.

Who Were the Addressees of Luke-Acts?

The Lucan community is believed to be comprised of both the destitute and those with considerable means, and others in between.[7] Many early Christians were believed to be property owners, what we would consider middle class today.[8] However, many would have also been from the lower end of the income-wealth spectrum judging from Luke-Act's message of hope and championing of the poor, its severe critique of the rich, and its call for the unselfish sharing of goods.[9]

Contrary to the popular characterization of Luke as the "evangelist of the poor," the growing consensus among scholars is that the writer should, in fact, be more aptly called the "evangelist of the rich and the respected."[10] The rich were most likely the primary addressees of Luke-Acts because of these works' prologues, the people highlighted in their narratives, and their message.

First, Luke-Acts were addressed to Theophilus, who is respectfully called "most excellent" (Lk 1:3; Acts 1:1). Such addressees were standard practice in that particular era as an acknowledgment of patrons and benefactors. Furthermore, the use of "most excellent" as part of the salutation indicates that this was a real person and not a generic literary construction to stand for all "lovers of God." The address suggests that Theophilus was a person of stature within the community. Furthermore, Luke-Acts were written in high Hellenized literary style, suggesting that the author was a person of some means from the upper class of that society who had the luxury of time and a quality education.[11] Consequently, these works stood a good chance of receiving not only a hearing, but even a sympathetic reading from the well-off and the leisurely classes because they were written by one of their own.

Second, the upper classes would have readily identified themselves with many of the characters in Luke-Acts because their narratives describe people from their own ranks: wealthy and powerful Zacchaeus (Lk 19:1–9); the tax collectors (Lk 3:10–14); the rich ruler in search of perfection (Lk 18:18–25); the Pharisees in whose homes Jesus dined (e.g., Lk 7:36); Jairus, the synagogue leader (Lk 8:40–56); property holders within the community (Acts 2:45; 4:34–37); homeowners hosting the early Church in breaking bread together (Acts 2:46); people with enough means to be able to support the ministry of Jesus, the apostles, and the early Church (Lk 10:38–42; 8:1–3; Acts 16:14–15, 40).

Consider, too, the many high officials who embraced the Gospel: Cornelius and his family (Acts 10), the pro-consul Sergius Paulus (Acts 13:4–12), prominent men and women in Beroea (Acts 17:11–12), the synagogue leader Crispus and his family (Acts 18:8), and many others who enjoyed status and honor within their communities. Clearly, Luke-Acts describe the early Church not as a fringe movement, but as a mainstream community that even upwardly mobile classes would be comfortable to be part of and be identified with. Even the characters in the parables of Jesus were about people they could relate to.[12]

Third, note Luke-Acts's concerns and message regarding proper economic conduct: caution on the idolatry of wealth and the need for detachment, the need to properly use and share wealth, the imperative of caring for the destitute, and the admonition to accept those "beneath" one's social class as an equal. These make sense only if they were addressed to the wealthy rather than the poor. Thus, recall the harsh woes to the rich in the beatitudes (Lk 6:24–26) and the numerous warnings concerning the impending reversal of fortunes between the rich and the poor. These were addressed particularly to the wealthy members of the community who had yet to change their attitudes vis-à-vis possessions.[13] In addition, the teaching on patron-client relationships made sense only for those affluent enough to be able to give substantial alms or to give banquets.[14]

In sum, the primary addressees of Luke-Acts were most likely the rich in light of these works' prologues, their concern over proper economic conduct, and their narratives of people whose lives had been changed by Jesus and his Gospel.[15]

LUKE'S THEOLOGY

We can better appreciate the theological context of Luke-Acts by examining two concerns they address, namely: (1) the question of God's fidelity to the promise made to the Chosen People and (2) the delay in the Parousia.

Problem #1: Theodicy

Luke-Acts are said to be a theodicy. Recall that these works were intended for a Hellenistic audience and were written sometime after the failed Jewish uprising (70 A.D.). Given the sorry plight of the Jewish nation at the hands of their Roman conquerors, how could they, the Gentile "God-fearers," take God's promises at face value? With the destruction of the Temple and the break-up of the nation Israel, who were supposed to be God's Chosen People, how seriously ought they take the Gospel of Jesus Christ since it is the same God who had seemingly broken the promise made to Abraham that had been repeatedly affirmed in the Covenant?

In response to these legitimate concerns, Luke-Acts point out that Jesus Christ is, in fact, the fulfillment of God's promise in the Old Testament. The Incarnation, life, passion, death, and resurrection of Jesus Christ, the Anointed One, are the crowning moment of the promise made to Abraham and the culmination of the Sinai covenant. It is Jesus Christ, the Messiah, who has brought salvation to the nation Israel. We find this to be a recurring theme throughout both works.

Narrative

Matthew establishes the link between his Gospel and the past by citing Old Testament passages that Jesus fulfills. In contrast, Luke-Acts are more subtle in showing the connection by carefully crafting details that would immediately be recognized by readers familiar with the Old Testament.[16] For example, the events leading up to the birth of John the Baptist and Jesus are reminiscent of the promise of a child made to Abraham and Sarah (Gn 17:15–8:15) and to Hannah (1 Sam 1).[17] Note the correspondence between Mary's Magnificat (Lk 1:46–55) and Hannah's prayer (1 Sam 2:1–10). In line with the twelve tribes of Israel, the new dispensation is founded on the twelve apostles (Lk 6:12–16). And even after the loss of Judas, the number twelve is preserved with the appointment of Matthias as a replacement (Acts 1:15–26). We find this traditional division of the twelve tribes of Israel even in the messianic banquet (Lk 22:28–30).[18]

Luke devotes a lengthy segment of his narrative to the journey to Jerusalem where the Gospel is preached (Lk 9:51–18:14). The Church ("reconstituted Israel") is born on Pentecost in Jerusalem and in the Temple (Acts 1–3). The Gospel is preached to all the nations and to the ends of the earth from Jerusalem (Acts 1:8).[19] Even the description of the early Church community in which goods are shared in common and no one is in want (Acts 4:34) brings to mind the Deuteronomic vision of having no poor in the land of Israel (Dt 15:4).

Observance of the Law

Jesus notes that in inaugurating the reign of God, he is not abrogating the law. In fact, he is emphatic it is easier for heaven and earth to pass away, than for one dot of the law to become void (Lk 16:17). The Ten Commandments and the two great commandments are to be observed (Lk 18:20; 10:25–28).

We see a similar deference for the law in Acts. Even as the Council of Jerusalem does not require Gentile Christians to observe Mosaic dietary laws and circumcision, the Gentiles are nonetheless admonished to abstain from food sacrificed to idols, from blood, from the meat of strangled animals, and from sexual immorality (Acts 15; 21:25).

Paul not only readily identifies himself as a product of Pharisaism, but is also proud of his heritage. He is not antinomian or against the Temple. In fact, he even employs the law to defend himself in the face of accusations trumped up by his own people that ultimately lead to his imprisonment in Rome (Acts 21–28).[20]

Prophetic Literature

Of the Synoptic Gospels, it is Luke that puts repentance and conversion front and center (e.g., Lk 3:8–9; 11:32). This is very much along the lines of the prophetic call for contrition and renewal.[21] Acts 3:22–23, 25 explicitly identifies Jesus as the forthcoming prophet along the lines of Moses described in Deuteronomy 18:15–19. Jesus, innocently condemned to death, is the "righteous martyr" of the wisdom literature. Compare, for example, the Wisdom of

Solomon 2:12–13, 17–20 and Acts 3:13–15; 7:51–52. In contrast to Mark's mournful lament of abandonment as Jesus is dying ("My God, my God, why have you forsaken me?" [Mk 15:34]), Luke opts for the royal lament psalm (Ps 31:5) with Jesus peacefully committing himself to the Father (Lk 23:46). Indeed, whether as the Isaianic Suffering Servant, or the forthcoming prophet, or the righteous martyr, Luke's description of Jesus relies heavily on the Old Testament as a reference point. He goes to great lengths to show the continuity of Luke-Acts with the Old Testament.[22]

Even more telling is the inaugural lecture of Jesus (Lk 4:16–30). Scholars agree that this passage is programmatic of the entire Gospel and mission of Jesus. It is a synopsis of the entire work and a concise statement on the identity of Jesus Christ (the Anointed One on whom God's Spirit rests), his mission (to preach the good news), and the concrete effects of preaching the good news (freedom for prisoners, sight to the blind, release to the oppressed, and a year of favor from the Lord).

At the heart of this inaugural lecture are Isaiah 61:1–2; 58:6 and the Jubilee Year (Lev 25). Isaiah uses the image of the Jubilee Year (Is 61:1–2) to give the Babylonian exiles hope for their eventual redemption. Isaiah 58:6 is about the centrality of justice in God's divine order. And, indeed, captive Israel regained her freedom, recovered the land promised to Abraham and his descendants, and worshiped once again in the Temple. The assurances of the prophets had been fulfilled and a remnant did survive to reconstitute Israel.

Luke wrote for people who were keenly aware that God's plan of salvation was yet incomplete and continued to unfold. They found themselves in "exile" too and awaiting their own liberation. Luke addressed a people awaiting the fulfillment of God's long-promised Messiah. In using Isaiah 61:1–2 and 58:6 to describe the mission of Jesus, Luke was in effect reassuring the Chosen People that their days of waiting had come to an end, just as their Babylonian exile ended. It was now their turn to find release from their captivity. God has faithfully lived up to the promise in the person of Jesus Christ, the Anointed One on whom God's spirit rests. Jesus is the "spirit-empowered servant" described by Isaiah.

Thus, this inaugural lecture affirms the recurring theme of "promise and fulfillment" that runs throughout the Gospel. Indeed, the use of Isaiah 61:1–2 and 58:6 is not about Jesus enforcing the Jubilee Law ("the year of favor from the Lord") in his own time. Luke 4:16–30 is not about a legislative Jubilee, but an eschatological Jubilee.[23] Jesus is inaugurating a new age and bringing to fruition and completion God's plan of salvation.

Finally, we have the early Church's community sharing of goods. The followers of Jesus are of one heart and one mind. They generously give according to their means and take only what they need. As a result, no one in the community is left in want (Acts 4:34). Clearly, this is the fulfillment of

Deuteronomy 15:4. This is once again Luke showing how the early Church is indeed the restored people of God in continuity with the Old Testament.[24]

Summary

What we have is not an abandoned Chosen People of God, but rather a divided people, with a righteous remnant welcoming and accepting the fullness of God's self-revelation in the person of Jesus Christ, and the rest not only rejecting him but also putting him to death. The promise lives on; it is fulfilled in those who have accepted Jesus Christ as the Messiah. In fact, these can be called the "bearers of the fulfilled promise."[25] But there is more, for the fulfillment of the promise continues to unfold.

As early as the Old Testament, it was already understood that God will extend salvation to all the nations of the earth through Israel. Thus, in the New Testament, we see the Gospel of Jesus Christ preached by the righteous remnant of Israel to the Gentiles, indeed, to the ends of the earth. Luke presents the formation of a "new" people of God comprised of Jews, Samaritans, and Gentiles—a new community that transcends ethnic, cultural, and social differences. Far from questioning the trustworthiness of God's word, the Hellenistic audience of Luke-Acts has, in fact, reason to be joyful because they themselves, as followers of Jesus Christ, are living proof of God's unfolding plan of salvation. They, too, just like their Jewish peers are aptly called "bearers of the fulfilled promise."

In sum, Luke puts in a great effort to establish the continuity between the Old and the New Testament. Luke-Acts are the reassurance of God's fidelity. God has a plan. And it is a plan of salvation that will inevitably come to fruition.

Problem #2: Delayed Parousia

In both the Pauline letters and in the Gospel of Mark, we see the expectation of an imminent Parousia. Paul is driven by a deep sense of urgency. He admonishes, pleads, and cajoles the church communities to embrace decisively the Gospel of Jesus Christ and to let their newfound faith be reflected in the way they lived and loved. There is no time to waste, no room for temporizing, for the day of judgment is close at hand with the second coming of Jesus Christ. In the Gospel of Mark, the suffering Church is encouraged to persevere. For with the Lord's imminent second coming, their pain and sacrifices for their faith are at an end.

By the time of the writing of Luke-Acts, this belief in an imminent Parousia was becoming a problem, indeed, even an embarrassment. The Lord seemed to be taking a long time in coming back. Meanwhile, the suffering continued, with no relief in sight. In addition, there was a constant shadow of uncertainty in which God's reign, while already inaugurated, still waited to be completed. It was the tension of living in an age of the "already" and the "not yet."

An important contribution of Luke-Acts to biblical theology and ethics is its resolution of this dilemma of a much-delayed Parousia.[26] Prior to Luke-Acts, human history was divided into two time periods: the age prior to Jesus and the end-time. The Jesus event is the dividing line separating these two ages. Because of the belief in the imminent second coming of Jesus Christ, the inauguration of the reign of God in the public ministry of Jesus was believed to be the prelude to the end-time.

Luke-Acts resolve the problem of a delayed Parousia by introducing a third age, a middle period of waiting. This is the era of the Church and its mission. Salvation history is divided into three main periods: (1) the time of the law and the prophets all the way up to John the Baptist (Lk 16:16); (2) the Incarnation, ministry, death, and resurrection of Jesus Christ; and (3) the era of the Church and its mission, from the ascension onwards (Lk 24:51).[27] Only after this third period do we have the Parousia, and no one knows how prolonged this third period might be.

Instead of Jesus Christ returning, it is the Holy Spirit that comes down to empower the Church. Instead of immediately bringing the kingdom of God to completion, Jesus elicits the Church's participation in bringing to fruition the reign of God in the here and now. Again, just as in establishing continuity with the Old Testament, Luke is subtle in deflecting the focus from an imminent Parousia to a much longer period of waiting. To be sure, Luke echoes Mark and Paul on the need to be always ready for the Lord's second coming (Lk 21:34–36). Nevertheless, Luke dials down the sense of urgency and immediacy. Consider the following distinctive Lucan touches.

In all the Synoptic Gospels, we find Jesus preaching for the first time soon after his temptation in the desert. Note the similarities and the differences in the presentation of the materials. Unlike Mark 1:15 and Matthew 4:17, Luke removes reference to the kingdom of God being at hand (Lk 4:15). In the parable of the sower and the seeds, Mark 4:20 and Matthew 13:23 emphasize the superabundance of heeding the Word of God. In contrast, Luke 8:15 stresses the importance of patience in producing fruit from the Word of God.

All the Synoptic Gospels state the conditions of discipleship similarly, with the exception of Luke adding and accentuating the daily nature of such demands (Lk 9:23; cf Mk 8:34; Mt 16:24). What might appear to be an insignificant addition of the word "daily" in Luke is, in truth, pivotal. Instead of describing discipleship as a one-time decision, Luke presents it as a commitment that has to be reaffirmed in the harsh and tedious day-to-day struggles of people.[28]

The parable of the pounds is part of the Triple tradition.[29] Mark 13:33–37 puts this parable within the context of the Parousia, starting from the prediction of the destruction of the temple, the signs and the troubles of the end-time, the timing and the coming of the Son of Man, and the parable of the fig tree (Mk 13:1–32). All point to the need and the urgency of being prepared for the coming of the Lord. Similarly, Matthew 25:14–30 situates the parable within the context of the Parousia and preserves the same account and order in Mark. However, Matthew goes even further than this and appends materials from Q that highlight the forthcoming Parousia: the need for watchfulness (Mt 24:37–42), the requisite vigilance as that of a householder taking the necessary precautions against a break-in (Mt 24:43–44), and the model of the faithful and wise steward whom the master rewards on his return (Mt 24:45–51). Matthew also adds the parable of the ten maidens and their lamps awaiting the arrival of the bridegroom. Five were wise, but five were foolish in not bringing enough oil for their lamps (Mt 25:1–13). And after his account of the parable of the pounds, Matthew once again adds materials unique to him in the parable of the last judgment, with the separation of the sheep from the goats. Clearly, the message is unmistakable in both Mark and Matthew: getting ready for the forthcoming day of judgment.

Luke 19:11–27 uses the same parable of the pounds to make a different point. Unlike Mark and Matthew, he does not situate it within the context of an imminent Parousia or of the final judgment. Instead, Luke places the account of the parable by itself, toward the end of the journey to Jerusalem, immediately after the episode with Zacchaeus. Even more telling, however, is the twist that Luke adds to parable. Observe how he carefully prefaces his account of the parable with the following: "he [Jesus] proceeded to tell a parable, because he was near to Jerusalem, and *because they supposed that the kingdom of God was to appear immediately*" (Lk 19:11, emphasis added). Instead of using the parable to stress the need to produce fruit in preparation for the coming of the Lord, as in the case of Matthew and Mark, Luke emphasizes the *long-drawn effort* of producing abundant fruit for the Lord. In Luke's account, Jesus employs the parable to disabuse people of their belief in an imminent Parousia. It has even been claimed that the nobleman of the parable who went away on a trip is, in fact, Jesus himself who now sits at the right hand of God (Acts 2:33).[30]

These are but some of the subtle changes Luke employs in shifting the focus from an imminent Parousia to the importance of faithful discipleship in the present moment. Luke-Acts accentuate the immediate task facing the followers of Jesus Christ, both as individuals and as a Church. By getting over the uncertainty of a world about to come to an end, followers of Christ could devote their full attention to building a community together. Thus, instead of being otherworldly in their outlook and planning, the faithful could invest themselves fully in the here and now.

IMPLICATIONS OF LUKE-ACTS' THEOLOGY FOR LUCAN ETHICS

"Long-Haul" Ethics

As a consequence of the addition of this middle period of the Church in God's unfolding plan of salvation, moral conduct receives even greater attention. The longer wait for Christ's second coming makes it even more important to teach people how to live upright lives.[31] An imminent versus a delayed Parousia has different implications and demands for ethical behavior. To begin with, an imminent Parousia requires an immediate, decisive acceptance of the faith. Given the urgency of the moment and a looming day of judgment around the corner, the focus is on securing a 180-degree turn in people's fundamental priorities. An imminent Parousia is a de facto short-term commitment given that temporal existence is at its end. All it requires is one final, major sprint to the finish line.

In contrast, a delayed Parousia has a much different, indeed an even more exacting, set of ethical requirements. Not only does it call for a radical reorientation of priorities, but it also demands a sustained commitment. It requires endurance and staying power. It is aptly viewed as a "long-haul" ethics in which one's commitment to the faith will be repeatedly tested and will have to be reaffirmed continually for an indefinite period of time. To make matters worse, it also turns out to be a period of suffering and persecution, with no end in sight. Thus, a delayed Parousia leads to even greater demands on the moral life. Not surprisingly, Luke's ethics has also been called an "ethics of martyrdom."[32] Recall that in describing the cost of discipleship, all three Synoptic Gospels see the need to take up one's cross and to follow Jesus. However, in contrast to Mark and Matthew, Luke adds that this is a task that has to be done *daily* (cf, Mk 8:34, Mt 16:24, Lk 9:23).

Elicited Discipleship

The fulfillment of God's promise in a reconstituted Israel requires a response. The Gospel of Jesus Christ is "inevitably self-involving."[33] Those who form part of the reconstituted Israel are invited to a discipleship that entails (1) repentance and conversion and (2) the imitation of Christ.

Repentance and Conversion

Repentance and conversion involve a fundamental reorientation of lives. To begin with, it requires people's truthful acknowledgment of their sinfulness and failures, followed by a genuine contrition that seeks to make amends and to lead a new way of life. Repentance and conversion are critical themes that run across all three Synoptic Gospels. But it is Luke who stresses them more than either Mark or Matthew.[34] And then, of course, we have the account of the events at Pentecost. Moved by the Peter's preaching on Pentecost, the crowds ask what they are supposed to do. Peter responds by inviting them to repent and to be baptized in the name of Jesus (Acts 2:37–38). Repentance, conversion, and baptism are the keys to becoming part of the reconstituted Israel.

The true measure of such repentance and conversion is in the fruits they produce. Thus, responding to the tax collectors, soldiers, and the multitudes who wanted to repent but did not know what to do, John the Baptist notes that repentance must bear concrete fruit in their actions—in being just in discharging their daily duties and in being generous in their treatment of others (Lk 3:4–14). The Gospel message necessarily leads to right conduct.[35]

For Luke, hearing and doing, while distinct, are inseparable in genuine discipleship. Thus, in the parable of the sower, the seeds that produced prodigiously are those who hear the word of God and let it bear fruit in patience (Lk 8:11–15). The true relatives of Christ are those who both hear and do the word of God (Lk 8:21). In contrast, Mark 3:35 and Matthew 12:50 mention only the doing, but not the hearing. Mary is lauded not merely for having borne Jesus in her womb, but for having heard and kept the word of God (Lk 11:28). Judgment is more severe for the servant who knew the will of the master but failed to do it (Lk 12:47).

Consider, too, a non-traditional reading of Luke 10:38–42.[36] The usual interpretation of this pericope on Mary and Martha is the greater perfection of the contemplative over the active life. This narrative, however, is better read in the context of the parable of the Good Samaritan that precedes it.[37] The immediate context of the parable of the Good Samaritan is the question of which is the greatest commandment. Mark 12:29–31 and Matthew 22:37–40 note that love of God and love of neighbor are the first and the second most important commandments. In contrast, Luke 10:27 does not speak of two commandments, but only of one—love of God and love of neighbor. The two are inseparable. The parable of the Good Samaritan clearly underscores the importance of action. Nevertheless, in putting the incident with Mary and Martha immediately after this parable, Luke also emphasizes the importance of listening to the word of God and not to be completely preoccupied with action alone. Thus, by juxtaposing the parable of the Good Samaritan and the incident of Mary and Martha, Luke can be said to highlight both hearing and doing as constitutive of genuine discipleship.[38]

Imitation of Christ

Such receptive and responsive obedience must ultimately result in the imitation of Christ. After all, Jesus Christ is the paradigm of one who listens and does the will of the Father. To believe in Christ is to follow Christ. Thus, the location of the Lucan story should not come as a surprise. The travel narrative—Jesus on the road to Jerusalem (Lk 9:51–19:44)—constitutes a substantial part of the Gospel and contains most of the ethical materials. It is an invitation to accompany Jesus, to walk with Jesus, indeed, to follow Jesus on his journey to Jerusalem.

But there is more to this invitation than meets the eye. Jesus is on his way to Jerusalem to suffer and to die. To follow Christ is to suffer with Christ. The disciple is repeatedly reminded of the enormous cost of following Christ (Lk 9:57–62; 12:49–53; 13:22–30; 14:25–35).[39] Thus, note the exacting nature of discipleship, whether it is in matters of marriage and sexuality, of money and possessions, or of violence and enemies.[40]

Empowered Discipleship

No doubt about it. It is daunting to be a disciple of Jesus Christ. Much is expected from one who follows Christ. But much too will be given to those who seek to imitate Christ. For the Spirit of God that descends upon Christ at his baptism (Lk 3:21–22) and fills him in his public ministry (Lk 4) is the same Holy Spirit that descends on the apostles on Pentecost to transform them into courageous and eloquent preachers of Christ's Gospel. Thus, it is said that Luke 4 is to Jesus, as Pentecost is to the Church.

Empowered by the Holy Spirit, the apostles begin to do the work of Christ in preaching, healing, and even raising the dead to life (Acts 9:36–43). And it is the same Spirit that provides them with constant guidance on what they are supposed to do and how they are to go about preaching the Gospel to the ends of the earth. Thus, it is the Spirit that guides them to set apart Paul and Barnabas for a mission to the Gentiles (Acts 13). It is the Holy Spirit that instructs Peter to go to the house of Cornelius (Acts 10), and the Holy Spirit that tells Philip to catch up with the Ethiopian eunuch (Acts 8:27–29). Christ has indeed fulfilled his promise to the apostles to send them the Holy Spirit (Acts 1:4–8).

But there is more. This is an empowerment that is not reserved only for the apostles or a select few. Christ is lavish in sending the Holy Spirit "in a comprehensive and egalitarian way to the whole people of God."[41] Peter himself clearly points this out in his preaching using the prophetic words of Joel 2:28–29 as he describes how God's Spirit will be poured out on all—young and old, men and women, slave or free—so that they, in their own turn, might prophesy for the Lord, dream dreams, and see visions (Acts 2:17–18). And indeed, the Holy Spirit that descends on the apostles in the locked room also moves the three thousand that day to hear and embrace wholeheartedly the Word and become the first converts of a new-born Church (Acts 2:41). It is the same Spirit that comes down on the Gentiles (Acts 11:1–18), on the family of Cornelius (Acts 10), and on the Ethiopian eunuch (Acts 8:26–39). Indeed, the entire Acts of the Apostles is, in fact, a chronicle of the Holy Spirit at work in the early Church. Some have even observed that the "Acts of the Holy Spirit" would have been a far more accurate title for the book.[42] It is still the same Holy Spirit that has since come down in every age to touch hearts and minds, transform lives, and animate men and women to embrace the demanding Gospel of Christ. It is the same Holy Spirit that has supplied the middle period with its boundless energy, dynamism, and enthusiasm despite the evils and opposition that shadow it. Instead of Jesus Christ coming back in the Parousia and marking the end-time, it is the Holy Spirit that has come down to empower all who sincerely hear and respond to the Word of God.

Clearly, the middle period of the Church and its mission is fraught with much suffering and pain. It requires patient endurance. Luke is emphatic on this point. As mentioned earlier, Luke's "ethics of martyrdom" is an ethics for the long haul, with people taking up their cross daily and following Christ. However, Luke is also quite clear that, with grace, disciples are up to this challenge.

Luke-Acts are more complete than either Mark or Matthew because they move from Christology to soteriology, especially in Acts where we read an account of what unfolded after Jesus' ascension.[43] The Acts gives readers an appreciation for what the redeemed are now capable of accomplishing, even that which is difficult. Through the gifts of the Holy Spirit, God provides the means not only to persevere and complete this journey, but also to continue the very work of Jesus Christ. In fact, this Spirit-empowered middle period of the Church will be the occasion for creating something beautiful, for theirs is a discipleship that is also sacramental.

Sacramental Discipleship

God fulfilled the promise made to Israel through the saving death and resurrection of Jesus Christ. Discipleship is the telltale sign of God's fulfillment of that promise. The followers of Christ—the Church, reconstituted Israel—are the "bearers of the fulfilled promise."[44] The transformation of sinful men and women into a community of faith, and aflame with mutual love and love of God, is evidence of God's in-breaking and healing touch. A Spirit-animated people who are able to do that which is humanly impossible is confirmation that God has indeed fulfilled the promise made to Israel.

But there is more. Not merely is reconstituted Israel (the Church) the "bearer of the fulfilled promise," it is in fact the *sacramental* "bearer of the fulfilled promise." The disciples of Christ are not merely living proof of the inauguration of the reign of God, but they are also instruments by which God brings the promise made in the Old Testament to completion. This is yet another gift from God. For the followers of Christ have been given a role in bringing to fruition the kingdom of God, which will find its perfection in the end-time. To follow Christ and to suffer with him is to be sacramental, both in being a sign of God's fulfilled promise and in serving as a divine instrument in such fulfillment. It is the gift of participation in the divine governance of creation.

For example, in making a fourfold restitution to all whom he had defrauded and in giving half of his wealth to the poor, Zacchaeus (Lk 19:1–10) is not merely a sign of the arrival of the reign of God. The gift given to Zacchaeus that day entails much more than that. He does not merely herald the advent of the kingdom of God; he in fact participates in that reality. The same is true of the fellowship (*koinōnia*) of the early Church community. By sharing their goods in common, contributing according to what they have and getting only according to what they need, no one in their midst is said to be in want, clearly a reference to Deuteronomy15:4–5. Thus, Christian discipleship is not merely proof of the fulfillment of God's promise and a sign of the reign of God in our midst, it is also sacramental in effecting that which it signifies. It participates in bringing to completion the reality of God's kingdom in which it participates.

An even better example of the sacramental ethic of Luke is Paul. As mentioned earlier, Luke's theology centers on how God has fulfilled divine promises in the person and ministry of Jesus. Within the Old Testament itself, there is the understanding that the trajectory of God's saving action will ultimately extend to all the nations of the world through Israel. Thus, in Acts, we see the fulfillment of this aspect of salvation history with the call of the Gentiles. The Gentiles are invited not because Jews failed to heed the Gospel of Christ. Rather, Gentiles are also called to holiness as part of God's unfolding plan all along, as part of salvation history. And Paul, as part of reconstituted Israel, becomes the divine instrument of this outreach to the Gentiles. Paul's repentance, conversion, and discipleship in Christ are sacramental because in his acceptance of God's earlier proffered graces, he becomes the vessel by which God's grace is in turn offered to the Gentile world.

Proleptic Discipleship

But more than just being sacramental, such discipleship is also proleptic. In loving God and neighbor, disciples already live in the here and now how they are to live in the end-time. As "bearers of the fulfilled promise," disciples anticipate eternal life by living and loving in a manner consistent with those who are destined to spend an eternity with God. They live and love in a manner that is consistent with being the children of God. They live today in the period of the "not yet," what is to be. Thus, people bridge the eschatological gap between the already and the not yet by simply living in the here and now the first installment of what is to come.

This-Worldly Affirmation

A third important implication of Luke-Acts' theology for Lucan ethics is the latter's this-worldly affirmation. This is evident in the importance accorded (1) to action in the here and now and (2) to an open and enthusiastic engagement with the larger world.

Action in the Here and Now

By downplaying the imminence of the Parousia, Luke-Acts shift the attention to the here and now. The expectation of Christ's imminent coming no longer takes center stage. Instead, attention moves to what the Church community ought to be doing today in this middle period of patient waiting and endurance.[45] The urgency lies in putting disciples' current affairs in order, and in such a manner as to continue the work of Jesus. Here again, we find the inaugural lecture of Jesus Christ to be important (Lk 4:16–30). In proclaiming the in-breaking of the kingdom of God and a year of favor from the Lord, Jesus speaks of providing relief to the poor, the unwell, and those who are oppressed. And Jesus is not merely talking metaphorically or of an eschatological, future Jubilee. No, Jesus is talking of alleviating those in distress right now. The clear reference to Isaiah 61:1–2 and 58:6 is not to be allegorized. Thus, when John the Baptist sends his disciples to inquire if Jesus is indeed the Anointed One they had been waiting for, Jesus responds by asking them to tell John of what they themselves had witnessed—the blind regaining their sight, the lame walking, the dead rising to life, and the poor receiving the good news (Lk 7:18–23).

The fulfillment of the promise to the poor does not have to wait until the end-time. Luke uses the present tense in the beatitudes in assuring the poor that the kingdom of God is theirs (Lk 6:20). Similarly, in the account of the rich ruler in search of eternal life, Luke uses the present tense in referring to how hard it is for the rich to enter the kingdom of God (Lk 18:24). In contrast, Matthew 19:23 and Mark 10:23 use the future tense. Moreover, in Acts 4:34, we already see a community without anyone destitute among them.[46]

The reign of God preached by Jesus is not reserved for some unknown apocalyptic future. Such kingdom has immediate, tangible effects in the present. And as mentioned earlier, empowered, sacramental discipleship is about joining Jesus in the building of the kingdom. The Church community can do no less in this middle period of waiting.[47] It is not one of idle waiting, but a lively, proleptic period of pro-active expectation. The kingdom of God is not merely potent; it is dynamic. Thus, Luke-Acts offer not merely a future eschatological salvation, but a this-worldly redemption as well. It is wrong to spiritualize or to romanticize poverty. God has an active interest in providing for people's material well-being.[48] We see this reflected both in the history of the nation Israel, in the prophetic indictments, in the wisdom literature, and in the public ministry of Jesus.

Furthermore, recall that for Luke, the Church is the reconstituted Israel as part of the fulfillment of God's promise. Thus, the Church continues the journey of Israel. It is one and the same journey, one and the same trajectory of a salvation history unfolding.[49] Recall that even as they awaited the fulfillment of God's promise, the Israelites strove to live as a nation different from all the other nations in the manner by which they cared for one another. Their religion shaped their economics and their politics. Their faith life and their understanding of their special election by God were supposed to be evident even in the most ordinary tasks of their daily lives. Nothing less than this kind of fidelity is expected of the Church in this middle period. For just like the Chosen People of the Old Testament, reconstituted Israel also has to strive to live up to the same special election during this middle period of patient waiting as the new Chosen People of God.

Openness

Luke-Acts' this-worldly affirmation is also reflected in the optimism and the confidence with which the Church engages the non-Christian community. Unlike the Essenes and the Johannine community who withdraw from the world, Luke's community locates itself in its midst. It engages it in dialogue. Far from viewing itself vis-à-vis the world in terms of light versus darkness, good versus evil, it sees goodness beyond the Christian community. Thus, Luke-Acts are not dismissive of the Gentile world, but reaches out to them. Gentiles can be reasonable, kind, and enlightened. On account of the Roman centurion's faith in Jesus, his slave is healed (Lk 7:1–10; Mt 8:5–13). At the crucifixion, it is a Roman centurion who acknowledges the innocence of Jesus (Lk 23:47).[50] The Roman Empire is not blamed for the death of Jesus. Acts 10–11 gives an extended account of the dramatic conversion of Cornelius and his entire household. Roman troops save Paul from being beaten to death by a mob in Jerusalem (Acts 21:31–40). Paul is treated fairly by the Roman commander according to Roman law (Acts 22:22–29). And it is a Roman commander who protects Paul from ambush by his Jewish enemies (Acts 23:16–35). While the warning of John the Baptist to Roman soldiers to stop their plunder and false accusations (Lk 3:14) is not flattering, Luke-Acts present a positive picture of Romans for the most part.[51]

Even the literary composition of Luke-Acts reflects this open engagement with the world and its appreciation for that which is good and beautiful beyond the community. Luke employs Hellenistic literature in writing the

Gospel and Acts, an affirmation that Christianity and culture are compatible.[52] Indeed, in contrast to the isolation of the Qumram community, Luke-Acts choose to be in the midst of the world.

Kingdom of God

Luke-Acts have the second most references to the kingdom after Matthew. And just as in the Gospel of Matthew, the kingdom is an important and perennial reference point for Christian conduct. Disciples ought to be concerned with the kingdom rather than be preoccupied with worldly anxiety (Lk 12:22–32). The kingdom is a reward for those who give alms (Lk 12:33). Those burdened with riches will enter the kingdom with difficulty (Lk 18:24–25). The kingdom belongs to those who have abandoned all for the sake of Christ (Lk 18:29–30). Not only will the poor find their liberation through the kingdom (Lk 4:16–21), but they will also receive it as their home (Lk 6:20).

Discipleship is about proclaiming the kingdom inaugurated by Jesus (Lk 4:16–21). They are now the ones to continue the work of Jesus on behalf of the kingdom (Lk 9:60; 10:9; Acts 1:8; 8:12; 19:8; 20:25; 28:23, 31). And part of this task is to bear witness to Jesus as the Messiah (Lk 24:26–27; Acts 17:3; 28:23, 31). Moreover, such a kingdom will bring its share of persecution and tribulations (Acts 14:22). Indeed, just as in Matthew, the kingdom of God is an important reference point for Lucan ethics.

LUCAN MATERIALS ON ECONOMIC LIFE

Luke reproduces 65 percent of Mark in contrast to Matthew, who reproduces 80 percent of Mark.[53] Thirty-five percent of Luke is from Mark, 20 percent from Q, and anywhere from a third to 40 percent are neither from Mark nor from Q.[54] Luke goes beyond both Mark and Matthew (1) by amplifying the economic teachings they share and (2) by adding materials on economic morality that are unique to Luke.

Luke carries forward all the Marcan materials directly or indirectly related to economic conduct with the exception of two passages. Luke drops Jesus' critique of the Pharisees who claim their gains are *qorban* (reserved for God) and are, therefore, excused from being used to support their parents (Mk 7:10–13; Mt 15:4–5). Luke also changes Mark's account of Jesus' anointing in Bethany. This second change is best explained in the next section.

Triple-tradition and Q Texts Amplified by Luke

Luke amplifies materials from Mark to intensify even further his concerns on economic morality. Similarly, with respect to materials drawn from Q, Luke accentuates the economic dimensions of certain passages far more than Matthew.

Triple Tradition

Consider Luke 5:11 (cf. Mk 1:18, 20), the call of Simon, James, and John, and Luke 5:28 (cf. Mk 2:14), the call of Levi. In both cases, Luke adds that they left everything in order to follow Jesus. Luke uses all the Marcan materials on the rich and the poor but removes the statement attributed to Jesus in Mark 14:7 on how the poor will always be with us. Matthew keeps this passage (Mt 26:11), but not Luke (Lk 7:36–50). The instruction to the twelve apostles to preach and to carry no bag or gold (Lk 9:1–6; Mk 6:7–11) is also given the seventy other disciples (Lk 10:3–4). Moreover, unlike Mark, Luke specifies that they are not to carry even a walking stick. Luke 18:18–23 intensifies the encounter between Jesus and the rich man in Mark by noting that the man is a ruler, and a very wealthy one at that. Even more telling is the manner by which Luke amplifies the episode by emphasizing that the very rich ruler had to sell all that he had and to give to the poor. And in the concluding reassurance of the rewards the apostles are to receive for having left everything to follow Jesus, only Luke (18:29) explicitly includes leaving even the spouses as part of such radical dispossession.

In both Mark's and Matthew's account of the anointing of Jesus in Bethany (Mk 14:3–9; Mt 26:6–13), the ointment used by the woman is described as incredibly expensive. As a result, many, including some of the disciples, are critical, saying that the perfume could have been sold and then given to the poor. Jesus responds by noting that the poor will always be with them, but not Jesus. Luke renders a different account of the encounter.[55] There is no mention of the enormous cost of the perfume or that it could have been sold instead for the benefit of the poor. Luke makes no mention of Jesus' remark on how there will always be the poor.[56] The evangelist merely describes the repentant woman washing the feet of Jesus with her tears and then anointing them from her alabaster flask of ointment (Lk 7:36–50). These changes suggest Luke's concern for the destitute by not conceding that there will always be the poor. Moreover, in being silent on the extravagant cost of the perfume that had been seemingly wasted, Luke strengthens the many other passages in his Gospel on almsgiving and the proper use of wealth by not making it appear that Jesus condones such indulgent use or show of wealth.

Both Mark and Matthew put Jesus' rejection in the Nazareth synagogue well into his public ministry (Mk 6:1–6; Mt 13:54–58). In contrast, Luke presents it right at the start of the ministry of Jesus (Lk 4:16–30). Moreover, Luke makes this particular event programmatic of the mission of Jesus and uses Isaiah 61:1–2 to describe Jesus' self-understanding of his task: to provide relief to the distressed and to proclaim the good news to the poor. Luke underscores the nature of Jesus' ministry by using the language of the Jubilee year.[57]

Q

Matthew 5:42 urges disciples not to refuse those who seek to borrow from them, while Luke 6:34–35 calls on disciples not only to lend, but also to lend without expecting anything in return.[58] In contrast to Matthew 6:19–20, Luke 12:33 explicitly calls on disciples to sell their possessions and to give alms as part of building treasure in heaven. Both Matthew 3:7–10 and Luke 3:10–14 insist on repentance as the proper response to John the Baptist's preaching. However, Luke goes further to suggest explicitly concrete actions for such contrition. Those who have food and two coats are to share these with others (Lk 3:11). Tax collectors are to take no more than what is just. Soldiers are to stop robbing others and to desist from making false accusations; they are to be content with their wages (Lk 3:13–14).

We have the difference in the beatitudes with Matthew "spiritualizing" them by referring to the poor in spirit and those who hunger and thirst for righteousness (Mt 5:3, 6), while Luke takes a more down-to-earth economic approach by simply referring to the poor and the hungry (Lk 6:20, 21). Moreover, Luke provides a corresponding set of woes against the rich and the complacent to accentuate the beatitudes even more (Lk 6:24–26). On the teaching regarding loving one's enemies, Luke, unlike Matthew, illustrates such love with the concrete example of doing good and lending without expecting repayment (Lk 6:35). Similarly in the admonition not to judge others, Luke adds an extra call to give, with the surprising result of receiving even more in return (Lk 6:38). In the critique of the Pharisees (Mt 23:26), Luke stresses the importance of almsgiving in order to be truly made clean (Lk 11:41). In the passage on not being anxious about procuring material provisions (Mt 6:25–33), Luke 12:33–34 surprisingly concludes the pericope with a call to sell one's possessions and to give the proceeds as alms. In Matthew's account of the parable of the great feast (Mt 22:9), the servants let into the banquet all whom they meet along the thoroughfares. In Luke's version of the parable, the first preference is accorded to the poor, maimed, blind, and lame (Lk 14:21).[59]

Explicitly Economic Pericopae Unique to Luke

On the inevitable reversal of fortunes: In Mary's hymn of thanksgiving, God will cast down the proud and the mighty and lift up the lowly (Lk 1:51–53).

The woes accompanying the beatitudes foretell the coming fate of the rich, the comfortable, and the complacent (Lk 6:20–26). *On how the poor are special to God*: Using Isaiah 61:1–2, Jesus characterizes his ministry as bringing the good news to the poor, release to the oppressed, and relief to the distressed (Lk 4:14–21).

On how repentance leads to upright economic conduct: In response to people's queries on what they ought to do in repentance for their sins, John the Baptist instructs tax collectors, soldiers, and other listeners to be honest and generous with others (Lk 3:10–14). In anticipation of getting fired by his master and in the hopes of currying favor with people who might later employ or help him, the dishonest steward marks down the debts owed to his master, and in so doing, corrects past injustices (Lk 16:1–9). Moved by the unconditional love and respect he receives from Jesus, Zacchaeus promises to recompense fourfold anyone whom he might have defrauded and to give half his wealth to the poor (Lk 19:1–10).

On generosity: Jesus calls on his listeners to lend even without expecting repayment (Lk 6:33–35). In criticizing the hollow external ritual observances of the Pharisees, Jesus teaches that it is almsgiving that makes people holy and righteous (Lk 11:41). *On the dangers of wealth*: Responding to someone asking Jesus to arbitrate a fight with his brother over their inheritance, Jesus warns of the danger of covetousness and the abundance of one's possessions (Lk 12:13–15). In the parable of rich fool who built a large barn to store his gains for years to come, Jesus warns his listeners on the impermanence of wealth and the folly of anchoring one's security on it (Lk 12:16–21). The Pharisees are severely taken to task for being "lovers of money" (Lk 16:13–15). In the parable of Dives and Lazarus, wealth and self-indulgence can harden people into indifference and to ignore the plight of their neighbors in need. They will be held to account for this on the day of judgment (Lk 16:19–31). "Dissipation and drunkenness and the worries of this life" can dull people's vigilance as they await the end-time (Lk 21:34–36).

On associating with the marginalized: Jesus urges his host that in giving a banquet, he should invite the maimed, the lame, and the blind—people who could not return his favor (Lk 14:7–14). *On faithful stewardship*: Unrighteous mammon ought to be used for good ends. Faithful stewards will be entrusted with even more (Lk 16:9–13). *On fellowship*: The early Church shares goods in common, and no one in their midst is found wanting. They are of one heart and one mind (Acts 2:44–45; 4:32–35).

In sum, in addition to the passages on economic morality from Mark (Triple tradition) and Matthew (Q), Luke has the following explicitly economic pericopae that are unique to his Gospel: an inescapable reversal of fortunes between the poor and the mighty, hope for the distressed, and a warning against complacency for the wealthy and the powerful (Lk 1:51–53; 6:20–26); the special status of the poor before God (Lk 4:14–21); upright economic conduct as the fruit of repentance (Lk 3:10–14; 16:1–9; 19:1–10); generosity (Lk 6:33–35; 11:41); the dangers of wealth (Lk 12:13–15, 16–21; 16:13–15; 16:19–31; 21:34–36); a critique of the Greco-Roman ethos of patronage[60] (Lk 14:7–14); faithful stewardship (Lk 16:9–13); and genuine fellowship as the ideal for economic life (Acts 2:44–45; 4:32–35).

Insights on Economic Morality by Inference

On the poor as special and beloved to God:[61] Jesus is born under poor circumstances, and the shepherds are the first to receive the good news of the birth of the Messiah (Lk 2:1–17). Simeon and Anna are blessed to behold and to recognize the child Jesus for who he truly is (Lk 2:25–38). Mary and Joseph offer the sacrifice of poor people in the Temple (Lk 2:24; cf. Lev 12:1–8). Jesus and the apostles lead a simple life dependent on the goodwill of others. *On gratitude*: Those who have been forgiven much have even greater reason to be grateful (Lk 7:41–43). Ten lepers are cured, and only one, a Samaritan, comes back in gratitude (Lk 17:11–19).

On material support to the preaching of the Gospel: Many provide material support to the public ministry of Jesus and his apostles (Lk 8:1–3). Samaritan villages refuse to extend hospitality to Jesus who is headed to Jerusalem (Lk 9:51–56). The disciples are to eat whatever is set before them as they are received in the towns in which they preach (Lk 10:8). Lydia, a seller of purple goods, supports the ministry of Paul (Acts 16:11–15). *On using one's own goods generously for the needs of others*: The Good Samaritan expends time and material resources to care for the man who fell in with the robbers (Lk 10:29–37). Deacons are charged with the daily distribution of food in the community (Acts 6).

On balancing daily tasks with contemplation: Mary chooses the better part in sitting to listen to Jesus (Lk 10:38–42). *On the value of perseverance*: The persistent friend of the baker gets his bread in the middle of the night for an unexpected guest (Lk 11:5–8). The unjust judge gives in to the persistent widow (Lk 18:1–8). *On accountability and bearing fruit*: People receive in the measure they have given (Lk 6:38). More will be demanded from those who have been given much (Lk 12:42–48). The fig tree is given another year to produce fruit before being cut down (Lk 13:6–9).[62] Judas meets a bad end for his wickedness (Acts 1:18–19).

On prudential planning and action: There is need to count the cost before building or going to war (Lk 14:28–32). With his imminent arrest and death, Jesus tells the apostles to provision themselves for what lies ahead (Lk 22:36). *On sharing one's joy with others*: The woman finds her lost coin and shares her joy with her friends and neighbors (Lk 15:8–9). The father welcomes his prodigal son with a feast to rejoice over the return of the wayward son (Lk 15:11–32). *On generosity*: The parable of the prodigal son is also a story of unconditional forgiveness and generosity.

On humility for one's accomplishments or service: At the end of a long day in the field, the servant continues to work with household chores without looking for praise or gratitude. Such devoted work is expected of the servant (Lk 17:7–10). There is nothing people can boast to God as their own or as God's due to them. *On repentance*: The tax collector is repentant and is justified as a result (Lk 18:9–14). *On itinerant mendicancy and trust in divine providence*: The apostles lack nothing even as they head off to their preaching without provisions (Lk 22:35).

On the importance of almsgiving: Peter and John have no money to give as alms but heal the cripple instead (Acts 3:2–10). Tabitha is praised for her almsgiving (Acts 9:36). Cornelius is rewarded for his almsgiving (Acts 10:2, 4, 31). Alms are provided for the relief of the poor brethren in Judea (Acts 11:29). Paul brings alms and gifts for the relief of the Jerusalem community from the other churches (Acts 24:17). Paul reminds his listeners on the importance of solicitude for the poor and generosity (Acts 20:35).

On the importance of a work ethic: Paul's work ethic is a model for emulation (Acts 18:3; 20:28–35). *On dishonesty*: Ananias and Sapphira are punished for their dishonesty (Acts 5:1–11). *On simony*: Peter warns Simon that the gifts of the Spirit cannot be bought (Acts 8:18–25).

Synthesis

Consider the following observations on the Lucan passages related to economic life. First, Luke-Acts have by far the most teachings on economic morality in the New Testament by any measure: in terms of volume, substance, intensity, and tone. Luke retains nearly all of Mark's and Q's teachings on economic life and even intensifies many of them. Clearly, Luke shows a relatively greater interest in economic morality compared with the other evangelists.[63] Not surprisingly, most studies dealing with New Testament economic ethics have focused on Luke-Acts.[64]

In addition, Luke-Acts use many more Greek terms that are related to the world of economics and business compared with other books of the New Testament, indicative of Luke and the Lucan community's concerns or greater familiarity with economic life.[65] Furthermore, even as many of the parables are not about economic morality, they nonetheless use economic imagery: the Good Samaritan's payment to the innkeeper (Lk 10:35), economic stewardship of servants (Lk 12:44–46; 19:11–27), the finding of the coin (Lk 15:8–10), the squandered inheritance by the prodigal son (Lk 15:11–32), the use of debt to underscore God's mercy and forgiveness (Lk 7:36–50), and the Jubilee language in the inaugural lecture of Jesus (Lk 4:16–21).[66]

Second, many of these insights on economic morality are not original to Luke-Acts since we find them in Mark, Q, the Old Testament, and ANE and intertestamental literature. Nevertheless, Luke accentuates many of these teachings and makes them an integral part of discipleship.

Third, an important point of convergence between Mark and Luke is their emphases on sacrificial discipleship. As we saw earlier, Mark highlights patient suffering as characteristic of Christian discipleship. Similarly, Luke (9:23–27; 14:25–33) repeatedly stresses the demands of discipleship. In fact, we find the fulfillment of such sacrificial discipleship in the death of Stephen (Acts 7:54–60) and James (Acts 12:1–2) and in the severe opposition encountered by the early Church in Jerusalem that ultimately cause the dispersion of the community (Acts 8:1). Just as Jesus is resolutely on his way to Jerusalem knowing full well the persecution that awaited him (Lk 9:51), so too is Paul resolute on his way to Jerusalem where he foresees great suffering and opposition (Acts 19:21; 21:10–14). And of course, Acts ends with the many privations and imprisonment of Paul (Acts 21:27–28:31).[67] Indeed, Acts is not merely a chronicle of the early Church's history, but it is also an account of its birth pangs.

Fourth, note that the bulk of teachings on economic morality from Q and those that are unique to Luke can be found within the travel narratives as Jesus is on his way to Jerusalem (Lk 9:51–19:44). In fact, we find three big blocks of materials on the subject of possessions within these narratives (Lk 12:13–34; 14:12–33; 16:1–31). If disciples take this courageous journey of Jesus to Jerusalem as a paradigm for their own journey of discipleship, then the sayings, the teachings, and the parables of Jesus on economic morality take added significance. Upright economic conduct and even suffering for it become constitutive of discipleship. These economic teachings become an integral part of the road that disciples themselves have to travel in this middle period.

Fifth, Luke's theology and setting in life (*Sitz im Leben*) partially account for the greater importance of economic morality in Luke-Acts relative to Mark and Matthew. To begin with, recall that a major contribution of Luke to theology and ethics is his shift in focus from an imminent Parousia to the middle period of the Church and its mission. Because of the delayed Parousia, it becomes even more important to set guidelines on how disciples ought to live during this period of waiting and how they ought to act together as an *ekklēsia*. In other words, ethics has become even more critical in light of the longer temporal existence caused by a delayed Parousia. This lengthened temporal existence has an unavoidable economic dimension to it, because of the embodied and social nature of humans and the finitude of the earth's resources. It should not be a surprise that Luke stresses economic morality even more than either Mark or Matthew given the much longer temporal horizon faced by the Lucan community.

Furthermore, most scholars believe that Luke wrote for a Hellenized audience that was steeped in a Greco-Roman socio-economy (e.g., patronage-subservience, disdain for the poor). Moreover, it was a community comprised of a wide spectrum of classes, from those with substantial means, to the destitute. As mentioned earlier, there is an emerging consensus among Lucan scholars that Luke was addressing the rich and propertied Christians in these works. Moreover, these Gentile converts had to be initiated into the Jewish ethos of almsgiving and solicitude for the poor and the outcast, so dissimilar from the Greco-Roman practice of self-serving benefactions. In addition, there was also the prophetic tradition that had to be passed on to these new Christians on the centrality of justice and the future reversal between the rich and the poor—values that are contrary to the Greco-Roman world's pursuit of power, privilege, and status.[68] Some even suggest that the stress on Christian fellowship (*koinōnia*) was meant to prevent the early Church from splintering along class or ethnic lines.[69] All these provide Luke with reason to devote much space and attention to questions of economic morality. Besides, in conveying to the Gentile converts the Hebrew tradition of care for the marginalized and the prophetic justice tradition, Luke also achieves the theological goal of showing how Jesus is the fulfillment, rather than the abrogation, of the Old Testament.

ISSUES IN LUCAN ETHICS

Who Are the Poor in Luke-Acts?

There is no consensus on who are the poor in Luke-Acts, or in the Gospels for that matter. We find a wide variety of views in the literature. Some hold that the poor refer to those who are destitute. One could take the term literally. Others claim that the poor are those who suffer on account of their covenant fidelity. Still, others note that the poor pertain to those who are in any way outcasts—socially, economically, religiously, and ritually. These include those who are deemed unclean either because of their illness, physical impairment, or non-observance of the law. And, of course, there are those who use the term "poor" to refer to all of the above. After all, the aforesaid views are not mutually exclusive.

Metaphorical Poverty

The poor are those who find their true wealth only in God. It is spiritual (not economic or social) poverty that is properly the concern of the Gospels.[70] Some scholars read Jesus' programmatic lecture (Lk 4:16–30) and its reference point (Is 61:1–2; 58:6) in an unconventional manner. The poor mentioned in these passages are not literally the destitute, but long-suffering

Israel. The poor are to be understood in the context of Isaiah 55–66, as those who have been oppressed for the sake of righteousness and those who have chosen to remain faithful to the Torah and have consequently paid a price for it. The poor are the "righteous remnant," the "eschatological people of God," that is, those who are being singled out for "eschatological deliverance."[71] Luke uses "poor" not only in its material but also in its spiritual sense. This inclusive use of "poor" is consistent with the prophets and psalms in their usage, as in Isaiah 57:15; 66:2 and Psalm 34:17–19.[72]

Contrary to the claims of people who use Luke-Acts as scriptural justification for radical social change and social justice, some scholars argue that Luke devotes much attention, not to the economically destitute, but to ordinary people with some means.[73] Thus, we have Jesus encountering self-employed fishermen, the centurion, Jairus, Mary and Martha, Joanna (wife of Herod's steward Chuza), Zacchaeus, tax collectors, and Pharisees. He attends banquets and dines in the houses of people with means (Lk 7:36; 11:37; 14:1). He is not an ascetic like John the Baptist (Lk 7:34).

Jesus does not condemn private property ownership or the wealthy per se. He does not idealize divestment, even as he himself is a mendicant preacher. Luke-Acts do not advocate a radical overhaul of first-century Palestine's political economy. Jesus moves around the social circles of the rich, the powerful, and the Pharisees, just as he associates with the poor, lepers, publicans, and public sinners. Even in death, his connection with people of means comes through as seen in Joseph of Arimathea asking for Jesus' corpse from Pilate and laying it in a tomb (Lk 23:50–53). And even Jesus' parables are about people of means: the housekeeper who had ten silver coins, lost one, and then found it; the shepherd who owned a hundred sheep and searched for a lost lamb; the prodigal son from a wealthy family; the shrewd steward about to lose his employment; the landowner and the servant; and the contrite tax collector (Lk 15; 16:1–7; 17:7; 18:11).

To be sure, Jesus ministers to the poor and is deeply concerned about the poor. After all, Luke-Acts are about the unconditional welcome, love, and care extended by Jesus to all—Jews and Gentiles, the sick, sinners, the outcasts, and certainly the destitute. Nevertheless, many believe that Luke-Acts are not solely or even primarily focused on the economically destitute themselves or on unjust socioeconomic structures. Luke-Acts are concerned with those who are oppressed and in need of God's salvation. Recall from the exilic and post-exilic prophetic tradition that the nation Israel is described as poor, suffering, and in dire need of God's salvation. Thus, the "poor" in Luke-Acts may, in fact, be shorthand for the nation Israel or those who suffer on account of their fidelity to the law of God.[74]

Truly Destitute

Social scientific research supports the view that the poor mentioned in the Gospels are actually those who are destitute. It is believed that ordinary citizens were driven to debt and extreme poverty during the time of Jesus. Land had been appropriated by the Herodian client kings, the peasants were heavily taxed by the Romans and by the Temple, and many were heavily indebted to the wealthy elite and unable to pay their loans.[75] Some believe that the tax burden on the population may have been as high as 40 percent of what the peasants produced.[76] In fact, some go so far as to claim that the relations between the city and the countryside were strained because produce from the rural areas were siphoned off by absentee landlords and creditors who lived in idle opulence in the city.[77] Given this socioeconomic milieu, there is reason to believe that the "poor" truly pertain to those who are destitute.

The texts themselves provide evidence that the poor refer to those who are truly impoverished. Recall Luke's use of Isaiah 61:1–2 and 58:6 in the inaugural lecture of Jesus (Lk 4:16–30). These passages refer to those who suffer from their oppression and their distress. And to ensure that these passages are not allegorized, Jesus responds to the query of John the Baptist on whether he (Jesus) is the Messiah by pointing to the blind, the poor, the lame, and the poor who have found relief in his (Jesus') ministry (Lk 7:22). Consider, too, the differences between Matthew and Luke in their presentation of the beatitudes. Unlike Matthew who refers to those who are poor in spirit and who hunger and thirst for righteousness, Luke does not spiritualize the beatitudes and simply refers plainly to those who are poor and those who are hungry.[78]

Furthermore, the inaugural lecture of Jesus must be taken within the larger context of ANE literature and practice. In the Ancient Near East, the king was the defender of the poor and those who were unable to fend for themselves. The poor were completely at the mercy of the whims of the rich and the powerful, and it was only the king who could level the playing field and provide relief to the poor. Thus, kings occasionally proclaimed debt forgiveness and slave release in an effort to provide respite for the weak. It is in this context that one can gain a better appreciation for Jesus' use of Isaiah 61:1–2 and 58:6. YHWH is king of Israel, and it is YHWH who is the defender of the poor and who will provide comfort and relief to all who are oppressed and in distress. Thus, in the same way, it is Jesus, in his own turn and in his own time, who brings that loving and caring concern of God to the poor and the weak.[79]

This is confirmed in the birth, life, and public ministry of Jesus. Consider the circumstances surrounding the birth of Jesus in the Gospel of Luke. Jesus is born to a poor family. His birth occurs under dire circumstances and humble surroundings. The shepherds (among the dregs and the most insignificant people of that time) are the first to receive the good news of his birth and the first to visit the family. In Mary's Magnificat, Luke clearly affirms the privileged place of the poor.[80]

Jesus is among the poor. He is not merely born in their midst, but he chooses to be one of them in his itinerant preaching and teaching, dependent on the generosity and assistance of others. Furthermore, he preaches the good news to the poor and offers them the hope of an eventual reversal in their fortunes. Moreover, we cannot gloss over the invitation to the rich ruler to sell all and to give to the poor (Lk 18:22). Similarly, we have Zacchaeus sharing half his wealth with the poor (Lk 19:8). Clearly, these passages do not make sense unless they refer to the destitute. Why should the rich ruler or Zacchaeus provide for those who are spiritually poor or socially, ritually, or religiously outcasts? Furthermore, note Jesus' choice of inconsequential, lowly people to be his apostles, the beneficiaries of his healing, and the banquet guests of the rich (Lk 14:12–14).

Finally, recall the nature of God. Critics argue that there is nothing intrinsically meritorious to being impoverished as to deserve eternal reward. Why should this social class be worthy of inheriting the kingdom of heaven? Why does social class determine the state and the quality of one's moral life? These are valid questions. In response to these, one must remember that the privileged position of the poor stems not from their meritorious acts or from their moral disposition. Rather, their preferential treatment is founded on the very nature of God who stands up against evil and who restores the good in the divine order of creation that is at risk. Thus, one should not romanticize economic poverty. It is abhorrent to God, an "insult to his honor," an "affront to the royal justice of God."[81] Destitution is a jarring contrast to God's gift of material plenitude when the fruits of the earth were entrusted to human stewardship (Gn 1:28–30). God is concerned for those who wallow in economic poverty.

The Vulnerable

In the eastern Mediterranean world, "poor" does not necessarily nor is exclusively reserved for those who are destitute. Rather, the poor are those who are weak and are unable to recover from the sudden vicissitudes of life, such as illness, debt, accident, family death, being in a foreign land, or any other contingency in life. They are unable to maintain their inherited status in life. Consequently, the poor are not a permanent underclass, but a revolving class of people.[82] The elite viewed those working for a daily wage as "in need" and "poor" because of their precarious socioeconomic condition and class.[83]

In other words, the formal defining characteristic of what it is to be poor is to have little control over one's life. Economic destitution is merely a possible cause or a consequence, or both. Moreover, there is a self-reinforcing effect in that such economic deprivation may in fact precipitate or at least worsen such helplessness. Thus, there is an overlap between this understanding of the poor as the vulnerable and the earlier definition of the poor as those who are economically destitute.

Outcasts

The poor in Luke-Acts need not be limited only to the economically destitute or even to the spiritually poor, or even to the "righteous remnant of Israel." The notion of the "poor" in Luke-Acts is both broad and robust enough to be able to accommodate all these and more. This is the view of many scholars.

The "poor" in Luke-Acts is best understood in the context of the Greco-Roman notion and practice of status-honor. Status and honor are important in that particular age and culture because these determined the respect one was able to command within the community and whether or not one belonged to a group. Such status-honor were a function not only of wealth, but also of ethnicity, class, blood line and ties, education, gender, religious observance, family history, and occupation. One may be wealthy, but may nevertheless still be accorded little standing if one was from a family of no consequence.

In a Jewish setting, we must add physical integrity as an additional condition. At Qumran, the lame, the blind, the deaf, the dumb, or those with any physical debility were barred from the general assembly. In the War Scrolls, boys, women, the lame, the sick, the disabled, and anyone with a physical defect were excluded from the coming eschatological battle. The blind, deaf, beggars, and the dumb were not permitted in the Holy Place in the Temple (Lev 21:16–23).[84] Furthermore, Jewish practice was keen on separating the pure from the unclean, those observant of the law from those who were not, and those who belong to the Chosen People from the Gentiles. In addition, sinners were clearly set apart for scorn and condemnation. Thus, Luke-Acts were written in the context of a society governed by norms of status-honor and purity-impurity that segregated people. There was a clear demarcation between (1) those who were in the group and with whom one associated and (2) those who were outside one's circle of friends whom one had to avoid or have nothing to do with.

Many scripture scholars believe that in Luke-Acts, the "poor" refers not only to the destitute but to all who in one way or another are outcasts, that is, people who do not belong, who have no social standing, and who are vulnerable. In proclaiming the good news to the poor and in extending an unconditional welcome to all, Jesus reaches out to all who have been excluded socially, economically, religiously, or physically. The poor are all those who are vulnerable, ostracized, and left at the mercy of others, with no one to take their cause or to come to their defense. These are the despised people who often literally live at the fringes of the community. They are the people who could be ignored, scorned, or treated as inferior, such as women, widows, strangers, foreigners, Samaritans, and Gentiles. These also include the lepers, the crippled, the blind, public sinners, and the tax collectors. These are the groups that receive special attention in Luke-Acts. The rich are those who enjoy power, prestige, and social standing. Those who have none of these deserve to be excluded. It is to these social and religious outcasts that Luke-Acts refer to as the poor.[85] In sum, the poor in Luke-Acts are the destitute, the rejected, the despised, the vulnerable, and the marginalized. These are the people and groups who receive preferential consideration.

SUMMARY AND CONCLUSIONS

The Gospel of Luke and the Acts of the Apostles stand out among the New Testament writings in the abundance of materials they bring to bear on economic morality. We find this reflected as well in the volume of scholarship on economic issues (primarily on wealth and possessions) coming out of Lucan studies compared to other areas of New Testament studies.

Luke's economic teachings reveal an evident concern and attention to affairs in the here and now. Unlike Mark and Matthew, Luke stresses the present dimension of salvation. Even as the eschatology is still to come, the fruits of such salvation have begun to be felt and enjoyed, thereby giving contemporary disciples incentives to live upright lives. In fact, these fruits of salvation that are already being felt in the here and now are tangible evidence of Christ's Gospel at work.[86]

Moreover, Luke-Acts exude an optimistic this-worldly affirmation[87] and a willingness to accommodate Rome and to coexist with unbelievers. Disciples are to engage the larger world and to live their Christian witness in the midst of the mundane needs, obligations, and activities of economic life. The evangelist believes in the goodness of creation and has an appreciation for economic life's possibilities in contributing toward the building of the kingdom of God.

NOTES

1. I refer to these two works from hereon as Luke-Acts for brevity.
2. Brown (1997, 268)
3. See, for example, Brown (1997, 270), Donahue (1989, 141), Esler (1987, 44), and Squires (2006, 160).
4. Burridge (2007, 231); Marshall (1978, 161)
5. Brown (1997, 272); Donahue (1989, 142); Esler (1987, 222); Squires (2006, 160); Thielman (2005, 148)

6. Brown (1997, 274) sets it around 85 A.D., plus or minus five to ten years. Donahue (2005, 28) puts it between 85 and 95 A.D. Burridge (2007, 246) gives a date of anywhere from the late 70s to the mid-80s. Esler (1987, 44) sets it between the mid-80s and the mid-90s.
7. Karris (1978); Kim (1998)
8. Porter (1990, 114)
9. Brown (1996, 270)
10. Schottroff and Stegemann (1986, 87–105)
11. Burridge (2007, 230); Gillman (1991, 24)
12. Gillman (1991, 25–26); Squires (2006, 175, 180, fn 22, 23)
13. Pilgrim (1981, 107)
14. Gillman (1991, 26–27); Harvey (1990, 126, 138)
15. Donahue (1989, 142–43; 2005); Esler (1987); Gillman (1991, 24–27); Karris (1978); Pilgrim (1981, 107); Schottroff and Stegemann (1986, 87–105)
16. This supports scholars' conclusion that the target audience of Luke-Acts were the Gentile "God-fearers," that is, people who were already familiar with the Old Testament. After all, it did not make sense for the author of Luke-Acts to take the trouble of carefully incorporating vestiges from the Old Testament that would simply be lost on readers.
17. Hays (1996, 113–14)
18. Karris (1991, 676); Squires (2006, 173)
19. Karris (1991, 676)
20. Karris (1991, 676)
21. See Squires (2006, 173).
22. Hays (1996, 115–20); Seccombe (1998, 371)
23. Pilgrim (1981, 69–72)
24. Johnson (2004, 162)
25. Hays (1996, 114)
26. Hays (1996, 131)
27. Conzelmann (1960). See also Burridge (2007, 247–50); Duling (1992, 58); Hays (1996, 129–32); Marshall (2004, 173–74); and Schrage (1988, 154–55).
28. Hays (1996, 130)
29. The Triple tradition pertains to materials found in Mark, Matthew, and Luke.
30. Hays (1996, 129). All the preceding examples are from Hays (1996, 129–32), where one could find even more illustrations. See also Burridge (2007, 247–50).
31. Burridge (2007, 247–50); Schrage (1988, 154–55)
32. Conzelmann (1960, 231–34). See also Sanders (1975, 34–39).
33. Verhey (1984, 34)
34. There is a more frequent call for repentance in Luke. See Squires (2006, 173).
35. Gillman (1981, 42–44)
36. Donohue (1988, 128–39) proposes this non-traditional reading of this pericope.
37. Note that both the story of Mary and Martha and the parable of the Good Samaritan are unique to Luke.
38. Thus, Donohue (1988, 128–39) calls this entire account on Mary and Martha a "parabolic narrative."
39. Squires (2006, 164)
40. Burridge (2007, 56–58)
41. Hays (1996, 121)
42. Hays (1996, 131)
43. Matera (2007, 68)
44. Hays (1996, 114)
45. Hays (1996, 131); Pilgrim (1991, 108)
46. Harvey (1990, 138, 226, fn 66)
47. Esler (1987, 193–97); Matera (1996, 67–68); Schrage (1988, 154); Verhey (1984, 12–16)
48. Dupont (1977, 41); Lohfink (1987)
49. Hays (1996, 134)
50. In Mark 15:39 and Matthew 27:54, the centurion calls Jesus the "Son of God."

51. M. Davies (1995, 333)
52. Hays (1996, 134)
53. The following pericopae pertain to economic morality according to Donahue (1989), Esler (1987, 165–69, 196), Gillman (1991), Johnson (1981, 12–13), Karris (1978, 117), Oakman (1986, 8–9), Pilgrim (1981, 184), Schmidt (1987), Squires (2006, 179), and Zimmerman (2003). See also Verhey (2002, 262–87).
54. Brown (1997, 263, 265)
55. It is unclear if Luke is reworking Mark 14:3–9 or if he is drawing from another source about the same event. In fact, it may even be a completely different event.
56. To get an idea of just how extravagant the anointing was, Esler (1987, 166) notes that two hundred denarii could feed five thousand (Mk 6:34–44). The perfume was believed to be worth three hundred denarii in the market. This was a year's worth of wages.
57. Esler (1987, 166–67)
58. We cannot determine definitively whether Matthew or Luke was more faithful in preserving the materials they drew from Q. Thus, we are unable to say whether or not Luke intensified Q pericopae on economic morality. All we can do is to compare Luke and Matthew relative to one another.
59. Esler (1987, 196); Donahue (1989, 131–35); Fitzmyer (1981, 247–48); Gillman (1991, 14–16); Pilgrim (1981, 85); Scott (1989, 128); Schelkle (1973, 309)
60. We will examine this practice in greater depth in the chapter on interpersonal relationships.
61. Donahue (1989, 134–35) notes that Luke presents Jesus in the tradition of the Old Testament prophets who take the side of the oppressed, the distressed, or the vulnerable, as in the cases of the widow (Lk 7:11–17; 18:1–8), the alien (Lk 10:25–37), and the marginalized (Lk 15:1–2; 14:12–13, 21). See also Nardoni (2004, 256–59) on how Luke was promoting the status of women.
62. See Hanson and Oakman (1998, 105–6) for their exposition on how the fig tree refers to the nation Israel and its failure to live up to her calling.
63. See Donahue (1989, 131–35) and Fitzmyer (1981, 247). Other scholars disagree and note that Luke was merely repeating the hostility to wealth in Mark. In other words, the economic pericopae in Luke are merely drawn from tradition and should not be interpreted as proof of Luke's greater concern with economic morality (Mealand, 1981, 16–20).
64. For example, see Balch (1995), Beavis (1994), Danker (1983), Donahue (1989), Gillman (1991), Green (1994), Heard (1988), Johnson (1981; 2004), Karris (1978), Kim (1998), Kirk (2003), Metzger (2007), Moxnes (1988), Nickelsburg (1978–79), Pilgrim (1981), Seccombe (1982), and Zimmerman (2003).
65. Gillman (1991, 17–18). This is also consistent with the earlier observation that there were people of means in Luke's audience.
66. Donahue (1989, 134–35)
67. Hays (1996, 122)
68. Beavis (1994, 365)
69. Karris (1978, 117)
70. Gelin (1964, 107–8)
71. Heard (1988, 75, 57–58)
72. Nardoni (2004, 220)
73. Heard (1988, 75–77)
74. Heard (1988, 77); Seccombe (1982, 38)
75. Gillman (1991, 18–20)
76. Horsley and Hanson (1985, 55); Oakman (1986)
77. Oakman (1991)
78. Dupont (1977, 34–36); Fitzmyer (1981, 248)
79. Dupont (1977, 38–41)
80. Beavis (1994, 359–60); Burridge (2007, 232)
81. Dupont (1977, 41); Lohfink (1987). See also Donohue (1989), Esler (1987), and Johnson (1981).
82. Malina (1987, 356)

83. Malina (1987, 356), citing Philo (*The Special Laws* IV, 195–96; LCL VIII, 128–29)

84. Green (1994, 69); Pilgrim (1981, 74, 83)

85. Bok (2004, 362); Burridge (2007, 264–68); Green (1994, 65, 68–69; 1995, 76–94); Marshall (2004, 144); Verhey (1984, 92–102)

86. Matera (2007, 74–75)

87. Hays (1996, 134)

Chapter Ten

Pauline Letters and James

In both the Pauline letters and James, faith without good works is not faith at all. The two are inseparable. Despite their primary focus on the divine, these letters are nevertheless concerned with moral conduct in the here and now, including economic life.

PAULINE LETTERS

Life Setting

Most scholars believe that seven letters can be attributed to Paul himself: 1 Thessalonians, 1 and 2 Corinthians, Philippians, Galatians, Philemon, and Romans. Three are disputed letters believed to have been written by disciples of Paul and called Deutero-Pauline (2 Thessalonians, Colossians, and Ephesians). The remaining three are called the Pastoral Letters (1 and 2 Timothy and Titus) and are considered pseudepigraphical. The earliest letter is 1 Thessalonians, written around 51 A.D. Tradition holds that Paul was martyred in Rome around the mid-60s.

Theology

Pauline theology is an account of what God had accomplished through the Christ-event, that is, the life, passion, death, and resurrection of Jesus Christ, the Son of God, the Anointed One.[1] The letter to the Romans is particularly illuminative on this point. In this letter, God's righteousness overshadows the kingdom of God as a theme (Rom 14:17). Divine righteousness consists of God's sovereign power to forgive sins and to save humanity from its iniquity. This salvation was affected through Christ's self-immolation on the cross

(Rom 3:25; 5:8–11). It is a sacrifice that flows from a profound divine love (Rom 8:29–39).

This redemption re-creates humans. As new creatures, they are set free through faith in Jesus Christ (Rom 1:17; 3:21–24). Humanity can now look forward to the future with hope (Rom 8:19–39). Salvation imbues them with the twin gifts of righteousness and a restored relationship with God. As a consequence, they have been empowered to bear much fruit through upright moral conduct. Such ethical righteousness is in itself a divine gift made possible by their transformation through Jesus Christ.

Thus, there is a threefold movement: from eschatology to Christology to anthropology and ethics. We understand and appreciate better the new possibilities now open to humanity on account of the life, death, and resurrection of Jesus Christ.[2]

Ethics

There are at least three points from Pauline ethics that are relevant for Pauline economic norms: the integral link between theology and ethics, community-building through mutual burden-bearing following Christ's example of self-emptying, and the call to active engagement with the larger world.

Indicative-Imperative

Pauline ethics is not merely an ad hoc addition to its theology in response to the many practical problems and questions posed by the churches Paul had established. Rather, the ethics of these letters flows from the Gospel that they preach. Ethical norms are the natural extension of the good news proclaimed. Ethics is merely a subset of theology in Paul. In fact, there "is no meaningful distinction between theology and ethics in Paul's thought, because Paul's theology is fundamentally an account of God's work transforming his people in the image of Christ."[3]

This inseparable link between theology and ethics has been described as the indicative-imperative nexus. The indicative is a description of how God re-created human life through Jesus Christ. It gives rise to attendant duties, that is, the imperative on how humans ought to live in light of their new freedom in Christ. In other words, people are invited to be true to who they are and to live accordingly. "Become who you are," so to speak.[4] One should not put a false dichotomy between the message of the Gospel (*kerygma*) and its teachings on moral conduct (*didachē*).[5] The two, while distinct from each other, mutually feed off one another. They constitute a seamless whole.

This mutual dependence is important because of the longstanding debate on whether salvation is wrought through faith alone or through good works. Faith is not merely or simply an intellectual assent. Rather, faith finds its full expression in a lived response to what is believed. In other words, faith without consequent good works is not faith at all. As Paul notes, "the only thing that counts is faith working through love" (Gal 5:6).[6]

A concrete way by which this imperative is fulfilled is to imitate Christ. This is central to Paul's ethics. Thus, the Christological hymn of Philippians 2:5–11 presents the selflessness and humility of Jesus as the norm for Christians (e.g., Rom 15:1–3). Paul himself openly acknowledges his great striving to be like Christ, and then presents his own example for his congregations' emulation (1 Cor 4:16–17; 11:1; 1 Thess 1:6–7). In fact, Paul sees his own suffering as an opportunity for making Christ visible to others (2 Cor 4:10). Indeed, the imitation of Christ is an excellent example of this indicative-imperative nexus. Christians are held to higher standards of moral conduct because they are now the children of God, brothers and sisters to Christ. They are to "put on the Lord Jesus Christ" (Rom 13:14).[7] Through the example of his life, Jesus shows concretely what righteousness looks like in practice. We also see such righteousness in the Pauline lists of debasing vices to be shunned and ennobling virtues to be embraced.[8] In sum, Pauline ethics flows from and is inseparably linked to its theology. Pauline theology necessarily leads to its ethical prescriptions.

Community Building

A distinctive feature of Pauline ethics is the individual and collective duty to build up the community (Rom 15:1–13; 1 Cor; Gal 3:26–29; Phil 2:1–13; Col 3:13; Eph 4:1–5:21). After all, the person is "justified by faith alone but never justified alone."[9] There is an integral communal dimension to salvation. It is not merely a personal gift or a private affair or a matter between the person and God alone. God invites the re-created person to be a channel of grace for others and to participate in divine governance. There is a constitutive social dimension to both the righteousness conferred by God and the consequent ethical righteousness that flows from it.

Thus, the redeemed community becomes the body of Christ.[10] Paul is emphatic in his letters on the importance of moral conduct that promotes, rather than destroys, this special bond among Christians. Everyone has a unique contribution to make in serving this body through the diverse gifts that God has given individuals within the community. Living according to the Spirit builds up this body, while giving in to the desires of the flesh erodes and ultimately destroys it (Gal 5:19–26).

Community building is necessarily rooted in emulating the example of Christ who emptied himself and freely gave his life so that sinners might be saved and live. Christ's self-sacrifice is the model for Christians in serving one another (Phil 2:5–11; Rom 15:1–7; 2 Cor 8:9; Col 3:13; Eph 4:32; 5:2).[11] The practical implication of this is the imperative of mutual burden-bearing within the community. We see this particularly in the letter to the Galatians in which Paul vehemently disagrees with the legalists who insisted that even the Galatians were subject to the Mosaic Law. Paul responds that it is the law of Christ that is binding, not the Mosaic law. And the law of Christ is none other than the paradigm of Jesus' self-emptying for others. Thus, Christians are invited to give of themselves in mutual burden-bearing, following the footsteps of Jesus Christ.[12] Paul himself lives up to what he preaches. He suffers much and gives up much, for love of God and for the sake of building up the communities to which he had been sent (1 Cor 8:1–11:1).[13]

Confident Engagement with the World

Despite fierce opposition from non-Christians, Paul's response was not to withdraw from the world just like the Essenes. Instead, the mandate, the desire, and the joy that come with preaching the Gospel compelled Paul to endure and adapt to whatever demands were made of him, no matter how exacting. Thus, 1 Corinthians 9:19–23 describes the great lengths to which he would go to win people over to the Gospel. Not only does he engage the larger world, but he also perseveres and adapts, even as he is persecuted. "Do not be overcome by evil, but overcome evil with good" (Rom 12:21). Christians are called not to a "sectarian isolationism," but to a spirit-filled witness to the Gospel.[14] This is consistent with the perennial theme of the goodness of the world that we find running throughout Sacred Scripture, from the account of creation (Gen 1), to the Word becoming flesh, to the table-fellowship of Jesus, and to the commission to preach the Gospel to the ends of the earth.

This confident interaction with the world is also reflected in Paul's willingness to cooperate with civil authority (Rom 13:1–7), but not out of necessity, expediency, dread, or servility. Rather, he is animated by the Christian regard and concern for the well-being of others (Rom 8–10). Nevertheless, in working vigorously with the world and its structures, Christians do not acquiesce to its flaws, but serve as a leaven instead. This selective and discerning engagement with the world is seen in Paul's admonition to the people to dissociate themselves from the "works of darkness," such as debauchery and licentiousness, and to put on instead the "armor of light" that permits one to live honorably (Rom 13:12–14).

Economic Norms

Taking Responsibility for Oneself: Work Ethic

The ancient Greeks and Romans abhorred manual labor as a curse, fit only for the lower classes. We find this disdain for work in classical literature and philosophy.[15] In contrast, Christianity has an entirely different view of work, including manual labor, which it deems to be both dignified and an obligation. Thus, in the Christian community, everyone is to work, and not merely women or people from the lower classes, such as farmers and poor craftsmen. This is most vividly seen in the stern Pauline warning that the able-bodied who refused to work were not to be fed (2 Thess 3:6–12).

Honest work is constitutive of Christian discipleship. More than anybody, Paul is keenly aware of the urgency of getting ready for Christ's second coming. An imminent Parousia changes temporal life to one of expectant waiting and intense preparation. Despite his focus on this supernatural end, Paul is not altogether otherworldly to the point of disregarding important temporal obligations, such as working to provide for one's own keep and not to free-ride on the efforts of others (1 Thess 4:9–12; 5:14; 2 Cor 9:8; cf. 2 Thess 3:6–12; Titus 3:1). He harshly criticizes those who have given up work on account of the looming eschatological age. They are slothful and do not deserve to be supported (2 Thess 3:6–12). Moreover, honest work enables people to provide material assistance to those who are genuinely unable to work for themselves. In addition, work is an effective way of avoiding the temptation to steal (Eph 4:28) and provides the means to fulfill one's civic duties, such as paying taxes (Rom 13:6).

Work is "an ordinance of creation" and an "obligation of justice."[16] To begin with, it prevents imposing unnecessary burdens on others (2 Thess 3:8). Thus, families with widows are encouraged to take care of them on their own, to the extent possible, so that the Church may devote its limited resources to the genuinely needy and helpless. Otherwise, the Church will be overwhelmed with demands it could not meet (1 Tim 5:16). People ought to do what they are able to do for themselves. Besides, idle people run the risk of becoming busybodies (1 Tim 5:11–13). Work is also a matter of justice, because family members have an obligation to provide for kin who are unable to fend for themselves or who are in distress. In fact, material support of dependents or needy family members is a requirement of faith (1 Tim 5:8).

Paul not only preaches a stringent work ethic, but also exemplifies this requisite work ethos.[17] Scripture clearly shows that the apostles and those who preach the word of God have a legitimate claim for material sustenance from their congregations. In the Synoptic Gospels, Jesus instructs the disciples not to take anything with them, but to depend on the goodwill and support of the people to whom they were sent to preach (Mt10:1–16; Mk 6:8–11; Lk 9:2–4; 10:4–7). Paul himself asserts his right for such compensation as an apostle (1 Cor 9:1–15). Moreover, this seems to have been an established practice in the early church (1 Tim 5:17–18; 3 John 1:5–8; 1 Cor 9; 2 Cor 11:7–9; Phil 4:10–19).

Such support for the apostles is not only a matter of justice or tradition or precept from the Lord, but also an issue of practical necessity, so that the Gospel might be preached more efficiently and effectively. Cast in economic terms, there are gains to be reaped from a communal division of labor where complex tasks are divided, and people specialize in one or two functions alone. Not only are specific jobs better performed due to specialization, but the entire community benefits from having more and better quality outcomes. Thus, the apostles appointed the first deacons so that they (the apostles) could concentrate full-time on preaching the Gospel (Acts 6:1–3).

Nevertheless, Paul voluntarily gives up this right to material support from the churches. Instead he opts to work for his own keep, so as not to burden the churches (Acts 18:3; 20:32–36; 1 Thess 2:6–9; 1 Thess 4:11–12; 1 Cor 9:12, 15; 2 Cor 11:7–9; 12:11–18; cf. 2 Thess 3:6–12;).[18] This is significant because by his own account, Paul already bore heavy burdens for the sake of the Gospel—arrest, shipwreck, floggings, persecution, destitution, cold, hunger, thirst, and homelessness. Far from seeking relief from these privations, Paul adds to them by refusing to claim his right for compensation and instead toils night and day to provide for his needs (1 Cor 4:12; 2 Cor 11:27; 2 Thess 3:8). This only underscores further the tremendous importance he accords to assiduous work. Nevertheless, despite the advantages and value of self-sufficiency, one ought to be gracious and thankful in receiving assistance from others. For example, Paul is deeply appreciative and grateful to the Philippians for coming to his aid on many occasions when he was in need (Phil 4:10–20).

While there are similarities between Paul's work ethic of self-sufficiency and the views of Greek moralists, Paul differs in his motive. Unlike the Cynics and Stoics who valued self-sufficiency for the independence, security, and personal integrity that it confers, Paul calls for providing for one's own needs, to the extent possible, because it is an obligation as part of right relationship with God. It is an act of charity not to burden others and to earn a livelihood with which to help those who are in distress.[19] By his own account, Paul does not want to be an economic burden on the people to whom he preached so that (1) they might focus only on his preaching, (2) there is clearly no ulterior motive that can be ascribed to his preaching, such as angling for people's money or free-riding on their labors (cf. Acts 20:33–34), and (3) he could set an example of how hard work is a means to helping the poor (cf. Acts 20:35).

Outreach to the Distressed and Needy

Paul's collection for the poor of Jerusalem affirms the importance of sharing one's substance with those who are in distress (Rom 12:13; 1 Cor 16:1–4; 2 Cor 8–9; Eph 4:28; cf. Acts 20:35). Solicitude for the poor is central to Pauline ethics.[20] The rich in the Christian community are reminded that wealth is meant for good works and generosity (1 Tim 6:17–19). Thus, Paul chides the wealthy in the Corinthian community because of the scandalous manner by which they celebrated the Eucharist (1 Cor 11:22). He admonishes wealthier members of the community to wait for their poorer brethren in the celebration of the Lord's Supper and to share their food with them. After all, they are all children of God (Gal 3:26). Besides, it is more in line with the self-emptying example of Christ (Rom 14:9; 1 Cor 8:11–13).[21]

Such generous sharing is duly rewarded by God (2 Cor 9:6–11; Gal 6:7–10). Moreover, it gives rise to thankful hearts all around: the giver thanks God for blessings received and the recipient thanks God for the donor's generosity and witness to the Gospel (2 Cor 9:11–15). Neither the expected reward from God nor earning one's own righteousness is the rationale for almsgiving and sharing. Rather, genuine generosity is animated by thanksgiving for God's benefactions.

Finally, sharing one's wealth is "sacramental" because it affects the Church's fellowship and unity in Christ. It becomes a concrete means by which Christian Jews and Christian Gentiles care for one another.[22]

Proper Attitude toward Possessions

Pauline economic norms differ from the rest of the New Testament in at least two ways. First, unlike James, the prophets, and Synoptic Gospels, they do not condemn or use harsh language against the rich. Second, unlike the synoptic evangelists, Paul does not call for radical voluntary divestment. In fact, he preaches on the duty to provide for one's own keep and not to be a burden on others. Dispossession is not extolled.

While the Pauline letters do not indict the rich, the latter are cautioned nonetheless on the dangers of possessions.[23] Wealth can cause people to anchor their identity, sense of security, and hopes on riches, rather than on God. Greed is the idolatry of riches (Col 3:5). The pastoral letters warn against the corrosive nature of avarice. An inordinate love of money leads to many disorders and evils. Arrogance and wealth crowd out the good works people ought to be doing (1 Tim 3:3, 8; 6:9–10, 17–19; Tit 1:7). Greed is both a symptom and a cause of sin (Rom 1:29; Eph 4:19). It is not proper conduct for the people of God and is subject to punishment (1 Cor 6:10; Eph 5:3, 5).[24]

Possessions are not to be treated as ends in themselves, to be accumulated as much as one can. Rather, the goods of the earth are to provision everyone. Work and possessions are meant to help people maintain themselves and their dependents in self-sufficiency (*autarkeia*) (1 Thess 4:11–12). Thus, even Paul himself acknowledges that there are limits to almsgiving. It should be proportionate to one's means and should not impoverish the giver (2 Cor 8:12–13). The proper attitude is not an acquisitive ethos, but a humble attitude of service and stewardship. Moreover, godliness is not to be used for financial gain (1Tim 6:2–12).

In addition to stewardship, contentment is another virtue presented to Christians. Simplicity of life and moderation in desire and the use of the goods of the earth are values worth pursuing (1 Tim 6:6–8). Thus, Paul is at peace and thankful, both in times of plenty or want (1 Cor 4:11–13; Phil 4:11–13).

Pauline Economic Norms in the Context of Pauline Theology and Ethics

Do Pauline economic norms flow from Pauline theology and ethics? If so, how? Clearly, Paul was not a social reformer. He was not intent on rectifying the injustices of his age. Rather, he was set on preaching Jesus Christ (Phil 1:21–24). Not surprisingly, the Pauline letters are principally concerned with the salvation wrought by Christ, not with social, much less economic, ethics. Nevertheless, upright moral behavior in economic life is an imperative. Pauline economic norms flow seamlessly from these letters' theology and ethics. Consider the following examples.

First, the death and resurrection of Jesus Christ inaugurate a "newness of life" (Rom 6:4). Paul's contrasts are not between heaven and earth or the material and spiritual, but between the old and the new age (2 Cor 5:17).[25] There is a new dispensation that radically alters moral life. There is a new freedom. It is a freedom from self-indulgence and sin, and a freedom for serving and loving others (Gal 6:2). It is a freedom for self-giving. Christians now have the opportunity to offer themselves as "instruments of righteousness"—agents for God's unfolding divine providence (Rom 6:13, 18).[26] Indeed, Christ's resurrection is transformative and empowering; it dispels fear and replaces it with a boundless liberty. Unlike the early days when the disciples locked themselves in a room for fear of the Jews (Jn 20:19), Christians could now live openly and courageously as witnesses to God's saving work (e.g., Acts 4:32–37; 1 Cor 1:18–31; Phil 3:10). Their very lives could become a blazing testimony to what God has accomplished in human life.

However, this empowerment has attendant obligations. In particular, living in the freedom wrought by Christ is not merely an option but a duty, so that the saved might live up to the fullness of life. The transformation, the empowerment, and the freedom that flow from Christ's resurrection demand corresponding changes in how people live and love. Thus, it is a false dichotomy to juxtapose faith and good works as if they were mutually exclusive. They are, in fact, necessary conditions to each other. We find this in the distinctive indicative-imperative dynamic of the Pauline letters.

Pauline economic ethics does not espouse a salvation won through good works. Rather, it is about a divinely conferred righteousness whose manifold fruits include good works. "Christians are not saved by works of love but definitely for works of love" (Eph 2:8–10).[27] Thus, sharing with the poor of

Jerusalem, an assiduous work ethic, and stewardship of possessions are not the means by which Christians earn their own salvation. Rather, these actions flow from their being saved and made righteous by Christ.

Second, as we have seen earlier, the imitation of Christ is a perennial and important theme in Pauline theology and ethics. For example, Paul encourages the Corinthians to give generously to the Jerusalem collection based on the example of Jesus Christ, who, though he was rich, made himself poor so that humans in their poverty might become rich (2 Cor 8:8–15). The Incarnation of Christ and his subsequent passion and death serve as the model and basis for people's own self-emptying love.[28] Christ's saving self-immolation is an unmerited gift that compels people to extend to others the same favors that they in their own turn had received in their own moment of need.[29]

Thus, Paul justifies the collection for the poor of Jerusalem as part of the law of Christ. After all, Christians are to bear one another's burden, following Christ who had laid down his life on the cross so that others might live (Gal 6:2; cf. Gal 1:4; 2:20).[30] Recall that the immediate context of Paul's collection was the need to assist the brethren in Judea who were ill prepared to deal with the drought (Acts 11:28–30) given their voluntary dispossession (Acts 2:44–45; 4:32–5:10). The community is one body in Christ (1 Cor 12:3–7, 12–13), and "if one member suffers, all suffer together with it" (1 Cor 12:26). Moreover, everyone has a unique gift that is meant to build up and to serve the whole body. For example, in the realm of work and possessions, it is an imperative to work and to share one's substance with those in distress.

Thus, they took responsibility for one another's well-being.[31] Some of such sharing was profoundly sacrificial, as in the case of the Macedonians who gave freely to the collection despite being hard-pressed themselves in what little they had (2 Cor 8:1–6). This, after all, is what Christian love is all about—heroism in what it is able to achieve (1 Cor 13) because of its endless reservoir found in Christ's love (Rom 8:35–39). This is what "fulfilling the law of Christ" is all about.

A third link between Pauline economic norms, theology, and ethics is the recurrent contrast between giving in to the desires of the flesh and living up to the desires of the Spirit. Paul's call for honest work, generosity, and moderation in consumption and property acquisition falls well within his characterization of the moral life as a choice between indulging the desires of the flesh, on the one hand, and living a new life in the spirit, on the other hand. Concupiscence is not only about sexual excesses, but also about inordinate economic conduct—hedonism, avarice, selfishness, oppression, and exploitation. Clearly, the aforesaid Pauline economic norms are among the collateral effects of the fruits of the Holy Spirit: "love, joy, peace, patience, kindness, generosity, faithfulness, gentleness, and self-control" (Gal 5:22–23). These sharply contrast with the works of the flesh, such as licentiousness, envy, drunkenness, and enmity that are characteristic of a dysfunctional economic life. Pauline economic norms are but part of the new life in the Spirit.

Fourth, note that the Pauline letters do not call for institutional or social changes, but focus instead on personal conversion and behavior. The Pauline stance is moderate in its counsels and simply accepts the social status quo. For example, as mentioned earlier, these letters do not harshly condemn the wealthy or call for radical voluntary poverty, but merely caution against the excessive pursuit of wealth and its dangers (1 Tim 6:2–12). Nevertheless, the rich in the community are urged not to anchor their hopes and life on riches, but to put such wealth instead to good use by sharing and helping the distressed.[32] Or take the case of runaway Onesimus. Much to the discomfort of modern-day commentators, Paul seems to acquiesce to the practice of slavery during his time; he does not challenge it. He sends Onesimus back to his master and simply instructs Philemon that the new freedom inaugurated by Christ changes the relationship between masters and slaves. The former were now to treat the latter as brothers and sisters.[33]

The imminence of the Parousia could possibly account for Paul's seeming indifference to social change. Recall how he had advised the Corinthians not to be concerned about their social status, much less seek to change it (1 Cor 7:17–24). After all, the "appointed time" is growing shorter and the "present form of this world is passing" (1 Cor 7:29–31). In the face of this looming day of reckoning, it makes more sense to employ their remaining time in interior conversion, rather than in a roundabout social change.

Nevertheless, as we see in his severe rebuke of malingerers and freeloaders who had given up work, there is a hard-nosed realism to Paul. He is not completely otherworldly in his concerns. He appreciates the pragmatic dimension to the tension between the eschatological "already here" and the "not yet." On the one hand, money matters little in the face of a passing age (1 Cor 7:29–31). On the other hand, this should not become an excuse to walk away from our temporal responsibilities, such as work, providing for our own keep, and feeding the widows and the genuinely helpless. Paul balances both effectively. After all, Christian communities must still be able to function as they awaited the Parousia. Note how he calls for sharing possessions rather than the complete renunciation of property. Neither does he advocate almsgiving to the point of impoverishing oneself (2 Cor 8:12–13).

Summary and Conclusions

Despite their pragmatism and down-to-earth concerns, why are there so few economic norms in the Pauline letters? The first possible explanation is Paul's imminent Parousia. The world as they knew it then was slipping away

(1 Cor 7:29–31).[34] This could also account for the mere handful of economic norms in Mark, in contrast to the wealth of economic teachings in Luke and Matthew. Recall that the Gospel of Mark, too, is marked by the expectation of an imminent eschatology. A second possible explanation is that Paul concentrates only on the death and the resurrection of Jesus Christ. In contrast, the Gospels have a broader scope that includes giving a narrative account of the ministry and the preaching of Jesus.[35]

On the surface, Pauline economic norms are not unique to Christians alone, but merely echo many commonsensical norms in the wisdom literature, such as the importance and virtuous nature of hard work, self-sufficiency, and generous sharing.[36] Nevertheless, what is distinctive about Pauline economic norms is not their content, but their motivation—love of God and neighbor, in emulation of Jesus Christ.

Finally, Pauline economic norms are vivid examples of the indicative-imperative dynamic in which ethics necessarily flows from theology. Good works and faith do not provide competing accounts of justification. They are inseparable complements—two sides of the same coin. Good works merely reflect a vibrant, overflowing faith that finds expression in upright moral conduct. In other words, Pauline economic norms merely invite Christians to live up to who they have become—redeemed by Christ and empowered by the Spirit.

JAMES

Life Setting

The letter of James is addressed to a community of Jewish Christians. Reference to the twelve tribes in the salutation (Jas 1:1) alerts us to the intended Jewish audience of the letter. It also explains what some observe to be the desultory nature of the work. After all, the letter seems to be disjointed in jumping from one point to another without further elaboration. This is because the writer of James presupposes that the readers are thoroughly familiar with and steeped in the Torah. The writer is merely reminding readers of what they already know and should be practicing to begin with.

This community was most likely comprised of different socioeconomic classes—the rich, the middle class, and the poor. This is inferred from the letter's critique of the well-off and its encouraging words for the poor. Note, for example, the severe reprimand of the rich for scorning the poor (Jas 2:1–4). The letter is believed to have been written toward the end of the first century when many urban Christian churches were increasingly dominated by wealthy benefactors who were part of the local elite.[37]

There is scholarly disagreement on whether the letter of James was occasioned by a problem in one of the churches or whether it was merely following the wisdom tradition in piecing together aphorisms, teachings, and exhortations on living life in a good and proper manner. Most scholars believe that the letter of James flows from the wisdom tradition. After all, James has many of the features of Hellenistic paraenesis:

- the letter is traditional and unoriginal in its teachings (e.g., critique of the rich, concern for the poor);
- it merely states general principles that can then be applied across time and culture;
- it is meant either to "juggle people's memories" or to move them to action, or both, because addressees have heard these exhortations/admonitions before;
- it presents concrete examples for emulation;[38]
- it reminds the rich of their obligations;
- there is a close relationship between teacher and student, teacher and addressee;[39] and
- hearing-forgetting (e.g., Jas 1:19–27) and knowing-doing (e.g., Jas 4:13–17) are favorite themes.

The paraenesis in the letter of James may have been part of new converts' initiation into the Christian community by spelling out what was expected of them.[40] Other scholars disagree because James does not follow the literary form and subject matter of the wisdom or paraenetic text of that era. They believe that James' literary and textual evidence heavily point to the letter being written with a specific social problem in mind.[41]

Theology

The goal of James is practical rather than doctrinal.[42] Nevertheless, there is a theological foundation undergirding the ethical admonitions of this letter. In particular:

- Faith is central to the letter. Complete trust in God is necessary if one is to endure and rise above the sufferings of the present age. It is faith that produces the harvest of good works, which are constitutive of a vibrant relationship with God.
- The letter is theocentric, rather than Christocentric, as it relies heavily on reference to God rather than to Christ.[43] God is presented as Father, Lord, lawgiver, and judge. The disciple faces a stark choice of friendship with God or with the world, but not both. Humans are created in God's image (Jas 3:9), and the goal is to live up to this image by imitating God.
- The letter has an eschatological horizon with its acknowledgment that this is a passing world. The eschaton is on the way, and the present is a call to

> prepare for it. This ought to be the context and reference point of moral conduct, the reason for the believer's paradoxical joy even in the midst of great distress.[44]

These provide the overarching theological context of the letter's ethical admonitions.

Ethics

The ethics of James is eschatological, social and communal, based on divine precept and command, and paradigmatic in which models are held up for emulation (e.g., Jas 5:10–11).[45] Regardless of whether James flows from the wisdom or the prophetic tradition and despite its seeming desultory and cursory nature, the letter offers a coherent ethical vision. We examine three different accounts of the letter's ethical vision. These are not mutually exclusive but overlap one another. They differ only in their emphases.

Moral Life as a Choice of Friendships

Humans have to choose between friendship with God and friendship with the world. They cannot have both since these are mutually exclusive (Jas 4:4). To be a friend is to be a "soul mate" with deeply shared values. Everything is shared in common, and there is a particular kind of intimacy and comfort in being with the other who is deemed to be "another self." It is to be able to identify oneself with the other. Friendship with the world leads to vicious speech (Jas 3:6–8) and the exploitation of the poor and defenseless by the rich and powerful (Jas 5:1–6). Friendship with the world results in the denial or haughty disregard of the fundamental equality of all (Jas 2:1–7), the centrality of divine providence in life (Jas 4:13–16), and the nature of creation as God's gift to humans (Jas 1:17). In contrast, to be a friend of God is to appreciate everything as an unmerited divine benefaction (Jas 1:17–18), to live up to the Word of God (Jas 1:22), and to love one's neighbor (Jas 2:8). Moral life is a constant struggle to move away from friendship with the world to a lively friendship with God. Hence, there is need for conversion (Jas 3:13–4:10) and ceaseless vigilance against complacency.[46] The best way to sustain this conversion is to live a faith that overflows into action.

The ethics of James is concerned, not with an individualistic ethics, but with building a faith community (e.g., Jas 5:12–20). It is, therefore, critical of those who erode the bonds of community through their sinful conduct. It frowns on conformity to the ethos of the larger culture and invites readers to give witness to their faith. Hence, there is a dualistic dimension to the letter's theology and ethics, as seen in the juxtaposition of contrasts between truth and error (Jas 1:16, 18), peace and war (Jas 3:17–18; 4:1–2), generosity and envy (Jas 1:17; 4:1–3, 6; 3:16), wisdom and folly (Jas 1:5, 26; 3:13), purity and impurity (Jas 1:21, 27; 4:8), blessing and curse (Jas 3:9), the lowly and the arrogant (Jas 4:6), and the innocent and the oppressor (Jas 5:6; 2:6).[47] These contrasts suggest that the letter's audience is a faith community living in the midst of unbelievers who subscribe to radically different values.

An Effective Faith

James 1:3 can be viewed as the hermeneutical key to the letter. It suggests a community that is being sorely tested in its faith. The unifying theme to James is its description of the nature of faith. The vibrancy of faith is seen:

- in its readiness and openness to listen and to act on the Word of God (Jas 1:19–27),
- in its impartiality in treating rich and poor alike as deserving of respect (Jas 2:1–13),
- in its fruits—the good works that spontaneously result from it (Jas 2:14–26),
- in its self-control (Jas 3:1–16) and consequent virtues (Jas 3:17–18),
- in its abhorrence of strife, division, presumption, exploitation, and injustice (Jas 4:1–5:12), and
- in its prayer life (Jas 5:13–18).

In other words, genuine faith is effective and distinctive in its resulting moral conduct. It is a "living faith."[48] Thus, far from being in competition with faith, good works flow from faith. They are a necessary condition of faith. The letter unambiguously and forcefully stresses this point (Jas 2:14, 20, 26). Some have even gone so far as to describe James as a "severe and pragmatic spirituality" in which faith and action are inseparable. James is not concerned with how to attain salvation, but with what to do and how to behave after being saved.[49] Believers must be both hearers and doers of the Word.[50]

Fidelity to the Torah

The writer sees no need to elaborate further on the letter's admonitions because readers are assumed to know the provenance of these teachings, the Torah. Note the reference in James 1:25 to the perfect law. Thus, all the writer is doing is to remind them of the moral precepts of the Torah they are already familiar with (cf. Jas 2:8 and Lev 19:18). Fidelity to the law is the letter's overriding concern. It advances four admonitions, namely: endurance in the face of suffering, control of speech, faith manifested in action, and concern for the poor.[51]

Economic Norms

The letter of James offers at least three insights on economic life: the insidious nature of favoritism, the obligations of the rich and the dangers they face, and a requisite concern for the poor.[52] First, it is shameful to judge people by what they have or what they lack (Jas 2:1–13). In particular, the letter is critical of those who are obsequious to the rich and disdainful of the poor (Jas 2:2–4, 6). This is scandalous and completely contrary to the faith, no different from breaking the commandments (Jas 2:14–26). After all, everyone shares a fundamental equality, having been created in the image of God (Jas 3:9). It is wrong to favor some and discriminate against others. Readers are reminded that at the end of the day, people will get their just deserts, with mercy for the merciful (Jas 2:13).

Second, the rich are condemned for defrauding their workers in withholding their wages and in corrupting the justice system, even as the poor are unable to defend themselves (Jas 2:6; 5:6). The wealthy are warned of their arrogance in thinking that they control their own destinies and future with no appreciation for their dependence on God's providence (Jas 4:13–17). They are rebuked for their failure to use the gift of wealth to do good (Jas 4:15–17) despite the law's clear mandate to love their neighbor (Jas 2:8). There is a forthcoming reversal: riches are evanescent and are about to be lost (Jas 5:2–3), God listens to the cries of the poor and will respond accordingly (Jas 5:4), and the wealthy's opulence will be judged (Jas 5:5). The letter's harsh condemnation of the rich for their abuse and failure to care for the poor (Jas 2:14–17; 5:1–6) is very much along the lines of the prophetic indictments, especially those of Amos.[53]

Third, the poor are consoled and encouraged to endure, to be patient, and to continue living up to what God expects of them despite their burdens, want, and oppression (Jas 5:7–11; cf. 1:9–11). The rebuke of the wealthy for their maltreatment of the marginalized is an affirmation that the poor are special to God and their pleas are heard (Jas 5:4). This age is passing and their sufferings are at an end (Jas 5:8). There is a looming reversal in their fortunes along with that of their rich, powerful oppressors (Jas 1:9–10; 4:9–10; 5:1–6).[54] So important is this concern for the poor that the letter of James has even been described as having a theology of social concern. Two hallmarks of a community of believers is the care for the weak and marginalized and an impartiality in according respect and love to all. Such care for the poor is part of their imitation of God.[55]

Note that in all this, the letter of James does not call for radical voluntary divestment or for social-institutional change despite the scandalous abuses of the rich and the powerful. This may be due to the writer's belief in an imminent Parousia (Jas 5:2–3).

James clearly shows how these norms flow from his theology and ethics when he notes:

> "Religion that is pure and undefiled before God, the Father, is this: *to care for orphans and widows in their distress*, and to keep oneself unstained by the world" (Jas 1:27; emphasis added).

This brings us back again to the fundamental choice faced by humans: friendship with God or friendship with the world. Clearly, there is an economic dimension to friendship with God. This concern for the poor is consistent with the Torah as a reference point for James.

SUMMARY AND CONCLUSIONS

Paul and James are often presented in the literature as polar opposites in their understanding of the role of good works vis-à-vis faith in salvation. This is a false dichotomy. Both Paul and James see the inseparability of faith and good works. The true believer acts on the Word that has been received. Because of this integral link, belief in Jesus Christ necessarily translates to upright moral conduct. This includes economic life. Thus, even as the Pauline letters and James were not written as ethical or even as economic treatises, they nevertheless offer insights on what constitutes proper economic behavior. These economic norms are the natural outflow of these letters' theology and ethics. Furthermore, both converge on the central importance of care for the poor. This should not come as a surprise since both are steeped in Jewish social thought and praxis.

NOTES

1. Pauline theology is an extensive field of study. The following account is merely a brief sketch of some of its insights directly relevant for Pauline economic ethics.
2. Dunn (1998; 2004); Fitzmyer (1990); Osborn (1976, 15–20)
3. Hays (1996, 46)
4. Ancient words of Pindar cited by Bultmann (Schrage 1988, 169)
5. Furnish (1968); Hays (1996, 18). Schrage (1988, 169–72) surveys four different accounts of the indicative-imperative dynamic in Paul.
6. Hays (1987, 288–89)
7. Davies (2006, 744–47)
8. 1 Cor 5:10–11; 6:9-10; 2 Cor 6:6–7; 12:20–21; Gal 5:19-23; Rom 1:29–31; 13:13; Col 3:5–8, 12–14; Eph 5:3–5; cf. Rev 21:8; 22:15; Mt 5:3–12; 25:31–46 (Fitzmyer, 1990, 1413; Osborn, 1976, 19).
9. Osborn (1976, 18)
10. Hays (1996, 32–36)
11. Hays (1987); Perkins (1984)
12. Hays (1987)
13. Hays (1996, 41)
14. Perkins (1984, 272–73, 280)

15. Homer in the *Iliad* (10, 71) describes work as "the most oppressive misfortune that Zeus imposes upon men from their very birth" (Schelkle 1973, 286). Plato and Aristotle note that "the confining nature of the life of a manual laborer is damaging to virtue and soul" (Schelkle 1973, 287). Cicero (*De Officiis* 1, 42) looks down on manual labor as shabby business. It is a dishonor to have to be compelled to do manual labor. There are unusual exceptions such as Marcus Aurelius, who holds a positive attitude toward work.
16. Schelkle (1973, 293)
17. Gordon (1989, 46–54); Matera (1996, 134–37); Perkins (1994, 56)
18. Perkins (1994, 56)
19. Dahl (1977, 23–25); Perkins (1994, 55–59)
20. See Longnecker (2010) for a detailed exposition on how care for the poor is integral to Pauline thought.
21. Donohue (2005, 30–31)
22. Dahl (1977, 32, 35)
23. Dahl (1977, 22)
24. Hays (1996, 70); Perkins (1994, 46)
25. Donohue (2005, 29)
26. Donohue (2005, 29–31)
27. Nürnberger (1978, 164)
28. Nürnberger (1978, 164–65); Rhyne (1987)
29. This is the same dynamic that we find behind Old Testament laws.
30. Hays (1996, 27–28)
31. Nürnberger (1978, 163)
32. Hays (1996, 70)
33. Lohfink (1986, 229)
34. Dahl (1977, 25)
35. Matera (2007, 8)
36. Dahl (1977, 24)
37. Harvey (1990, 117); Kidd (1990, 61–95); Perkins (1994, 46); Schelkle (1973, 306); cf. Johnson (2004, 169–70).
38. For example, we have Abraham and Rahab in James 2:14–26, Job and the prophets in James 5:7–11, and Elijah in James 5:13–20.
39. Note the writer's use of "my brethren" in James 1:2; 2:1, 14; 3:1, 12; 5:7, 10, 12, 19 and "my beloved brethren" in James 1:16, 19; 2:5. Johnson (1995b, 82) concludes that the writer of James is egalitarian rather than authoritarian in tone and language. There is only one father, and that is God (Jas 1:17–18, 27).
40. Perdue (1981, 241–46, 251–56; 1990b)
41. See Johnson (1995a; 1995b, 193–97). Maynard-Reid (1987) uses social scientific criticism to show that James flows from the prophetic tradition in its harsh critique of unjust social relations. It addresses a real need and problem within the community.
42. Heibert (1978, 223)
43. Hartin (2003, 31)
44. Hartin (2003, 29–38)
45. Chester and Martin (1994, 35). See Johnson (1995b, 81–82) for a slightly different characterization of the ethics of James.
46. Johnson (1985, 173–75)
47. Johnson (1995b, 81–88)
48. Hiebert (1978)
49. Hartin (2006)
50. Donohue (2005, 26–27)
51. Hartin (2006)
52. Hartin (2006, 466–68); Nardoni (2004, 235–39); Wheeler (1995, 98–105)
53. Donohue (2005, 26–27)
54. Chester and Martin (1994, 34); Schelkle (1973, 305)
55. Hartin (2003, 37–39)

III

Toward a Biblical Theology of Economic Life

Chapter Eleven

A Divine Order of Conditional Prosperity

The economic ordinances, aphorisms, and paraeneses of Sacred Scripture do not arise in a vacuum. Neither are they the arbitrary norms of a whimsical deity who pulls them out of thin air without rhyme or reason. As we have repeatedly seen in the preceding chapters, these teachings on economic life flow from the theology and ethics of the books in which they are found. Thus, the laws mandating assistance to the distressed stemmed from the nation Israel's understanding that God was merely asking the Chosen People to extend to others the same favors that they themselves had received from God in their own moment of need. The prophets were appalled by injustice because they knew that such iniquity was antithetical to Israel's special Covenant relationship with YHWH. The sages' sayings on proper economic conduct arose from their understanding of a world that was steeped in the wisdom of God. The evangelists cautioned against the idolatry of wealth and power because of the certain reckoning that is to come with Christ as judge seated at the right hand of his Father. Indeed, the economic teachings of these sacred texts reveal something much larger than themselves—the building of the nation Israel and the Kingdom of God. In other words, *the economic teachings of Sacred Scripture point to a much larger divine plan and order, of which they are a part and to which they contribute.*

Biblical economic norms give us a glimpse into God's order of creation and its attendant requirements. This divine order of creation (1) communicates the goodness, perfection, and wisdom of God; (2) subjects all creatures to the absolute sovereignty of God; and (3) specifies a particular order both in the natural world and in moral life. While we are not able to understand fully everything that can be known about this divine order, we can nevertheless discern enough of it through Revelation, reason, and human experience.

Based on the ordinances, aphorisms, and admonitions on economic conduct from the preceding chapters, we can discern features of this divine order. In particular, we can draw the following inferences that are relevant for our study:

- The natural world and human affairs are governed by the divine order of creation.
- There is an underlying act-consequence dynamic in God's order of creation.
- God has given humanity the gift of material sufficiency, albeit one that is conditional on upright moral conduct.
- Such conditionality turns out to be yet another divine gift—the gift of human participation in divine providence. In other words, God effects the gift of conditional prosperity through human agency itself.

We examine each of these in the following sections.

AN OVERARCHING DIVINE ORDER

Nothing escapes the sovereignty of God. After all, every creature comes from God. Moreover, all creation has to be sustained by God for every moment of its existence. What emerges clearly from Sacred Scripture is that there is an order with very specific requirements that are embedded in God's creation. In other words, the natural world and human affairs are governed by a particular set of laws and dynamics that have been set by no less than God. We find such divine order implicitly or explicitly undergirding Sacred Scripture, from Deuteronomy's teachings on just deserts, to the wisdom literature's ethics of order, to the prophets' warnings on the dreadful consequences of injustice, to the New Testament's constant reminder of a forthcoming day of judgment and surprising reversals.

Consider some of the characteristic features of this divine order, especially as described in the wisdom literature.[1] First, God's cosmic order (*tzedeq*) originated from the very beginning of creation. It permeates creatures' existence and all of reality. It continues down through temporal time and is actively maintained by divine governance, providence, and justice. Thus, there is regularity and constancy observed in natural and human phenomena (Prov 6:6–8; 30:24–31).

Second, God deals with pre-existent chaos and makes it orderly, intelligible, and good. God is the architect of a well-ordered functioning cosmos, including its structures. Third, justice permeates creation itself. It is in the very fabric of creation, having been embedded in it from the initial moment of creatures' existence. Thus, even social institutions are steeped in this cosmic order and must conform to it if they are to be functional. It also means that justice is a constitutive element of upright human conduct.

Fourth, this cosmic order is a dynamic phenomenon.[2] Chaos has to be continuously kept at bay by the creative act of God. This is consistent with the theological understanding of creation as an ongoing event. Only God has necessary existence. Creatures are merely contingent in their existence; they decay, die, and revert to dust. They need not exist nor can they guarantee their own existence. Thus, God has to sustain creatures in continued existence for every moment of their existence (divine providence). Since the cosmos is a creation of God that has to be continuously sustained, creation is not a one-time divine act, but an ongoing vibrant activity.

Fifth, Wisdom is the first of God's creation, God's divine child who is a source of delight. It shows humanity the pathway to living in harmony within the cosmic order. Sixth, God elicits human participation and cooperation in keeping chaos at bay and in maintaining the order of divine creation. God as creator offers the bounty of creation to the wise and the righteous—to those who live in harmony with the cosmic order and who participate in the unfolding creative act of God. The outcome for human conformity is their well-being and flourishing.

Seventh, God transcends the world, yet also dwells within it. God creates the world, but also judges it. Eighth, the cosmos with all its wonders is the work of God. However, despite the wonders of creation and what it reveals and despite all that Lady Wisdom can teach, God is not and cannot be fully known. There is an impenetrable mystery to God (cf. Job) that humans cannot fathom or access.

All these characteristic features of the divine order underscore a fact of life—humans are subject to a particular nature with its specific constraints and obligations. Moreover, with the help of divine grace, humans can know and live up to the objective requirements of such a nature. Not only are they knowable, but they are also doable. These objective requirements encompass all of human life, including economics. Of interest to us for our study are two features of this divine order, namely: (1) God's gift of material sufficiency and (2) an act-consequence (cause-and-effect) dynamic.

DIVINE GIFT OF MATERIAL SUFFICIENCY

As part of this order, humans receive God's gift of material prosperity in which no one is in want and there are adequate material provisions for all. God not merely freed Israel from her Egyptian bondage but went even further in setting her in a land "flowing with milk and honey" (Ex 3:8, 17; 13:5; 33:3; Lev 20:24; Num 14:8; Dt 6:3). It was a land of great bounty (Num 13:17–27; Dt 6:10–11; 8:7–10; 11:10–12; 26:9, 15). Furthermore, the people were instructed to divide the Promised Land so that every family had a plot, the proportions of which were determined by the fertility of the soil and the household size. Every household was to be an independent landholding family providing for its own keep. It was their inheritance from God. These idyllic descriptions bring home the point that God intends all to be free from want. Moreover, as we have repeatedly seen in the preceding chapters, the Old Testament abounds with narratives, laws, and motive clauses that reveal God's gift of material prosperity for Israel.

Unlike the Old Testament, the divine gift of economic security is not a recurring theme in the New Testament. However, we can infer such a gift from the Gospel, life, and ministry of Jesus Christ himself. The assurance of material sufficiency in Matthew 6:25–34 and Luke 12:22–31 is supported by the larger witness of the New Testament. First, humans are special in God's unfailing providence (Mt 10:28–32; Lk 12:4–7). Both evangelists reassure disciples that, even in the face of suffering and persecution, the watchful gaze of God never misses anything that happens to them. Such encouragement is directly relevant and transferrable to economic affairs because it is the same divine providence that is attentive to human needs, even before people ask. Furthermore, the filial relationship of humans to God is yet another reason for why it is fitting for them to enjoy material sufficiency. In reference to persistence in prayer and in a clear allusion to the Father's unfailing solicitude, Jesus tells his listeners that no father would ever let his child go hungry (Lk 11:9–13; Mt 7:7–11).

Second, an underlying refrain in the mission and preaching of Jesus is that he came so that people might have life and have it to the full (Jn 10:10). The plenitude of the gift that God intends for all is also revealed in Jesus' inaugural preaching when he proclaims the in-breaking kingdom and affirms the Jubilee nature of his mission (Lk 4:16–21). It is a "year of favor from the Lord" in which, true to the spirit of the Jubilee Law, no one will be in want. Of course, in speaking of life, liberation, and favor from the Lord, Jesus might have been referring primarily to the spiritual dimensions of the future eschatology when the fullness of God's reign will be revealed. Nevertheless, even as these promises deal ultimately with the immaterial matters of the heart, they have constitutive material dimensions. In other words, the promise of a future eschatology has particular, concrete effects even in the temporal here and now. We see this in the mission and life of Jesus.

By his own account, Jesus is inaugurating not a kingdom of this world but of heaven (Jn 18:36–37). Nonetheless, Jesus does not limit himself and his concerns to people's spiritual lives. More often than not, we find Jesus healing and ministering to the physical needs and material wants of the destitute, the sick, the hungry, and the marginalized. The kingdom of God is not merely about the promise of a spiritual liberation at some point in the future when the eschaton comes; it is also a promise of freedom in the here and now. Thus, in speaking of the gift of life and its abundance, we cannot merely limit ourselves to an exclusively spiritualized reading of Christ's mission. Such plenitude and fullness also pertain to human affairs in the earthly order. In fact, such contemporary abundance is integral to an in-breaking kingdom. Contrary to the eschatological reading of the Lord's Prayer, it is said that the bread requested is not about the messianic banquet, but about the daily bread that assuages hunger in the here and now.[3]

Third, whether in bestowing spiritual or material gifts, there is an unfailing, characteristic liberality to how Jesus dispenses his benefactions. For example, in ministering to people's ailments, Jesus does not merely ameliorate their debility by providing relief. Rather, he takes away the very condition itself and effects a complete healing. Jesus does not merely feed a few; he fills a multitude, and with such leftovers (Jn 6:5–13; Mt 14:13–21; Mk 6:32–44; Lk 9:10–17). Jesus does not merely provide an ordinary catch; he supplies such a great catch of fish to the point of nearly swamping the boats themselves (Lk 5:1–7; Jn 21:1–14). Jesus does not merely provide wine to save a newlywed couple from embarrassment; it has to be wine of the finest quality and in flowing abundance (Jn 2:1–11). Even if some claim that these are metaphorical images meant to make a larger theological point rather than actual historical events, they nonetheless point to God's characteristic abounding generosity in everything God does. They all herald the copious nature of the Messiah's work.

What is critical is not whether these events are historical or theological in nature or whether they refer to abundance in the present or in the eschaton. What is important to note is the hallmark quality of a God so lavish and persistent in bestowing gifts upon gifts on humans. And if God is so prodigal in dispensing such blessings, it would be completely uncharacteristic of divine liberality to limit its bounteous gifts only to the spiritual realm and not to the material conditions of human life. Might we not infer that the benevolence of God in dispensing spiritual gifts—as in the untiring divine forgiveness proffered (Mt 18:21–35), or as in the fruitfulness of the branches of the vine (Jn 15:1–8), or as in the bread from heaven that satisfies and saves (Jn 6:24–35), or as in the Incarnation and death of Jesus Christ—is the same liberality that will surely satisfy human needs in the here and now, both physical and spiritual? God has an established track record of beneficence that dates all the way back to that moment of creation when humans were given not merely existence, but were made in the very image and likeness of God itself. Moreover, they were made the stewards of the earth that was to provide for their needs. Indeed, the Old and New Testament reveal a God who is keenly interested in providing the earth and humans with signal plenitude.[4]

ACT-CONSEQUENCE DYNAMIC

Besides this gift of material sufficiency, the divine order is also characterized by an act-consequence dynamic. In other words, effects follow their causes. There are consequences to moral choices. We find this in the numerous biblical passages dealing with just deserts, forthcoming reversals, and prosperity in the wake of fidelity to the law. This act-consequence nexus is important for economic ethics because (1) it highlights people's accountability for their economic conduct, and (2) it points to life's overarching natural and moral order.

Divine justice-retribution is an important theological theme across the books of Sacred Scripture. There is clearly a cause-and-effect dynamic that is operative. We encounter it right from the very start in Genesis with the expulsion of Adam and Eve from Eden, the endless wandering of Cain for the murder of Abel, the dispersion of the people at Babel, the great flood in which only Noah and his family survived, and the destruction of Sodom and Gomorrah. We still find the same accountability at work in the book of Revelation with the separation of the saved from the condemned. Indeed, divine justice is at work throughout Sacred Scripture. The day of reckoning is a certainty, and all will be held to account for their moral choices. This phenomenon has sometimes been referred to as the Deuteronomic doctrine of divine retribution. It has also been called the act-consequence nexus, character-consequence link, reward-retribution dynamic, or wisdom-virtue-prosperity connection.[5]

Such cause-and effect dynamic is intuitively appealing. Humans expect nothing less than this from divine justice, since God is all-good, all-knowing, and almighty. For the sage:

> [B]asic to the wisdom of the ancient world was the conviction that the Creator had established the universe in an orderly fashion, that a principle of the right or appropriate deed held the created order together, and that man's purpose was to act in harmony with this principle at all times. . . . Any action that was not in accord with the governing principle of the universe was thought to have upset the balance of nature, to have reintroduced an element of chaos into the created order, hence to be deserving of punishment or death. Conversely, the appropriate deed was rewarded, since it sustained the universe, so that religion became highly utilitarian. (Crenshaw, 1970, 292)

An important caveat: This cause-and-effect dynamic in life is not always evident in every instance. In fact, as we have seen in the Psalms, we have the supplicant lamenting before God that the wicked prosper, while the just and the virtuous wallow in destitution. We have to remember that what is important is the underlying structure of reality rather than the empirical verifiability of this cause-and-effect dynamic. The goal is not so much as to "give evidence so much as to *make evident*."[6] Act-consequence rhetoric is not about empirically verifying or validating such a causal link. Rather, it is about pointing to wisdom[7] and the unfailing justice of God's order of creation, even if they are not always perceptible in the here and now.

In sum, undergirding the act-consequence nexus are the theological axioms (1) that God always takes care of the righteous (Ps 37:25) and (2) that God, the Creator, takes an active interest in maintaining the order of the universe, punishing iniquity, and rewarding the good.[8] Thus, moral choices, including economic ones, are consequential. There is a convergence between religious life and economic life as a practical activity. Both are oriented toward the same end—participating in the maintenance and upbuilding of the divine order of creation. In fact, they are complementary. Religious life seeks for and reflects on the goals that are truly worth pursuing in life, while economic life contributes toward actualizing such ends.

CONDITIONAL PROSPERITY

The aforesaid act-consequence dynamic of the divine order underscores the conditional nature of God's gift of material abundance. The gift of material abundance comes about because of the nature of creation itself in which God has created a bountiful world. But such material prosperity is enjoyed only to the degree that humans conform to the will of God, love and care for one another, and exercise stewardship over the earth. Material sufficiency is contingent on human's right relationship with God, with one another, and with the earth. In other words, God affects the divine gift of material prosperity through human agency. In fact, a perennial theme running across both the Old and the New Testament is the cause-and-effect dynamic of the divine order in economic life. The prophet, the priest, the sage, the evangelists, and St. Paul all believe in the efficacy of upright moral conduct. There is a direct link between good works and earthly rewards.[9]

Fidelity to God (whether through observance of the law or pursuit of the kingdom) leads to material prosperity or, at least, material sufficiency. We see this in the legal codes, among the prophets, and in the wisdom literature. Deuteronomy 28, Leviticus 26, and Psalm 37 assure the Chosen People that by not having idols, by observing the Sabbath, and by keeping God's statutes and ordinances, Israel will never want for rain, her harvests will flow in great abundance, she will prevail over her adversaries, and peace will reign in the land. She is repeatedly told that she will conquer the whole land flowing with milk and honey for herself, possess it, live on it, and, indeed, thrive on it, but only if she is faithful to God's decrees (Dt 6:1–15; 7:12–14; 8:6–20; 11:8–17; 16:20; 19:8–9; Lev 26:1–26; Jer 7:5–7; Is 58; Hg 1:1–11; 2:15–19; Mal 3:9–12). The Deuteronomist reassures those who observe the Sabbath fallow that God will bless them with such plentiful harvest in the sixth year as to feed them until the ninth year's harvest (Lev 25:18–22). The law provides repeated reminders on the blessings and the condemnation that come with its observance or violation. Israel's tenure on the land flowing with milk and honey depends on her conformity to the law (e.g., Dt 28; 30:16). Israel will be blessed if she observes the ordinances of the Lord (Dt 7:13; 14:29; 15:10, 18; 24:19; 30:16).

Similarly, the prophets preach, plead, and cajole the nation to reform its ways and to live up to its part of the Covenant. Fidelity brings good fortune, while continued disobedience spells doom and destruction. In fact, the prophets are emphatic in their warnings on the imminent punishment Israel and Judah are about to bring down upon themselves. Injustice and evil lead only to want and impoverishment (e.g., Is 5:8–10). Israel will be suckled as a child feeds from her mother's breasts, if only she were faithful (Is 66:11–13). And, indeed, Judah enjoys peace and prosperity because of Hezekiah's and Josiah's covenant obedience (2 Kgs 18–20; 22:1–23:30). Jeremiah 22:13–16 reminds the wayward King Jehoiakim that his father King Josiah (640–609 B.C.) never lacked for food or drink because he was just in all that he did. Similarly, Daniel flourishes because of his righteousness before the Lord (Dn 1:8–20). Vineyard fruitfulness is a favorite metaphor for what awaits those who are faithful to the Lord (Is 5:1–7; Hos 10:1; Jer 2:21; cf. Jn 15).[10] The book of Lamentations describes the fate of those who spurn God's ordinances. Israel loses the manifold material blessings she had abused wantonly.[11]

The sages repeat the same message. Wisdom literature describes the same cause-and-effect phenomenon. Wealth and prosperity are the fruits of virtue, hard work, and wisdom. In contrast, destitution is the lot of the indolent, the frivolous, and the wicked. There is a near mechanical correspondence in which wrongdoing brings about punitive consequences (e.g., Prov 26:27; Ps 7:15). Long life and wealth are the rewards for fidelity to the law and a life of virtue. Bitter troubles and early death await vice and disobedience to the law. God's favor and blessings are evident in one's numerous descendants (Ps 112:2; 128:3; Jb 42:13) and in the abundance of one's land, livestock, and possessions (e.g., Prov 3:9–10; 10:4, 6, 15–16, 22; 18:11; 19:4; Ps 37:22; 112:1–3; Jb 1:10; 42:12).[12] And, of course, recall the great prosperity of Abraham. This Deuteronomic doctrine of just deserts (Dt 28; 30) can admit occasional adversity even for the just, but only as a test of that person (e.g., Jgs 2:22–3:6; Job).[13]

Unlike the Old Testament, we do not find repeated promises of material prosperity for fidelity to the law in the New Testament. Instead, we have Matthew 6:25–34 and Luke 12:22–31 assuring readers that they need not worry about what they are to eat or drink, for the Lord knows all that they need. What is important is that they seek the kingdom of God first, and all else will be provided. The apostles leave everything, and Jesus promises them that they are to receive a hundredfold in return both in this life and in the next (Mk 10:29–30).

Dives is held liable for his indifference to Lazarus (Lk 16:19–31). And, at the end-time, Jesus Christ will reward or punish people according to whether or not they had fed the hungry, clothed the naked, and comforted the distressed (Mt 25:31–46). Good deeds are always rewarded (Mk 10:28–30; Mt 6:4, 33).[14] Paul tells the Galatians (6:6–10) that they will reap what they sow. Abraham prospers and is the father of a multitude of nations because of his faith (Rom 4:3–5).

Indeed, a consistent theme from the Old and New Testament is the certainty of God's judgment. People get their just deserts. Psalm 37:25 says it well: "I have been young, and now am old, yet I have not seen the righteous forsaken or their children begging bread." God's gift of material abundance is conditional on (1) humans' obedience to the will of God, (2) their mutual respect, solicitude, and love for one another, and (3) their respect and care for the earth. Far from being a burdensome imposition, such requisite upright moral conduct, in fact, provides humans with the occasion to avail the fullness of God's other prior gifts, to wit:

- the gift of divine friendship (chapter 12)
- the gift of one another (chapter 13)
- the gift of the earth (chapter 14)

We examine each of these in greater depth in the following chapters.

SUMMARY AND CONCLUSIONS

Sacred Scripture's ordinances, aphorisms, and admonitions on economic life reveal features of the divine order undergirding the natural world and human affairs. All creatures are subject to the objective requirements stemming from this pre-defined order. Thus, economic freedom, or human freedom for that matter, is not absolute but is delimited by both constraints and positive obligations.

Biblical morality and economics dovetail each other well. After all, both emphasize the importance of getting relationships right. Righteousness in Sacred Scripture is defined as living up to the requirements of our manifold relationships. Economic life can be characterized as a thick and complex web of relationships, given people's division of labor and dependence on shared resources. Not surprisingly, flourishing in both moral and economic life is largely a function of getting our relationships right: our relationships with God, with one another, and with the earth. As mentioned earlier, there is a convergence, indeed a complementarity, between religious life, on the one hand, and economic life as a practical activity, on the other hand.

Getting these relationships right through upright moral conduct should not be viewed as an inconvenient divine imposition or a burden. After all, living up to the demands of these relationships is not for God's sake (who is self-sufficient and does not need anything or anyone), but for our own sake, so that we might appreciate God, one another, and the earth for what they truly are—unmerited gifts.

NOTES

1. Most of the following points on the theology of creation are from Perdue (1994, 121–22).
2. Perdue (1990a, 458–59)
3. Gordon (1989, 44–45). See also Baker (1973).
4. Hiers (1996–98, 175–76); Lohfink (1987, 5–15). See also Ps 65:9–13; 104.
5. van Leeuwen (1992, 27); Sandoval (2006, 61–62)
6. Sandoval (2006, 63, 64, original emphasis)
7. Sandoval (2006, 130)
8. Crenshaw (1989, 31)
9. Crenshaw (1970, 292–93)
10. Anderson (1978, 41)
11. Blomberg (1999, 71–81)
12. See also Psalm 34:10; 35:27; 37:25; 103:3; Josh 1:8; Ex 15:26. See Kaiser (1988, 152–53) and Wittenberg (1978, 141).
13. di Lella (1966, 144)
14. Schelkle (1973, 301, 307)

Chapter Twelve

Gift of Divine Friendship

Imitatio Dei

As seen in the preceding chapters, Sacred Scripture is clearly demanding in its teachings on proper economic conduct. Whether it is lending to others without interest, forgiving debt, or letting the landless glean from one's property, the Old Testament requires great liberality in sharing with those who are in distress. The New Testament for its part is just as, if not even more, exacting as it invites people to sell all and to give to the poor, so that they might follow Christ. All this requisite sacrifice leads to the question, "Why be moral in one's economic conduct?" The simple and direct answer is for love of God and neighbor (Dt 6:5; Mk 12:29–31).

Any reasonable account of human flourishing and the common good must necessarily include, as a requirement, uprightness and integrity in the key relationships constitutive of human life—one's relationship with God, with other humans, and with the earth. Neither human flourishing nor the common good can be achieved if there is malaise in any of these relationships. Furthermore, not all of these relationships are equal in their importance or in their claims. In particular, the human person's relationship with God is *the* primary relationship that defines and shapes the nature and the requirements of all the other relationships. Thus, recall how one's love of God necessarily leads to the love of neighbor. Genesis vividly describes how the human duty to care for the earth stems from the divine gift of creation.

Biblical economic norms carry weight and are binding because it is God who makes such claims. We find this particularly in the Old Testament motive clauses and in the New Testament invitation to follow Christ. In order to understand fully the nature of biblical economic teachings, it is necessary to appreciate how they flow from one's relationship with God, the human person's primary reference point.

TELEOLOGICAL *IMITATIO DEI*

Old Testament

The economic ordinances of the Old Testament are exacting and require considerable personal sacrifice. Proof of this can be inferred from the repeated failures of the nation Israel to live up to them, as seen in the prophetic indictments, the sages' writings, and the priestly redactions of the law that reiterated these economic provisions. In the editing and finalization of the law, recall how motive clauses were appended to coax the nation to persevere in following the law (see chapter 3).

Care for the marginalized was constitutive of the Chosen People's self-understanding, both as individuals and as a nation. YHWH had liberated them from oppression and slavery out of divine righteousness, and it was YHWH who now asked them to extend to others the same favors they had received from God (e.g., Dt 15:12–15). It is not surprising that YHWH came to Israel's rescue or that God should now ask the Chosen People to be righteous themselves in the way they treated one another. After all, evil is abhorrent to God. Thus, at its root, the formal characteristic that made Israelite legal thought and practice different from all the other nations was that YHWH commanded it. It was the will of God.

On the surface, it appears to be a simple deontological approach to morality—conformity to the will of some authority, God's! Moral excellence is about obedience, plain and simple. In the case of Israel, YHWH's liberation of the Chosen People, the gift of the Promised Land, and the Covenant relationship were merely the prelude to a whole chain of many other gifts God had in store for the nation. What appeared to be a deontological morality was, in fact, teleological. God asked Israel to be loving and just in her conduct because YHWH wanted Israel to be everything God created her to be: a nation different from all the other nations in the manner by which people truly cared for one another, in their economy of equality and mutual respect, and in their politics of service.[1] Work on behalf of the poor was constitutive of Israel's identity because it actualized Israel's potential—to be holy as God is holy (Lev 19:2). The law merely specified the minimum requirements; it identified the boundaries that should not be crossed. However, Old Testament laws go beyond that minimum to propose ideals that must be pursued, such as loving God and being holy (e.g., Lev 11:45; 19:18; Dt 6:5).[2]

Imitatio Dei, to the extent humanly possible, summarized Israel's full potential. The Chosen People understood that Leviticus 19:2 was an invitation that came from no less than God, for holiness is a quality that is wholly God's alone. They also knew that this was no ordinary invitation because to be holy is to be wholly other from the world, to be set aside solely for God, and for nothing and no one else. *Imitatio Dei* goes way beyond the account of humanity being created in the image of God (*imago Dei*). To be an *imago Dei* is to be a representative of the image whose likeness one bears. *Imitatio Dei* goes beyond mere likeness or being God's representative among the creatures of the earth. *Imitatio Dei* entails voluntarily and deliberately appropriating the qualities of God, to the extent humanly possible. Justice, righteousness, and steadfast love are intrinsic to God. Israel was invited to be nothing less than these.

Thus, the divine command to be just and righteous appears on the surface to be just another of God's rightful claim—the Creator merely exercising absolute sovereignty in eliciting obedience from creatures, God's handiwork to begin with. But at a deeper level, it turns out that far from being a burdensome imposition, living up to social justice is, in fact, a special divine gift. It is a divine gift because it is an avenue by which one can be holy as God is holy. It is a divine gift because it is in reality a summons to the people to actualize fully their latent *imago Dei* through *imitatio Dei*. Clearly, the demands of living up fully to the requirements of social justice are not easy to fulfill: returning land to their original owners, forgiving debt, releasing slaves, lending to those who ask, and without interest at that. But it is precisely the difficulty of the task, indeed, the sacrificial nature of the task that should alert people that the stakes involved are high—nothing less than emulating the righteousness and the holiness of God. This was the bedrock quality that differentiated Israel from other Ancient Near Eastern nations in their legal thought and praxis on social justice.

Finally, note that care for the poor is a venue by which people participate in God's providence and governance, yet another divine gift. As we have repeatedly seen in Sacred Scripture, people at the margins are ever present in the gaze of God. They are special to God. The marginalized, the oppressed, and the distressed elicit extra help and attention from God. It is for this reason that YHWH had liberated Israel from her slavery and oppression, gave her a land she could call her own, and formed her into a nation. After all, recall that righteousness is in the very nature of God. In other words, God has a track record of challenging evil and rectifying wrongs. The poor are beloved to God.

This being the case, *imitatio Dei* should necessarily lead to the same concern and work on behalf of the poor and the oppressed. Thus, far from being an onerous divine command, the call to live up to social justice is, in fact, an invitation to work alongside God in challenging evil, rectifying wrongs, and maintaining the divine order of creation. It is an unmerited gift of participating in God's providence and governance of the created world. In extending to the poor and oppressed the same compassion and steadfast love she had received from YHWH in her own moment of liberation from slavery, Israel made God present to those who were in need. Through her holy works, Israel incarnated the holiness of God in the world. *Imago Dei* is revealed in its fullness in *imitatio Dei*.

New Testament

We find the same phenomenon in the New Testament. The economic demands in the Gospels are no less demanding and sacrificial as those of the Old Testament. Thus, they were to minister to the needs of the vulnerable and the distressed. The well-being of those who were cold, hungry, naked, ill, or in prison were to be their own concern (Mt 25:31–46). Disciples were to be generous in sharing what they had, even to the point of radical divestment (Acts 2:44–45).

Jesus personified the kingdom of God in the way he lived and loved. In contrast to the Greco-Roman practice of patronage that looked down on those considered to be unclean and unworthy because of their low social class, Jesus engaged in table-fellowship and associated with one and all, rich and poor alike. He risked being considered unclean himself by freely associating with sinners, publicans, and lepers. Everyone was a child of God.

Jesus repeatedly taught the value of generosity in forgiving others and lived up to it on Calvary. He had served others, instead of seeking to be served or to be first. And he asked his apostles to do likewise and to serve one another (Jn 13:1–17). The rich ruler who yearned for eternal life discovered to his chagrin that he had to sell all he had, give to the poor, and then follow Christ (Mt 19:16–22). In fact, a common feature of all four Gospels is the invitation to discipleship—to imitate Christ—by dying to self, taking up one's cross, and following Christ.

The fifth chapter of the Gospel of Matthew vividly and succinctly shows the centrality of *imitatio Dei* even in the New Testament. The evangelist goes through an extended list of very difficult mandates for the disciple starting from the beatitudes, to being the salt and the light of the earth, to living up to the law, to loving one's enemies. Matthew caps all these demands with a simple summary and invitation, "Be perfect, therefore, as your heavenly father is perfect" (Mt 5:48).

Indeed, this simple invitation reveals an important insight relevant for our study of economic ethics. What seems to be an endless list of demanding and onerous norms and mandates turns out to be a gift. These norms and mandates turn out to be the very building blocks of perfection. Biblical economic ethics take on new light when viewed as stepping-stones to holiness, to the imitation of Christ.

JUSTICE AND WORSHIP

The quality of one's relationship with God is necessarily reflected in, indeed spills over into, one's relationship with one's neighbors. Consequently, justice and cultic worship, while distinct from one another, are inseparable.

Old Testament

The prophets preached the complementarity of social justice and cultic observances. Besides social injustice, idolatry and apostasy are other perennial prophetic concerns. The prophets took Israel and Judah to task for turning away from YHWH and worshiping idols instead.

Worship and just conduct mutually reinforce one another. In fact, they are necessary conditions to each other. On the one hand, worship lays the groundwork for justice. It facilitates just conduct. The prophetic critique of Israel is an excellent example. The Chosen People had forgotten all that God had done for them (Hos 13:4–6; cf. 2:8) and how God stood by an enfeebled Israel against her powerful enemies (Am 2:9). In exchange, Israel rebelled against the God who had given her all that she enjoyed (Is 1:2; cf 5:1–7). Israel forsook God (Jer 2:13). As a consequence, the Chosen People also lost knowledge of truth, love, justice, and righteousness (Hos 4:2; 6:6), and they spurned the law and rejected God's offer of salvation (Is 5:24; 30:12).[3] Indeed, Israel is an excellent illustration of how memory is important because it makes for gratitude, which in turn increases the likelihood of fidelity to the law. Remembering is an integral part of worship life. It is in this roundabout manner that worship life nurtures just conduct.

On the other hand, just behavior is an important venue for actualizing prayers. Justice can be said to be sacramental in that it effects the interior disposition that comes with prayer. It is also a telltale sign that people have internalized their worship life. People act on what they utter with their lips. The heart's promptings and prayers overflow into action. Furthermore, it is just behavior that gives substance and meaning to prayers. In addition to their indictments of injustice and apostasy-idolatry, the prophets constantly warned the Chosen People of their empty worship (e.g., Jer 7:4–7). Cultic observances without social justice are useless. The people's sacrifices and holocausts were, in fact, abhorrent before God because of their evil deeds. What the lips boldly or piously professed must be consistent with what brimmed over their hearts and what was evident in their deeds. Without this fundamental appreciation of the nature of prayer, worship runs the risk of developing or encouraging the mindset that people can put God in their debt (the domestication of God!) through their holocausts and sacrifices (Am 4:4–5; 5:21–24; cf. Is 1:10–17; Jer 7:3–7). The motive for prayer is misplaced and people adopt heathen cultic practices (Hos 4:6, 8, 12–13).[4]

Authentic worship comes with the proper and just treatment of others (Is 58; Zech 7:4–14). It is justice, not burnt offerings, that God requires. In fact, the prophets and psalmists are clear that God abhors sacrificial offerings (Am 5:21–24; Hos 6:6; Is 1:11–17; Ps 50:8–14). Jeremiah 7:21–23 and Amos 5:25 even go so far as to chide Israel that YHWH never did command such burnt offerings.[5] Instead, it is mutual solicitude and justice that God requires.

One explanation for this disconnect between their moral lives and their cultic observances was the people's false sense of security in thinking that they, as a nation, were in good standing before God because of their cultic practices (Jer 7:10). They were strengthened in such mistaken belief by two assumptions: (1) that Jerusalem and Mount Zion were inviolate (nb. Is 37:33–35), and (2) that the monarchy was secure because of God's promises regarding the preservation of the Davidic line of kings (2 Sam 7). The consequences of such presumption were a fatal complacency and a lack of urgency or concern over their moral duties.[6] By juxtaposing genuine worship with righteous conduct, the prophets underscored two features of their economic ethics: (1) the theological foundations of economic life and (2) the need to internalize norms.

Theological Foundations of Economics

The prophetic literature is distinctive in Sacred Scripture for explicitly calling attention to the close link between theology, liturgy, and ethics. Three seemingly separate prophetic concerns turn out to be a single issue. Idolatry-apostasy (theology), empty cultic observances (liturgy), and social injustice (ethics) give rise to and mutually reinforce one another in a malign self-feeding dynamic.

Sacrifices, holocausts, and rituals give people a false sense of security in thinking that they are righteous before God and have satisfied all that God expects of them because of their cultic observances. Such complacency and presumption lead to an unexamined moral life. As a result, they persist in their unjust treatment of others, even as they faithfully observe the requirements of worship to their minute detail (cf. Pharisees in Mt 23:23). After all, sacrifices, holocausts, and rituals are much easier to perform than reforming one's conduct toward others.

Apostasy and idolatry make living a moral life that much more difficult because people fail to appreciate the example provided by God. They expose their ignorance of who God truly is (Jer 9:23–24). They do not recognize and, consequently, fail to avail of the graces to speed them along an upright life. They fail to internalize God's laws and do not use them as welcome aids to a full life. For its part, a derelict moral life leads one farther away from God, makes worship purely mechanical and hypocritical, and paves the way ultimately for turning away from God and worshiping idols.

Of course, the opposite dynamic is true. There is a beneficial, virtuous self-feeding cycle: better knowledge of God nurtures a more fervent and meaningful worship and a more vibrant moral life, which in turn lead people to desire to know God even better.

All these matter for economic ethics because they are prerequisites to an economic life that is truly alive to God. *There is a necessary theological dimension to economic life.*[7] Theology is neither antithetical nor irrelevant for a complete economics. The prophetic literature underscores the theological foundations of economic morality.

The Need to Internalize Norms

By criticizing Israel and Judah's hollow cultic observances, the prophetic books highlight the need to internalize moral norms. This is particularly important for economic morality, and for social ethics for that matter, because it is not always clear what is right or wrong when it comes to living together in community. Social issues are often complex, and much prudential judgment is needed in resolving the dilemmas they pose. In many of these cases, there is no social consensus, and individuals are left to decide on their own in the internal forum of their hearts and minds. Thus, it is all the more important for people to understand and appreciate these norms. Herein is another contribution of the prophetic literature to economic ethics.

Prophetic ethics has been described as perfectionist, because the prophets were intent on moving the divided kingdoms beyond the minimum requirements of the law. They called for a more "internalized" behavior on the part of the people.[8] The prophets were often reacting to the never-ending tension between legality and righteousness, between law and value, between institutional order and justice.[9] After all, these are separate sets of norms.

On the one hand, we have law in the usual sense of the word, such as legal codes and oral or customary law. On the other hand, we have moral exhortations and commands from God. These address every person directly, such as the *Shema* (Dt 6:4–5) and the Decalogue (Ex 20:2–17; Dt 5:6–21). One could call the latter "rules of righteousness."[10] In an ideal world, legal codes and customary law should serve or at least be consistent with the moral norms from Revelation. Unfortunately, this is often not the case since the powerful often shape jurisprudence to serve their own interests.

The royal exactions of taxes and forced labor and the landlords' demands for high rents and fines may have been legal, but they were not righteous, because they were exploitative and drove many to indebtedness and eventual slavery. These were contrary to the Covenant's call for mutual solicitude and for an economy in which no one was to be in want.

Or take the case of justice at the city gates. While the actions of the wealthy and the powerful in claiming their due may have been legal (e.g., land foreclosure, the enforcement of creditors' rights, the garnishment of loan pledges), they were unrighteous because they went against the intention and the spirit of the Covenant for a compassionate society. While the rich and the powerful may have been within legal rules to rewrite laws and to change administrative procedures to their own advantage, they were immoral in doing so, especially since it led to the oppression of the weak and the poor. Not surprisingly, the prophets condemned the corruption of the judicial system (e.g., Am 5:7, 10; Is 1:21–26; Mic 3:1–3).

The crown and the elite (including religious leaders) were slavish in observing cultic requirements to their minute details, even as they ignored the spirit and intent of the law on how righteousness before God requires righteousness in their treatment of their neighbors and the poor. They failed to understand the nature of the Covenant, much less to value the gracious favors of God.

This is a tension that we find even in modernity, indeed, in every age. What is legal or permissible is not necessarily moral. There is a gap between what is legal and what is righteous because people fail to appropriate the spirit of God's norms. The prophets' critique of Israel's and Judah's empty worship is important for economic ethics because (1) it is a vivid reminder that what is moral takes precedence over what is legal, and (2) it is a call for the community to internalize the spirit and intent of God's norms.

New Testament

The New Testament likewise shows the inseparability of theology, liturgy, and ethics. Conflict stories abound in the Gospels. The Pharisees and Jesus were constantly at loggerheads over the observance of the law, especially the Sabbath. Mark 7:1–23, Luke 11:37–54, and Matthew 23 are particularly pointed in exposing the Pharisees' hypocrisy in observing the minutest details of the law, yet violating the more important matters of the law—justice, mercy, and faithfulness. Referring to the Pharisees' corruption and greed, Jesus reminds them that it is the inside of the cup, not the outside, that matters. It is not what comes from the outside that renders a person unclean. Rather, it is what comes from within the person that defiles a person. Thus, Jesus tells the Pharisees that if they truly want to be clean, they should be generous to the poor (Lk 11:41).

We see the same teaching on internalizing norms beyond the Gospels. In talking about faith and good deeds, James 2:14–17 notes that a follower of Christ cannot pass by a neighbor who is cold and hungry and do nothing about it. Such inaction is contrary to the faith. Similarly, Paul reproves the Corinthians in their scandalous celebration of the Eucharist (1 Cor 11:17–34). Their indifference to one another, especially for those from a different class or status, belied the unity that the Eucharist represents. In other words, the prayers that flow from our lips and hearts find their fullest expression only in our deeds.

SUMMARY AND CONCLUSIONS

Biblical economic norms arise from our relationship with God. Both the Old and New Testament elicit great and sacrificial deeds in our economic lives because of who we are as individuals and as a community—people invited to rise to the holiness and perfection to which God has invited humanity. In other words, our relationship with God ought to animate and provide direction to our economic conduct. After all, it is our love of God that provides the larger context of our love of neighbor and our care for the earth.

So, let us end with the question at the start of this chapter. Why be moral in our conduct? Far from being an onerous imposition, the invitation to love God with its manifold and exacting duties is, in fact, a gift—the gift of a divine friendship being proffered. In requiting this divine friendship and love, we are transformed and become moral in our conduct along the way, including how we treat one another in the marketplace. In other words, *there is an economic dimension to imitating God, to following Christ. Love of God and love of neighbor are necessarily manifested in people's economic conduct.* Such an economic dimension and its requirements are revealed in the manifold teachings and admonitions of Sacred Scripture on upright economic conduct.

NOTES

1. Birch (1991)
2. Wenham (2006, 357–59). In fact, Williamson (2012, 105–9) notes that Israelites strived to live up to the demands of social justice, not only because of the law but also because of their longing to follow the example of God, as seen in the prophetic and wisdom literature.
3. Wolff (1978, 27–28)
4. Wolff (1978, 27–28)
5. See also Hiers (1984b, 53–54).
6. Bracke (2002, 392). A separate, additional issue is the inappropriate use of the goods of the earth. Blomberg (1999, 71–81) associates idol worship with the improper use of material goods (e.g., Is 2:7–8, 19–21; 44:12–20; Hos 2:8). Haggai 2:8 notes that even the precious metals in the Temple are not the people's gifts to God for these precious metals belong to God to begin with.
7. This is the mirror image to the last chapter's point that there is a necessary economic dimension in God's order of creation. Economics is not peripheral to a complete theology.
8. Eichrodt (1967, II, 327)
9. Mays (1987, 151–53)
10. Mays (1987, 152)

Chapter Thirteen

Gift of One Another

Mutual Solicitude and Care for the Poor

Mutual solicitude, especially for the poor and the distressed, is a perennial theme in Sacred Scripture. Indeed, a distinctive formal characteristic of any community steeped in biblical values is the mutual love that animates it. This ethos of mutual solicitude is evident across the Old and New Testament, from the law codes' admonition to take care of the distressed, to the prophetic condemnation of injustice, and finally to the Gospels' call for interior conversion and fellowship.

LAW

Old Testament ordinances on economic life are not organized in any systematic manner, as one would expect in a genuine code of laws, but are randomly spread out. They are interspersed with statutes on seemingly unrelated topics, such as ritual and cultic obligations. Consequently, readers often get the impression that these economic teachings have no rhyme or reason to them; they are merely random economic "do's and don'ts." However, closer inspection will show that these economic precepts can, in fact, be organized as a coherent set of prescriptions for a morally upright economic life.

It is rare for scripture scholars to come to a near-consensus on anything. The central importance of care for the poor in Old Testament law is one of these exceptional points of agreement. Most scholars agree that a distinctive feature of Old Testament law that clearly stands out is its recurring admonition on solicitude for those at the fringes of society. It is, in fact, an impressive convergence.

To begin with, recall that these law codes were written over a span of centuries, from the pre-monarchic period (parts of the Covenant Code), to the seventh-century reform (Deuteronomic Code), and finally to the post-exilic completion of the Holiness Code. Furthermore, as mentioned earlier, each collection of laws is undergirded by a different tradition: the Elohists (*E*) for the Covenant Code, the Deuteronomist reformers (*D*) for the Deuteronomic Code, and the priestly class (*P*) for the Holiness Code. Each tradition had its own agenda. The Elohists were bent on counterbalancing the Yahwist (*J*) tradition's unabashed promotion of the monarchy by reminding Israel that the Exodus was her defining moment. The Deuteronomic reformers were keen on bringing Israel back to covenant fidelity and saving her from the precipice of an imminent self-destruction. The priestly writers were intent on promoting their own interests and on consolidating their power base in the post-exilic restoration. Despite these differences, however, it is remarkable that these disparate traditions espouse similar views on economic morality. Let us examine this convergence in greater detail.

Overarching Principle: Care for the Poor

Running across the economic ordinances is the larger goal they share of caring for the poor. Old Testament economic norms are predominantly about providing relief to those who have fallen on hard times. Solicitude for the marginalized clearly stands out as a hallmark of Hebrew Law. The law codes, and even the prophetic literature, agree in their conclusion that "there is a concrete measure of God's holiness, namely, the ritual system's own treatment of those who are poor."[1] Israel was presented with a wide variety of measures she could take in addressing the problem of poverty. Clearly, the Chosen People were called to respond robustly in alleviating destitution and in dealing with the chance and contingencies of life.

The provisions of Old Testament law on the security of life and property, honesty in commercial transactions, and protection of family relationships are all found in ANE legal literature. What truly stand out, however, are the length and the persistence to which Old Testament laws set out to protect the poor, aliens, widows, and orphans.[2] Care for the vulnerable in their midst was a defining formal characteristic of their election as the Chosen People. Such active and genuine concern was constitutive of their self-identity as a nation. In fact, using modern terminology, some have described the Old Testament laws as "a well-developed social welfare system" or as direct and indirect income transfer mechanisms.[3] Economic security for everyone was a practical goal of the law.[4]

This overlap among different Old Testament traditions (*J*, *E*, *D*, *P*) and disparate economic statutes underscores the centrality of taking responsibility for the well-being of the poor in Covenantal theology and praxis. Such consistency, multiple attestation, and repeated emphasis across the law codes point to the strength, historicity, and importance of this particular teaching. (Recall the hermeneutical rule of weight-of-Scripture-as-a-whole from chapter 1.)

Reciprocity

The Israelites relied on an agricultural ethos. As we have seen in chapter 2, many Old Testament norms were practiced as a strategy of mutual survival. Rural life was demanding because of its hostile environment marked by great uncertainty. Given such conditions, the best chance for an individual's survival was to belong to a group (such as a family, clan, and tribe) that can provide assistance in the face of life's uncertainties. In agriculture, providing assistance to others was, in fact, a rational strategy of self-preservation. After all, by helping others, people were able to ask the rest of the community for the same kind of assistance in their own moment of need. Thus, mutual solicitude had a self-interested component to it. It was a strategy adopted at all levels, from individuals helping other individuals, to families assisting other households, all the way up to clans and tribes helping other clans or tribes. The importance of belonging to a group for survival may also partly explain the statutes on land return and on the redemption of land and kin. In a limited-goods or traditionalist society, the goal of the clan or tribe was to preserve and to hold on to its most important wealth: its members and its land. This was a rational response to a precarious setting of great or chronic scarcity. Not surprisingly, kinship and belonging were important social values.[5]

The expectation of reciprocity held the key to this self-enforcing social "safety net." There was relative equality because all shared the same fate as members of the same family, clan, or tribe. Wealth was used to entertain others, extend hospitality, or assist the poor because wealth was fragile and could easily be lost to predation or natural disaster. It was better to use such bounty in building social capital, relationships, and good will. The latter are various forms of riches, too, and in an ancient world of constant uncertainty, it was much easier and safer to "bank" such wealth in good deeds that could then be reciprocated later. Thus, among rural residents, wealth was not used to exploit or to accumulate even more riches.

Besides ensuring assistance in the face of life's chance and uncertainties, a second reason for the importance of belonging to a group was protection from others' rapacity. This explains why Hebrew law singles out aliens, widows, and orphans for special consideration. In the absence of a modern state that guarantees individual and collective security, kinship rather than citizenship furnished the necessary protection. Strangers in the land were all alone and were an inviting target for exploitation, robbery, or violence. Without relatives or friends in the land, aliens could not avail of safety in numbers and were literally at the mercy of their hosts' good or bad intentions. In the absence of modern-day human rights and laws, the hospitality and protection of the host became extremely important for the stranger.

Widows were on their own, belonging neither to their own blood families nor to their husbands' families. Similarly, orphans lost their natural connection to both their maternal and paternal families. Moreover, orphans were especially vulnerable to people stealing or taking advantage of their inheritance. In other words, strangers, widows, and orphans were easy prey and required special protection and aid from the rest of the community. Widows, orphans, and resident aliens depended on the protection of the law to help them in their poverty since they had little family support, if they even had it at all (Ex 22:21–27; Dt 10:18–19; 24:17–21; 26:12–13; 27:19).[6] Not surprisingly, these three groups were frequently the object of the apodictic Hebrew economic ordinances. In fact, the word pair "widows and orphans" became shorthand to refer to those in need.[7] The threefold formula of "the stranger, the orphan, and the widow" was often used from Deuteronomy to the rest of the Old Testament to connote the vulnerable, the poor, and the distressed (e.g., Dt 10:18–19; 16:11, 14; 24:19–21; Jer 7:6; 22:3; Ps 94:6; 146:9).[8]

There is a further reason for the alien's need for special concern and treatment. In addition to being defenseless, vulnerable, and at the mercy of their hosts, strangers were most likely to be in deep distress to begin with. In all likelihood, they had been driven to migrate because of oppression, persecution, or famine (economic migrants), as in the many cases we find in the biblical narratives (Gen 12:10; 47:4; Ru 1:1; 2 Kgs 8:1; Ex 2:15; Mt 2:13–15).[9] Given the nature and circumstances of migrants and refugees in the ancient world, the inclusion of aliens in the threefold formula and in Israel's laws takes on even greater significance (e.g., Ex 22:21; 23:9; Lev 19:10, 33–34; 23:22; Dt 10:18–19). It reveals Israel's compassion and empathy, in addition to her sense of justice. After all, the Chosen People were themselves strangers in Egypt and in Babylon and had firsthand experience of the distress of being economic nobodies (Dt 10:19; Lev 19:34; Ex 22:21; 23:9).

In other words, Israel's solicitude for the poor was longstanding and deep, dating all the way back to her earliest days. This concern for the poor was neither a late development nor merely an adaptation of ANE laws. It was embedded as part of Israel's earlier ethos, right from the start of her life as a community.

Care for the Poor as a Duty for All

A third pattern we can discern is how everyone—even the common person—was obligated to discharge these poverty-alleviation measures. In the Ancient

Near East, kings were deemed to be chiefly responsible for providing relief to the poor. They were expected to be the advocates for the poor and the defenseless at the city gate. In other words, ANE kings were the dispensers and the guarantors of justice in their realms. We see evidence of this especially in the prologues or epilogues, or both, of the ANE law codes. For example, in the prologue of the famous Code of Hammurabi, the king touts his record of having defended and provided for the poor. He claims that the weak and the defenseless who read the Code can have the peace of mind in knowing that the king has secured them from the dangers of injustice or oppression. In truth, however, there is not a single piece of legislation in the entire Code of Hammurabi that provides relief or extra protection for the poor.[10] It turns out that these ANE prologues or epilogues served another function: self-promoting royal propaganda. They were intended to create a public image of the king, not only as just, but also as a champion of the poor and the marginalized. Such royal propaganda was intended for the consumption of the gods, the public, and posterity. It highlights the widespread expectation of that time that the monarchy was synonymous with justice.

Israel extends this even further by emphasizing that ensuring justice was not the responsibility solely of the king. Everyone among God's Chosen People was charged with dispensing justice in the land, with protecting the defenseless, with releasing those in bondage, with providing interest-free loans, and with assisting the poor. Carefully note the addressees of the economic ordinances of the Old Testament. It was contingent on every Israelite to live up to these economic statutes. Israel broadened economic responsibility.[11] The nation did not rely solely on the state or the Temple in taking care of the poor because protecting the latter's well-being was everyone's moral obligation. Besides, unlike the highly organized, centralized, and bureaucratized Pharaonic Egypt and the Canaanite states, early Israel was a group of peasants without a central government, a capital, a sovereign, or a standing army.[12] Ordinary people had to do their part of the work. In fact, their share of this duty was based on their ability to provide aid. Note how the cost of these "welfare safety nets" was borne by those with the resources to lend, to give, or to make available to the poor. It has even been suggested that a rationale of Old Testament economic statutes, such as debt forgiveness, land return, slave release, and gleaning, was to moderate accumulation in the face of a limited-goods society. Those who had the good fortune of accumulating surplus circulated these back into the community.[13]

Old Testament laws merely tell us the ideals that were meant to be pursued in the nation. Sacred Scripture does not tell us whether or not, or to what extent, these moral exhortations were actually implemented in practice. Nevertheless, there is evidence to suggest that these economic ordinances were demanding and required enormous personal sacrifice. For example, we know that the three law codes had undergone considerable further development, with earlier laws being refined or revised. Most scholars hold that the Deuteronomic Code reworked and "humanized" the Covenant Code. There are also indications of rampant violations. The wisdom and prophetic literature repeatedly condemn abusive lending practices and the unjust expropriation of land.[14] The divided kingdoms, Israel and Judah, were headed for exile and near-destruction partly for ignoring these ordinances. Legal devices like the *prosbul*[15] were created to provide loopholes from the observance of the debt laws. Ironically, all these attest to how everyone was bound by the obligation to assist the poor. Had these duties been merely the king's alone, Israel would not have had to be condemned by the prophets for her violations, or would not have had to be repeatedly reminded by the sages that true Wisdom entails caring for the poor. Israel would not have had to invent creative legal devices (e.g., *prosbul*) to get out of the requirements of the law. The well-being of the poor and the vulnerable in their midst was supposed to be every Israelite's concern.

Codifying Care for the Poor

Another feature of Old Testament law is the codification of care for the poor. In the ANE, kings proclaimed economic releases (e.g., debt forgiveness) at their pleasure—on their ascension to the throne, to celebrate a noteworthy royal anniversary, as a strategy to win public support in times of war, or to revive a stalling debt-laden economy. In contrast, economic releases were regularized in Israel. They were made an integral part of Israel's public morality. These releases were not dependent on the whims of the king but occurred on a regular cycle: the release of slaves after six years of service, the forgiveness of debts after seven years, land-fallow every seven years, poor-tithes every third year, rest from work every seventh day, and, of course, the Jubilee Law with its land-return provision every fifty years in addition to slave manumission and debt write-off. These economic statutes were codified and regularized just like cultic observances, at least in theory. Besides these releases, other protections were codified, such as, the gleaning privileges of the poor for whatever grows on the land during the fallow year (Ex 23:10–11) and measures to ensure justice at the city gates, especially for the weak (Ex 23:2–3, 6–8).[16]

The Jubilee Law restrains wealth and income inequalities. In an agrarian setting, land is the primary engine of wealth creation. By mandating the return of ancestral land to their original owners, Israel, in effect, sought to prevent the inordinate accumulation of large tracts of land, and with it, the concentration of economic and political power in the hands of a few. The Jubilee Law could thus be described as a built-in mechanism that provided stability to the community. It could be viewed as a safeguard against the formation of large estates. Regular debt forgiveness and slave manumission can also be described as structural measures because they periodically corrected imbalances from getting out of hand and provided those in distress with a fresh start. However, despite these mechanisms, many biblical commentators are nevertheless critical that these economic statutes merely addressed the symptoms (e.g., destitution, indebtedness, slavery, loss of land), rather than the root causes of deep-seated problems (e.g., oppression by the elite, abuse and monopoly of power, and heavy royal exactions).

Proximate Goals of Restoration and Independence

Another discernible pattern in the biblical law codes is the underlying principle of restoring those who had fallen on hard times. It was not sufficient merely to provide the vulnerable and the destitute with their basic needs of food, clothing, or shelter. Debt slavery, after all, could provide these as well. No, this was not good enough for the Chosen People. The goal of these economic ordinances, taken as a whole, was not merely the provision of basic needs, but the restoration of those who had fallen on hard times to their former independence. Restoring their livelihood was a critical intermediate step in attaining this goal of self-sufficiency.[17] The care with which every family was provided with land during the formation of the nation (Num 26:52–56; 33:54) speaks volumes of their ideal of ensuring a livelihood for all. In fact, the writers of the Old Testament were careful to note that land was parceled out according to the size of the family and the productivity of the land—reflective of the desire to ensure the economic security of every family.

Agricultural life is fraught with chance and contingencies, such as, the vagaries of weather, crop failure, drought, disease, and blight. As mentioned earlier, in order to give families a better chance of surviving these unavoidable downturns in life, Israel had laws (moral admonitions) on mutual assistance, such as mandatory lending without interest, almsgiving, gleaning, poor-tithing, shared feasts, and many others. These were emergency measures to tide the family over. And if, despite these measures, the families that had fallen on hard times still found themselves mired in debt and ultimately sold into debt slavery, there was a second set of measures to ensure that such destitution was not their permanent lot. Thus, the Israelites had provisions for debt forgiveness after seven years and slave manumission after six years of service. Moreover, such former debt slaves were to receive goods and provisions upon their release (Dt 15:13–14) to give them a realistic chance of starting anew and not find themselves driven to debt once again. In addition, kinfolks were obligated to assume the role of *go'el* (redeemer) in buying back their enslaved relatives or family land that had to be sold. And then there was the Jubilee Law in which ancestral land was returned to their original owners, in addition to the release of debts and slaves. Referring to the law, "one cannot help but be impressed with the range of provisions that were made to cushion the blows engendered by a life filled with want."[18]

There is a common spirit running across these ordinances, namely, that those who had fallen on hard times needed a fresh start and assistance to be able to stand on their own again as free landholding families. Misfortunes in life are inevitable. These laws ensure that those who found themselves in trouble can be restored to their former livelihood and independence. One could call this the principle of restoration, or the principle of second chances. The Chosen People were to build an economy of hope: no matter how unfavorable life's circumstances might be, there will always be the possibility of recovery and renewal because of others' assistance. In sum, not only did the law codes converge in their goal (caring for the poor), but they also espoused similar measures.

PROPHETIC JUSTICE

Despite their wide diversity, the prophetic books consistently indicted Israel and Judah for their oppression of the weak, theft, general dishonesty, inordinate consumption, avarice, and subversion of the justice system. Land-grabbing was forcefully condemned by the prophets (e.g. Mic 2:1–5, 9; Is 5:8–10; Hos 5:10; Ez 46:16–18).[19] In the face of the gross injustice perpetrated by the very leadership charged with protecting the poor and the defenseless, it is not surprising that justice is a cardinal theme of the prophetic literature. Micah 6:8 is held up as the "epitome of the message of the eighth century prophets."[20] "To do justice, and to love kindness, and to walk humbly with your God" is the "linguistic trinity" in the classic message of the eighth-century prophets. All three are action words and not merely abstract principles, thereby, underscoring the importance of deeds, rather than mere words (cf Am 5:24, Hos 6:6, Is 7:9; 30:15).[21]

And, of course, we have the combination of steadfast love (*hesed*)[22] and justice (*mišpāt*). Note, too, the "synonymous parallelism" in which justice (*mišpāt*) and righteousness (*tzědāqâ*) are paired (Am 5:7, 24; 6:12; Hos 2:19; Is 1:21, 27; 5:7; 9:7; Jer 22:15). Such justice and righteousness are at the heart of prophetic preaching and moral vision.[23] Thus, social reform is not about individual conversion or a one-on-one relationship with God. Rather, it is about changing sinful social structures and permitting all to participate in society, and to do so in a substantive and meaningful manner, with dignity and shared responsibility.[24]

However, not only did the prophets criticize what was wrong, but they also articulated what was right and what God expected from the Chosen People. Thus, the people were to be particularly solicitous of the weak, in what we have come to call today as the preferential option for the poor (e.g.,

Is 3:14–15). Care for the marginalized was a measure of a just community.[25] Justice, too, was to be dispensed on their behalf (Is 1:17; 58:6–7; 61:1–2; Jer 22:13–17; Ez 16:49; 18:5–9). The widow, orphan, alien, and the poor were not to be oppressed (Zech 7:10). In fact, their cause and their welfare were to be championed by the able and the strong (Am 5:21–24; Hos 10:12–13; Jer 22:13–17; Is 58:6–9; 61:1–2).[26]

The ownership and use of possessions were to be marked by generosity (Mal 3:8–10). All were to have access to what was essential for a livelihood, identity, the means to participate in the community, and a life of freedom. Administrative and judicial systems were to be put in the service and pursuit of these goals.[27] Righteousness was about fulfilling the requirements of one's relationships within the community and with God. It was meant to permeate institutions and laws. The outcome is *šālôm* (peace or welfare).[28] It was a "community-centered" justice.

NEW TESTAMENT: FELLOWSHIP RATHER THAN PATRONAGE

People's respect and care for one another are evident in how they interact in the marketplace. The Old Testament laws on gleaning, lending without interest, debt forgiveness, and land return were social mechanisms that taught the Chosen People how to care for one another. Recall, too, how the vineyard owner kept hiring the unemployed in the square until the last hour of the day and then paid everyone a full day's wage regardless of their contribution (Mt 20:1–16). "[E]conomic exchanges encode social relationships and make statements about the relative value of different groups of people before God."[29] We find an example of this in the New Testament's admonitions against the Greco-Roman practice of patronage and Jesus' call for an alternative relationship based on fellowship (*koinōnia*).

Patron-Client Relationships

Sociological Background

Ancient economic life functioned differently compared with the modern marketplace. Pre-modern economies operated on the basis of custom, law, and usage, while contemporary exchange is driven by the price mechanism. There are four foundational social institutions: kinship, religion, economics, and politics. In the modern era, each of these is independent and is governed by its own set of laws.[30] For example, we have the Western practice of separating Church and State. Laissez-faire capitalism keeps the market and government apart from each other. In contrast, economics was embedded within religion, politics, and kinship in the Ancient Near East, including Israel.[31]

The practice of patronage-subservience predates the Hellenistic-Roman period. In fact, scholars believe that this was characteristic of Israel's political economy during the Iron Age II, the era of the monarchs.[32] Nevertheless, an easy way of understanding patron-client relationships is to examine the Greco-Roman ethos of honor-status.

Ethos of Honor-Status

In the Greco-Roman world, honor-status was everything. Where one stood within the community was important because it determined the degree of respect one received and the resources one could command. Many factors shaped one's honor-status, the most obvious one being the individual's role in the community. There was a clearly defined hierarchical order in the ancient social world in the following descending order of importance and rank: emperor; representatives of the emperor in Palestine and Syria, such as Roman consuls/procurators and Herodian kings; high priests, Jerusalem aristocracy, and major landowners; officials acting on behalf of the preceding groups; village leaders such as wealthy farmers and synagogue leaders; landholding peasants; and finally, the outcasts such as sinners, social deviants, tax collectors, the destitute, and the unclean.[33]

A second determinant was wealth. Status pertained to social acceptance, while class was about economic standing.[34] A third determinant was the individual's social network. A household was defined by the status of its extended family, its friends, the people they associated with, and the people who were subservient or indebted to them. This social stratification was bound by the following strictures: (1) Anyone higher in the preceding list acted as patron to those below them in the pecking order, that is, the clients. (2) Patrons provided clients with economic resources and political protection, favors, or access to power. (3) Clients for their part accorded their services, respect, and loyalty to their patrons. (4) People were most comfortable only among their social equals and did not cross class lines, neither being presumptuous to move around a higher social class nor stooping down to associate with lower classes.[35]

Patronage in an Agrarian Setting

Patron-client relationships easily arose in the context of a limited-goods society. The political economy of the ancient, agrarian world was conducive to breeding domination-subservience within communities. In particular, (1) agricultural life was inherently a precarious source of livelihood, and (2) there was a great disparity in power between the wealthy and the poor.

First, given the fragile nature of agricultural life, the poor were vulnerable to the vagaries of the weather and the circumstances of life. They had little or no cushion to fall back on in the event of a failed harvest or a family emergency that entailed unforeseen expenses. Given the rudimentary state of agricultural technology, peasants lived an uncertain life because of the chance and contingencies that came with farming. The surplus they could accumulate in good years could easily disappear from unforeseen events, such as a bad harvest, the breadwinner's illness, or arbitrary exactions from rulers. Peasants were easily driven into penury, debt, and slavery.[36]

In the event of such exigencies, their first line of defense was to ask for assistance from their neighbors or kin who had surplus. This, however, was not possible if the contingency had affected the entire community. In this case, they had to ask help from other communities. If this was also not feasible, then appealing to the king or the Temple was an option. In addition to this, looking for a patron with the necessary resources was always a viable alternative.

A second reason for the emergence of patronage-subservience was the unequal bargaining power between the wealthy and the impoverished. In hard times, the peasants' desperate need for assistance put them at the mercy of the demands of the rich and left them vulnerable to exploitation. In exchange for the benefactor's aid or protection, the poor pledged their loyalty. Thus, we have a patron-client relationship characterized by domination and subservience.[37]

In sum, the patronage system was a strategy for mutual security amidst the dangers of the ancient world. In a social setting of precarious subsistence and ill-defined laws, banding together as a group was a survival mechanism to deal with the uncertainties and the unforgiving nature of life. Kinship and belonging were extremely important, and the stranger was particularly vulnerable and literally at the mercy of others.[38] It was vital to have the protection of a powerful benefactor, either to deter others from harming them or to exact retribution or redress in the event of injury. Such a benefactor became even more important in a world governed by the rule of might rather than the rule of law. Justice was commonly dispensed by judges and officials subjectively, according to relationships.[39] Thus, acceptance, honor, and status within the community were paramount.

Patron-Client Relationships in the Old Testament

We can infer patron-client relationships in monarchic Israel from Old Testament text. Thus, Saul buys the loyalty of his troops against David by plying them with gifts of land and military rank (1 Sam 22:7–8). David's relationship with Saul was clearly as a subordinate to a patron. David addresses Saul his "father" and Saul reciprocates by calling him "son" (1 Sam 24:11;

26:17–25). We find a similar relationship of mentor and mentee between Elijah and Elisha (2 Kgs 2:12) or of patron and dependent in the case of Naaman and his servants (2 Kgs 5:1–19). Note how Tiglath-pileser protects Ahaz from his enemies in exchange for the latter's gifts, tributes, and loyalty (2 Kgs 16:5–9). Even YHWH is described by some as patron to David (and Israel).[40] The Old Testament does not explicitly challenge such patron-client arrangements. It is simply accepted as a regular feature of socioeconomic life. Not so in the New Testament.

Patron-Client Relationships in the New Testament

Luke is believed to be reacting to the Greco-Roman practice of patronage in writing about the social conflict and economic relations of first-century Palestine.[41] We find evidence that such patron-client relationships were a significant feature of social life at that time. For example, recall how the centurion seeks healing for his slave from Jesus.[42] Instead of approaching Jesus directly, he asks the local elders to intercede with Jesus on his behalf. The request of the elders is most revealing: "He [referring to the centurion] is worthy of having you do this for him, for he loves our people, and *it is he who built our synagogue for us*" (Lk 7:2–5, emphasis added). The elders consider it their obligation to reciprocate the past kindness and assistance of the Roman officer in his own moment of need. The centurion, as benefactor to the village, has certain claims on the local community which he was now exercising to good effect. This is an example of a balanced reciprocity—a favor exchanged for a favor.[43]

Fellowship in Lieu of Patronage and Domination

Subservience and domination have no place in the kingdom of God and are contrary to the fundamental equality that is shared by all in their common justification in Christ. Taken together, four pericopae provide the most telling indictment of the Greco-Roman practice of patronage: Luke 6:27–36, Luke 14:12–14, Acts 2:42–47, and Acts 4:32–35. Each of these texts challenges the Greco-Roman system of patronage and subservience: the ethos of reciprocity, honor-status consciousness, and segregation.

Non-reciprocity

Balanced reciprocity is an interpersonal relationship governed by a strict parity in what each party gives to the other. Market exchange is a typical example. Luke calls for much more than parity in exchange. Luke 6:27–36 is clearly a summons to go beyond reciprocity. It is a call to move away from an "ethics of strict reciprocity" to one that is animated by a spirit of generous self-giving. It is an invitation to be prodigal in one's benefactions and not to be measured or calculating in the manner they treat others. This is the complete antithesis of a relationship based on utility. Patronage is motivated by a *quid-pro-quo* mindset, of giving with an eye to getting something in return. In contrast, disinterested generosity is being God-like in giving liberally and indiscriminately. This is a distinctively Christian virtue. It has been described as "Jesus' rigorous ethic of giving without expectation of return." The goal is to "decenter" the self (that is concerned with self-serving reciprocity) and to "center" the other (founded on altruism).[44]

Indiscriminate Table-Fellowship

The call to associate with those whom society considers to be inferior is another direct challenge to patron-client relationships. Luke 14:12–14 is a striking illustration of this in which Jesus admonishes his dinner host to invite the poor, the lame, the crippled, and the blind—people whom the host would be mortified to fraternize with, much less invite to his household for a meal. What is at stake here is not only giving up the ethos of strict reciprocity and the expectation of a return invitation or a favor down the road. There is much more involved here. In the Greco-Roman world in which honor-status meant everything, one's circle of friends or relations determined one's social standing. Similarly, given the Jewish concern for purity, one associated only with those who were considered clean. Thus, whether for Jews or Hellenized Gentiles, one is never indiscriminate when it comes to whom one eats with, much less invite to one's home. Table-fellowship and the admonition against patron-client relationships are related norms. Meal-fellowship is particularly important for Luke.[45] Meals are an important occasion for fellowship. Thus, Jesus asked his host to do the unthinkable—invite (and associate with!) the poor, the maimed, the lame, and the blind.

The parable of the great feast (Lk 14:15–24) immediately after the abovementioned pericope reinforces the point made by Jesus. In this parable, recall that after the invited guests refused to attend the banquet with their excuses, the host orders his servant to bring in the poor, the maimed, the blind, and the lame and anyone else along the highways and hedges. Using social scientific models, scholars have shown that the parable is about the need to treat one another as equals.[46] Again, this stands in sharp contrast to the Pharisees who excused themselves from having anything to do with those at the fringes of society by invoking the purity laws.[47]

We also find class barriers breaking down in the early Church. In Joppa, Peter had no qualms about staying with Simon the tanner (Acts 9:43). (Tanning was a despised occupation at that time.) By accepting the hospitality of a tanner and his household, Peter affirmed the dignity of the work and the breakdown of distinctions by status.[48] Similarly, Peter had no problems obeying the instructions of the Holy Spirit to go to the household of Cornelius, a Roman centurion. Not only did he stay with them, but he also partook of their Gentile meals (Acts 10–11). Class distinctions and dietary restrictions that held people apart from one another were trumped by a newfound fellowship accorded by the Holy Spirit.

Consider the consequences of heeding Jesus' call for undiscriminating table-fellowship. First, it is a de facto lowering of one's own social standing in the eyes of others. It is to be the laughing stock of the Hellenized community. Within the Jewish community, it is to be rendered unclean oneself. In both cases, the indiscriminate will be shunned and isolated by their own social circle of friends and relations for fear of putting their own social status at risk by associating with those who are unselective in the company they keep. It is sheer folly, social and religious suicide. It is to invite scorn and ridicule from one's peers and the rest of society.

Second, people who associate with others beneath their social class or status erode their own power base. Patronage, after all, is about accumulating as much influence as one can by putting people in their debt or by liberally dispensing favors to others who will feel obligated to return the favor in the future. By following the advice of Jesus in inviting those who are unable to reciprocate, one is in effect wasting one's time and material resources that could have otherwise been used to amass even more prestige and power.

Third, the indiscriminate invitation called for by Jesus also means that besides consorting with people who are considered one's social "inferiors," one may also have to welcome and associate with people whom one may despise or perhaps even hate or have reason to hate. In other words, it is to follow the example of Jesus in accepting and loving one and all. His table-fellowship is an example of how to accord others the respect and regard they deserve as children of God. This is perhaps no less demanding than foregoing one's social standing or power base because it entails giving something that is not merely external, but internal and from the heart: one's time, attention, respect, love, and friendship. It means a radical transformation deep in one's heart and mind.

Christian Alternative

The early Church community is an example of both an ethics of non-reciprocity and an ethics of indiscriminate table fellowship. Acts 2:42–47 is a particularly vivid account of how they held property in common, prayed together, shared meals, and genuinely enjoyed one another's company.

In lieu of domination and subservience, the New Testament calls for friendship, one that blossoms into fellowship and communion (*koinōnia*), which in turn find expression in a generous sharing of material goods. In Acts 2:42–47, those who sold their possessions did not simply give alms to the poor. They also provided table-fellowship. In that era, shared meals were part of the Palestinian culture's community of goods. Philo describes the Essene community of goods as one in which wages were pooled together to buy food for their common meals (the evening meal-fellowship) and to procure the needs of the community.[49]

The self-giving in Luke 6:27–36 and the indiscriminate table-fellowship of Luke 14:12–14 are not merely exacting in what they require, they are downright difficult, if not impossible, to fulfill. Such unmeasured self-giving and indiscriminate table-fellowship is ultimately a call for a *koinōnia* founded on genuine friendship. There are four different uses of the term *koinōnia*: as fellowship-communion, as generosity, as the concrete sign of such communion (e.g., a gift or proof of such a special relationship), and as the act of sharing.[50] All four senses of the word are relevant for our study.

The call to put an end to patron-client relationships actually demands much more than just giving up power over others. It is to extend friendship to people whom one would have never chosen to associate with on their own. In fact, breaking down class barriers is a perennial undercurrent in Luke-Acts, from the voluntary dispossession of the apostles, to the invitation to the rich ruler in search of eternal life, to the scandalous table fellowship of Jesus, to the community sharing of goods in Acts.[51]

In Greco-Roman literature, there are theological motifs and themes (*topoi*) which are a loose collection of proverbs, maxims, and other materials that point to the same thought. In the New Testament, we find the Greco-Roman motif on friendship, even if the word friendship (*philia*) is not used.[52] Hellenized readers will immediately recognize the Greek ideal of friendship in Luke's description of the early Church as being of one heart and one mind (Acts 4:32).[53] This is the essence of *koinōnia*. It is the same language and understanding of Greek proverbs on friendship.[54]

The Greek notion of friendship entails unity and equality (manifested in reciprocity). It is oriented toward the same vision of the good for one another. It carries with it genuine obligations, as in the case of Luke's narrative of the importunate friend at midnight (Lk 11:5–8). And it involves the "full sharing of all things, spiritual and material" and a real "active participation, sharing, and help between partners."[55] In Greek literature, friends enjoy things in common.[56] Thus, Acts 2:42–47 and Acts 4:32–37 exemplify the true essence of friendship. The sharing is voluntary and sacrificial so that others might be provisioned (Acts 5:1–11). And it is a friendship and fellowship based on unity in having received the same Holy Spirit (Acts 2:38; 4:31) and in having acknowledged the authority of the apostles (Acts 4:34–35, 37; 5:1–2). The New Testament uses the Greek language and concept of friendship to stress how the early Church was going to be an intentional community of *koinōnia*.[57]

Note that the early Church members did not divest themselves of property as an end in itself. Rather, they sold their properties in order to provide relief to the needy among them. This goes back to the earlier point on equality and sharing among friends.[58] In their communion of goods, the early Church combined the Old Testament ideal of covenant community (the economy of equality) and the Greek ideal of friendship. We find other instances of such fellowship and communion in the early Church, even between Gentile and Jewish Christians. The Gentile churches took up a collection to send alms for the poor brethren in Jerusalem (Acts 11:29–30; 24:17).

It is perhaps not surprising that the admonitions against a socioeconomic system of patronage and domination-subservience are found mostly in Luke-Acts. After all, the Lucan community consisted of Gentiles. They were most likely unfamiliar with the Old Testament laws on mutual assistance and were probably also steeped in the Hellenistic-Roman ethos of patronage. Moreover, there were many people of wealth and social standing in this community—the group that would have practiced such social stratification. Not surprisingly, unlike Mark or Matthew, Luke accentuates the importance of fellowship and communion. In effect, Luke-Acts also challenge the Jewish Christians to embrace the Gentile Christians and the poor in table fellowship.[59]

Beyond Luke-Acts: Patronage

The admonition against the Greco-Roman practice of patronage and subservience is not limited to Luke and Acts alone. We can infer it from the narratives of the other Gospels, from Paul's own life, and from the Pauline letters.

Matthew 6:1–4 calls for untrumpeted almsgiving, preferably done in secret. This is the antithesis of the Greco-Roman practice of self-serving almsgiving in which benefactions are made for the express purpose of winning public adulation and putting people in their debt. Such negative almsgiving was driven by expediency and expected returns, in contrast to Matthew's call for disinterested giving.

In response to the mother of James and John seeking to let her sons be seated on the left and right of the Lord, Jesus clearly warns the apostles not to emulate "the kings of the Gentiles [who] *lord it over them*" and "*are called benefactors*" (Lk 22:25; cf. Mt 20:20–28; Mk 10:35–45, emphasis added). Rather he invites them to be the servant of all if they want to be great.

Jesus sends forth his disciples to preach, teach, and heal just as he has, and asks them not to take any gold, silver, copper, or any means of economic support for themselves. Rather, they were to depend on the hospitality and kindness of the people and communities to whom they were sent (Mt 10:7–14; Mk 6:8–11; Lk 9:2–4; 10:4–7). Scholars interpret this as a reaffirmation of Jesus' precondition of radical dispossession for those who would follow him in his ministry.[60] However, we could probably add a secondary point: a reverse patron-client relationship. The disciples are to become humble supplicants in meeting their basic needs. In relying on people's support and sustenance, disciples are, in effect, precluded from building patron-client relationships for themselves as they go about healing and preaching. This is the complete antithesis, indeed an indictment, of the ethos and practice of the Pharisees whom Luke disparagingly describes as "lovers of money."[61]

Of course the prime counter-example to the Pharisees, the scribes, and the elite of the time is Jesus himself. More than anybody else, Jesus is in a unique position to build a circle of people beholden to him for their miraculous healing. Jesus could have turned his large following into subservient clients who would shower him with praise, adulation, honors, loyalty, money, power, status, service, and favors. And yet, Jesus never takes the role of a benefactor, much less lord it over people. On the contrary, it is Jesus who puts himself in a position of mendicancy and humbly accepts material support from friends and followers (Mt 27:55; Lk 23:55). This dependency is completely unnecessary considering that Jesus could have chosen to accumulate wealth and power for himself given what he had done for many. Indeed, Jesus himself lives, preaches, and travels in the manner that he asks his disciples—no gold, silver, or staff for himself, but reliant only the kindness of the people to whom he preached. Most important for our purposes, this is the Jesus who, far from holding his disciples in subservience, calls them friends and even washes their feet in humble service.

Paul is another example of one who does not fall for the lure of patron-client relationships. We can infer this in the way he interacts with the churches he had established. Paul urges the Thessalonians to work quietly and assiduously so that they might edify others and not be dependent on anybody (1 Thess 4:11–12). With such an "artisan ethos of self-sufficient independence,"[62] there would be less reason to attach oneself to a benefactor. And Paul practices what he preaches. He is keenly aware that just like the other apostles, he is entitled to support from the people he serves. However, far from adding further burdens on the churches, Paul voluntarily foregoes whatever material claims he may have and pursues a separate livelihood, even while preaching the Gospel (1 Cor 9:1–23; 1 Thess 2:6–10; cf. Mt 10:8–11). And he is explicit in stating why he chooses this more laborious path: so that "I am free with respect to all" (1 Cor 9:19), clearly referring to avoiding being beholden to a patron.

Nevertheless, despite his preference to be self-supporting, Paul graciously accepts provisions sent to him (Phil 4:10–20; 2 Cor 11:8–9; 12:13). This reveals a humility that would not be found in anyone wishing to put together a retinue of subservient clients for oneself.[63] Thus, for Paul, the ideal economic exchange between people ought to be based on charity and self-sufficiency. Charity precluded the benefactor from engaging in self-serving almsgiving, while self-sufficiency minimized the need for a benefactor.[64]

Class and status consciousness and self-selected segregation seem to have been rife in some of the early churches. However, Paul is firm in correcting such conduct from the converts' previous lives. In particular, Paul takes the Corinthians to task for their poor table-fellowship in which the rich and the powerful simply ignored the poor and the lower classes (1 Cor 11:17–34). Meals were to be shared with one another, rich and poor alike.[65] In fact, rich Christian benefactors even had to forgo the honorific titles that were standard at that time even in Jewish synagogues.[66]

Beyond Luke-Acts: Friendship and Material Sharing

Just like the critique against patron-client relationships, the call for friendship and fellowship in the early Church community goes beyond Luke-Acts. In his letter to the Philippians, Paul urges them to be a community of friends.[67] This is evident in Philippians 2:1–4 in which the community is "of the same mind" and "sharing in the Spirit," in contrast to ambition and conceit. They are to embrace a humility that puts others ahead of self. It is a *koinōnia* founded on the Holy Spirit that leads to like-mindedness, fellowship in the life of the Gospel, service to others, a readiness to suffer, and a Christ-like kindness so different from Greco-Roman patronage. This friendship and fellowship find concrete expression in the generous sharing of material goods. Note how the Philippians generously supported the ministry of Paul even after he was long gone to preach and found other churches (Phil 4:15, 18–19; 2 Cor 11:9).[68] We also find such fellowship manifested in the sharing of material goods among the churches, as seen in the alms and collections taken up for the poor in Jerusalem (Gal 2:9–10; 6:2; 1 Cor 16:1–4; 2 Cor 8–9; Rom 15:25–27).[69]

We find the same phenomenon of fellowship in the mutual assistance and sharing of material goods in James and the Johannine literature. In the letter of James, friendship with God entails a low-mindedness (Jas 4:7–10) and a complete readiness to share everything and to give all for God, as in the case of Abraham (Jas 2:23). This friendship will then overflow to the poor and the sick (Jas 2:1–5; 2:15–16; 5:13–16). Such friendship is in marked contrast to envy, arrogance, and the inordinate pursuit of profits (Jas 4:13–17; 2:6; 5:1–6). The Johannine literature also shows how friendship and fellowship lead to a sharing of material possessions (Jn 15:13–15; 1 Jn 1:3, 7; 3:16–18; 3 Jn 1:4–8).[70] In sum, friendship as a theme is seen not only in Luke-Acts, but also in the rest of the New Testament. Such fellowship necessarily overflows into a sharing of material goods.

Admonition for Both Rich and Poor

What does *koinōnia* mean in practice? Clearly, the rich will have to give up much in the Christian indictment of Greco-Roman patronage. They are to be generous in sharing their wealth. They are to go against the prevailing Hellenistic-Roman ethos of honor-status as a basis for how they treat others. In fact, they are not to make class distinctions at all. They are to give up their upper-class privilege, treat as equals those who are deemed to be beneath their social standing, and extend them friendship and communion. By doing all these, the rich are to put their own social standing in jeopardy. In fact, some suggest that the Gospels' account of the Pharisees' disdainful criticism of Jesus for his shocking indiscriminate table-fellowship (Lk 5:30; 7:33–35; 15:1–2; Mk 2:15–16; Mt 9:10–11) may have been the evangelists' way of consoling rich Christians who were enduring social criticism and ostracism themselves for associating with people beneath their class.[71]

But this admonition against patronage and the call for *koinōnia* apply just as well to the poor and also demand much from them. For example, Luke 6:27–36 can be read in the context of the Hellenistic-Roman social stratification of patron-client relationships. The lower classes, which despise and hate the rich for maltreating them, are summoned to love those who have made their lives difficult or who have been indifferent to their plight.[72] In effect, the poor are also addressees of this call to love one's enemies. Furthermore, the poor are also invited to be generous. Wealth does indeed bring power and self-sufficiency, and this becomes the occasion for the rich to cut themselves off from the rest of the community in luxurious self-sufficiency and abundance (e.g., Lk 16:19–31). But being mean and miserly is not reserved for the rich alone. We have the account of the unmerciful servant who could not forgive a fellow servant's debt (Mt 18:23–35), or the workers who took offense at the vineyard owner's generosity in paying everyone a full day's wage (Mt 20:1–15).[73]

Thus, whether rich or poor, all are invited to treat one another with magnanimity. All are to imitate God's generosity, to the extent humanly possible. *Koinōnia* requires much of all, from the rich and the poor and those in between. Heroic self-giving (whether of wealth or forgiveness) becomes the norm. They are to give without regard for recipients' merit. They are to give even to those who do not deserve their love and gift, and even to those who hate or oppress them. It is to be completely unmeasured, indiscriminate, and unconditional in self-giving.

Theological and Ethical Insights from the Caution Against Patronage

The admonitions against the Greco-Roman practice of patronage and subservience enrich our understanding of longstanding ethical teachings. First, to give up dominating and reducing others to servility in favor of mutual respect is to make present the kingdom of God. This kingdom calls for an entirely different interpersonal relationship, one based on mutual love, solicitude, and respect: *koinōnia*. To live in *koinōnia* is to be proleptic, that is, to live today how we are to live in the eschaton. To freely associate with one another without class distinction is to have a foretaste of the Messianic banquet.

Second, parties to a patron-client relationship are shown the utter futility of their efforts. On the one hand, it is pretentious of patrons to lord it over others and to build up a clientele of people indebted and subservient to them. In truth, there is only one true benefactor, God, from whom all things come into being and who provides people according to their needs and deeds.[74] All relationships based on power and domination will be revealed for what they truly are—hollow, fleeting, and subject to a day of eschatological reckoning (Lk 14:14).

On the other hand, clients ought to remember the call not to be anxious about what they are to eat or drink because of the reassurance that the Father knows what they need and will provide for them with far more care and love as God takes care of the lilies of the fields and the birds of the air (Lk 12:22–31). For the poor and the powerless, there is no need to be anxious, much less to have to worry about attaching themselves to a benefactor-protector-provider. For those who seek the kingdom of God, it is sufficient to put their trust in the providential care of a loving God, a good shepherd, an indulgent Father.

Third, to give up patron-client relationships is to imitate Christ and be God-like in the way they conduct themselves vis-à-vis their neighbors. The paradigm of heroic and prodigal *koinōnia* is no less than God. God, the Lord of creation, brought the world into existence, when there was no need to do so and created humans for their own sake to share in divine life and happiness, and in God's own image and likeness at that. God, the Lord of history, took the initiative of self-revelation, offered the gift of divine friendship, and pursued a vibrant relationship with humans (e.g., Old Testament covenants). God has a proven track record of radical fidelity in never taking back gifts, despite repeated human betrayal. God even restores lives and communities shattered by sin (e.g., Babylonian exile).

And then, of course, there is the gift and example of Jesus Christ. In the gift of the Incarnation, God took on human flesh. The Incarnate Word did not come to condemn or to lord it over creatures, but to preach, teach, and heal those who are suffering. Jesus died on the cross, forgiving and loving even those who had brutalized him.

The one true patron and benefactor, God, could have rightfully lorded it over humans, but instead gave them the gift of divine friendship and made them heirs of heaven, children of God, brothers and sisters of Jesus Christ. Can one do any less than follow the example of God?

Fourth, renouncing patronage-domination and embracing *koinōnia* instead sheds light on the many teachings and narratives on almsgiving, sharing, and generosity (e.g., Lk 6:30, Acts 4:32–37). *Koinōnia* makes the motive for almsgiving clear: treating others as brothers and sisters, as equals, as fellow children of God, as members of the same Church and Body of Christ in need of assistance. Most of all, *koinōnia* is founded on friendship. This is foundational, indeed the starting point, for all the biblical economic norms. All the caritative activities of people, whether as individuals or as a community, flow from this.

Even more important than the amount people share is the spirit with which they share. This spirit determines whether they limit themselves to sharing their material goods, or whether they go so far as to share their very selves. Thus, the widow with her two small copper coins gave infinitely far more than all the others who were giving vast sums (Mk 12:41–44) because in giving all she had to live on, she was giving of herself and holding nothing back. Only friendship and love lead to the latter kind of sharing.

The goal of almsgiving is not merely the relief of a neighbor's destitution or need, but the offer of fellowship and friendship. Friends bind themselves to each other with a mutual concern for one another's well-being. Such sharing goes beyond mere poverty-alleviation; it is an affirmation of *koinōnia*. Such proffered friendship is consistent with the table-fellowship of Jesus who freely associates with and extends an unconditional welcome to all, regardless of whether one was in the in-group (e.g., the Pharisees) or the out-group (e.g., tax collectors, sinners). Thus, the sin of Dives was not so much his opulent lifestyle or stinginess, but his indifference and lack of empathy for Lazarus.[75] Genuine almsgiving must find its completion in friendship.[76]

Fifth, friendship, as a motive for sharing, is much more profound than kinship, pity, or compassion. Friendship goes beyond blood ties, emotions, or even the imagination. Friendship is reliant on love, an act of the will. Thus, Christian *koinōnia* is not merely a willingness to share everything with a friend, but a willingness to extend *koinōnia* and its underlying friendship even to enemies, with those who do not mean you well.

Sixth, the exacting call to forego patron-client relationships in favor of *koinōnia* is possible in the Spirit-empowered discipleship to which all are invited. The early Church's table-fellowship stemmed from their common rebirth and life in the Holy Spirit (Acts 2:38; 4:31) that allowed them to be of one heart and one mind (Acts 4:32).[77] After all, it is God who makes possible that which is difficult or impossible for humans. It is friendship with God that animates and sustains one's friendship with others. One's friendship with God overflows into one's friendship with neighbors. Authentic *koinōnia* is possible only because of divine grace.

Seventh, the invitation to radical voluntary poverty is not merely about giving up possessions. Since wealth is an important basis of honor-status and power in the Greco-Roman world, the rich are, in effect, being asked to give up not only their properties, but also all that come with such wealth. By divesting themselves of riches, they are also giving up their honor, status, and power. More than that, they are voluntarily reducing themselves to the ranks of the poor, the defenseless, and the vulnerable. From being a benefactor, provider, and protector, they voluntarily cross the social divide and take the opposite position of being dependent on the good will and mercy of others. Indeed, Jesus' invitation to complete divestment is much more demanding than it appears on the surface. It is not a surprise that the rich man left Jesus, sad and unable to give up all that he possessed (Mk 10:17–22). In fact, unlike Matthew and Mark, note how Luke even describes this rich man as a ruler (Lk 18:18).

Eighth, in the pericope critical of Greco-Roman patronage (Lk 14:12–14), Jesus assures his host that he will be rewarded in the resurrection of the righteous. Righteousness (*tzĕdāqâ*) is about fulfilling the obligations that come with relationships. Fellowship (*koinōnia*) is righteous behavior because people treat one another as equals, as brothers and sisters, as fellow children of the same God. Clearly, Greco-Roman patronage falls far short of righteousness.

In sum, the New Testament calls for fellowship in lieu of the Greco-Roman practice of patronage. It is a fundamental condition of the mutual respect and solicitude that humans owe to one another.

WORK ETHIC AS A SERVICE TO OTHERS

Both mutual solicitude and *koinōnia* call for a responsible work ethic from every member of the community. We can infer this from the Old Testament's account of how every family receives an ancestral land, its norms on land return and land redemption, and its laws on interest-free debts, slave release, and debt forgiveness. The goal is clearly to have independent landholding families in Israel that supported themselves and contributed to the upkeep of the nation and the Temple through their tithes and offerings. Moreover, the value of hard work is repeatedly affirmed in the wisdom literature.

In the New Testament, we find the same call for an upright work ethic in the Pauline letters. Despite their expectation of an imminent Parousia, members of the early Church are nevertheless still expected to work and earn a living so that they are not a burden on anyone and instead are able to assist the poor. Moreover, families are to support their relatives who have fallen on hard times so that the community's limited resources could be devoted to helping those who are genuinely needy. Paul himself sets an example of this work ethic and this desire not to be a burden on others in spite of his rightful claims for support as an apostle.

In contrast to the Greco-Roman disdain for manual labor, both the Old and New Testament laud work not only as a gift from God (Gen 1), but also as an important means of caring for others and promoting the good of the entire community. Work is not merely a gift; it is also an obligation. This averts a moral hazard problem whereby slothful people take advantage of others' solicitude. There is no obligation to feed, and thereby enable, the indolent (2 Thess 3:6–12).

SUMMARY AND CONCLUSIONS

The Old and the New Testament converge in what they teach on interpersonal relationships despite the wide disparity in their life setting, in the socioeconomic problems they were addressing, and in their theological concerns. In the Old Testament, interpersonal relationships must be imbued with the triad of steadfast love (*hesed*), justice (*mišpāt*), and righteousness (*tzĕdāqâ*). As a result, the Chosen People were to care for the stranger, the widow, and the orphan, and there was to be no poor in their midst (Dt 15:4). In the New Testament, the early Christians were not to be class- or status-conscious like the larger Greco-Roman culture. They were to associate freely with those whom they deemed to be beneath their social standing. In contrast to calculated reciprocity, this entailed genuine friendship and disinterested gift-giving with no expectation of return. *Koinōnia* was to be their formal characteristic as a Christian community. As a result, they looked after one another's need, and there was said to be no poor in their midst (Acts 4:34). Indeed, *tzĕdāqâ* and *koinōnia* are distinct concepts, but they, nevertheless, converge on the same point of treating one another with mutual respect, as an equal, and with justice, mercy, compassion, and love.

These striking similarities between the Old and New Testament should probably not be surprising because both *tzĕdāqâ* and *koinōnia* have similar roots in the importance of anchoring interpersonal relationships on family values. Of course, the key difference is that New Testament *koinōnia* is anchored on an even deeper and more profound foundation: all are now adopted brothers and sisters of Christ, children of the One God, and members of the one Body of Christ in the redemption won for them by Christ through his Incarnation, passion, death, and resurrection. In other words, the scope of disciples' obligations is even wider, and the grounds for treating one another with justice, respect, and love are even deeper and stronger. They have even greater cause to treat each other with steadfast love, mercy, righteousness, and, best of all, friendship.

NOTES

1. Pleins (2001, 65). For a sampling of scholars who conclude that solicitude for the poor is central to the law, see Barton (2003, 163); Donahue (1977, 73–77); Ogletree (1983); Otto (1995, 162, 164); Pleins (2001); von Waldow (1970); and Wenham (2006, 357–59).

2. Von Waldow (1970) calls these the *personae miserabiles*. This concern may stem from (1) inherited materials from ANE literature, (2) Israel's Covenant relationship with God, and (3) their reaction to the declining socioeconomic conditions of their day. See also Fensham (1962).

3. Hiers (2002, 56). See also Soss (1973).

4. Rosner (1978)

5. Perkins (1994, 47). Recall the safety net provided by the clan in the *go'el*, that is, a relative who redeems an enslaved kin or family land that had been sold.

6. Perdue (1994, 102)

7. Lohfink (1991, 34)

8. Von Waldow (1970, 182); Lohfink (1991, 40)

9. Cohn (1984, 77) notes that these migrants are what we call today "refugees." See also Hiers (2002, 62).

10. Lokfink (1991)

11. Fensham (1962, 138) holds a different view. He argues that in the ANE nations, the obligation to care for the weak applied to the general populace as well and not only to the king. The vertical command from the gods had to be reflected in people's horizontal, interpersonal relationships.

12. Blomberg (1999, 69)

13. Perkins (1994, 49)

14. Harvey (1990, 119)

15. This was a declaration made before the court and in front of witnesses that the Sabbatical debt remission did not apply to the loan being incurred.

16. Pleins (2001, 52–53) notes that codifying these practices is a distinctive feature of the Covenant Code relative to its ANE counterparts.

17. We find this ideal in the prophetic literature as well in which every person has the peace of mind in having a secure home and inheritance (Mic 4:4).

18. Pleins (2001, 53). See also Davies (1981, 72–75).

19. See Premnath (2003) for an in-depth exposition.

20. Anderson (1978, 36)

21. Anderson (1978, 47)

22. Anderson (1978, 47) notes three variants of *hesed*, namely: (1) as mercy, loving-kindness, steadfast love, loyal love, loyalty, and constancy, (2) as a response to God, such as when it is paired with righteousness (Hos 10:12) and justice (Hos 12:6), and (3) as an unequal relationship between a superior and an inferior. For the superior, such concern is not noblesse oblige, but a genuine and spontaneous desire to work for the welfare of the other. For the inferior, it is a desire to perform faithfully one's duties. Anderson (1978, 47) defines "love" as "the energetic devotion of one's whole being—will, thought, and feeling—toward or against an object."

23. Wittenberg (1978, 148–49)

24. Anderson (1978, 44)

25. Mays (1987, 154–55)

26. Pilgrim (1981)

27. Mays (1987, 156)

28. Anderson (1978, 43)

29. Perkins (1994, 57)

30. Gillman (1991, 29); Malina (1987, 358). See also Malina (1987), Moxnes (1988, 28–32), and Polanyi (1944) for a description of the embedded economy.

31. Thus, recall from part I how the Covenant model's economy of equality and politics of service were ultimately shaped by religion (Birch, 1991). This also explains why, by modern standards, the Israelite economy was encumbered by many efficiency-distorting rules, such as the prohibition on the charging of interest (e.g., see Silver, 1995).

32. Domeris (2007, 80–81); Simkins (1999; 2004)

33. Moxnes (1988, 73)

34. Mott (1987, 234–37)

35. Moxnes (1988)

36. Oakman (1986). Thus, there was a perennial concern for debt-slaves even as the nation Israel was rewriting its laws during the different phases of her history.

37. See Hanson and Oakman (1998, 72) for a succinct listing of the features of a patron-client relationship. See also Elliott (1996) and Eisenstadt and Roniger (1980; 1984).

38. Perkins (1994, 47–48)

39. Even in our own contemporary era of rights and laws, social networking is still a valuable resource.

40. For example, see Simkins (1999, 128–29).

41. Moxnes (1988)

42. Capper (1998) sees Luke 4:1–13 (Mt 4:1–11) as another example of patron-client relationships.

43. For a description of the social stratification in Hellenistic-Roman life, see Esler (1989, 171–79). See also Donahue (1989, 142); Dupont (1977, 32–34); Gillman (1991, 29–31, 33–35, 56–57, 76–80); Hays (1996, 123); Moxnes (1988); Nardoni (2004, 252–55); Perkins (1994, 48–49, 58); and Schottroff and Stegemann (1986, 111–16, 118).

44. Kirk (2003, 668, 671)

45. See Capper (1998, fn 51).

46. Rohrbaugh (1991). See also Hanson and Oakman (1998, 74–75) on this parable.

47. Moxnes (1988)

48. Davies (1995, 333)

49. Capper (1998)

50. Dupont (1979, 85)

51. Perkins (1994, 56–58) notes that while Jesus criticizes the Pharisees' rules of purity and honor, Luke attacks the Greco-Roman patronage system.

52. For example, fellowship (*koinōnia*) connoted friendship (*philia*) for Greek readers (Johnson 2004, 163).

53. See Johnson (2004, 159–61) for some of the motifs (*topoi*) on friendship as used in the New Testament.

54. See Beavis (1994) and Capper (1998).

55. Johnson (2004, 160)

56. For example, see *Nicomachean Ethics* VIII:11, 1159B, 31; IX:8, 1168B, 8.

57. Johnson (2004, 161–62)

58. Dupont (1979, 95)

59. Esler (1987, 71–109)

60. For example, see Johnson (1981, 23–25) and Pilgrim (1981, 96–98).

61. Moxnes (1988)

62. Perkins (1994, 55–59)

63. See also Perkins (1994, 56).

64. See Perkins (1994, 55–59).

65. Perkins (1994, 55)

66. Meeks (1983, 81)

67. Paul heavily uses terms associated with friendship and the Greek prefix "syn-" pertaining to "with or together." See Johnson (2004, 163) for such specific instances.

68. Johnson (2004, 162–65)

69. Johnson (2004, 165–67)

70. Johnson (2004, 169–70)

71. Perkins (1994, 58)

72. Schottroff and Stegemann (1986, 111–16)

73. Perkins (1994, 60)

74. Gillman (1991, 35); Perkins (1994, 58)

75. Scott (1989)

76. After all, there are many possible motives for almsgiving: out of fear and desire to conform to the law; for social prestige and praise; to develop patron-client relationships; to flaunt one's wealth; as a form of social insurance ("banking" favors that can be returned in the future); giving to others what one had received as a gift; assisting those who are beloved of God; as part of the duties of kinship.

77. Johnson (2004, 162)

Chapter Fourteen

Gift of the Earth

Stewardship

God intends a flourishing life for all—humans and other living creatures—as part of the divine order in the natural world and in moral life. To this end, God extended to humanity a third gift—the gift of the earth. Sacred Scripture has much to say on the blessings and the obligations attendant to such divine gift.

RESPECT AND CARE FOR THE EARTH

Genesis 1:26–28 has been misunderstood and misinterpreted to the point of even being blamed for human abuses of the environment. Critics assert that these passages give humans carte blanche over the fruits of the earth, with predictable disastrous results.[1] Scripture scholars vigorously contest these claims. They note that far from giving humans absolute authority over the use of the earth and its fruits, Genesis 1:26–28, in fact, calls for great human care and respect for the earth.[2]

To begin with, the abuse of the earth is contrary to the will of God. At the end of each day of creation, the priestly account in Genesis 1 has the constant refrain on how God saw creation to be very good. Note, too, the purposefulness of God's activity. God acts in a methodological and deliberate manner. There is a purpose to everything, and creation is in equilibrium. Nothing is superfluous. Everything has a place and a role to play. Everything is good and has a purpose.[3]

Second, it is also important to note that Genesis 1 is not exclusively, or even principally, about the human person. The chapter is about God!

> The biblical world view is not so much anthropocentric as theocentric. That is why it speaks of creation and not nature. For all this deep appreciation of the natural environment, neither Psalm 104 nor Job 38–39 is nature poetry. The world is good because it is God's creation, not because it is divine. (Tucker, 1997, 17)

Psalm 104 is a celebration and praise of God as creator and God's creatures. It is an affirmation of how God provides for creatures and cares for creation. In other words, Genesis 1 is not about the human person's domination of the earth, but about God's sovereignty as creator of a beautiful world marked by goodness.

Third, the Old Testament has a strong land ethic. Land belongs to God (Ex 9:29b; 19:5; Dt 10:14; Ps 24:1–2; 50:10–12; 89:11; Lev 25:23; Jer 27:5), and it is God who cares for it and makes it fertile (Dt 11:11–12; Ps 65:9–13; 147:8–18; Job 38:25–27). Even land is given rest (Ex 23:10–11; Lev 25: 2–12; 26:34–35, 43). Note, too, the explicit call for the proper care of trees (Lev 19:23–25). Cutting down fruit trees when besieging an enemy city is proscribed (Dt 20:19–20). Sennacherib is punished for wantonly destroying cypresses in Lebanon (2 Kgs 19:23–24).[4] Indeed, the Old Testament calls for conservation and respect for the earth.

Fourth, contrary to widespread belief, the earth was not made exclusively for use by the human person. Non-human creatures are celebrated for their beauty. Such beauty is a reflection of God's wisdom (e.g., Ps 8). For example, God sends rain to the desert where no humans live (Jb 38:25–27). It would have been unnecessary to do so if the earth and its fruits had indeed been created primarily and exclusively for human use. Moreover, the fruits of the earth are also for the use and benefit of animals (Ex 23:11; Lev 25:7).

Fifth, the divine mandate to subdue and have dominion over the earth does not confer humans with absolute freedom of action. Job 38–39 is a forthright reminder that human knowledge and control of the world is limited. It is God who manages the world, not humans. For example, humans do not know how the world came about nor do they exercise control over wild animals.[5]

Sixth, to be made in the image and likeness of God does not mean that humans are divine or that they can lord it over all the other creatures. Rather, it means that they are the representatives of God on the earth.[6] This means that they are to act on God's behalf and in accord with divine will.

Finally, God cares for all creatures and not only for humans.[7] The words "subdue" and "dominion" in Genesis 1:26–28 must be taken in the context of God's call for the other creatures to be fruitful and to multiply (Gen 1:20–22, 28; 8:17). God ordered Noah to build an ark large enough to accommodate animals too (Gen 6:20; 7:14–15). God wanted these species to survive. In fact, the divine bidding to be fruitful and to multiply is renewed after the flood (Gen 8:17). Note, too, the major biblical covenants. In the covenant struck with Noah, God made such a covenant not only with humans but also with all living things. We see repeated reference to "every living creature" as part of this post-diluvial covenant (Gen 9:8–17). Moreover, the new creation in the eschatology is not only for the benefit of humans, but also for animals and other creatures as well. In the new dispensation there will be no more violence, even among animals (e.g., Is 11:6–9). Every creature has a specific place and role in God's order of creation. After all, all creation is good (Gen 1:20–31).

Laws on animal sacrifice can, paradoxically, be used as an illustration of God's respect for life. The substitution of animals for humans in sacrifice suggests that animals are valued, to the point of even being used as a substitute for humans. Restrictions on the disposal of their blood are also indicative of respect for these creatures. "Life" is believed to be contained in the blood. People may eat other creatures, but not their blood (Gen 9:3–4). "Life" is to be returned to the ground. Note the Jewish law governing the slaughter of animals for food (Lev 7:26–27; 17:10–14; Dt 12:23–24, 27).[8]

Laws calling for the respect and humane treatment of animals are yet another indication of the goodness of God's creation and God's care for the earth and its creatures. Note, for example, the extensive laws on tending to new-born animals, the care for distressed or lost animals, the proper feeding of oxen which are not to be muzzled as they work, rest even for the animals on the Sabbath and the sabbatical year, and respect for a bird's nest with a mother sitting on the eggs or on fledglings (Dt 22:6).[9] In addition, there are non-legal texts that also show sensitivity to animals (Num 22:21–35; Prov 12:10; Sir 18:13). And, of course, we have the New Testament passages on God's care even for the lilies of the field and the birds of the sky (Mt 10:29; Lk 12:24–28). Not a single sparrow falls to the ground without God knowing it. The writers, editors, and compilers would not have devoted so much time, attention, and space to such duties on the proper respect and care for animals had it not been a genuine concern.

In sum, on the surface, it would seem that care for the earth is yet another issue in which we find contradiction in the Bible. On the one hand, there is the "dominion" model with human beings at the top of the food chain and with all the other creatures existing only to serve and provide for human needs (e.g., Ps 8; Gen 2:15, 19–20; 6:19–20; 8:15–19; Wis 9:1–2) . On the other hand, we have the "integration" model in which humans are only one of many other creatures in the world. The former is an anthropocentric model; the latter is "geocentric, earth-centered" model (as in Ps 104).[10] This is a false dichotomy. These two models are not mutually exclusive because "dominion" has to be properly understood in the manner that many exegetes have emphasized, namely: (1) that the human person acts as God's representative on earth, discharging God's will, and (2) that human conduct has to be consistent with God's care and plans for the world and in accord with the intrinsic goodness of the earth. The two creation stories underscore that:

- God is the creator of everything and values every creature as good.
- Humans are bound to other creatures as fellow creatures and are charged with special responsibilities for their care.[11]
- Humans should be imbued with a spirit of stewardship, rather than a proprietary attitude in dealing with the earth.

In other words, the world is God's and it is good. Clearly, there is a need to take care of it.[12] These points are subsequently affirmed in the rest of the Old Testament.

The Old Testament is also explicit about the consequences of human failure to care for the earth. Genesis 6:11–13 has to be understood in the context of Genesis 1:26–28. Humans failed to live up to their call to be God's representative and, as a result, they brought down destruction upon themselves and the earth.[13] Human sinfulness pushes creation into "de-creation" with its resulting chaos and disequilibrium. In fact, pre-creation in Genesis is described as *tohu vevohu*, which is translated as "formless and empty" or "a formless void."[14] The only other place these two words are used is in Jeremiah 4:23 as he describes the consequences of the nation's sinfulness.[15] Human sinfulness has adverse consequences for the earth, as we find in Hosea 4:1–3 and Leviticus 18:24–25. After all, caring for the earth is an act of worship of God. And, thus, the Law was given by God as a "temporary" means of minimizing and slowing down the ravages of this "de-creation." And indeed, the only real remedy for this process of "de-creation" is the redemption wrought by Christ. The "seed of the woman" will crush the "seed of the serpent" (Gen 3:14–19), and will inaugurate the new creation in Revelation 21:1–4.[16]

Humans undoubtedly have a special place and role in all of creation. But far from endowing humans with a free hand in using the earth in any way they please, the priestly account of creation, in fact, imposes limits, positive obligations, and special responsibilities on human agency. Nevertheless, this should not be viewed as an onerous duty. Rather it is a blessing, because caring for the earth provides an occasion for humans to truly shine forth in the fullness of their being made in the image and likeness of God. In other words, Genesis 1:26–28 does not mean license to abuse, but a call to responsibility and stewardship. It entails maintaining the order of God's creation in accord with the divine will.

PROPERTY

The biggest block of materials in biblical economic morality pertains to wealth and possessions.[17] Not surprisingly, wealth and possessions have also received the most attention from scripture scholars. Undergirding these teachings are at least three recurring themes: (1) the call to trust in God alone, including the invitation to radical divestment and warnings against idolatry and the folly of worldly anxieties; (2) the importance of sharing; and (3) material support for worship and the preaching the Gospel.[18] This chapter examines each of these themes and concludes with an examination of the jarring incongruity between the invitation to radical voluntary divestment and the private property ownership implicit in the call to share the use of possessions.

Trust in God Alone

Idolatry and the Dangers of Wealth

Even as it lauds wealth as a sign of favor from God and as the well-earned reward for hard work and virtue, the wisdom literature is nonetheless wary of riches. After all, wealth can distract people from righteousness (e.g., Prov 11:24–26; 22:16, 22–23). It can ensnare and lead them to complacency and destruction (Sir 31:1–7). It can mislead many to pursue ends that have no intrinsic worth and are not enduring (Ps 49). Qoheleth views its wanton and assiduous accumulation as a wasted effort, as vanity.

The Decalogue is emphatic that there should be no other god than YHWH in all Israel (Ex 20:3; Dt 5:7). This necessarily includes anything and everything, such as possessions, that compete with God for human attention and devotion. The prophets vehemently indict the rich and the elite. Their avarice in acquiring ever more land and ever more wealth has led them to oppress and to rob their fellow Israelites. Their inordinate desire for gain has driven them to shed blood and to corrupt justice at the city gates. Indeed, wealth can ruin lives, not only of the victims, but also of the perpetrators themselves. The legal codes, the wisdom writings, and the prophetic literature are vigilant over wealth and its dangers. This skepticism is evident in the undercurrent of hostility to wealth that we find in the Old Testament.[19]

The New Testament is even more cautious about wealth. Treating possessions and economic activity as ends in themselves is idolatry. This teaching is among the most sustained and the clearest in New Testament economic morality. The choice is stark and is set in unequivocal terms in Matthew 6:24 and Luke 16:13. Humans love and serve either God or mammon, but not both. God above all else! This is not a condemnation of wealth per se or of temporal affairs. Rather, it is about the folly of juxtaposing God with something or someone else as if they were comparable and, therefore, properly subject to a trade-off. Divine claims over creation stand singularly by themselves and cannot be put on a par with the claims of anything or anyone else.

The early Church was alert to the consequences of idolatry and other attachments that keep people away not only from God but also from one another. James 4:1–4, 13–17 notes that coveting wealth ruins the community through competition and conflict, besides misleading people to pursue ends that are ephemeral and of no lasting value. The day of reckoning will reveal the fleeting and impermanent nature of wealth, and the injustices people committed in its pursuit will be exposed and punished (Jas 5:1–6). Love of money destroys that sense of contentment that is critical to leading a life of righteousness, godliness, faith, love, steadfastness, and gentleness (1Tm 6:6–11). Instead, lovers of money fall prey to a multitude of vices that lead to alienation from God and others (2 Tm 3:1–5). This obsession with wealth severely hurts the individual and the community, so much so that it is an impediment to the appointment of bishops, deacons, and other elders in the early church (1 Tm 3:1–9; Ti 1:5–9).

At the heart of the idolatry of wealth and power is an insidious premise that people might have unwittingly internalized from the larger culture without even being aware of it:

> *Being and worth are dependent on having*; having more means being more, and having less means being less. By this logic, therefore, humans are essentially in competition with each other for being and worth, and the surest way to succeed is to eliminate the competition. (Johnson, 1995b, 83, emphasis added)

This flawed understanding of being and worth inevitably gives rise to conflict. An erroneous anthropology leads to a misdirected ethics.

A humble acknowledgment of human dependence on God is a sure guard against the hazards of wealth. Disciples are invited to find their security in God alone, and to do so with such confidence to the point of not being anxious about their needs. Thus, Jesus teaches his followers to ask God for their daily bread in their prayers (Lk 11:3; Mt 6:11).

Voluntary Radical Dispossession

Related to the admonitions on the dangers of wealth and idolatry is the possible response of divesting oneself of possessions. Voluntary poverty is a perennial teaching in the Gospels and Acts. But divestment is not an end in itself nor is it pursued as an ideal.[20] Rather, dispossession has value only in connection with following Christ, or materially supporting the Church (Acts 4:32–36), or putting one's trust in God alone, as in the case of the widow's mites (Mk 12:41–44; Lk 21:1–4). Poverty should not be romanticized because destitution is not what God intends for humanity.[21] There is nothing meritorious in destitution per se that automatically imbues people with moral perfection.

The invitation to radical divestment is associated with the call to follow Christ. We see this in the narrative of the rich young man who has lived an exemplary life and asks Jesus what else he could do to reach perfection. Jesus invites him to sell everything for the benefit of the poor and to come follow him (Mt 19:16–22; Mk 10:17–31; Lk 18:18–30). The call of Peter, Andrew, James, and John also attests to the need for radical divestment in becoming Jesus' disciples (Mt 4:12–22; Mk1:16–20; Lk 5:1–11). The same pattern is repeated in the call of Levi, the tax collector (Mt 9:9–13; Mk 2:13–17; Lk 5: 27–32). They all left everything behind immediately and decisively—family, work, friends, and property—to follow Jesus. And should there be any doubts about this complete renunciation, we see reference to it again later when Peter, in response to Jesus' comparison of the rich to the camel passing though the eye of the needle, reminds Jesus that they had left everything to follow him (Mt 19:27; Mk 10:28; Lk 18:28).

Religious-Ethical Principle: Gottvertrauen ("God-trust")

The warnings on the dangers of wealth and the call for radical dispossession have been viewed as "hostility to wealth." Some believe that this disparagement of riches did not emerge in response to the dismal socioeconomic conditions of the time, but was inherited tradition from Ancient Near Eastern literature and the Old Testament, particularly the wisdom sayings.[22] Wealth is spurned so that people might put their trust in God alone, "God-trust" (*Gottvertrauen*).[23] Such "God-trust" is the path that leads to eternal, heavenly reward. The striving for possessions is pejoratively described as typical of "pagan anxiety" in which one anchors one's security in material possessions rather than in God (Mt 6:25–34).[24]

Unlike the Synoptic Gospels, the Old Testament does not call for voluntary divestment in pursuit of such exclusive trust in God. Instead, the Chosen People actualize their trust in God through their monotheism and their belief that God will deliver them in their adversity (e.g., Psalms). Moreover, trust in God alone is also manifested in Israel's faithful observance of the law despite the practical difficulties it posed. For example, to observe the sabbatical fallow is to trust that God will provide such an abundance of harvest in the sixth year that they will have more than enough tide them over until the harvest of the ninth year (Lev 25:18–22).

Duty to Share

Almsgiving

Almsgiving is an act of compassion and beneficence. It is a central tenet of Old Testament morality (e.g., Sir 29:8–13; Tob 4:7–10, 16; 12:8–9).[25] Even the gleaning law (Lev 19:9–10; 23:22) falls under almsgiving. This is in sharp contrast with Greco-Roman thinking in which almsgiving was more of a cultural, civic practice, "commendable but not especially meritorious."[26] However, one should not automatically assume that the motive for almsgiving is compassion for the poor. It may, in fact, be driven by the desire for eternal or temporal reward for oneself. In fact, many of the injunctions to dispossession and even almsgiving are not out of concern for the poor but for the sake of the donor.[27] After all, almsgiving is an important venue for atonement.[28] It is an effective way to pay debts incurred because of sin.[29] We find this in Jesus' critique of the Pharisees for their hypocrisy and for their hollow observance of the law. What is more important is the internal disposition of the person, and almsgiving is an example of how one can truly be made clean inside (Lk 11:41).

Generosity

The proper use of possessions is a perennial teaching of Sacred Scripture. "Wealth is consistently colored by eschatological considerations."[30] It is never an end in itself but is used as a means for greater ends, such as building community, caring for one another, almsgiving, and satisfying basic human needs. This is an important point of continuity in both the Old and New Testament. There is a strong, clear mandate to give alms and not to refuse loans to the needy (Dt 15:7–11; Mt 5:42; Lk 6:30). There is need to feed and care for the hungry and the needy (Prov 22:9, Tob 1:7; 4:16; Lk 14:13; 16:19–31; Mt 25:31–46; 1 Jn 3:17).

The invitation to liberality extends to everyone and is all the more praiseworthy in the measure that it is given from one's own need and substance, rather than from one's abundance and surplus, as in the common interpretation of the pericope on the widow who put everything she had to live on in the temple treasury (Mk 12:41–44; Lk 21:1–4), or of the Macedonians who insisted on giving to the poor of Jerusalem despite their own pressing needs (2 Cor 8:1–5). And, of course, we have the parable of the Good Samaritan (Lk 10:25–37) who unhesitatingly expended his time and treasure in caring for the man who fell in with the robbers. Generosity is a duty, indeed a privilege, not reserved exclusively for the Jewish nation. Even as charity in the early Church was initially limited to the community alone and "centered on the meal" (Acts 2:44–47; 4:32–37), there is, in fact, no limit on who may be the recipient of one's liberality in the admonition to give and to lend without expecting anything in return and to love even one's enemies (Lk 6:30, 35).[31]

Generosity is also a concrete way of imitating God. Far from calling for retribution or even reciprocity, Jesus' Golden Rule (Lk 6:31) is, in fact, a summons for unbounded generosity for one another, in imitation of God's limitless benevolence. Consider the immediate context of this pericope on the Golden Rule: the Sermon on the plain (Lk 6:27–36), love for one's enemies (Lk 6:27–30), rejection of the Greco-Roman practice of reciprocity in exchange and the expectation of a *quid pro quo* in interpersonal relationship (Lk 6:32–34), and the imitation of God, to the extent possible, of being perfect and merciful, just as God is perfect and merciful (Lk 6:35–36; Mt 5:39–48).[32]

Such disinterested and generous sharing is a constant theme: in the admonition to "unreciprocated remission of debt" (Mt 6:12; 18:23–35); in the praise of untrumpeted almsgiving (Mt 6:2); in the undiscriminating hiring practices of the vineyard owner who was also unmeasured in giving a full day's wage to all regardless of their contribution (Mt 20:1–15); and in the account of the final judgment in which feeding the hungry, clothing the naked, and visiting the sick and imprisoned are rewarded (Mt 25:31–46).[33]

Material Support for the Practice and Promotion of the Faith

In the Old Testament, Levites receive no share in the partition of the Promised Land. Instead of earning their livelihood from the land, they are to serve the Lord and minister at the altar and the holy sanctuary. God, rather than land, is to be their heritage. In lieu of land, the Levites are entitled to share in the tithes collected. After all, they serve the people through their priestly function. In addition to these tithes, Levites are to have a share in people's various offerings and special gifts to the Lord during the festivals (Num 18; cf. Neh 13:10–12).[34]

Jesus is a mendicant in his itinerant preaching, with not even a place to lay his head (Mt 8:20). He and his disciples are supported by benefactors that include many women, some of whom have social standing, as in the case of Joanna, wife of Chuza, Herod's steward (Lk 8:2–3). Even in death, Jesus has to be laid in somebody else's unused tomb (Mt 27:57–60; cf. Mk 15:43–47; Lk 23:50–53; Jn 19:38). Throughout his public ministry, Jesus is dependent on the material support of the people among whom he preached and healed.

Despite Paul's giving up his pecuniary entitlements as an apostle and despite his desire to work with his own hands and be self-sufficient, many of the churches nonetheless support him long after he had left them to preach in other regions. The Macedonians provide sustenance for Paul in his work in Corinth (2 Cor 11:8–9). The Philippians provision Paul in Macedonia, Thessalonica, and beyond (Phil 4:14–20). And, of course, there is the unflagging support of his fellow tentmakers, Aquila and Priscilla in Corinth and in Ephesus.[35] Clearly, material possessions can be put to good use in the worship of God and in the preaching of the Gospel. It is a worthy use of wealth and property.

DIVESTMENT OR OWNERSHIP?

Scholars have long grappled with the seeming contradictions in the New Testament on private property ownership and use.[36] On the one hand, readers are confronted with Jesus' incessant call for radical divestment as a condition of discipleship. On the other hand, numerous passages and practices suggest widespread private property ownership among disciples at the time of Jesus' public ministry and in the early Church. Some frame the tension as the difference between the "forgoers" and the "stewards."[37]

Jarring Disparities

More than any other New Testament writer, Luke is passionate in writing about the poor and is forceful in his treatment of wealth, money, and possessions.[38] As we have seen earlier, Luke presents additional materials on wealth and possessions not found in Mark or in Matthew. Despite the many studies done on Luke's teachings on possessions, there is as yet no consensus or clear idea of what it is exactly that Luke teaches about possessions because of his two sets of seemingly contradictory teachings.[39] There is no consistent perspective in Luke-Acts on the question of voluntary dispossession because both divestment and ownership with sharing are lauded.[40]

Both blocks of teachings on radical voluntary poverty and on the just use of privately held property can be found in his Gospel and in Acts. Thus, Luke has been described as having a "twofold attitude" when it comes to material possessions, namely: (1) a moderate attitude that calls for the prudential use of possessions to alleviate the suffering of the poor (e.g., Lk 3:11; 8:3; 11:41) and (2) a radical attitude that calls for complete divestment (e.g., Acts 4:33–37; 2:44–45).[41] These differing positions have often been cited by scholars as evidence of the lack of a homogeneous economic message in the New Testament. Luke comfortably slips back and forth between a radical and a more moderate outlook on possessions, whether the evangelist is working with Markan, Q, or uniquely Lucan materials. We find the same admixture of teachings on property in both Matthew and Mark.

Jesus lives a life of voluntary poverty (Mt 8:20; Lk 9:58) and instructs those who wished to follow him to sell all their possessions, give to the poor, and acquire heavenly treasure (Lk 12:33; Mt 6:19). At the same time, Jesus sanctions property ownership and use even among his disciples. Mary and Martha welcome Jesus to their home (Lk 10:38–39). He and his disciples are followed by women who minister to their needs and provide them material support (Mk 15:41; Mt 27:55; Lk 8:2–3). These women can furnish such support only if they are propertied and have resources from which to give. The repeated calls to almsgiving must presuppose that people have something to share to begin with. Zacchaeus gets to keep as much as half his wealth, even as he is commended by Jesus and becomes his follower (Lk 19:1–10). Jesus has no problems accepting invitations to banquets (Mk 14:3–9; Mt 26:6–13; Lk 7:36–50; 14:1; 19:1–10). He does not condemn property ownership in his parables but accepts it as routine in the ordinary course of life, as we see in the cases of Dives and Lazarus (Lk 16:19–31), the Good Samaritan (Lk 10:25–35), the unjust steward (Lk 16:1–8), the talents (Mt 25:14–30), the vineyard owner (Mt 20:1–16), the prodigal son (Lk 15:11–32), and many others. Jesus does not criticize his host for his wealth, but instead asks him to invite the lame, the maimed, the blind, and the poor (Lk 14:12–14).

The Acts of the Apostles describes examples of voluntary divestment of properties with the proceeds being given to the Church for distribution accordingly. At the same time, however, there are even more passages that suggest private property ownership as the prevailing norm rather than the exception in the early Church. The faithful gather in the houses of believers, presumably the more affluent ones (Rom 16:3–5, 23; 1 Cor 16:19; Phlm 1:2; Col 4:15). By Paul's own account, there are disparities in wealth and power within the churches themselves (1 Cor 11:17–22), contradicting the claim of a common ownership of properties. The Macedonians, Philippians, Corinthians, and Thessalonians contribute to Paul's collection for the poor of Jerusalem, again suggestive of some property ownership. Lydia, Aquila, Priscilla, the Macedonians, and Philippians provide Paul with material support that most likely came from their privately held surplus. Philemon is a Christian even as he owns property, including the runaway slave Onesimus. Many early Christians are believed to be middle-class property owners.[42] For example, immediately upon his miraculous release from prison, Peter goes to the house of Mary the mother of John (also called Mark) where disciples are gathered and praying (Acts 12:12). Some believe that Mary must have been wealthy to have a house big enough to accommodate so many people. Lydia is a dealer of purple cloth (luxury goods) and is, therefore, most likely to be wealthy herself. She, too, must have had a big house in pressing Paul to stay with her household while in Philippi and in being able to host a gathering of the disciples after the release of Paul and Silas from prison (Acts 16:14–15, 40).[43] As mentioned earlier, the Gospel of Luke was most likely written for a Hellenistic church community that included wealthy believers.

In stark contrast to Jesus' preaching, Paul makes no mention of voluntary radical divestment as a prerequisite of discipleship. For the Pauline writings, it is sharing and just use that are critical, not dispossession.[44] In fact, true to form, Paul follows the Jewish tradition in cautioning people that while they ought to give alms, they should not do so to the point of penury themselves (2 Cor 8:12–15).

Quantitative and Qualitative Assessment of the Shift

Old Testament

In his book *Hostility to Wealth*, Schmidt (1987) proposes a typology with which to organize scriptural teachings on wealth. We can use his work to quantitatively and qualitatively assess the radical shift in the views on wealth in moving from the Old Testament to the Synoptic Gospels. He proposes five stages leading up to the Gospels' aversion to riches.

In the first stage, injustice is equated with avaricious conduct. To be greedy is to be unjust. For example, "All day long the wicked covet, but the righteous give and do not hold back" (Prov 21:26).[45] In the second stage, injustice is associated with being rich. Being rich is prima facie evidence of greed and injustice. In other words, the presumption is that wealthy people are unjust and greedy. Wealth and injustice are synonymous, that is, two sides of the same coin. For example, "Such are the wicked; always at ease, they increase in riches" (Ps 73:12).[46]

The third stage is the "comparative devaluation" of wealth in which people are urged to attach a higher value to other laudable goals, such as one's relationship with God and care for the poor. For example, "Treasures gained by wickedness do not profit, but righteousness delivers from death" (Prov 10:2).[47] The fourth stage is the "alternative valuation" of wealth which urges people not to value wealth at all, but to pursue other worthwhile aims in life. (Recall that in the third stage, wealth is still valued even if at a much lower scale.) For example, "Take my instruction instead of silver, and knowledge rather than choice gold" (Prov 8:10).[48]

The fifth stage is the "teleological devaluation" in which wealth is actively spurned and devalued so that one might be completely free and unhindered in the pursuit of greater and more enduring ends. Job 22:23–30 is a prime example of this.[49] At its root, teleological devaluation is motivated by the religious-ethical tenet of sole reliance on God alone (*Gottvertrauen*). People strip themselves of anything (such as wealth) or of anyone that may deceive them as reliable anchors of stability and security.

Schmidt identifies 214 Old Testament passages that refer to wealth. Of these, more than half (126) value wealth as a consequence of virtue, wisdom, or Covenant fidelity; 65 refer to the justice imperative; and 78 are critical of wealth. Of these 78 passages classified as hostile to wealth, only 4 make it beyond stage 3. In other words, there are only 4 Old Testament passages out of the 214 examined that reach stages 4 and 5 in Schmidt's categories. And only one of these (Jb 22:23–30) can be considered as an active spurning of wealth for the sake of reaching higher ends.

New Testament

In contrast, most of the materials on wealth in the Synoptic Gospels fall under the last stage: teleological devaluation (wealth is spurned in order to attain something else of greater value). And, indeed, one distinctively New Testament teaching on economic life is the repeated call to radical dispossession, that is, to sell all or to leave all in order to follow Jesus. Consider Schmidt's assessment of the pericopae related to wealth in the Synoptic Gospels.

Mark

Schmidt (1987) notes that the teleological devaluation of wealth clearly stands out in the Gospel of Mark. Jesus warns about the dangers and deceitfulness of wealth in choking off the Word of God from producing much harvest (Mk 4:19). He admonishes those who want to be disciples to deny themselves and to take up their cross as a precondition to following Christ (Mk 8:34–37). The rich man longing for eternal life is told by Jesus to sell all his wealth, give the proceeds to the poor, and then follow Christ (Mk 10:21). Peter, Andrew, James, John, and Levi are decisive in leaving behind their livelihoods and their families, indeed everything, in order to follow Christ (Mk 10:28; 1:16–20; 2:14). Jesus commends the widow who gives up what little she had—her entire livelihood—to the Temple (Mk 12:44). The common theme running through these pericopae is the importance of turning away from possessions in order that one might attain a much more enduring value—treasure in heaven, perfection, or discipleship in Christ. Possessions are voluntarily foregone in the quest for a much greater treasure.

We can infer a similar teaching in the narratives of Mark. Thus, we have John the Baptist dressed in camel's hair and subsisting on locusts and wild honey (Mk 1:6). The twelve apostles are sent off by Christ to preach and to heal, as mendicants dependent on the generosity and support of people to whom they had been sent. Taking no food or money with them, the apostles are to trust that God will provide for them (Mk 6:8–9). The woman who lavishly anoints Jesus with an alabaster of costly spikenard worth three hundred days' wages spares nothing but the best for her Lord. Jesus defends the woman from criticisms of waste and extravagance (Mk 14:3–9). These narratives suggest that radical divestment is often necessary to pursue a much greater good.

Schmidt concludes that both the explicit and implicit teleological devaluation of wealth in the Gospel of Mark stand in continuity with earlier ANE and Old Testament materials concerning wealth. There is a marked similarity in their distrust of possessions as an obstacle to one's relationship with God and with one's neighbors. Moreover, there is nothing in Mark to indicate that these economic teachings were in response to dire socioeconomic conditions at that time. Furthermore, Schmidt (1987, 118) observes that the Gospel "contains little evidence of concern for the poor."[50]

Matthew

Matthew incorporates the Marcan materials that point to a teleological devaluation of wealth: the call of the apostles (Mt 4:18–22; 9:9); mendicant preaching (Mt 10:9–10); the seeds choked by deceitful wealth (Mt 13:22); taking up one's cross (Mt 16:24–27); the rich man in search of eternal life (Mt 19:16–30); the anointing of Jesus with expensive perfume (Mt 26:6–13). In addition, Matthew draws materials from Q that also directly or indirectly call for the teleological devaluation of wealth: the third temptation of Jesus (Mt 4:8–10); the beatitudes (Mt 5:3); to give to all who ask (Mt 5:40–42); to store up treasure in heaven (Mt 6:19–21); the light of the body (Mt 6:22–23); no anxiety (Mt 6:25–34). Furthermore, Matthew adds materials that are not found in either Mark or Q: purchasing pearl and treasure of great value (Mt 13:44–46); the goats and the sheep in the last judgment (Mt 25:31–46).

The quintessential teleological devaluation of wealth is Matthew 6:19–21 in which Jesus invites all to store up enduring treasure in heaven rather than setting one's heart on earthly wealth that can be stolen, lost, or destroyed. Similarly, Matthew 6:24 is forthright in asserting that people can follow only one master in life; God and mammon are mutually exclusive. This follows the teaching on the importance of generosity and the evil of greed (Mt 6:22–23).

Just like in Mark, the "hostility to wealth" and its goal of engendering trust in God alone are fundamental themes in the Gospel of Matthew. Schmidt also notes that the poor are of secondary concern in Matthew.

Luke

Luke maintains the pericopae from Mark and Q that point to the teleological devaluation of wealth. Moreover, Luke further intensifies many of these passages and adds materials not found in either Mark or Matthew.

The distinctive woes in the Lukan beatitudes (Lk 6:24–25) and the parable of the rich fool (Lk 12:16–21) warn of the folly of preoccupation with wealth and comfort. Luke presents numerous examples of conduct vis-à-vis wealth to be avoided: the Pharisees as lovers of money (Lk 16:14–15), the brothers fighting over their inheritance (Lk 12:13–15), and the rich man dressed in purple coming to a bad end in his indifference to the plight of Lazarus (Lk 16:19–31). And then there are the people who are caught up in worldly affairs and concerns as to be heedless to the invitation of Christ (Lk

14:18–20)[51] and those who are oblivious to the coming judgment, eating and drinking all the way to the last days (Lk 17:28–33). Instead, disciples are invited to be free of worldly anxiety (Lk 12:22–32), to repent and live upright lives as in the case of Zacchaeus (Lk 19:1–10), and to set their hearts and minds on serving and trusting in God alone rather than mammon. In all this, Luke keeps and intensifies further the pericopae on the teleological devaluation of wealth drawn from Mark and Q, and adds even more passages with the same treatment of wealth.

Summary

In sum, Schmidt (1987) argues that we can trace a familiar theme across the synoptic passages on wealth and property, to wit:

- Dispossession is an integral part of what it is to follow Christ unhindered.
- Such divestment is an affirmation of utter trust in God alone (*Gottvertrauen*).
- It is a complete trust that will be more than amply rewarded in this and the next life.

Thus, the Synoptic Gospels are characterized by a teleological devaluation of wealth (stage 5) whereby possessions are foregone with the hope of ultimately attaining eternal life.

Discontinuity with the Past

The New Testament teachings on radical dispossession and voluntary poverty are a sharp departure from Old Testament economic teachings. In the first place, private property rights are deeply entrenched in both ANE and Old Testament laws. We see this in the Old Testament legislation against thievery and in the many positive obligations attendant to such ownership. In addition, recall the tort laws that hold proprietors responsible for injuries or damages caused by properties under their care.[52] The prophetic literature is not hostile to property ownership. In fact, the prophets are propertied themselves. Amos is a successful sheep-breeder; Isaiah belongs to the upper circles of society. They are not ascetic at all. They do not laud destitution as a value in itself.

The prophetic literature does not condemn wealth per se, but the manner of acquiring it: if done through dishonesty or oppression, if it drives others to debt slavery, or if it diminishes the welfare of others. Wealth accumulation is reprehensible if it fosters inordinate, conspicuous consumption, especially in light of others' unmet needs. It deserves censure if it violates the requirements of righteousness in putting economic gain above personal values. Wealth acquisition is immoral if those in authority responsible for the well-being of others use their power for their own enrichment instead. Moreover, by indicting unconscionable land-grabbers, the prophets are standing up for the interests of the small landholding farmers who are unable to fend for themselves. This is a de facto affirmation of these families' right to private property ownership.[53]

Second, while the Essenes and the wandering charismatics embraced voluntary poverty[54] and even as we find Jewish examples of complete dispossession,[55] such radical divestment is not the norm for Old Testament religious-ethical teachings or praxis. In fact, traditional Jewish practice was characterized by measured almsgiving in which liberality was balanced with not impoverishing oneself. A rabbinic rule of thumb was to give away no more than one-fifth of one's capital and no more than one-fifth of one's income.[56] Paul follows this tradition and asks for contributions only in the measure his communities can afford (2 Cor 8:13–15). In contrast, radical dispossession figures prominently in the synoptic teachings on economic morality.

Destitution is not romanticized in the Old Testament. It is viewed as a negative state of affairs that has to be avoided, rectified, or, at least, alleviated. In the wisdom literature, prosperity is a divine gift and reward for wisdom, virtue, and hard work. Poverty is the lot of the wicked and the indolent. The prophets vehemently censure the rich and the powerful for depriving people of their land and driving them into destitution and debt slavery. Scholars have consistently concluded that poverty (as destitution) per se is never idealized in Sacred Scripture. In the pre-exilic period, the prophets and the three law codes see impoverishment as something negative. The prophets view destitution as an evil that must be redressed both at a personal and at a communal level. It is a disorder that God will correct at some point in the future.

However, there is a subtle change in the aftermath of the exile. Deutero-Isaiah changes the views on poverty by describing the entire nation Israel as poor on account of her oppression and exile. She is poor because she only has God. And this relationship with God is a treasure in itself and will eventually be manifested in their liberation from bondage. Herewith begins the association between piety and poverty. This is also consistent with and builds on the earlier observation that God is close to the poor. This also accounts for the positive view of poverty in the psalms.

Observe that what is lauded is poverty as dependence on God and not poverty as destitution. Poverty can be an ambiguous term, and one should not confuse a religious attitude (dependence on God) with a socioeconomic condition (indigence). The former is lauded, but not the latter. There has been a misunderstanding of the term "poor," which refers to piety, or a humble attitude of submission in which God is the only source of people's security. Thus, the term could refer to any person of whatever socioeconomic class for as long as there is that genuine emptiness and reliance only in God.[57] The ideals are Micah 4:4 (in which people will sit under their own vine and fig tree) and Proverbs 30:7–9 (in which one is neither rich nor poor, but self-sustaining).

Third, there are numerous references in the Old Testament on how wealth, including tenure on the land, is a consequence of Covenant fidelity (though not automatically or immediately apparent). In the New Testament such reward for fidelity to the Lord is "christified."[58] Such promises cannot be taken in a literal materialistic sense, but only metaphorically—abundance in the kingdom of God. For example, the meek inherit the earth in Matthew 5:5 compared with the meek in Israel who are promised an inheritance in the Promised Land in Psalm 37:11.

Fourth, could such call for divestment be due to an imminent Parousia, as in the case of Mark and his teaching on the rich man? This is doubtful. To begin with, dispossession is not called for even in the apocalyptic segments of the Old Testament. Or consider the Pauline writings. Despite his belief in an imminent Parousia, Paul never calls for radical divestment and is, in fact, completely quiet about it. Luke-Acts are distinctive for their acknowledgment of a possible long middle period of waiting on the part of the Church, and yet, it is in these writings that we find many of the passages on radical dispossession. In other words, the teaching on radical dispossession does not necessarily follow as a response to belief in an imminent Parousia.

In sum, the New Testament calls for radical voluntary divestment is a sharp discontinuity from Old Testament teachings on possessions. We must account for such divergence.

Making Sense of Incongruities

How then are we to reconcile these seemingly incompatible teachings? Are they truly contradictory? Schmidt (1987) notes that "hostility to wealth" is not original to Mark, Matthew, and Luke because we find the same attitude in ANE, Old Testament, and inter-testamental non-canonical literature. Even synoptic language and vocabulary can be traced back to these earlier materials. For example, the Triple traditions' call to give alms is merely a continuation of longstanding ANE and Old Testament teachings and practice. The Gospels' admonition not to store earthly riches but to lay up enduring heavenly treasure (Mt 6:19–21; Lk 12:33–34) is reminiscent of Tobit 4:9 (almsgiving as a form of storing up treasure for a day of necessity) and Sirach 29:11–12 (almsgiving as a form of laying up heavenly treasure).[59] The term "mammon" used in Matthew 6:24 and Luke 16:13 is found in ANE and Rabbinic literature as well and connotes corruption, dishonesty, and injustice associated with property and wealth. The theme on the deceitfulness of wealth in the parable of the sower (Mk 4:19; Mt 13:22; Lk 8:14) is, in fact, a "very old allegory and homily."[60] Wealth is viewed with suspicion in the Ancient Near East.

Scholars propose various theories to account for the divergence in the Old and New Testament treatment of property. Some say that divestment is not really about impoverishing oneself but about redistributing wealth. Moreover, such action should not be viewed as supererogatory almsgiving, but as conformity to the justice of God.[61] Others propose that divestment is only for the initial period of the Church, a sort of utopian ideal of "primordial beginnings."[62] Some claim that the abandonment of wealth and family is pre-Markan and is associated with wandering charismatics.[63] Still others suggest that these teachings come from two different time periods in the ministry of Jesus, with Caesarea Philippi as the turning point. Prior to this, we have the more moderate wisdom sayings. But after this, with the looming confrontation in Jerusalem and the imminent sacrifice of Jesus, the teachings switch to the more radical, apocalyptic sayings.[64]

Let us take a closer look at some of these theories. In the first place, we have to affirm the goodness of creation. Radical dispossession is not on account of an intrinsic evil to material goods. In responding to those who forbid certain foods, the Pauline tradition holds that everything God created is good and nothing is to be rejected (1 Tm 4:1–5). By extension, this also includes wealth. Moreover, in contrast to John the Baptist's ascetic lifestyle, Jesus eats and drinks in table fellowship with one and all, to the point of being accused as a glutton and a drunkard (Mt 11:19; Lk 7:34). Furthermore, in the parable of the dishonest steward who writes off huge portions of his master's claims, Jesus lauds those who are worldly-wise in using the goods of this earth at the service of the world that is to come (Lk 16:8–9).

Second, the simultaneous practices of voluntary poverty and private property ownership within Christian discipleship merely parallel the need to satisfy both temporal and transcendent obligations. Both have their proper roles and are not mutually exclusive. Far from fleeing from the world, the disciple, just like Jesus, engages the world. Temporal obligations still have to be discharged, as Jesus points out in the case of the *qorban* and the Pharisees' avoidance of their obligations to their parents (Mk 7:10–13). The same applies in the matter of paying taxes or obeying legitimate public authority (Mt 22:15–22; Mk 12:13–17; Lk 20:20–26). There is a non-rival nature to rightful temporal and transcendent duties. Grace and nature are not at odds with one another. On the one hand, the problem with idolatry is in absolutizing the temporal against the transcendent. On the other hand, being dismissive of the world as an evil to be avoided and withdrawing in isolation (e.g., Essenes) exalt the transcendent to the exclusion of the temporal. The latter has its legitimate claims too.

Radical dispossession is an anticipation of the end-time; it is looking ahead to the reversals of God's forthcoming reign. Thus, there is an eschatological undercurrent to the pericopae on voluntary divestment.[65] This eschatological orientation also accounts for why, in addition to properties, even normal relationships are given up, such as father, mother, family, spouse, and children (Lk 14:26–27, 33; Mt 10:37–39). It also explains why there is even no time to fulfill one's filial duty to bury one's father or even to say farewell to those left at home (Mt 8:21–22; Lk 9:59–62). Indeed, radical dispossession is merely part of a much larger proleptic living of the end-time in the here and now.

At the same time, as we have seen earlier, Luke is keenly aware that we are in the middle period, in the age of the Church's mission and ministry prior to the Parousia. And during this patient waiting, there is still need to address the temporal plight of the poor, the neglected, and the outcasts. Moreover, there is need to imbue Luke's wealthy Hellenistic audience with an appreciation for the Jewish ethos of charity. Thus, we also see teachings on the importance of generosity and sharing from one's means.

In other words, we see a tension between the demands of daily life and the Gospel's larger eschatological horizon. The passages on sharing, almsgiving, and generosity stem from the wisdom sayings and pertain to carrying on with the duties of daily life. In contrast, the more radical calls for divestment are apocalyptic in their vision.[66] Rightful temporal and transcendent obligations are not in competition with one another. Luke illustrates this well in his deft handling of these two seemingly competing teachings on possessions. The temporal and the transcendent meld together not only in Luke, but also across the New Testament.

Third, another possible explanation behind this seeming confusion over radical divestment versus property ownership is the wide diversity of religious-ethical tenets in the New Testament. In particular, *Gottvertrauen* and *koinōnia* can account for these teachings on property. On the one hand, there is a long-standing hostility to wealth in ANE and in Sacred Scripture. The repeated warnings on the deceitfulness of wealth are driven by the call to put one's trust in God alone. Such "God-trust" (*Gottvertrauen*) finds its clear and full expression in radical dispossession. On the other hand, as we will see in the preceding chapter, fellowship (*koinōnia*) is another important Christian religious-ethical principle. Such fellowship can find expression in the liberal sharing of one's goods, besides outright divestment. In other words, both radical voluntary poverty and generous property ownership and sharing are consistent with early Christian moral tenets and praxis. After all, "God-trust" (*Gottvertrauen*) and fellowship (*koinōnia*) are not mutually exclusive.

Fourth, in looking at the textual evidence, one can only conclude that both radical divestment and private property ownership must have been practiced and accepted at the time of Jesus and in the early Church. The two are, in fact, complementary because members of the same Body of Christ differ in their roles and functions. There is a universal call to discipleship and holiness, but not a universal call to voluntary, complete poverty as part of that discipleship.[67]

One could say that there are two possible tracks to discipleship. Total dispossession (Mk 10:28–30) is not an absolute requirement for every disciple. The co-existence of these two sets of teachings on property merely reflects the wide "latitude of response" available to the followers of Jesus at that time.[68] On the one hand, there was the inner circle of disciples who accompanied Jesus to Jerusalem for the expected big confrontation. They had left everything behind in preparation for sharing the same fate as Jesus. The radical demands of divestment applied to this group.

On the other hand, there was the larger public. These disciples were not expected to disrupt their lives, but were to continue with their livelihoods and to follow Jesus by living the Gospel values, such as generosity in sharing and mutual solicitude. What was asked of them was to furnish the material support needed to sustain the community of faith according to their means. However, in both cases, followers of Christ had to give up whatever it was that stood in the way of loving God and neighbor. Mark 10:23–24 may, in fact, be an allegory for whatever it is that may hold disciples back from God, wealth included.[69]

Indeed, ownership of wealth is not the issue as it is not intrinsically evil. As mentioned earlier, what is critical is the manner by which possessions are accumulated and used. Wealth becomes evil when used to oppress others or when it enslaves the owner.[70] Dispossession is not an end in itself, but is valued in the context of the decisive claim that God has on humans. Thus, what is vital for discipleship is that nothing and no one should get in the way between the person and God. By the nature of the task assigned to some, this may include the renunciation of property as a means to a more effective and undistracted discipleship. For others, such property ownership may be the means by which they contribute to the Church. Thus, both radical divestment and private property ownership share a similar instrumental function—a venue by which people serve the Lord and partake of the building of the kingdom.

Fifth, another possible explanation is that the call to voluntary poverty may be part of Jesus' prophetic urgency in getting the message through and in shocking people into seeing what they were doing to themselves. The teachings on radical dispossession have been described as merely part of a much broader pattern of "unconditional generality" in the teachings of Jesus. Thus, when asked how many times ought people to forgive, Jesus responds not seven times, but seventy-seven times (Mt 18:21–22). When asked whether or not personal obligations can interfere with following Jesus, the response is no. One does not even have the time to bury one's father or to say goodbye to kin left at home (Mt 8:21–22; Lk 9:59–62).[71]

We could find many more examples of such "unconditional generality" in Jesus' preaching. What do we give up to follow Christ? Not only possessions, but even houses, family, spouses, and children (Lk 18:28–30). Disciples are not to appeal to *lex talionis*, but are to love even their enemies, walk the extra mile, turn the other cheek, and give to all who ask without expecting repayment (Mt 5:38–48; Lk 6:27–36). And who are mother, brother, and sister to Jesus? Only those who do the will of God (Mk 3:35). Moreover, only those who deny themselves and take up their cross can follow Christ (Lk 14:27).

What is asked is total commitment, as in the case of the widow's mites and the apostles. Such "unconditional generality" on the part of Jesus is meant to provoke "us to question all our normal assumptions about vocations, priorities and responsibilities and to glimpse the depth of personal commitment that God demands of each of us."[72] This is the deeper aim behind the call to radical dispossession. It is the shock value, the "sharp edge"[73] meant to awaken readers.

If correct, this explanation brings out the prophetic dimension in Jesus' ministry. Just like the Old Testament prophets who struggle mightily, but ultimately to little effect, in getting Israel and Judah to repent and reform their sinful ways, and just like John the Baptist who warns people of a looming winnowing fan, Jesus is also apocalyptic in his preaching, reminding everyone of a day of judgment when the kingdom of God will appear without warning. Just like the prophets and John the Baptist, Jesus calls for immediate repentance and decisive action.

Sixth, the variety of traditions that interpenetrate and shape Sacred Scripture is another possible explanation.[74] There are many conflicting economic teachings and norms in the Old and New Testament. Besides the question of property ownership versus radical dispossession, recall the seeming contradictions in the wisdom literature on whether or not wealth and poverty are associated with virtue and wickedness respectively. Recall, too, the seeming contradictions even within the laws themselves. A plausible explanation for these incongruities is that they come from different traditions with their respective theologies, agendas, needs, and settings in life. After all, the process of putting Sacred Scripture in writing took over a millennium.

We have not exhausted the many plausible theories proposed in the literature on resolving the clash between the teachings on radical poverty and property ownership. Many of these explanations are not mutually exclusive and can in fact work together. It is sufficient for our study to note that despite this apparent inconsistency on the question of voluntary divestment, the Old and New Testament converge in many of their teachings on wealth and poverty. Property and wealth are never ends in themselves. Others' property must be respected. Property ownership is a necessary part of human survival and flourishing (e.g., ancestral land for each family). It is morally permissible to pursue prosperity and to own property, but only as means and never idolized as ends, and with restraints and not to excess or at the expense of others driven into poverty. Land and its produce are to be used, not only for personal needs, but also for the welfare of as many as possible. Land belongs to God. Material blessings are from God meant to be shared with generosity and compassion for the poor. A critical measure of morality is how well one cares for the distressed and the weak. Those who possess more have even greater obligations toward the poor. Material possessions are gifts from God; they are good. But they can also be dangerous obstacles to a vibrant relationship with God. Sincere stewardship is a clear sign of a life transformed by grace. Put in another way, faith must be manifested in one's economic choices and conduct. Moderation is critical; there are limits to inequalities in wealth. Severe inequalities are symptomatic of malaise and sin. Beneficence and deeds of charity are at the core of Covenant election and Christian discipleship.[75] It has been suggested that the gist of Sacred Scripture's views on property and wealth are "respect and restraint."[76]

ACCOUNTING FOR HOSTILITY-TO-WEALTH WORLDVIEW

Sociological models provide tools and frameworks of analysis that are helpful in understanding pericopae on wealth and property. In particular, the notion of the limited-goods society is helpful in understanding the preceding discussion on the hostility to wealth and the previous chapter's patron-client relationships.

In the Ancient Near East, people believed that no one had to go without necessities because there were sufficient supplies to go around.[77] Of course, exceptions were natural and man-made disasters, such as droughts, famines, or wars.[78] Nevertheless, despite this belief in sufficiency, ancient cultures also thought that they lived in a limited-goods society.[79] Given the absence of growth in a primitive economy, an increase in people's wealth came about only by depriving somebody else of such goods (a zero-sum phenomenon). Societal resources were limited, and one's use of these left that much less for others. Not surprisingly, in such a setting, there was a prima facie case against the rich because of the presumption that they amassed wealth only by crowding out others from the common social trough.[80] Thus, the term "rich" carried a pejorative connotation in the eastern Mediterranean world.[81] The rich person was deemed to be inherently evil because wealth accumulation came from avarice.[82] Inherited wealth was seen as stolen wealth: "Every rich person is a thief or the heir of a thief."[83]

Consider the following implications of a limited-goods society for New Testament hermeneutics. First, the call for dispossession can be interpreted as the redistribution of wealth and not about self-impoverishment. Second, almsgiving and assistance to the poor are not about "self-satisfying charity" but about "God-ordained, socially required restitution."[84] Third, the purpose of wealth is the sustenance of human beings in a happy life. The goal is self-sufficiency (*autarkeia*) (2 Cor 9:8; Phil 4:11; 1 Tm 6:6; 1 Thess 4:12). Everyone should be able to live life without undue care (Mt 6:25–32).[85] Fourth, inequality in the distribution of wealth is not the issue in the New Testament. Rather, it is the failure of the rich to re-circulate the wealth back into the community in terms of debt relief and almsgiving, because of their self-indulgent consumption and comforts. In accumulating wealth, they leave that much less for others.[86]

This limited-goods worldview provides a sociological explanation for the hostility to wealth in ANE literature. The rich are viewed as necessarily evil by the nature of how they acquire and amass so much to begin with, at the expense of everybody else in a limited-goods society.

SUMMARY AND CONCLUSIONS

Property and wealth are perennial concerns in Sacred Scripture. There is both continuity and change in these teachings across the Old and New Testament. Both testaments affirm the obligation to use possessions to assist those who are needy and to support cultic worship or the preaching of the Gospel. Wealth is never to be one's anchor of security or self-identity. That would be idolatry. Instead, people are called to put their trust in God alone, and not on anyone or on anything else. These are unchanging bedrock teachings in Scripture.

There is a major shift between the Old and New Testament when it comes to the question of whether or not God asks people to divest themselves of property. In particular, it is unclear if voluntary poverty is a necessary condition for Christian discipleship. Most scholars take the position that there is room for both private property ownership and voluntary dispossession in the new dispensation inaugurated by Christ. In most cases, what is critical is the use rather than the ownership of property. But in all cases, property ownership and use must be characterized by trust in God alone (*Gottvertrauen*) and by an attitude of grateful stewardship that manifests itself in generous sharing.

NOTES

1. For example, see White (1967).
2. For a history of the exegesis of Genesis 1:26–28, see Westermann (1984, 147–58).
3. Johnson (2009, 7); Tucker (1997, 8)
4. Tucker (1997, 6–7, 12–17); Hiers (1984b, 54–55). See Kay (1988) for references to other instances of punishment for cutting down trees.

5. Tucker (1997, 13–16)
6. Sharp (1995, 306–7); Westermann (1984, 146); Vawter (1977, 59); Von Rad (1961, 60)
7. For example, see Psalms 104; 148. See Hiers (1984b, 48–49).
8. Hiers (1996–98, 134, 140, 148, 152)
9. Hiers (1996–1998, 155–68)
10. Limburg (1994, 344–45)
11. See Hiers (1984b, 50–53).
12. Hiers (1984b, 47–48)
13. Sharp (1995)
14. New International Version (NIV) and New Revised Standard Version (NRSV), respectively.
15. Johnson (2009, 6)
16. Johnson (2009, 9–10)
17. Heard (1988, 80) counts 450 separate passages on wealth in Sacred Scripture.
18. M. Davies (1995, 322–35) suggests that the key themes of New Testament norms on property are (1) to trust in God rather than wealth, (2) generosity to the destitute in what he calls the "charity of consumption," and (3) support of the missionaries.
19. See Schmidt (1987).
20. Schelkle (1973, 301)
21. Lohfink (1987)
22. This is the thesis of Schmidt (1987).
23. Schmidt (1987, 108)
24. Schelkle (1973, 308)
25. Nardoni (2004, 228)
26. Harvey (1990, 119)
27. Harvey (1990, 120, 136). Recall, for example, the invitation extended by Jesus to the rich young man.
28. Harvey (1990, 123)
29. Anderson (2009, 135–51)
30. Schelkle (1973, 307). See also Johnson (1981) and Pilgrim (1981).
31. M. Davies (1995, 326–27)
32. Topel (1998)
33. Perkins (1994, 49–50); Schelkle (1973, 301); Schottroff (1984)
34. See Goldingay (2002, 203–4) for a brief sketch of the origins and history of tithes in the Old Testament.
35. Lohfink (1986, 228–29)
36. Some examples are Donahue (1989), Gordon (1989, 59–78), Harvey (1990, 126), Johnson (1981), Pilgrim (1981), Schnackenburg (1965, 121–32), and Wheeler (1995).
37. Pemberton and Finn (1985)
38. Fitzmyer (1981, 247–51); Johnson (1981); Pilgrim (1981)
39. Johnson (1981, 13)
40. Donahue (1989, 135)
41. Fitzmyer (1981, 249–50)
42. Porter (1990, 114)
43. M. Davies (1995, 333)
44. See Dahl (1977, 22–39) for Paul's views and practices regarding material possessions.
45. Other examples are Psalm 10:3; Proverbs 15:27; Jeremiah 6:13. See Schmidt (1987, 57).
46. Other examples are Psalm 10:5a; 73:3; Isaiah 53:9; Jeremiah 5:26–28; Micah 6:10–12. See Schmidt (1987, 57–58).
47. Another example is Psalm 52:7. See Schmidt (1987, 58).
48. Schmidt (1987, 59)
49. Schmidt (1987, 59)
50. Many scholars disagree with Schmidt on this last conclusion regarding a lack of regard for the poor in Mark.
51. Schmidt (1987, 149)
52. Baker (2009, 15–43, 310); Schelkle (1973, 297–98)

53. Mays (1987, 149, 154); Wittenberg (1978, 142)
54. Theissen (1978, 10–14)
55. Harvey (1990, 125)
56. Harvey (1990, 121)
57. See Pleins (2001, 420–24), who synthesizes the works of Baudissin, Bruppacher, and van der Ploeg on this point. Lohfink (1987) concludes similarly that poverty goes against God's will for humanity. Van der Ploeg uses Psalms 10, 22, and 69 to distinguish poverty from piety. Recall, too, the earlier discussion on who are the "poor" in Luke.
58. Blomberg (1999, 93)
59. M. Davies (1995, 324) agrees with Schmidt that much of the teachings of Jesus is from the wisdom tradition.
60. Schelkle (1973, 308–9)
61. Gillman (1991, 31)
62. Conzelmann (1960, 233); Donahue (1989, 135); Johnson (1981, 128)
63. Theissen (1978, 10–14)
64. Burrows (1974, 239)
65. Fitzmyer (1981, 250–51); Perkins (1994, 64)
66. See Burrows (1974, 239).
67. Lohse (1991, 49); Johnson (1981)
68. Harvey (1990, 127). See also Burrows (1974, 239), M. Davies (1995, 335), and Harvey (1990, 127–32).
69. Via (1985, 137)
70. Perkins (1994, 46–47); Donahue (1977, 107)
71. Harvey (1990, 133)
72. Harvey (1990, 133)
73. Harvey (1990, 134)
74. Blomberg (1999, 92–97); Hanson (1977)
75. Blomberg (1999, 85–86, 243–47); Schelkle (1973, 299); Williamson (1985)
76. Brueggemann (1975, 354–55); Blomberg (1999, 83)
77. Cf. Clement of Alexandria, *Paidagogros*, II, 14, 5, SC CVIII, 36; Plutarch, *On Love of Wealth*, 523F; LCL VII, 8.
78. Malina (1987, 362)
79. Foster (1967); Gregory (1975)
80. Thus, Horsley (2009) differs from traditional exegesis in his views on the parable of the pounds (Mt 25:14–30; Lk 19:11–27). Far from underscoring the importance of using our talents and gifts well, the parable is, in fact, a condemnation of the greed of that era, with the rich having even more and the poor losing what little they have to begin with.
81. Malina (1987)
82. See, for example, Plutarch's treatise *On Love of Wealth* (LCL VII) and his characterization of the rich as people with an insatiable appetite for ever more wealth to the complete disregard of others. They pursued these with whatever means available.
83. This quote is from Malina (1987, 363) citing St. Jerome, *In Hieremiam*, II, V, 2, CCL LXXIV, 61; Tract de Ps LXXXIII, lines 29–30, CCL LXXVIII, 96; Epistle 120: To Hebedia, PL XXII, 984. This assumption is consistent with a limited-goods mindset.
84. Malina (1987, 366)
85. Malina (1987, 366). Similar sentiments have been expressed by the Stoics and the Cynics.
86. Perkins (1994, 50–51)

Chapter Fifteen

Summary and Conclusions

Economic Life as Participation in God's Providence

It has been suggested that in using Sacred Scripture as a basis for making pronouncements on a particular issue such as economic life, contemporary readers have to examine the consistency (or lack thereof) of biblical teachings on the subject matter, the multiple attestation and amount of attention devoted to the question, and the degree to which the topic is central to the Bible's concerns. This is the "weight-of-Scripture-as-a-whole" rule in hermeneutics,[1] and it is to this task that we now turn our attention in this concluding chapter.

COMPARISON OF OLD AND NEW TESTAMENT ECONOMIC ETHICS

The Old and New Testament teachings on economic morality are marked by continuity, further development, and differences in emphases and foci. We assess their points of convergence and divergence and explain such similarities and differences.

Points of Continuity

Both the Old and the New Testament are this-worldly in their outlook. The Old Testament is about enjoying the good life in the here and now (e.g., Qoheleth; Dt 28:2–13). Jesus feasts and enjoys the fellowship of one and all (e.g., Mt 11:19. Lk 7:34). Asceticism is not a core message of Judaism.[2] Nevertheless, even as both are this-worldly, they also see the primacy and the incomparable worth of the transcendent (e.g., Prov 1–9; Mt 6:31–33).

Both testaments stress the absolute sovereignty of God (e.g., Mk 1:15; Ps 93:2, 145:13). They point to an ultimate eschatological judgment (e.g., Mt 25:31–46; Ps 96:10, 13; 98:9). Moreover, in both testaments, God's will is revealed in the law and it is important to observe it (e.g., Mt 5:17–18; 8:4; Mic 6:8). Law is a gift of love (Dt 7:6–12; Hos 11:1). Jesus is not critical of the law, but of those who twist it for their own ends.[3] Just like the prophets, Jesus did not come to promulgate new laws, but only to call for the faithful observance of what had already been handed down. Both the prophets and Jesus appeal for justice and repentance (e.g., Mt 4:17; Is 55:6–7). The enforcement of the law relies on free human assent, besides divine sanctions.[4] Like the prophets, Jesus is critical of people substituting cultic practices for proper ethical conduct (e.g., Hos 6:6; Mt 12:1–7). There is need for forgiveness and love rather than vengeance (e.g., Mt 18:21–22; Lev 19:18).[5]

Duties attendant to property ownership and admonitions on the dangers of wealth are evident in the Old and New Testament. Both caution against the idolatry of wealth and the deceitfulness, emptiness, and impermanence of riches. Both call on people to furnish material support for cultic worship (e.g., Num 18:8–32) and the promotion of the faith (Lk 10:5–7).

Both testaments underscore accountability for human conduct. Thus, the prophets are adamant on an imminent day of reckoning, even as the New Testament parables repeatedly stress a forthcoming accounting for our sins of commission or omission (Mt 3:7–10; 25:31–46). Both the prophets and Jesus defend those unable to speak for themselves and take to task a delinquent and abusive religious and political leadership.[6] The New Testament condemns the opulent lifestyle of the royal court (Lk 7:24–26); the greed and grasping ways of the Pharisees (called lovers of money), who impose even heavier burdens on the poor and who corrupt the practice of religion (Mt 23); the Roman impositions (Revelation); the abuses of soldiers and tax collectors (Lk 3:12–14), and the venality of the Temple (Mk 12:38–42). Injustice is an issue for both the Old and New Testament.

The Old Testament invites Israel to be holy, as God is holy (Lev 11:44–45), while the New Testament calls on disciples to be perfect as the heavenly Father is perfect and to be Christ-like in the way they live, forgive, and love (Mt 5:48; 11:29). The prophets lambast Israel and Judah for their hollow cultic practices because of their injustice and indifference to the poor, even as Jesus repeatedly clash with the Pharisees over observance of the spirit of the law and not only the letter of the law.

Family and community are central to both testaments. The Israelites' shared corporate identity is central to their self-understanding and self-worth as the Chosen People of God. New Testament discipleship unfolds in the kingdom of God, characterized by the one Body of Christ to which everyone contributes their unique gifts. Thus, note the strong communal ethos of the early Church (Acts 4:32). Moreover, as part of belonging to these communities of faith, people are supposed to work for their own keep, to the extent possible. In the Old Testament, each family has access to land for its livelihood, and assistance is extended to households to ensure that they are able to hold on to such ancestral land through measures, such as land return, land redemption, and interest-free debt. In the New Testament, we have the Pauline work ethic.

Both affirm belief in a steadfast divine providence. Recall the bounty of creation (Gen 1) and God's gift of a land flowing with milk and honey to a formerly enslaved Israel. On the occasion of the fallow year, it is God who will grant such an increase on the sixth year (the eve of the fallow year) as to be able to provide enough for all until the next harvest in the ninth year (Lev 25:21–22). The evangelists assure disciples that in seeking the kingdom of God, there will be no need for anxiety (Mt 6:25–33). In both cases, economic cares and concerns are dispelled by faith in the goodness and kindness of God. Two points of convergence stand out in particular and deserve special mention: care for the poor and the forthcoming great reversals.

Care for the Poor

Mutual care and concern for the poor are central to Israel's self-identity, just as it is in the kingdom of God inaugurated in the new dispensation. Most scholars agree that at the heart of Old Testament economic ethics is the grave obligation to care for the poor. We find this in the many laws calling for solicitude and generous assistance to the poor. Given God's track record in providing relief to the oppressed, even if they do not merit it, people of the Old Testament have come to know God as a champion, indeed, as a steadfast protector of the poor, the distressed, the persecuted, and the vulnerable. The rich and the powerful are warned not to oppress the poor because God hears their cries and will be their defender. God will inflict punishment on their oppressors and effect an unexpected reversal in their lives. This reputation of God as a champion of the poor also becomes a motivation for people to follow the prescriptions of the law regarding their obligations to the marginalized.

Similarly, care for the poor is repeatedly affirmed in the New Testament. The poor continue to occupy a special position. The poor are beloved to God (Mt 5:3–10). Jesus is entrusted to parents of little means and from an inconsequential town (Lk 2:24; cf Lev 12:8). He is born under poor conditions. Shepherds, among the unclean and living on the fringes of society, are the first to receive the good news of the birth of the Messiah, and the first to behold him. In his programmatic inaugural lecture (Lk 4:16–21), Jesus announces the good news to the poor, the prisoners, the blind, and the oppressed. It is a year of favor from the Lord in which people are to be released from their bondage, whether it is poverty, illness, or injustice. And indeed, in response to the query of John the Baptist as to whether or not Jesus is the Messiah they had long been awaiting, Jesus responds by noting that the blind see, the lame walk, and the lepers are cleansed (Mt 11:1–5).

God's concern for the poor is also clearly shown in the manner by which Jesus welcomes them and makes them privileged members of the kingdom. In Jewish purity laws, the lack of physical integrity is an impediment to full participation in social and religious life.[7] In Luke 14:12–14, Jesus admonishes his host to invite the crippled, the lame, and the blind—precisely the people who would have otherwise been completely ostracized.

Jesus did not come to make the poor richer.[8] If not, then what is the good news Jesus is supposed to preach to them (Lk 4:16–21)? What does Jesus bring to the poor? In addressing the poor directly (e.g., the beatitudes in Lk 6:20–23) and in including them in his preaching, Jesus, in effect, recognizes their dignity. It is the affirmation that, just like the well-to-do, the poor could also fulfill moral ideals. Recall that a prevalent attitude at that time was to look down on the poor as people who did not know the law, much less satisfy its stipulations. We find this dismissive and condescending attitude toward the poor in Jeremiah 5:4: "These are only the poor, they have no sense; for they do not know the way of the Lord, the law of their God." And since they could not fulfill the requirements of the law, the poor are unclean, in addition to being ignorant. Thus, by preaching to them and by preaching about them, Jesus, in effect, acknowledges their dignity. "The poor are treated as responsible moral agents with serious options for behaviour worthy of the kingdom."[9] Jesus does not have qualms associating with them (e.g., touching the lepers), just as he does not hesitate to associate with people of means (e.g., Mary and Martha), with the hated collaborators (e.g., tax collectors, Zacchaeus), with the Roman centurion, or with the Pharisees. It is the universal table-fellowship of Jesus.[10]

And, of course, we see once again in the New Testament, the imperative to minister to the needs of the poor in the name of Christ (Mt 25:31–46). Such solicitude is the hallmark of a Christian, as seen in the admonition to the Gentiles to take care of the poor and in the Pauline collection. Indeed, Jesus identifies with the poor, and their relief and liberation are central to his mission (Lk 4:16–21).

In sum, mutual solicitude is central in both testaments. In the Old Testament we have neighbors and fellow Israelites extending assistance to one another. We find the same dynamic in the New Testament, as seen in the early Church whereby all were provided according to their needs, and there was no poor among them (Acts 4:32–35; 6:1).

Surprising Reversals

Another recurrent pattern we observe in both the Old and New Testament is the phenomenon of reversals. A vivid example of this is Exodus. God heeds the cry of the enslaved and frees them from their Egyptian overlords. In the end, we have a reversal of fortunes in that the Chosen People gain their freedom, occupy a land they could call their own, and, most of all, enjoy a Covenant relationship with an almighty God who cares for them. In contrast, the Egyptians lose their slaves, their army, and their firstborn. They receive their just deserts in going against the God of Israel.

Other instances of reversals, less dramatic but no less significant, can be found in the prophetic and wisdom literature. The prophets foretell the demise and ruin of Israel's and Judah's oppressive neighboring great empires. The prophets warn eighth-century Israel and Judah not to be complacent in thinking that God was pleased with them, given the unprecedented period of prosperity, peace, and political power they were enjoying then. They are about to lose all these because of their Covenant infidelity and rampant injustice. And, indeed, they endure a stunning reversal in their fortunes with the northern kingdom's destruction in 722 B.C. and the subsequent Fall of Jerusalem in 587 B.C. Both Israel and Judah are stripped of nearly all that their ancestors had received after their liberation from Egyptian slavery—their freedom, land, peace, and prosperity. The book of Lamentations is a poignant and sad account of what befalls them and all that they lose.

But in all this, they get to keep the most precious gift their ancestors received in the Sinai—their Covenant relationship with a loving God. Thus, we witness a third great reversal in the history of Israel. A remnant survives and finds its way back to Jerusalem. There, the Temple is rebuilt, and Israel is reconstituted as a nation. They regain some of their ancestral land. Once held captives in Babylon, the Chosen People are restored, yet again. This, too, is an unexpected reversal in their fortunes, unmerited just like their Exodus liberation.

And, of course, we find unimaginable reversals in the coming age in the New Jerusalem and in Old Testament apocalyptic literature. Thus, the lamb will lie with the wolf, the child will play near the cobra's den, and the lion and the ox will graze together (Is 11:6–9). There will be peace in place of violence, and love and harmony in place of strife. Nations, ever at odds with one another, will climb the mountain together, hand in hand as one (Is 2:3–4). All this should not come as a surprise because God's propensity to bring about stunning reversals is apparent right from the start. God passes over great and mighty nations and selects puny Israel, the most insignificant and stiff-necked of peoples, even by their own admission, to receive God's election of responsibility. God's choice of a Covenant partner speaks volumes on the reversals to which the people of the Old Testament have become accustomed.

We find the same reversals in the Palestinian Jewish understanding of the kingdom of God. In the Old Testament, God's absolute reign over all human sovereigns and kingdoms is unquestioned. It is God who will render the final judgment; it is God who will have the final word. And in this apocalyptic eschatology, there will be a reversal between those who had been mighty and oppressive in the world, on the one hand, and the "elect" who had been persecuted or marginalized, on the other hand.[11]

These characteristic divine reversals continue in the New Testament. A common feature of the New Testament writings is the reversal of values and outcomes. This requires a volume in itself and we could only sample and give a mere thumbnail sketch of some of these reversals. It is not the learned, the aristocracy, or the "clean" who are privileged to accompany the Messiah in his earthly ministry, but the poor, the sinners, the shunned, the unclean, and the disenfranchised. It is they who will enjoy the Messianic banquet (e.g., Lk 14:21). The beatitudes are among the most well known of these reversals. The rich, the complacent, and the proud, on the one hand, and the poor, the mourning, and the meek, on the other hand, will find their fortunes reversed (Jas 1:9–11; 5:1–6). Following the Old Testament (1 Sam 2:1–10), the Magnificat of Mary affirms how the mighty and the proud will be cast down and the lowly and hungry will be filled with good things. Lazarus and Dives have firsthand experience of this inevitable turnabout (Lk 16:19–31). Even the kingdom has been likened to a mustard seed, which when put in the ground is the smallest of all seeds, and yet grows to be the largest of shrubs (Mk 4:30–32).

We also find a reversal, this time with values, in the difficult teachings of Jesus regarding dispossession and dying to oneself so that one might live (Jn 12:24). Instead of anchoring their self-identity and security on wealth and power, the apostles and disciples are invited to give up all and to trust solely in God's providence.

Across the Gospels, we find yet another instance of a stunning reversal. In his ethics of servanthood, Jesus calls on his disciples to serve and to be the last (Mk 10:35–45). Jesus exemplifies this himself and reveals the fullness of his identity in his helplessness and suffering.[12] Christ is fully and profoundly revealed in the brutalized Jesus dying on the cross, a suffering and self-emptying voluntarily embraced. "The stone that the builders rejected has become the cornerstone" (Mk 12:10). Jesus' resurrection after death is the paradigmatic reversal.

In sum, both testaments are laden with paradoxes and unexpected outcomes. But how and why do these reversals come about? These reversals of values and outcomes come about because God will not stand idly by as evil wreaks chaos. Not only does God confront evil, but God also restores the good that had been marred. Creation is not a one-time event; it is an ongoing divine act in which every creature is sustained in continued existence by God. Evil and chaos are the antithesis of divine order. Thus, we can be certain of a forthcoming reversal in every instance in which evil and chaos seem to triumph over good and order. Both testaments are strewn with many unusual and surprising reversals that reiterate the point that God's ways are not our ways.

Reasons for Convergence

How do we account for such remarkable convergence in Old and New Testament economic ethics despite the rich diversity in their respective starting points, sociological settings, theology, ethics, social visions, problems addressed, and time periods? What factors have contributed to such continuity? The convergence in the economic teachings of Sacred Scripture should not come as a surprise, for a number of reasons.

First, later authors and editors used earlier writings. The laws may have been the basis for many prophetic indictments. The post-exilic priestly tradition that is believed to have finalized the text of the Old Testament as we receive it today was drawing from the earlier wisdom, prophetic, and legal traditions. And, of course, the Old Testament was the reference point for the New Testament writers as they wrote the Gospels around the life, preaching, death, and resurrection of Jesus Christ—the fulfillment of God's longstanding promise in the Old Testament.

Second, many sections of the Old Testament were written at the same time. Parts of the prophets and the laws were most likely composed, edited, or finalized at the same time, as were the wisdom writings. It is believed that the wisdom literature spanned the period from the monarchy all the way to the Hellenistic period.

Third, many of the biblical books may have been reliant on the same oral tradition. Fourth, New Testament ethics presupposes Old Testament morality. Jesus and Paul were said to be not advancing a new moral system but were merely reminding their hearers of the demands of the faith that they and their ancestors had already embraced.[13] They were preaching to communities of believers, even as they reached out to Gentiles.

Fifth, Jesus stands in the prophetic tradition, which emphasizes mercy and justice. Moreover, far from abrogating the law, Jesus calls for its observance, and from the heart! Sixth, despite differences in their foci and emphases, both the Old and New Testament share the same first principles. In the Old Testament, righteousness includes mercy, while in the New Testament, love includes righteousness.[14] Seventh, for all its diversity, the Bible describes the same divine order, the same God being revealed, the same human experience, and the same salvation history unfolding.

Points of Discontinuity

There are also points of discontinuity in the two testaments. For example, the principle of restoration stands out for its extensive treatment and emphasis in the Old Testament, only to be treated lightly, if at all, in the New Testament. Much of the Old Testament laws governing economic life revolve around providing assistance to those who had fallen on hard times. Thus, we have the debt legislation that encompasses interest-free loans, debt forgiveness, and restrictions on collateral that may be demanded. There is extensive legislation on the proper treatment of slaves, their manumission after six years of service, and the mandate to weight them down with provisions as they are freed. The Jubilee Law returns ancestral land to their original owners. The gleaning law; the third-year tithe; the admonitions on the caring for the alien, widow, and orphan; the fallow year; and the shared feasting from the cultic sacrifices provide a safety net for the landless and the vulnerable in society. These releases from work, slavery, and debt are important for people who fall prey to the inherent chance and contingencies of life because they speak of restoration. It is an economy of hope, of second chances because fellow Hebrews are morally obligated to extend a helping hand to those who are in distress and those who have fallen on hard times. There will always be a day of restoration when they could recover all that they may have lost—their freedom and their land—and start anew as a landholding family. There is an operative principle of restoration in the Old Testament economic ordinances. The New Testament neither develops further these economic ordinances nor refers to them. It is silent on these specific Old Testament measures for the most part, with the exception of the importance of almsgiving.

This silence on the part of the New Testament should not be construed either as a divergence from these teachings or as an implicit judgment of their unimportance. The New Testament's seeming lack of interest on these ordinances that take up much of early Old Testament economic norms may possibly be explained by the following reasons. First, the New Testament presupposes Old Testament law. Recall how the evangelists repeatedly stress that Jesus did not come to abrogate the law but to bring it to a higher level of observance. Many in the audience to whom Jesus preached would have already been familiar with these moral exhortations. There would have been no need to repeat them. For example, recall that the Gospel of Matthew was directed to the Jewish nation, and it would have already been conversant with Old Testament requirements.

Second, it is believed that the early Church was urban-based, and many of the Old Testament social safety nets were more suited for rural residents (e.g., fallow year, gleaning law).[15] Third, much of the New Testament is aimed at a Gentile audience (e.g., Mark, Luke-Acts, letters of Paul), and the

Mosaic laws may be of little interest or relevance to them in their particular circumstances or region (e.g., Jubilee Law, sabbatical year).

In sum, one glaring difference between the Old and New Testament is the latter's silence on the many Mosaic ordinances concerning economic life, such as debt legislation, land return, slave release, third-year tithing, and gleaning. The urban location of the early Church, in addition to the preaching of the Gospel to non-Jewish lands may account for this disparity.

Other points of discontinuity or difference in emphases have been the New Testament's repeated calls to radical voluntary divestment, the admonition against the Greco-Roman practice of patronage, and the invitation to service and servanthood. We do not find these in the Old Testament to the same degree that we read them in the Gospels. We have just examined these in the preceding chapters and need not discuss them further.

NATURE OF ECONOMIC LIFE

What do the Old and New Testament teach us about the nature of economic life? I suggest that Sacred Scripture gives us at least two important insights, to wit:

- That there is a constitutive economic dimension to God's order of creation;
- That economic life is a divine gift through which humans are able to participate in God's providence and governance of creation.

Constitutive Economic Dimension

One could easily dismiss economics as a profane, practical science with little to do with sacred theology. However, Old Testament narratives, ordinances, and statutes convincingly demonstrate that there is a constitutive economic dimension to God's providence and governance of creation.

> These events [from Exodus to the conquest of the Promised Land], in which the Israel of the Old Testament originated and from which it understood itself, would not be conceivable without their economic ingredients. *What Israel called "redemption" was concretely a change of economic systems effected by God.* (Lohfink, 1986, 220, emphasis added)

> Israel fell away again and again from the heights of its beginnings. Again and again it succumbed to the temptation to be like the other peoples. Again and again God led it back and then further on the way to the definitive revelation of the Kingdom of God. Especially through the prophets. *Again and again the decisive question was one of economic relations.* (Lohfink, 1986, 222, emphasis added)

Not surprisingly, economic morality is a perennial theme we see running across the Covenant and law.

Economic life became another channel through which the Israelites encountered and got to know more about God. In light of what YHWH had done for them (e.g., gift of land, law as a blueprint for upright living with its attendant prosperity), the Chosen People learned new insights about YHWH, such as: that God is actively interested in human material well-being; that poverty (as destitution) ought not to be viewed as the ideal and, consequently, passively accepted;[16] that economic security and material sufficiency are what God intends for humanity; that God provisions people through their mutual solicitude; that God is a good provider; that God is a defender of the poor and marginalized; that God is righteous in dealing with humans.

God is not an aloof, otherworldly God who leaves creatures to fend for themselves after their creation. In fact, theological creation means that God has to sustain creatures in continued existence. Were God to step back for even a moment, creatures would revert back into non-existence. In other words, creation is not a one-time act of God. It is an ongoing divine initiative. Creation entails divine providence, that is, God providing for creatures for every moment of their existence. Consequently, this is a God who is actively engaged in the here and now, a God who is deeply interested and involved in human affairs.

And indeed, we find this in the Old Testament. God breaks into human history to liberate Israel from her oppressive bondage in Egypt. Note the significant economic dimension to God's action. Israel is freed from the yoke of Pharaonic oppression. She lives in freedom and independence in the Promised Land. There is a bequest of land for each and a livelihood for all. There is supposed to be sufficiency for all, and people are to provide for themselves through their own labor. And, as we have seen earlier, there are social provisions in place to restore those who had fallen on hard times to their rightful place in the nation as free landholding households. Israel is no longer to be in want, nor is she to be subjected once again to the whims of capricious overlords. Nor is she going to be shadowed any longer by the fear and danger of landlessness. Israel is to live as a free nation on God's land.

We find the same central role for economic agency in the New Testament. The Synoptic Gospels are clearly about God's saving act in the person of Jesus Christ. Nevertheless, the evangelists, especially Matthew and Luke, teach so much about proper economic agency because of their understanding that faithful discipleship necessarily manifests itself in moral conduct. Ethics flows from theology. Similarly, James and Paul are emphatic that faith and good works, while distinct, are inseparable. They are mirror images. Consequently, in the parable of the sheep and the goats, people are held to account for what they did or failed to do for those who were needy. Similarly, Dives is held responsible for his indifference to Lazarus. And as the parable of the

Good Samaritan shows us, there is a large, unavoidable economic dimension when it comes to the question of who is our neighbor. Love of God and love of neighbor are not about lofty sentiments and words. Rather, they are ultimately measured and actualized by how much we are willing to devote our time and treasure, indeed our very selves, for the well-being of others. And, of course, recall the example of the early Church and how they held things in common, contributing according to their means and getting only according to their needs.

Economics matters in Sacred Scripture. After all, human beings are both social and embodied creatures. As social beings, people live in communities, and they need to share the finite goods of the earth. They have to make hard choices in allocating scarce resources to their many competing uses and users. As embodied creatures, they need food, clothing, shelter, medical care, and education. Human nature is extremely demanding in its material requirements for survival, basic health, growth, and development. Indeed, there is a constitutive material, economic dimension in God's order of creation. God is interested in humanity's material welfare. Economic life is not a peripheral concern for God. The Bible is about salvation history and God's manifold initiatives for human welfare. It is not about economics. Nevertheless, such divine concern for humanity has ramifications in the more "mundane" matters of economic life. This leads us to the following conclusions:

- Economic morality is not central to the kerygma of Sacred Scripture, but it is not peripheral either. There is a necessary economic dimension to the kingdom of God since it is being built in the here and now—in a temporal setting in which time, human capacities, and earthly resources are limited and need to be allocated in the face of their competing uses.
- Economic life, or the marketplace for that matter, is not a value-free or a value-neutral realm of life since faith makes demands of it. The reign of God will necessarily have to be reflected in people's economic conduct, both individually and communally.
- Economic life takes even greater moral significance because it presents manifold occasions of sin—from the allures of wealth, to the temptation of employing power to dominate and use others for one's own ends. Economic agency can either ennoble or demean human life. It can be a dangerous terrain for moral life. Far from reflecting Emmanuel (God with us) and engendering virtuous living, socioeconomic life has often proven to be a severe test of our moral rectitude.

Economic Life as a Participation in Divine Providence

There is a second reason for why economic life is a constitutive part of the divine order of creation. It turns out that economic agency is a venue through which humans participate in divine providence and governance.

Human Participation in the Divine Order

The underlying order in creation is all-encompassing and seeps into every facet of the universe, whether in cosmology, society, or human nature and affairs. There are three dimensions to this order:

- the righteous order of the cosmos (*tzedeq*) that encompasses even social institutions including royal governance (Prov 8:15–16; 25:5; 31:1–9);
- righteous behavior (*tzĕdāqâ*), that is, the conduct of those who actualize, contribute, or maintain the above righteous order in the cosmos and in human affairs (Prov 10:2; 11:4, 6, 19; 14:34; 21:3); and
- the righteous person (*tzaddîq*) (Prov 10:3, 16, 20, 21, 24), the antithesis of the wicked who ruin the above order (Prov 11:5; 13:6; 28:12; 29:2).[17]

Humans are instrumental in actualizing this cosmic order.

As part of God's wisdom and providence, the divine order of creation must be partially actualized by the righteous.[18] The goal of humans is to act in concert with God in maintaining this order. After all, some would go so far as to claim that "creation is the establishment of the order of the cosmos for the purposeful existence of human beings."[19] Moral agency is about conforming to this order and living in harmony with it. Consider the nature of this moral order:

- The order of the comos includes the moral order.
- There are consequences (reward or punishment, good or ill) to human acts and choices. The ideal response in the righteous order is righteous behavior.
- The righteous person lives according to the requirements of the order of the cosmos. This entails walking the path of wisdom, righteousness, and virtue (Prov 11:5; 12:28; 13:6; 21:21).
- As a consequence, the righteous person is blessed accordingly (Prov 10:25, 30). This includes "longevity, fulfillment, happiness, success, contentment, and health" (Prov 10:2; 11:4–6; 12:28).
- The righteous person is established forever in the manner by which the earth is established—solid, stable, and on a firm footing. The language employed to describe creation is also used to describe the righteous person (Prov 3:19–20; 10:30).

- The righteous person not merely lives in accord with the cosmic and social order, but also actively participates and shapes this cosmic and social order through moral action.[20]

All these point to human participation in God's divine governance. Such participation is entirely consonant with the understanding that the cosmic order, or God's creative act, continues to unfold. In fact, God uses creatures, especially human beings, as instruments in this divine providence. But such human participation is often fraught with difficulty and suffering.

> Job learns that *human righteousness entails actively participating with God in the struggle against chaos and its various incarnations. Suffering is inevitable* and mortality circumscribes human efforts, but the structures of life for creation and human communities are secured only by the struggle for justice. (Perdue, 1990a, 470, emphasis added)

Another significant point is how humans have a real impact on the cosmos, for good or for ill. They may choose to be part of the divine act of keeping the chaos at bay, or they may choose to contribute instead to that chaos through a life of wickedness and folly. However the human person responds, there is a second-order effect. Vibrant participation in God's creative activity enhances and imbues the righteous person's life, and others', with profound purpose—an "informed human participation in the shaping of a social and cosmic order that not only make[s] life possible, *but also [gives] it meaning.*"[21]

I would go further and claim that it is a meaning that redounds back to these human instruments to enrich their lives as well. After all, as humans imbue the larger order with meaning, they themselves are ennobled. In other words, upright economic life turns out to be a double benefaction in its own right, namely: (1) it is the gift of participation in divine providence and (2) it enriches the moral agent's life with meaning and purpose.

Economic Life

Far from being viewed as toil, economic agency should in fact be accepted as a gift. Equally important, far from being viewed as burdensome impositions, the Old and New Testament economic norms and ordinances turn out to be the very building blocks of yet another divine gift for humanity—the gift of actively taking part in God's creative activity.

God could have directly provided humans with material abundance, as in the case of manna in the desert. (After all, God is the creator of the heavens and the earth who brought everything into existence out of nothing.) Instead, God provides such abundance, but only through the people's own efforts and through their mutual care for one another.[22] Thus, in addition to the land flowing with milk and honey, God also gives the Law to the Chosen People. This, too, is another divine gift—that of being instruments in God's ongoing act of creation.

As we have seen in part I, the Old Testament legal codes provide an extensive safety net to deal with the chance and contingencies of life. Those who fall on hard times always have a chance to start afresh. Israelites are cushioned from life's vicissitudes through their ethos of mutual assistance: hardship loans at no interest, almsgiving, tithing, land and kin redemption, the provisioning of released slaves, and the preferential treatment of the stranger, widow, and orphan. Equally important, debt remission, slave release, land return, third-year poor tithes, Sabbath rest, sabbatical fallow, tithing, and shared feasts are institutionalized and practiced at regular intervals. Thus, the Deuteronomist can boldly proclaim that there will be no poor in Israel (Dt 15:4), and the prophet could envision how Israelites "shall all sit under their own vines and under their own fig trees" (Mic 4:4).

The description of the Promised Land as "flowing with milk and honey" is idyllic and metaphorical in that God is going to give Israel far more than a bounteous earth. Israel herself is to let the land bloom and blossom in abundance in the measure that she allows justice to flourish on the land. *In other words, God's gift to the nation is more than just a rich land, but a land that is animated by justice and mercy, which in turn bring peace and harmony. God is giving Israel the even greater gift of growth in righteousness and holiness.* Consequently, we repeatedly encounter Old Testament passages that remind Israel of what she must do to enjoy tenure on the land, namely: fidelity to her Covenant election of responsibility.

The Old Testament does not romanticize poverty. Destitution is not part of God's plan for humanity.[23] Rather, God is keenly interested in human material well-being. Thus, God is thoroughly engaged in providing Israel with a land flowing with milk and honey and in giving her a blueprint (the Law) on how to walk down a path of prosperity and peace. The Israelites are mandated to offer to God the first fruits of their land and vines and the firstlings of their animals. They tithe from the produce of their land. It is by way of thanking God and acknowledging all these as unmerited divine gifts and blessings. It is poignant to note, however, that these offerings are eaten by the families themselves, as an entire household, including the servants, slaves, and aliens living among them, and the Levites who depend on such support. And they share such feasting together in the presence of the Lord (Dt 14:22–27; Num 18). This is a foretaste of the eschatological banquet. Equally important, it is an affirmation that God continues to supply an abundance for the Chosen People in the Promised Land, with no one excluded, just as God did in providing manna when they wandered through the desert. Clearly, God intends the gift of material sufficiency, if not abundance, for all.

In the New Testament, God's gift of economic security is also conditional. A genuine pursuit of the kingdom of God is a necessary condition to living life without material anxieties (Mt 6:25–34; Lk 12:22–34). The early Church heeds this admonition. They give according to what they have and take only what they need. They are bold in holding everything in common. The Gentile churches take up a collection in order to provide relief for the poor of Jerusalem (2 Cor 8–9). Thus, God provides for people through their mutual assistance.

No one is said to be in want in the early Church community given their radical sharing of goods that come with *koinōnia* (Acts 4:34). This again is yet another sign of God's fulfillment of the Covenant promise in the reconstituted Israel. This early Christian community is, in fact, a fulfillment of the promise that had been made that if Israel followed the law, there should be no poor among them. Acts 4:34 accomplishes what was merely an aspiration in Deuteronomy 15:4.[24] Forgoing patron-client relationships and embracing *koinōnia* is, in fact, not merely a sign of God's reign in their midst, but it is also sacramental in bringing about such a state.

God's gift of material abundance comes about through the righteous person. It is the righteous person who creates harmony in the world and in the community. ("You will know them by their fruits" [Mt 7:16].) After all, there will be harmony only if all the requirements of relationships are fulfilled. The consequences and signs of justice are "peace, prosperity and fertility on the land."[25] And this is how the gift of material abundance is actualized.

Paul provides a down-to-earth account as he explains to the Corinthians the practical wisdom of contributing to the collection for the poor in Jerusalem. He suggests that just as their material surplus today fills deficiencies in other churches, these other churches will in their own turn and in their own surplus also provide for the Corinthians' needs someday (2 Cor 8:13–15). In other words, genuine solidarity can even out cycles of plenty and want. It is reminiscent of mutual assistance as a rational strategy of mutual survival that we find in early Israel.[26]

In sum, God affects the divine gift of material sufficiency through the people themselves. In other words, God's gift of economic security is conditional. It is contingent on moral conduct. The Deuteronomist puts it succinctly: "There will, however, be no one in need among you, because the Lord is sure to bless you in the land that the Lord your God is giving you as a possession to occupy, *if only you will obey the Lord your God by diligently observing this entire commandment that I command you today*" (Dt 15:4–5, emphasis added). It turns out that the Old Testament economic statutes and ordinances have an important function to them—it is through observance of these divine decrees that God provides for Israel's material needs. Similarly, God provisions the New Chosen People in the New Testament through their own individual efforts and, more importantly, through their mutual solicitude. God provides for us through each other. Thus, there is a second divine gift in the order of creation—human participation in God's providence.

SUMMARY AND CONCLUSIONS

Biblical economic norms attest to a divine order undergirding the natural world and human affairs. Economic life can be viewed as a series of unmerited gifts:

- the gift of divine friendship, which invites humans to emulate God's holiness and righteousness (to the extent possible) through upright economic conduct,
- the gift of one another, which calls for mutual respect and solicitude, and
- the gift of the earth, which requires stewardship and the generous sharing of the material world.

These gifts, in turn, open the door to other subsequent divine gifts. In particular, there are the two related gifts of (1) material sufficiency and (2) human participation in the divine providence and governance of the world. God affects the gift of material prosperity through human virtue, hard work, generosity, and mutual love.

Much can be said about the implications of Sacred Scripture for economic morality. First, biblical economic norms accentuate the constitutive economic dimension in the divine order. In other words, moral choices have consequences for economic life. We find this critical economic dimension illustrated in the liberation of Israel. An economy that functions properly and peaceably implies both divine blessings and a response of right moral action on the part of the people. After all, strife and immorality in the community can never lead to a genuinely sound, peaceful economic life. Not surprisingly, prosperity is often associated with upright moral conduct. The latter is a necessary condition for a genuine and sustainable material abundance. This is an axiom of the natural and moral order of divine creation. Economic life matters for human flourishing. This, in turn, underscores the importance of getting their economic ethics right.

Second, the act-consequence (cause-and-effect) nexus points to a natural and moral order that cannot be ignored in economic life. Effects follow their antecedents because both are part of a much larger order at work. God's creative act brought into existence not only creatures but also a natural and moral order in which they are to live and thrive. There is an end for which God acts. Every creature has an end (*telos*) for which it was created and is sustained by God. Divine will is not whimsical or arbitrary in its requirements. The demands of this divine will are discerned through Revelation and through the natural and moral world. Such an operative order means that there are objective requirements as part of human existence that are neither created nor subject to change by humans. (For example, justice, love, and mercy are necessary conditions to a harmonious society.) These objective standards come with God's order of creation. Humans simply have to accept them as part of the immutable facts of life. To conform to these objective requirements is to travel down the road to human flourishing. To ignore them, or worse, to go against them, is to set themselves for failure. This is the dynamic behind the act-consequence or cause-and-effect nexus.

Third, Deuteronomy 8:17–18 cautions against the dangers posed by riches in leading people to think that their accomplishments are due to their hard work and not God's gift.[27] Great wealth gives people an ever-larger scope for freedom of action. They become ever more autonomous and independent because of the self-sufficiency that riches bring with them. Wealth can make successful people arrogant or complacent in thinking that they are not accountable to anyone but themselves and that they have no need for others, sometimes not even God.

The forthcoming day of reckoning dispels such a misplaced proprietary attitude. To begin with, health, wealth, and success are all gifts from God. As gifts, they come with attendant obligations. Stewardship and its corollary—accountability—are the appropriate posture to take. The independence and autonomy that prosperity confers in this lifetime are illusory, more apparent than real, because riches or success are not the arbiters of life. God is. Biblical economic ethics brings the certainty of the day of judgment front and center and exposes the folly of self-satisfaction that is prevalent among the rich, the successful, and the powerful (e.g., Lk 12:16–21).

Fourth, Deuteronomy 15:4 ("There shall be no poor among you") is an affirmation that destitution is a scandal and is contrary to the will of God.[28] Thus, chronic poverty (in the sense of material want) should never be lauded as an ideal because this is not part of God's plan, but is the consequence of individual and collective moral failure. It is an unacceptable state of affairs that needs to be rectified. We find this consistently across the Bible, from the Pentateuchal narratives (e.g., land distribution with each family getting a plot), to the laws (e.g., social safety net), to the prophetic indictments, to the wisdom literature (e.g., Proverbs on the benefits of wealth and the toilsome nature of being poor), and even to the New Testament (e.g., parable of the sheep and goats, Lazarus and Dives).

Fifth, the twofold divine gift of economic security is conditioned on whether or not humans accept such a double benefaction. God does not force grace on humanity. God respects human freedom. In other words, God proffers such signal divine gifts, but it is up to humans to avail of them and to let them bloom in their fullness. Thus, God brought Israel to a land flowing with milk and honey. But it was left up to the Chosen People to do their part in treating one another with mutual respect and solicitude to ensure that the land truly flows with milk and honey. They had a role to play in allowing God's gift of (conditional) material abundance to come to fruition. Far from suggesting a miserly giver, such conditionality highlights two additional gifts: the gift of human freedom and the gift of human participation in God's providence. Contemporary generations face the same invitation as the Israelites and the early Church.

Finally, self-sacrifice and self-donation are copious in their ripple effects. Power is limited by its nature. One acquires more of it, but at the expense of others' power. Thus, in the view of many, to forswear wealth accumulation and its accompanying power is to weaken themselves relative to others who do not subscribe to these values. To live an upright economic life while others do not is to make oneself vulnerable (and a fool!), according to prevalent human thinking. This is yet another reason for why moral economic conduct can be viewed as a prophetic call to self-sacrifice and self-denial.

If all are equally willing to refrain from inordinate wealth accumulation as an end in itself, the community can reach an optimum solution to the perennial economic problem of finite resources, giving the entire community a social outcome far better than if each were to behave selfishly. Mutual selflessness produces a sustainable abundance that competitive self-interest cannot. Recall how the pursuit of the kingdom leads to sufficiency.

There is a self-reinforcing dynamism that feeds into material sufficiency. Luke 6:38 summarizes the phenomenon well: "[G]ive, and it will be given to you. A good measure, pressed down, shaken together, running over, will be put into your lap; for the measure you give will be the measure you get back" (cf. Mt 7:1–2; Mk 4:24–25). Generosity and self-forgetfulness in economic conduct unleash an inversion where self-emptying and self-deprivation bring returns that are even more copious than what had been foregone or given away (cf. Lk 12:33; 18:29–30; Mt 10:37–42). And as self-sacrifice and self-donation are generously rewarded with abundance, even this consequent abundance is shared further. It is a self-reinforcing virtuous cycle. To borrow imagery from the Synoptic Gospels, those who have more will be given even more, while those who have less will lose what little they have. Paul makes the same point as he encourages the Corinthians to be unstinting and ungrudging in giving to the poor of Jerusalem (2 Cor 9:6–10). Indeed, "the goods of this earth are the sign of the right relationship with Yahweh [YHWH] *as well as the means to create harmony within the community*."[29]

The nature of economic life dovetails well the operative dynamic of the kingdom. On the one hand, the ideal economic life demands much self-sacrifice and self-donation. On the other hand, the kingdom operates and thrives precisely on these same selfless qualities. In overlaying the two together, people unleash the plenteous consequences of self-giving and, in the process, produce abundantly not only for themselves but for all. Indeed, the

Bible is an account of the breathtaking possibilities humans face, thanks to the goodness and wisdom of a loving God.

Finally, let us close the circle by going back to where we started in our biblical theology in chapter 11: Our economic life is merely part of a much larger divine order of creation. This divine order of creation is animated and sustained by God's love, especially for humanity. Because of God's love for them, humans are able to love God in return and to love one another. It is this twin inseparable love that enables humans to live up to the heroic self-giving clearly demanded by Sacred Scripture's economic teachings. Such love of God and neighbor, burning fiercely, is the fullness of human flourishing.

NOTES

1. Cosgrove (2002, 195–96)
2. Burrows (1974, 229)
3. Hays (1996, 164, 167)
4. Burrows (1974, 232) describes Deuteronomy as "literature of persuasion."
5. The points from the preceding two paragraphs are drawn from Burrows (1974).
6. Donohue (2005, 25)
7. Nardoni (2004, 211)
8. Harvey (1990, 137–38) makes this point and the following observation on how Jesus gives the poor the dignity, respect, and recognition they deserve.
9. Harvey (1990, 138)
10. Burridge (2007)
11. Duling (1992, 52)
12. Hays (1996, 75)
13. Matera (1996, 255)
14. Lohfink (1982, 239–54)
15. Meeks (1983)
16. Lohfink (1987)
17. Perdue (1990a, 458–59)
18. Perdue (1990a, 472–73)
19. Yee (1992, 93–94)
20. Perdue (1990a, 459)
21. Perdue (1990a, 460, emphasis added)
22. Nardoni (2004, 82, fn 39)
23. Lohfink (1987)
24. Lohfink (1986, 228)
25. Donahue (1977, 71)
26. See chapter 2 and von Waldow (1970).
27. Kaiser (1988, 161)
28. Harvey (1990, 119)
29. Donahue (1977, 70, emphasis added)

References

Anderson, Bernhard. 1978. *The Eighth Century Prophets: Amos, Hosea, Isaiah, Micah*. Philadelphia: Fortress.

Anderson, Gary. 2009. *Sin: A History*. New Haven: Yale.

Applebaum, Shimon. 1976. "Economic Life in Palestine," in *The Jewish People in the First Century: Historical Geography, Political History, Social, Cultural and Religious Life and Institutions*. Volume 2. Edited by S. Safrai and M. Stern. Philadelphia: Fortress.

Balch, David. 1995. "Rich and Poor, Proud and Humble in Luke-Acts," in *The Social World of the First Christians: Essays in Honor of Wayne A. Meeks*. Edited by L. Michael White and O. Larry Yarbrough. Minneapolis, MN: Fortress.

Baron, Salo, Arcadius Kahan, and others. 1975. *Economic History of the Jews*. Edited by Nachum Gross. Jerusalem: Keter Publishing House.

Barton, John. 1978. "Understanding Old Testament Ethics," *Journal for the Study of the Old Testament* 9: 44–64.

Barton, John. 1982. "Approaches to Ethics in the Old Testament," in *Beginning Old Testament Study*. Edited by John Rogerson. Philadelphia: Westminster.

Barton, John. 2003. *Understanding Old Testament Ethics: Approaches and Explorations*. Louisville, KY: Westminster John Knox.

Beavis, Mary Ann. 1994. "'Expecting Nothing in Return': Luke's Picture of the Marginalised," *Interpretation* 48: 357–68.

Beed, Clive, and Cara Beed. 2012. "The Nature of Biblical Economic Principle, and Its Critics," *Faith and Economics* 59: 31–58.

Berlin, Andrea. 1997. "Between Large Forces: Palestine in the Hellenistic Period," *Biblical Archaeologist* 60: 2–51.

Berthoud, Pierre. 2005. "The Covenant and the Social Message of Amos," *European Journal of Theology* 14: 99–109.

Birch, Bruce. 1991. *Let Justice Roll Down: The Old Testament, Ethics, and Christian Life*. Louisville, KY: Westminster/John Knox Press.

Birch, Bruce. 1995. "Moral Agency, Community, and the Character of God in the Hebrew Bible," in *Ethics and Politics in the Hebrew Bible*. Edited by Douglas Knight. *Semeia* 66. Society of Biblical Literature.

Birch, Bruce. 2001. "Old Testament Ethics," in *The Blackwell Companion to the Hebrew Bible*. Edited by Leo Perdue. Malden, MA: Blackwell.

Blomberg, Craig. 1999. *Neither Poverty nor Riches: A Biblical Theology of Possessions*. New Studies in Biblical Theology #7. Series editor: D. A. Carson. Leicester, UK: Apollos.

Bracke, John. 2002. "Justice in the Book of Jeremiah," *Word and World* 22: 387–95.

Brin, Gershon. 1994. *Studies in Biblical Law: From the Hebrew Bible to the Dead Sea Scrolls*. Translated from the Hebrew by Jonathan Chipman. Journal for the Study of the Old Testament Supplement Series 176. Sheffield, UK: JSOT Press.

Broshi, Magen. 1987. "The Role of the Temple in the Herodian Economy," *Journal of Jewish Studies* 38: 31–37.

Brown, Raymond. 1997. *An Introduction to the New Testament*. Anchor Bible Reference Library. New York: Doubleday.

Brueggemann, Walter. 1975. "Reflections on Biblical Understandings of Property," *International Review of Mission* 64: 354–61.

Brueggemann, Walter. 1994. "Justice: The Earthly Form of God's Holiness," *Reformed World* 44: 13–27.

Burridge, Richard. 2007. *Imitating Jesus: An Inclusive Approach to New Testament Ethics*. Grand Rapids, MI: W. B. Eerdmans.

Burrows, Millar. 1974. "Old Testament Ethics and the Ethics of Jesus," in *Essays in Old Testament Ethics*. New York: Ktav Publishing.

Byargeon, Rick. 1995. "Amos: The Man and His Times," *Southwestern Journal of Theology* 38: 4–10.

Cahill, Lisa Sowle. 1990. "The New Testament and Ethics: Communities of Social Change," *Interpretation* 44: 383–95.

Capper, Brian. 1998. "Reciprocity and the Ethic of Acts," in *Witness to the Gospel: The Theology of Acts*. Edited by I. Howard Marshall and David Peterson. Grand Rapids, MI: W. B. Eerdmans.

Carter, Charles. 1999. *The Emergence of Yehud in the Persian Period: A Social and Demographic Study*. Journal for the Study of the Old Testament Supplement Series 294. Sheffield, UK: Sheffield Academic Press.

Ceresko, Anthony. 1992. *Introduction to the Old Testament: A Liberation Perspective*. Maryknoll, NY: Orbis.

Ceresko, Anthony. 1995. "The Function of 'Order' (*Sedeq*) and 'Creation' in the Book of Proverbs, with Some Implications for Today," *Indian Theological Studies* 32: 208–36.

Chaney, Marvin. 1986. "Systemic Study of the Israelite Monarchy," in *Social Scientific Criticism of the Hebrew Bible and its Social World: The Israelite Monarchy*. Semeia 37. Edited by Norman Gottwald. Society of Biblical Literature.

Chaney, Marvin. 1989. "Bitter Bounty: The Dynamics of Political Economy Critiqued by the Eight-Century Prophets," in *Reformed Faith and Economics*. Edited by Robert Stivers. New York: University Press of America.

Chester, Andrew, and Ralph Martin. 1994. *The Theology of the Letters of James, Peter, and Jude*. Cambridge, UK: Cambridge University Press.

Childs, Brevard. 1993. *Biblical Theology of the Old and New Testaments: Theological Reflection on the Christian Bible*. Minneapolis, MN: Fortress.

Clements, Ronald. 1984. "Christian Ethics and the Old Testament," *Modern Churchman* 26: 13–26.

Clifford, Richard. 1990. "Exodus," *New Jerome Biblical Commentary*. Englewood Cliffs, NJ: Prentice-Hall.

Cohn, Haim Hermann. 1984. *Human Rights in Jewish Law*. New York: KTAV.

Collins, Gerald, and Daniel Kendall. 1997. *The Bible for Theology: Ten Principles for the Theological Use of Scripture*. New York: Paulist.

Conzelmann, Hans. 1960. *The Theology of St. Luke*. Translated by Geoffrey Buswell. London: Faber.

Coote, Robert. 1981. *Amos among the Prophets: Composition and Theology*. Philadelphia: Fortress.

Coote, R. B., and K. W. Whitelam. 1986. "The Emergence of Israel: Social Transformation and State Formation following the Decline in Late Bronze Age Trade." *Semeia Supplements* 37: 107–47.

Cosgrove, Charles. 2002. *Appealing to Scripture in Moral Debate: Five Hermeneutical Rules*. Grand Rapids, MI: W. B. Eerdmans.

Crenshaw, James. 1970. "Popular Questioning of the Justice of God in Ancient Israel," in *Studies in Ancient Israelite Wisdom*. New York: KTAV.

Crenshaw, James. 1989. "Poverty and Punishment in the Book of Proverbs," *Quarterly Review* 9: 30–43.

Dahl, Nils Alstrup. 1977. *Studies in Paul: Theology for the Early Christian Mission*. Minneapolis, MN: Augsburg.

Danker, Frederick. 1983. "Reciprocity in the Ancient World and in Acts 15: 23–29," in *Political Issues in Luke-Acts*. Edited by Richard Cassidy and Philip Ministry. Maryknoll, NY: Orbis.

Davies, Eryl. 1981. *Prophecy and Ethics: Isaiah and the Ethical Traditions of Israel*. Journal for the Study of the Old Testament Supplement Series, 16. Sheffield, UK: JSOT Press.

Davies, Eryl. 1995. "Ethics of the Hebrew Bible: The Problem of Methodology," in *Ethics and Politics in the Hebrew Bible*. Edited by Douglas Knight. *Semeia* 66. Society of Biblical Literature.

Davies, Eryl. 2006. "The Bible in Ethics," in *Biblical Studies*. Edited by J. W. Rogerson and Judith Lieu. Oxford, UK: Oxford University Press.

Davies, Margaret. 1995. "Work and Slavery in the New Testament: Impoverishments of Traditions," in *The Bible in Ethics: The Second Sheffield Colloquium*. JSOT Supplement Series # 207. Edited by John Rogerson, Margaret Davies, and M. Daniel Carroll R.

Dearman, J. Andrew. 1984. "Prophecy, Property and Politics," Society of Biblical Literature Seminar Papers 23: 385–97.

Dearman, J. Andrew. 1988. *Property Rights in the Eighth-Century Prophets: The Conflict and its Background*. Dissertation series #106. Atlanta, GA: Scholars Press.

De Vaux, Roland. 1973. *Ancient Israel: Its Life and Institutions*. Second edition. London: Darton, Longman and Todd.

Domeris, William. 2007. *Touching the Heart of God: The Social Construction of Poverty among Biblical Peasants*. London: T and T Clark.

Donahue, John. 1977. "Biblical Perspectives on Justice," in *The Faith That Does Justice: Examining the Christian Sources for Social Change*. Edited by John Haughey. New York: Paulist Press.

Donahue, John. 1989. "Two Decades of Research on the Rich and the Poor in Luke-Acts," in *Justice and the Holy: Essays in Honor of Walter Harrelson*. Edited by D. A. Knight and J. Paris. Atlanta: Scholars Press.

Donahue, John. 2005. "The Bible and Catholic Social Teaching: Will This Engagement Lead to Marriage?" in *Modern Catholic Social Teaching: Commentaries and Interpretations*. Edited by Kenneth Himes. Washington DC: Georgetown University Press.

Duling, Dennis. 1992. "Kingdom of God, Kingdom of Heaven," *The Anchor Bible Dictionary*. Volume 4. Edited by David Noel Freedman. New York: Doubleday.

Dunn, James. 1998. *The Theology of Paul the Apostle*. Grand Rapids, MI: Eerdmans.

Dunn, James. 2004. "Paul's Theology," in *The Face of New Testament Studies: A Survey of Recent Research*. Edited by Scot McKnight and Grant Osborne. Grand Rapids, MI: Baker Academic and Apollos.

Dupont, Jacques. 1977. "The Poor and Poverty in the Gospels and Acts," in *Gospel Poverty: Essays in Biblical Theology*. Edited by A. George et al. Chicago: Franciscan Herald.

Dupont, Jacques. 1979. "Community of Goods in the Early Church," in *The Salvation of the Gentiles: Studies in the Acts of the Apostles*. New York: Paulist.

Edelman, Diana. 2007. "Settlement Patterns in Persian-Era *Yehud*," in *A Time of Change: Judah and Its Neighbours in the Persian and Early Hellinistic Periods*. Edited by Yigal Levin. London: T and T Clark.

Eichrodt, Walther. 1967. *Theology of the Old Testament*. Volume 2. Philadelphia: Westminster John Knox.

Elat, M. 1979. "The Monarchy and the Development of Trade in Ancient Israel," in *State and Temple Economy in the Ancient Near East*. Volume 2. Edited by Edward Lipinski. Leuven, Belgium: Katholieke Universiteit Leuven, Departement Oriëntalistiek.

Eldridge, Victor. 1981. "Jeremiah, Prophet of Judgment," *Review and Expositor* 78: 319–30.

Elliot, John. 1993. *What Is Social Scientific Criticism?* Minneapolis, MN: Fortress.

Elliott, John. 1996. "Patronage and Clientage," in *The Social Sciences and New Testament Interpretation*. Edited by Richard Rohrbaugh. Peabody, MA: Hendrickson.

Engels, Donald. 1990. *Roman Corinth: An Alternative Model for the Classical City*. Chicago: University of Chicago Press.

Esler, Philip Francis. 1987. *Community and Gospel in Luke-Acts*. Cambridge: Cambridge University Press.

Faley, Roland. 1990. "Leviticus," in *New Jerome Biblical Commentary*. Englewood Cliffs, NJ: Prentice-Hall.

Faust, Avraham. 2000. "The Rural Community in Ancient Israel during Iron Age II," *Bulletin of the American Schools of Oriental Research* 317: 17–39.

Faust, Avraham. 2003. "Judah in the Sixth Century B.C.E.: A Rural Perspective," *Palestine Exploration Quarterly* 135: 37–53.

Faust, Avraham. 2004. "Social and Cultural Changes in Judah during the 6th Century BCE and Their Implications for Our Understanding of the Nature of the Neo-Babylonian Period," *Ugarit-Forschungen* 36: 157–76.

Faust, Avraham. 2008. "Settlement and Demography in Seventh-Century Judah and the Extent and Intensity of Sennacherib's Campaign," *Palestine Exploration Quarterly* 140: 168–94.

Faust, Avraham, and Ehud Weiss. 2005. "Judah, Philistia, and the Mediterranean World: Reconstructing the Economic System of the Seventh Century B.C.E.," *Bulletin of the American Schools of Oriental Research* 338: 71–92.

Faust, Avraham, and Shlomo Bunimovitz. 2003. "The Four Room House: Embodying Iron Age Israelite Society," *Near Eastern Archaeology* 66: 22–31.

Fensham, F. C. 1962. "Widow, Orphan, and the Poor in Ancient Near Eastern Legal and Wisdom Literature," *Journal of Near Eastern Studies* 21: 129–39.

Finley, Thomas John. 1985. "Evangelical Response to the Preaching of Amos," *Journal of the Evangelical Theological Society* 28: 411–20.

Fitzmyer, Joseph A. 1981. Anchor Bible Commentary *The Gospel according to Luke: Introduction, Translation, and Notes*. Volume 28. Garden City: Doubleday.

Fitzmyer, Joseph A. 1990. "Pauline Theology," in *The New Jerome Biblical Commentary*. Englewood Cliffs, NJ: Prentice-Hall.

Fitzpatrick-Mckinley, Anne. 1999. The Transformation of Torah from Scribal Advice to Law. Journal for the Study of the Old Testament Supplement Series 287. Sheffield, UK: Sheffield Academic Press.

Fox, Michael. 2000. *Proverbs 1–9*. The Anchor Bible Series. New York: Doubleday.

Fretheim, Terence. 1991. *Exodus*. Louisville, KY: John Knox Press.

Freyne, Seán. 1988. *Galilee, Jesus and the Gospels: Literary Approaches and Historical Investigations*. Philadelphia: Fortress.

Freyne, Seán. 1994. "The Geography, Politics, and Economics of Galilee and the Quest for the Historical Jesus," in *Studying the Historical Jesus: Evaluations of the State of Current Research*. Edited by Bruce Chilton and Craig Evans. Leiden: E. J. Brill.

Freyne, Seán. 2004. "Galilee and Judea: The Social World of Jesus," in *The Face of New Testament Studies: A Survey of Recent Research*. Edited by Scot McKnight and Grant Osborne. Grand Rapids, MI: Baker Academic.

Friessen, Steven. 2004. "Poverty in Pauline Studies: Beyond the So-Called New Consensus," *Journal for the Study of the New Testament* 26: 323–61.

Furnish, Victor Paul. 1968. *Theology and Ethics in Paul*. Nashville, TN: Abingdon Press.

Gelin, Albert. 1964. *The Poor of Yahweh*. Translated by Mother Kathryn Sullivan. Collegeville, MN: Liturgical Press.

Georgi, Dieter. 1991. *Remembering the Poor: The History of Paul's Collection for Jerusalem*. Nashville, TN: Abingdon.

Gillman, John. 1991. *Possessions and the Life of Faith: A Reading of Luke-Acts*. Zacchaeus Studies. Collegeville, MN: Liturgical.

Goldingay, John. 2002. "Jubilee Tithe," *Transformation* 19: 198–205.

Gordon, Barry. 1989. *The Economic Problem in Biblical and Patristic Thought*. New York: E. J. Brill.

Gossai, Hemchand. 1993. *Justice, Righteousness and the social Critique of the Eighth-Century Prophets*. American University Studies 7. Theology and Religion 141. New York: Peter Lang.

Gottwald, Norman. 1976. "Israel, Social and Economic Development of," *Interpreter's Dictionary of the Bible*. Supplementary volume. Nashville, TN: Abingdon.

Grabbe, Lester. 1998. "Poets, Scribes, or Preachers? The Reality of Prophecy in the Second Temple Period," in *Society of Biblical Literature 1998 Seminar Papers, Part Two*. Atlanta, GA: Scholars Press.

Grabbe, Lester. 1999. "Israel's Historical Reality after the Exile," in "The Crisis of Israelite Religion" in *Transformation of Religious Tradition in Exilic and Post-Exilic Times*. Edited by Bob Becking and Marjo Korpel. Leiden: Brill.

Grabbe, Lester. 2002. "Israel Under Persia and Greece," in *The Biblical World*. Volume 1. Edited by John Barton. London: Routledge.

Grabbe, Lester. 2004. *A History of the Jews and Judaism in the Second Temple Period*. Volume 1. *Yehud: A History of the Persian Province of Judah*. London: T and T Clark.

Grabbe, Lester. 2007. *Ancient Israel: What Do We Know and How Do We Know It?* London: T and T Clark.

Green, Joel. 1994. "Good News to Whom? Jesus and the 'Poor' in the Gospel of Luke," in *Jesus of Nazareth: Lord and Christ*. Edited by Joel Green and Max Turner. Grand Rapids, MI: W. B. Eerdmans.

Green, Joel. 1995. *The Theology of the Gospel of Luke*. Cambridge: Cambridge University Press.

Greene, K. 1986. *The Archaeology of the Roman Economy*. Berkeley: University of California Press.

Gregory, Bradley. 2010. *Like an Everlasting Signet Ring: Generosity in the Book of Sirach*. Berlin: De Gruyter.

Gregory, James. 1975. "Image of Limited Good, or Expectation of Reciprocity?" *Current Anthropology* 16: 73–92.

Gustafson, James. 1978. *Protestant and Roman Catholic Ethics: Prospects for Rapprochement*. Chicago: University of Chicago Press.

Gustafson, James. 1984. "The Place of Scripture in Christian Ethics: A Methodological Study," in *The Use of Scripture in Moral Theology*. Readings in Moral Theology Series. Volume 4. Edited by Charles Curran and Richard McCormick. New York: Paulist.

Guyette, Fred. 2008. "Amos the Prophet: A Meditation on the Richness of 'Justice,'" *Jewish Bible Quarterly* 36: 15–21.

Habel, Norman. 1988. "Wisdom, Wealth and Poverty Paradigms in the Book of Proverbs," *Bible Bhashyam* 14: 26–49.

Hagner, Donald. 1992. "Righteousness in Matthew's Theology," in *Worship, Theology and Ministry in the Early Church*. JSNT supplement series #87. Sheffield, England: Sheffield Academic Press.

Hanson, K. C., and Douglas Oakman. 1998. *Palestine in the Time of Jesus: Social Structures and Social Conflicts*. Minneapolis, MN: Fortress.

Hanson, Paul. 1977. "Theological Significance of Contradiction Within the Book of the Covenant," in *Canon and Authority: Essays in Old Testament Religion and Theology*. Edited by George Coats and Burke Long. Philadelphia: Fortress.

Harland, Philip. 2002. "The Economy of First-Century Palestine: State of the Scholarly Discussion," in *Handbook of Early Christianity: Social Science Approaches*. Edited by Anthony Blasi, Jean Duhaime, and Paul-André Turcotte. New York: Altamira.

Harnack, Adolf von. 1901. *What Is Christianity?* Translated by J. R. Wilkinson. London: Williams and Norgate.

Hartin, Patrick. 2003. *James*. Sacra Pagina series 14. Edited by Daniel Harrington. Collegeville, MN: Liturgical Press.

Hartin, Patrick. 2006. "The Letter of James: Its Vision, Ethics, and Ethos," in *Identity, Ethics, and Ethos in the New Testament*. Edited by Jan G. Van der Watt. Berlin and New York: Walter de Gruyter.

Harvey, A. E. 1990. *Strenuous Commands: The Ethic of Jesus*. London: SCM Press.

Hauer, Christian. 1980. "The Economics of National Security in Solomonic Israel," *Journal for the Study of the Old Testament* 18: 63–73.

Hauerwas, Stanley. 1984. "The Moral Authority of Scripture: The Politics and Ethics of Remembering," in *The Use of Scripture in Moral Theology*. Readings in Moral Theology Series 4. Edited by Charles Curran and Richard McCormick. New York: Paulist.

Hays, Richard. 1987. "Christology and Ethics in Galatians: The Law of Christ," *Catholic Biblical Quarterly* 49: 268–70.

Hays, Richard. 1990. "Scripture-Shaped Community: The Problem of Method in New Testament Ethics," *Interpretation* 44: 42–55.

Hays, Richard. 1996. *The Moral Vision of the New Testament: Community, Cross, New Creation: A Contemporary Introduction to New Testament Ethics*. San Francisco: Harper.

Heard, Warren. 1988. "Luke's Attitude toward the Rich and the Poor," *Trinity Journal* 9: 47–80.

Hembrom, T. 1996. "Economic Policy in the Wisdom Literature of the Old Testament," *Bible Bhashyam* 22: 231–37.

Hiebert, D. Edmond. 1978. "The Unifying Theme of the Epistle of James." *Bibliotheca Sacra* 135: 221–31.

Hiers, Richard. 1984a. "Jesus, Ethics and the Present Situation," in *The Use of Scripture in Moral Theology*. Readings in Moral Theology Series 4. Edited by Charles Curran and Richard McCormick. New York: Paulist.

Hiers, Richard. 1984b. "Ecology, Biblical Theology, and Methodology: Biblical Perspectives on the Environment," *Zygon* 19: 43–59.

Hiers, Richard. 1996–1998. "Reverence for Life and Environmental Ethics in Biblical Law and Covenant," *Journal of Law and Religion* 13: 127–88.

Hiers, Richard. 2002. "Biblical Social Welfare Legislation: Protected Classes and Provisions for Persons in Need," *Journal of Law and Religion* 17: 49–96.

Himes, Kenneth. 1985. "Scripture and Ethics: A Review Essay," *Biblical Theology Bulletin* 15: 65–73.

Holladay, John. 1995. "The Kingdoms of Israel and Judah: Political and Economic Centralization in the Iron II A-B (ca. 1000–750 BCE)," in *The Archaeology of Society in the Holy Land*. Edited by Thomas Levy. New York: Facts on File.

Hopkins, David. 1983. "The Dynamics of Agriculture in Monarchial Israel," *Society of Biblical Literature Seminar Papers* 22: 177–202.

Hopkins, David. 1987. "Life on the Land: The Subsistence Struggles of Early Israel," *Biblical Archaeologist* 50: 178–91.

Hopkins, David. 1996. "Bare Bones: Putting Flesh on the Economics of Ancient Israel," in *The Origins of the Ancient Israelite States*. Edited by V. Fritz and P. R. Davies. Sheffield: Sheffield Academic Press.

Hoppe, Leslie. 2004. *There Shall Be No Poor among You: Poverty in the Bible*. Nashville, TN: Abingdon.

Horsley, Richard. 2009. *Covenant Economics: A Biblical Vision of Justice for All*. Louisville, KY: Westminster John Knox.

Horsley, Richard, and John Hanson. 1985. *Bandits, Prophets, and Messiahs: Popular Movements in the Time of Jesus*. San Francisco: Harper and Row.

Houston, Walter. 2008. *Contending for Justice: Ideologies and Theologies of Social Justice in the Old Testament*. London: T and T Clark.

Houston, Walter. 2010. "Exit the Oppressed Peasant? Rethinking the Background of Social Criticism in the Prophets," in *Prophecy and Prophets in Ancient Israel: Proceedings of the Oxford Old Testament Seminar*. Edited by John Day. London: T and T Clark.

Hudson, Michael. 1999. "'Proclaim Liberty throughout the Land': The Economic Roots of the Jubilee," *BR* (Washington DC) 15: 26–33, 44.

Jackson, Bernard. 1989. "Ideas of Law and Legal Administration: A Semiotic Approach," in *The World of Ancient Israel*. Edited by R. E. Clements. New York: Cambridge University Press.

Jackson, Bernard. 2006. *Wisdom-Laws: A Study of the Mishpatim of Exodus 21: 1–22: 16*. New York: Oxford.

Jensen, Morten Hoerning. 2006. *Herod Antipas in Galilee: The Literary and Archaeological Sources on the Reign of Herod Antipas and Its Socio-Economic Impact on Galilee*. Tübingen: Mohr Siebeck.

Jeremias, Joachim. 1969. *Jerusalem in the Time of Jesus: An Investigation into Economic and Social Conditions during the New Testament Period*. Translated by F. H. and C. H. Cave. Philadelphia: Fortress.

Johnson, Luke Timothy. 1981. *Sharing Possessions: Mandate and Symbol of Faith*. Philadelphia: Fortress.

Johnson, Luke Timothy. 1985. "Friendship with the World/Friendship with God: A Study of Discipleship in James," in *Discipleship in the New Testament*. Edited by Fernando Segovia. Philadelphia: Fortress.

Johnson, Luke Timothy. 1995a. "The Social World of James: Literary Analysis and Historical Reconstruction," in *The Social World of the First Christians: Essays in Honor of Wayne A. Meeks*. Edited by L. Michael White and O. Larry Yarbrough. Minneapolis, MN: Fortress.

Johnson, Luke Timothy. 1995b. *The Letter of James*. The Anchor Bible series. New York: Doubleday.

Johnson, Luke Timothy. 1999. *The Writings of the New Testament: An Interpretation*. Revised edition. Minneapolis, MN: Fortress.

Johnson, Luke Timothy. 2004. "Making Connections: The Material Expression of Friendship in the New Testament," *Interpretation* 58: 158–71.

Johnson, Luke Timothy. 2008. Review of *Poverty in the Roman World*. *Theological Studies* 69: 226.

Johnson, R. Boaz. 2009. "A Biblical Theology of the Environment in the Creation Narrative," *Covenant Quarterly* 67: 3–19.

Josephus, Flavius. 1980. *Jewish Antiquities*. Volumes 4–10. Translated by Ralph Marcus. Loeb Classical Library. Cambridge: Harvard.

Kaiser, Walter. 1983. *Toward Old Testament Ethics*. Grand Rapids, MI: Zondervan.

Kaiser, Walter. 1988. "The Old Testament Promise of Material Blessings and the Contemporary Believer," *Trinity Journal* 9: 151–70.

Karris, Robert. 1978. "Poor and Rich: The Lukan Sitz im Leben," in *Perspectives on Luke-Acts*. Edited by Charles Talbert. Edinburgh: T and T Clark.

Kay, Jeanne. 1988. "Concepts of Nature in the Hebrew Bible," *Environmental Ethics* 10: 309–27.

Keck, Leander. 1984. "Ethics in the Gospel according to Matthew," *Iliff Review* 41: 39–56.

Kidd, Reggie. 1990. *Wealth and Beneficence in the Pastoral Epistles*. Atlanta: Scholars Press.

Kim, Kyoung-Jin. 1998. *Stewardship and Almsgiving in Luke's Theology*. Journal for the Study of the New Testament. Supplement Series #155.

King, Philip, and Lawrence Stager. 2001. *Life in Biblical Israel*. Library of Ancient Israel series. Louisville, KY: Westminster John Knox.

Kirk, Alan. 2003. "'Love Your Enemies,' The Golden Rule, and Ancient Reciprocity (Luke 6: 27–35)," *Journal of Biblical Literature* 122/4: 667–86.

Kloppenborg, John. 1990. "Alms, Debt and Divorce: Jesus' Ethics in their Mediterranean Context," *Toronto Journal of Theology* 6: 182–200.

Knight, Frank. 1939. "Ethics and Economic Reform: III Christianity," *Economica* 6: 398–422.

Kyrtatas, Dimitris. 2002. "Modes and Relations of Production," in *Handbook of Early Christianity: Social Science Approaches*. Edited by Anthony Blasi, Jean Duhaime, and Paul-André Turcotte. New York: Altamira.

Lang, Bernhard. 1985. "The Social Organization of Peasant Poverty in Biblical Israel," in *Anthropological Approaches to the Old Testament*. Philadelphia: Fortress Press; London: SPCK.

Lee, Dorothy. 2002. *Flesh and Glory: Symbols, Gender and Theology in the Gospel of John*. New York: Crossroad.

LeFebvre, Michael. 2006. *Collections, Codes, and Torah: The Re-characterization of Israel's Written Law*. New York: T and T Clark.

Lella, Alexander di. 1966. "Conservative and Progressive Theology: Sirach and Wisdom," *Catholic Biblical Quarterly* 38: 139–54. Reprinted in *Studies in Ancient Israelite Wisdom*. Edited by James Crenshaw. New York: Ktav, 1976.

Lenski, Gerhard. 1966. *Power and Privilege: A Theory of Social Stratification*. New York: McGraw-Hill.

Lewis, Naphtali. 1983. *Life in Egypt under Roman Rule*. Oxford: Clarendon.

Limburg, James. 1994. "Down-to-Earth Theology: Psalm 104 and the Environment," *Currents in Theology and Mission* 21: 340–46.

Lipschits, Oded. 2004. "The Rural Settlement in Judah in the Sixth Century B.C.E.: A Rejoinder," *Palestine Exploration Quarterly* 136: 99–107.

Lohfink, Norbert. 1982. "Love," in *Great Themes from the Old Testament*. Translated by Ronald Walls. Edinburgh, UK: T and T Clark.

Lohfink, Norbert. 1986. "The Kingdom of God and the Economy in the Bible," *Communio: International Catholic Review* 13: 216–31.

Lohfink, Norbert. 1987. *Option for the Poor: the Basic Principle of Liberation Theology in Light of the Bible*. Berkeley, CA: Bibal Press.

Lohfink, Norbert. 1991. "Poverty in the Laws of the Ancient Near East and of the Bible," *Theological Studies* 52: 34–50.

Longenecker, Bruce. 2009. "Socio-Economic Profiling of the First Urban Christians," in *After the First Urban Christians: The Social-Scientific Study of Pauline Christianity Twenty-five Years Later*. Edited by Todd Still and David Horrell. London: T and T Clark.

Longenecker, Bruce. 2010. *Remember the Poor: Paul, Poverty, and the Greco-Roman World*. Grand Rapids, MI: Eerdmans.

Longenecker, Richard. 1984. *New Testament Social Ethics for Today*. Grand Rapids, MI: Eerdmans.

Lowery, Richard. 2000. *Sabbath and Jubilee*. St. Louis, MO: Chalice Press.

Malchow, Bruce. 1982. "Social Justice in the Wisdom Literature," *Biblical Theology Bulletin* 12: 120–24.

Malina, Bruce. 1987. "Wealth and Poverty in the New Testament and Its World," *Interpretation* 41: 354–67.

Marshall, Christopher. 1989. *Faith as a Theme in Mark's Narrative*. Society for New Testament Studies Monograph series 64. Cambridge: Cambridge University Press.

Marshall, I. Howard. 1978. *The Gospel of Luke: A Commentary on the Greek Text*. Grand Rapids, MI: Eerdmans.

Marshall, I. Howard. 1994. "New Occasions Teach New Duties? 2. The Use of the New Testament in Christian Ethics," *The Expository Times* 105: 131–36.

Marshall, I. Howard. 2004. *New Testament Theology: Many Witnesses, One Gospel*. Downers Grove, IL: IVP Academic.

Matera, Frank. 1996. *New Testament Ethics: The Legacies of Jesus and Paul*. Louisville, KY: Westminster John Knox Press.

Matera, Frank. 2007. *New Testament Theology: Exploring Diversity and Unity*. Louisville, KY: Westminster John Knox.

May, David. 2010. "Ancient Economics—Modern Interpreters: The World of Jesus," *Review and Expositor* 107: 481–98.

Maynard-Reid, Pedrito. 1987. *Poverty and Wealth in James*. New York: Orbis.

Mays, James. 1987. "Justice: Perspectives from the Prophetic Tradition," in *Prophecy in Israel: Search for an Identity*. Issues in Religion and Theology 10. Edited by David Petersen. Philadelphia: Fortress.

Mazar, Amihay. 2001. *Studies in the Archaeology in the Iron Age in Israel and Jordan*. Journal for the Study of the Old Testament Supplement series #331. Sheffield, England: Sheffield Academic Press.

McKenzie, John. 1990. "Aspects of Old Testament Thought," in *The New Jerome Biblical Commentary*. Englewood Cliffs, NJ: Prentice-Hall.

Meeks, Wayne. 1983. *First Urban Christians: The Social World of the Apostle Paul*. New Haven, CT: Yale.

Meeks, Wayne. 1986. *The Moral World of the First Christians*. Philadelphia: Westminster Press.

Meeks, Wayne. 1993. *The Origins of Christian Morality: The First Two Centuries*. New Haven, CT: Yale.

Meggitt, Justin. 1998. *Paul, Poverty and Survival.* Edinburgh: T and T Clark.

Mendenhall, George. 1954. "Ancient and Biblical Law," *Biblical Archaeologist* 17: 26–46.

Metzger, James. 2007. *Consumption and Wealth in Luke's Travel Narrative*. Leiden and Boston: Brill.

Miller, Patrick. 1985. "The Human Sabbath: A Study in Deuteronomic Theology," *Princeton Seminary Bulletin* 6: 81–97.

Morla Asensio, Víctor. 1998. "Poverty and Wealth: Ben Sira's View of Possessions," in *Der Einzelne und seine Gemeinschaft bei Ben Sira*. Edited by Ingrid Krammer and Renate Egge-Wenzel. BZAW 270. Berlin Walter de Gruyter, 151–78.

Mott, Stephen Charles. 1987. "The Use of the New Testament for Social Ethics," *Journal of Religious Ethics* 15: 225–60.

Moxnes, Halvor. 1988. *The Economy of the Kingdom: Social Conflict and Economic Relations in Luke's Gospel*. Philadelphia: Fortress Press.

Murphy, Roland. 1990a. "Introduction to the Pentateuch," in *New Jerome Biblical Commentary*. Englewood Cliffs, NJ: Prentice-Hall.

Murphy, Roland. 1990b. "Introduction to Wisdom Literature," in *New Jerome Biblical Commentary*. Englewood Cliffs, NJ: Prentice-Hall.

Nardoni, Enrique. 2004. *Rise Up, O Judge: A Study of Justice in the Biblical World*. Translated by Seán Charles Martin. Peabody, MA: Hendrickson.

Neufeld, Edward. 1955. "The Prohibitions against Loans at Interest in Ancient Hebrew Laws," *Hebrew Union College Annual* 26: 355–412.

Neufeld, Edward. 1960. "The Emergence of a Royal-Urban Society in Ancient Israel," *Hebrew Union College Annual* 31: 31–53.

Nicholson, Ernest. 1986. *God and His People: Covenant and Theology in the Old Testament*. Oxford: Clarendon.

Nickelsburg, George. 1978–1979. "Riches, the Rich, and God's Judgment in 1 Enoch 92–105 and the Gospel According to Luke," *New Testament Studies* 25: 324–44.

Noell, Edd. 2007. "A 'Marketless World'? An Examination of Wealth and Exchange in the Gospels and First-Century Palestine," *Journal of Markets and Morality* 10: 85–114.

Nürnberger, Klaus. 1978. "The Economics of Paul," in *Affluence, Poverty and the Word of God*. Edited by Klaus Nürnberger. Durban, Natal: Lutheran Publishing House.

Oakman, Douglas. 1986. *Jesus and the Economic Questions of His Day*. Lewiston, NY: E. Mellen Press.

Oakman, Douglas. 1991. "The Countryside in Luke-Acts," in *The Social World of Luke-Acts: Models for Interpretation*. Edited by Jerome Neyrey. Peabody, MA: Hendrickson.

Ogletree, Thomas. 1983. *The Use of the Bible in Christian Ethics: A Constructive Essay*. Philadelphia: Fortress Press.

Osborn, Eric. 1976. *Ethical Patterns in Early Christian Thought*. Cambridge: Cambridge University Press.

Otto, Eckart. 1995. "Of Aims and Methods in Hebrew Bible Ethics," *Semeia* 66: 161–79.

Paris, Peter. 1995. "An Ethicist's Concerns about Biblical Ethics," in *Ethics and Politics in the Hebrew Bible*. Edited by Douglas Knight. *Semeia* 66. Society of Biblical Literature.

Perdue, Leo. 1981. "Paraenesis and the Epistle of James," *Zeitschrift für die neutestamentliche Wissenschaft und die Kunde der älteren Kirche* 72: 3–4: 241–56.

Perdue, Leo. 1990a. "Cosmology and the Social Order in the Wisdom Tradition," in *The Sage in Israel and the Ancient Near East*. Edited by John Gammie and Leo Perdue. Winona Lake, IN: Eisenbrauns.

Perdue, Leo. 1990b. "The Social Character of Paraenesis and Paraenetic Literature," *Semeia* 50: 5–39.

Perdue, Leo. 1994. *Wisdom and Creation: The Theology of Wisdom Literature*. Nashville, TN: Abingdon.

Perdue, Leo. 1997. "Wisdom Theology and Social History in Proverbs 1–9," in *Wisdom, You Are My Sister*. Edited by Michael Barré. Catholic Biblical Quarterly Monograph Series. Washington, DC: Catholic Biblical Association of America.

Perkins, Pheme. 1984. "Paul and Ethics," *Interpretation* 38: 268–80.

Perkins, Pheme. 1986. "Taxes in the New Testament," *Journal of Religious Ethics* 12: 182–200.

Perkins, Pheme. 1994. "Does the New Testament Have an Economic Message?" in *Wealth in Western Thought: The Case for and against Riches*. Edited by Paul G. Schervish. Westport, CT: Praeger.

Pilgrim, Walter. 1981. *Good News to the Poor: Wealth and Poverty in Luke-Acts*. Minneapolis, MN: Augsburg.

Pleins, J. David. 1987. "Poverty in the Social World of the Wise," *Journal for the Study of the Old Testament* 37: 61–78.

Pleins, J. David. 2001. *The Social Visions of the Hebrew Bible*. Louisville, KY: Westminster John Knox Press.

Polanyi, Karl. 1944. *The Great Transformation*. Boston: Beacon.

Polanyi, Karl. 1968. *Primitive, Archaic and Modern Economies: Essays by Karl Polanyi*. Edited by George Dalton. Garden City, NY: Anchor Books.

Premnath, D. N. 1988. "Latifundialization and Isaiah 5.8–10," *Journal for the Study of the Old Testament* 40: 49–60.

Premnath, D. N. 2003. *Eighth Century Prophets: A Social Analysis*. St. Louis, MO: Chalice Press.

Premnath, D. N. 2008. "Amos and Hosea: Sociohistorical Background and Prophetic Critique," *Word and World* 28: 125–32.

Rathbone, Dominic. 2006. "Poverty and Population in Roman Egypt," in *Poverty in the Roman World*. Edited by Margaret Atkins and Robin Osborne. Cambridge, UK: Cambridge.

Rhyne, C. Thomas. 1987. "II Corinthians 8: 8–15," *Interpretation* 41: 408–13.

Ricoeur, Paul. 1976. *Interpretation Theory: Discourse and the Surplus of Meaning*. Fort Worth, TX: Texas Christian University Press.

Rodd, Cyril. 1993–1994. "New Occasions Teach New Duties? 1. The Use of the Old Testament in Christian Ethics," *The Expository Times* 105: 101–6.

Rohrbaugh, Richard. 1991. "The Pre-Industrial City in Luke-Acts: Urban Social Relations," in *The Social World of Luke-Acts: Models for Interpretation*. Edited by Jerome Neyrey. Peabody, MA: Hendrickson.

Rosner, Dor. 1978. "The Balance of Economic Security and Income According to the Mosaic Law," in *Affluence, Poverty and the Word of God*. Durban, Natal: Lutheran Publishing House.

Safrai, Ze'ev. 1994. *The Economy of Roman Palestine*. London: Routledge.

Sanders, Jack. 1970. "The Question of the Relevance of Jesus for Ethics Today," *Journal of the American Academy of Religion* 2: 131–46. Reprinted in *The Use of Scripture in Moral Theology*. Readings in Moral Theology Series 4. Edited by Charles Curran and Richard McCormick. New York: Paulist, 1975.

Sanders, Jack. 1975. *Ethics in the New Testament: Change and Development*. Philadelphia: Fortress.

Sandoval, Timothy. 2006. *The Discourse of Wealth and Poverty in the Book of Proverbs*. Leiden and Boston: Brill.

Schelkle, Karl Hermann. 1973. *Theology of the New Testament*. English version by William A. Jurgens. Collegeville, MN: Liturgical Press.

Schiedel, Walter. 2006. "Stratification, Deprivation and the Quality of Life," in *Poverty in the Roman World*. Edited by Margaret Atkins and Robin Osborne. Cambridge, UK: Cambridge.

Schmidt, Thomas. 1987. *Hostility to Wealth in the Synoptic Gospels*. Journal for the Study of the New Testament Supplement Series 15. Sheffield, UK: Sheffield Academic Press.

Schnackenburg, Rudolf. 1965. *The Moral Teaching of the New Testament*. Translated by J. Holland-Smith and W. J. O'Hara. Freiburg, Germany: Herder.

Schneiders, Sandra. 1991. *The Revelatory Text: Interpreting the New Testament as Sacred Scripture*. Collegeville, MN: Liturgical Press.

Schottroff, L., and W. Steggemann. 1986. *Jesus and the Hope of the Poor*. Maryknoll, NY: Orbis.

Schottroff, Willy. 1984. "The Prophet Amos: A Socio-Historical Assessment of His Ministry," in *God of the Lowly: Socio-Historical Interpretations of the Bible*. Edited by Luise Schottroff and W. Steggemann. Maryknoll, NY: Orbis.

Schrage, Wolfgang. 1988. *The Ethics of the New Testament*. Translated by David E. Green. Philadelphia: Fortress Press.

Scott, Bernard. 1989. *Hear Then the Parable: A Commentary on the Parables of Jesus*. Minneapolis, MN: Augsburg Fortress.

Seccombe, David. 1982. *Possessions and the Poor in Luke-Acts*. Linz: Studien Zum Neuen Testament und Seiner Umwelt.

Seccombe, David. 1998. "The New People of God," in *Witness to the Gospel: The Theology of Acts*. Edited by I. Howard Marshall and David Peterson. Grand Rapids, MI: W. B. Eerdmans.

Sharp, Donald. 1995. "A Biblical Foundation for an Environmental Theology: A New Perspective on Genesis 1: 26–28 and 6: 11–13," *Science et Esprit* 47: 305–13.

Silver, Morris. 1995. "Prophets and Markets Revisited," in *Social Justice in the Ancient World*. Edited by K. D. Irani and Morris Silver. Westport, CT: Greenwood.

Simkins, Ronald. 1999. "Patronage and the Political Economy of Monarchic Israel," *Semeia* 87: 123–44.

Simkins, Ronald. 2004. "Family in the Political Economy of Monarchic Judah," *The Bible and Critical Theory* 1: 1–17.

Smith, Mark. 2004. *The Memoirs of God: History, Memory, and the Experience of the Divine in Ancient Israel*. Minneapolis, MN: Fortress.

Spohn, William. 1984. *What They Are Saying about Scripture and Ethics?* New York: Paulist.

Spohn, William. 1986. "The Use of Scripture in Moral Theology," *Theological Studies* 47: 88–102.

Spohn, William. 1995. "Jesus and Christian Ethics," *Theological Studies* 56: 92–107.

Squires, John. 2006. "The Gospel According to Luke," in *The Cambridge Companion to the Gospels*. Cambridge: Cambridge University Press.

Stackhouse, Max. 1987. "What Then Shall We Do? On Using Scripture in Economic Ethics," *Interpretation* 41: 382–97.

Stager, Lawrence. 1998. "Forging an Identity: The Emergence of Ancient Israel," in *The Oxford History of the Biblical World*. Edited by Michael Coogan. New York: Oxford.

Theissen, Gerd. 1978. *Sociology of Early Palestinian Christianity*. Philadelphia; Fortress.

Theissen, Gerd. 1982. *The Social Setting of Pauline Christianity*. Translated by John Schütz. Edinburgh: T and T Clark.

Thielman, Frank. 2005. *Theology of the New Testament: A Canonical and Synthetic Approach*. Grand Rapids, MI: Zondervan.

Toombs, Lawrence. 1965. "Love and Justice in Deuteronomy: A Third Approach to the Law," *Interpretation* 19: 399–411.

Topel, John. 1998. "The Tarnished Golden Rule (Luke 6: 31): The Inescapable Radicalness of Christian Ethics," *Theological Studies* 59: 475–85.

Tucker, Gene. 1997. "Rain on a Land Where No One Lives: The Hebrew Bible on the Environment," *Journal of Biblical Literature* 116: 3–17.

Van Leeuwen, Raymond. 1992. "Wealth and Poverty: System and Contradiction in Proverbs," *Hebrew Studies* 33: 25–36.

Vawter, Bruce. 1977. *On Genesis: A New Reading*. Garden City, NJ: Doubleday.

Vawter, Bruce. 1990. "Introduction to Prophetic Literature," *New Jerome Biblical Commentary*. Englewood Cliffs, NJ: Prentice-Hall.

Verhey, Allen. 1984. *The Great Reversal: Ethics and the New Testament*. Grand Rapids, MI: Eerdmans.

Verhey, Allen. 2002. *Remembering Jesus: Christian Community, Scripture, and the Moral Life*. Grand Rapids, MI: W. B. Eerdmans.

Verhey, Allen. 2011. "Ethics in Scripture," in *Dictionary of Scripture and Ethics*. Edited by Joel Green. Grand Rapids, MI: Baker Academic.

Veyne, Paul. 1990. *Bread and Circuses: Historical Sociology and Political Pluralism*. Translated by Brian Pearce. London: Penguin

Via, Dan. 1985. *The Ethics of Mark's Gospel—In the Middle of Time*. Philadelphia: Fortress.

Von Rad, Gerhard. 1961. *Genesis; A Commentary*. Philadelphia: Westminster.

Von Rad, Gerhard. 1975. *Old Testament Theology*. 2 volumes. London: SCM Press.

von Waldow, H. Eberhard. 1970. "Social Responsibility and Social Structure in Early Israel," *Catholic Biblical Quarterly* 32: 182–204.

von Waldow, H. Eberhard. 1974. "Israel and Her Land: Some Theological Considerations," in *A Light Unto My Path; Old Testament Studies in Honor of Jacob M. Myers*. Edited by Howard N. Bream, Ralph D. Heim, and Carey A. Moore. Philadelphia: Temple University Press.

Walton, Steve. 2004. "Acts," in *The Face of New Testament Studies: A Survey of Recent Research*. Edited by Scot McKnight and Grant Osborne. Grand Rapids, MI: Baker Academic.

Washington, Harold. 1994. *Wealth and Poverty in the Instruction of Amenope and the Hebrew Proverbs*. Atlanta, GA: Scholars Press.

Weinfeld, M. 1961. "The Origin of the Humanism in Deuteronomy," *Journal of Biblical Literature* 80: 241–47.

Wenham, Gordon. 2006. "Law in the Old Testament," in *Oxford Handbook of Biblical Studies*. Edited by J. Rogerson and Judith Lieu. Oxford, UK: Oxford University Press.

Wessels, Willie. 1994. "A Theology of Renewal: A Perspective on Social Justice from the Book of Jeremiah," in *Spirit and Renewal: Essays in Honor of J. Rodman Williams*. Sheffield, England: Sheffield Academic Press.

Westerman, Claus. 1984. *Genesis 1–11*. Translated by John Scullion. Minneapolis, MN: Augsburg.

Wheeler, Sondra Ely. 1995. *Wealth as Peril and Obligation: The New Testament on Possessions*. Grand Rapids, MI: W. B. Eerdmans.

White, Lynn. 1967. "The Historical Roots of Our Ecological Crisis," *Science* 155: 1203–7.

Whybray, R. N. 1989. "Poverty, Wealth, and Point of View in Proverbs," *The Expository Times* 100: 332–36.

Whybray, R. N. 1990. *Wealth and Poverty in the Book of Proverbs*. Journal for the Study of the Old Testament Supplement Series 99. Sheffield, UK: JSOT Press.

Williamson, H. G. M. 1985. "The Old Testament and the Material World," *Evangelical Quarterly* 57: 5–22.

Williamson, H. G. M. 2012. *He Has Shown You What is Good: Old Testament Justice Then and Now*. The Trinity Lectures, Singapore 2011. Cambridge, UK: Lutterworth.

Wilson, Robert. 1995. "Sources and Methods in the Study of Ancient Israelite Ethics," in *Ethics and Politics in the Hebrew Bible*. Edited by Douglas Knight. Semeia 66. Society of Biblical Literature.

Wippel, John. 2007. *Metaphysical Themes in Thomas Aquinas II*. Studies in Philosophy and the History of Philosophy. Revised edition. Washington, DC: Catholic University of America.

Witherington, Ben. 2010. *Jesus and Money: A Guide for Financial Times*. Grand Rapids, MI: Brazos.

Wittenberg, Gunther. 1978. "The Message of the O.T. Prophets during the Eighth Century B.C. Concerning Affluence and Poverty," in *Affluence, Poverty and the Word of God*. Edited by K. Nürnberger. Durban, South Africa: Lutheran Publishing House.

Wittenberg, G. H. 1987. "Amos 6: 1–7," *Journal of Theology for Southern Africa* 58: 57–69.

Wolff, Hans Walter. 1978. "Prophecy from the Eight through the Fifth Century," *Interpretation* 32: 17–30.

Wolff, Hans Walter. 1990. *Micah: A Commentary*. Translated by G. Stansell. Minneapolis, MN: Augsburg.

Wright, Addison, Roland Murphy, and Joseph Fitzmyer. 1990. "A History of Israel," *New Jerome Biblical Commentary*. Englewood Cliffs, NJ: Prentice-Hall.

Wright, Benjamin. 1998. "The Discourse of Riches and Poverty in the Book of Ben Sira," SBL Seminar papers 37: 559–78.

Wright, Benjamin, and Claudia Camp. 2001. "'Who Has Been Tested by Gold and Found Perfect?' Ben Sira's Discourse of Riches and Poverty," *Henoch* 23: 153–73.

Wright, Christopher. 1990. *God's People in God's Land: Family, Land, and Property in the Old Testament*. Grand Rapids, MI: W. B. Eerdmans.

Wright, Christopher. 2004. *Old Testament Ethics for the People of God*. Downers Grove, IL: InterVarsity Press.

Yee, G. A. 1992. "The Theology of Creation in Proverbs 8: 22–31," in *Creation in the Biblical Traditions*. Edited by R. J. Clifford and J. J. Collins. Catholic Biblical Quarterly Monograph Series 24. Washington DC: Catholic Biblical Association.

Yoder, Christine. 2001. *Wisdom as a Woman of Substance: A Socioeconomic Reading of Proverbs 1–9 and 31: 10–31*. Berlin: Walter de Gruyter.

Zimmerli, Walther. 1964. "The Place and Limit of the Wisdom in the Framework of the Old Testament Theology," *Scottish Journal of Theology* 17: 146–58. Reprinted in *Studies in Ancient Israelite Wisdom*. Edited by James Crenshaw. New York: Ktav, 1976.

Zimmerman, John. 2003. "Yoder's Jesus and Economics: The Economics of Jesus or the economics of Luke?" *Mennonite Quarterly Review* 77: 437–50.

Index

Index of Scripture Passages

Isaiah

Jeremiah

Ezekiel

Luke

John

About the Author

Albino Barrera is professor of theology and economics at Providence College (Rhode Island). His books include *Market Complicity and Christian Ethics* (Cambridge, 2011), *Globalization and Economic Ethics: Distributive Justice in the Knowledge Economy* (Palgrave MacMillan, 2007), *Economic Compulsion and Christian Ethics* (Cambridge, 2005), *God and the Evil of Scarcity: Moral Foundations of Economic Agency* (Notre Dame, 2005), and *Modern Catholic Social Documents and Political Economy* (Georgetown, 2001).